THE
AUSTIN ★ BOSTON
CONNECTION

the AUSTIN/BOSTON connection

FIVE DECADES OF HOUSE DEMOCRATIC LEADERSHIP, 1937–1989

Anthony Champagne
Douglas B. Harris
James W. Riddlesperger Jr.
and Garrison Nelson

Texas A&M University Press
College Station

This paper meets the requirements of
ANSI/NISO Z39.48-1992 (Permanence of Paper).
Binding materials have been chosen for durability.

Library of Congress Cataloging-in-Publication Data
The Austin-Boston connection : five decades of House
Democratic leadership, 1937–1989 / Anthony Champagne . . .
[et al.]. — 1st ed.
    p. cm.
Includes bibliographical references and index.
ISBN-13: 978-1-60344-116-2 (cloth : alk. paper)
ISBN-10: 1-60344-116-6 (cloth : alk. paper)
ISBN-13: 978-1-60344-120-9 (pbk. : alk. paper)
ISBN-10: 1-60344-120-4 (pbk. : alk. paper)
1. United States. Congress. House — Leadership — History —
20th century. 2. United States. Congress. House — Speakers —
History — 20th century. 3. Democratic Party (U.S.) — History —
20th century. 4. Legislators — Texas — History — 20th century.
5. Legislators — Massachusetts — Boston — History — 20th
century. 6. Legislators — United States — History — 20th century.
I. Champagne, Anthony.
JK1411.A87 2009
328.73092'2744 — dc22
                  2008051136

CONTENTS

A gallery of photographs follows page 72.

Acknowledgments vii

1 Introduction 1

2 Joe Bailey 16

3 John Nance Garner 47

4 Sam Rayburn 73

5 John W. McCormack 119

6 Sam Rayburn's Boys: Who Will Lead? 148

7 Back to Boston: Tip O'Neill 188

8 Jim Wright: The Last Texan 219

9 Conclusion: The Impact of the Austin-Boston

   Alliance on House Politics 251

Notes 263

Index 317

ACKNOWLEDGMENTS

The research for this book required travel to many archival collections. We are grateful to several organizations that provided travel grants that allowed us to visit a number of collections: Dean's Fund, University of Vermont; Earlham Foundation; John F. Kennedy Presidential Library and Museum; Loyola College Summer Research Grant; Morris K. Udall grant from the University of Arizona; Texas Christian University Research Fund; the Carl Albert Center; the Everett McKinley Dirksen Congressional Research Center; and the Lilly Library, Indiana University. We gratefully acknowledge the assistance of the following undergraduate students who helped with the research: Alana Chain, Ryan Henry, Iris Kwong, Oren Lund, Maggie Taylor, Lissette Villaruel, and Donald Zinman.

Dr. Kenneth Moody provided valuable aid in researching materials at the Franklin D. Roosevelt Library.

The John J. O'Connor Papers are used courtesy Lilly Library, Indiana University, Bloomington.

We are grateful to the many librarians and other individuals who assisted us with this research. Special thanks to those who allowed us to interview them and to the librarians who were of enormous assistance in locating materials.

THE
AUSTIN ★ BOSTON
CONNECTION

 n 1940, the Speaker of the U.S. House was a Democrat from a district on the Texas-Oklahoma border. The majority leader was a Catholic Democrat from a Greater Boston district. Thirty six years later the Speaker was a Democrat from a district on the Texas-Oklahoma border and the majority leader was a Catholic Democrat from a Greater Boston district. While it may seem as if time stood still in the House, the 1940 occupants of these posts — Speaker Sam Rayburn and Majority Leader John McCormack — were not the occupants of these posts in 1976. And, rather than the same districts being represented, they were adjacent districts such that the leaders of the 1970s — Speaker Carl Albert and Majority Leader Tip O'Neill — were the neighbors and friends of their predecessors in the leadership. Even more unusual was that every Democratic Speaker from 1940 to 1989 came from either the North Texas–southern Oklahoma area or from the Greater Boston area. With one exception — Hale Boggs of Louisiana served as majority leader from 1971 to 1973 — in the years when the Democrats controlled the House, there was an alternation of the leadership such that when the Speaker was from North Texas–southern Oklahoma, the majority leader was from Boston, and when the Speaker was from Boston, the majority leader was from North Texas–southern Oklahoma.

This Austin-Boston alliance that dominated House Democratic leadership from the New Deal to the Reagan era was more than mere coincidence; rather, it was the manifestation of Franklin Roosevelt's New Deal coalition in the House of Representatives necessary to balance the regional interests of that broad coalition. Forged in the late 1930s in the wake of Roosevelt's failed efforts at recasting the Democratic Party, the Austin-Boston alliance took shape as Sam Rayburn of Texas, Roosevelt's preferred candidate over New Deal dissident John O'Connor of New York, won the House majority leadership post in 1937. Upon Rayburn's succession to the Speakership, another Roosevelt loyalist, John McCormack of Boston, bested southern conservative Clifton Woodrum of Virginia to become majority leader in 1940. Set in motion on the eve of Roosevelt's unprecedented third term in the White House, the Austin-Boston alliance was perpetuated by a string of personal alliances and leadership elections from the New Deal to the 1970s and 1980s, and it maintained the tenuous coalition amidst a series of threats including House Democratic electoral losses of the House majority in 1946 and 1952, the personal losses of key leaders who retired from the House or died, and the emergence of policy issues — most notably civil rights — that threatened to divide the party. Whereas many have argued that the New Deal party system ended as early as Richard Nixon's 1968 election or, at least, by Ronald Reagan's 1980 victory, the Austin-Boston alliance in the House outlasted the New Deal presidential coalition: Austin-Boston's remnants persisted until Jim Wright resigned the Speakership in 1989.

The Austin-Boston connection in House party leadership replicated, solidified, and, ultimately, outlasted the New Deal coalition at the presidential level. It was embedded in and representative of the broader party system, perpetuated by friendships and the often intensely personal politics of congressional leadership selection. Explaining this unusual leadership pattern, its remarkable longevity, and its eventual decline requires an examination of a century of regional and personal power in the House of Representatives.

Sectionalism and Regional Politics in the House of Representatives

One notable advantage of the Austin-Boston alliance was its ability to balance regional interests, especially the north-south divide, in Congress and the Democratic Party. Sectionalism, the politics of competing regional interests, is a recurrent, perhaps dominant, political force in U.S. political history, and the management of cross-regional differences has been a key aim of political parties and Congress throughout U.S. history.[1] Most notably, much of party politics, even prior to the Civil War, has been preoccupied with managing the divisions between "the industrial Northeast" and the "southern periphery."[2]

Between the Civil War and the New Deal, the Democratic Party in Congress was primarily a southern party, north-south regional politics separated Republicans from Democrats, and party politics exacerbated rather than ameliorated sectional divisions. Figure 1-1 shows just how southern the Democratic Party was prior to the New Deal: in the pre–New Deal era, normally over 50 percent of the House Democrats hailed

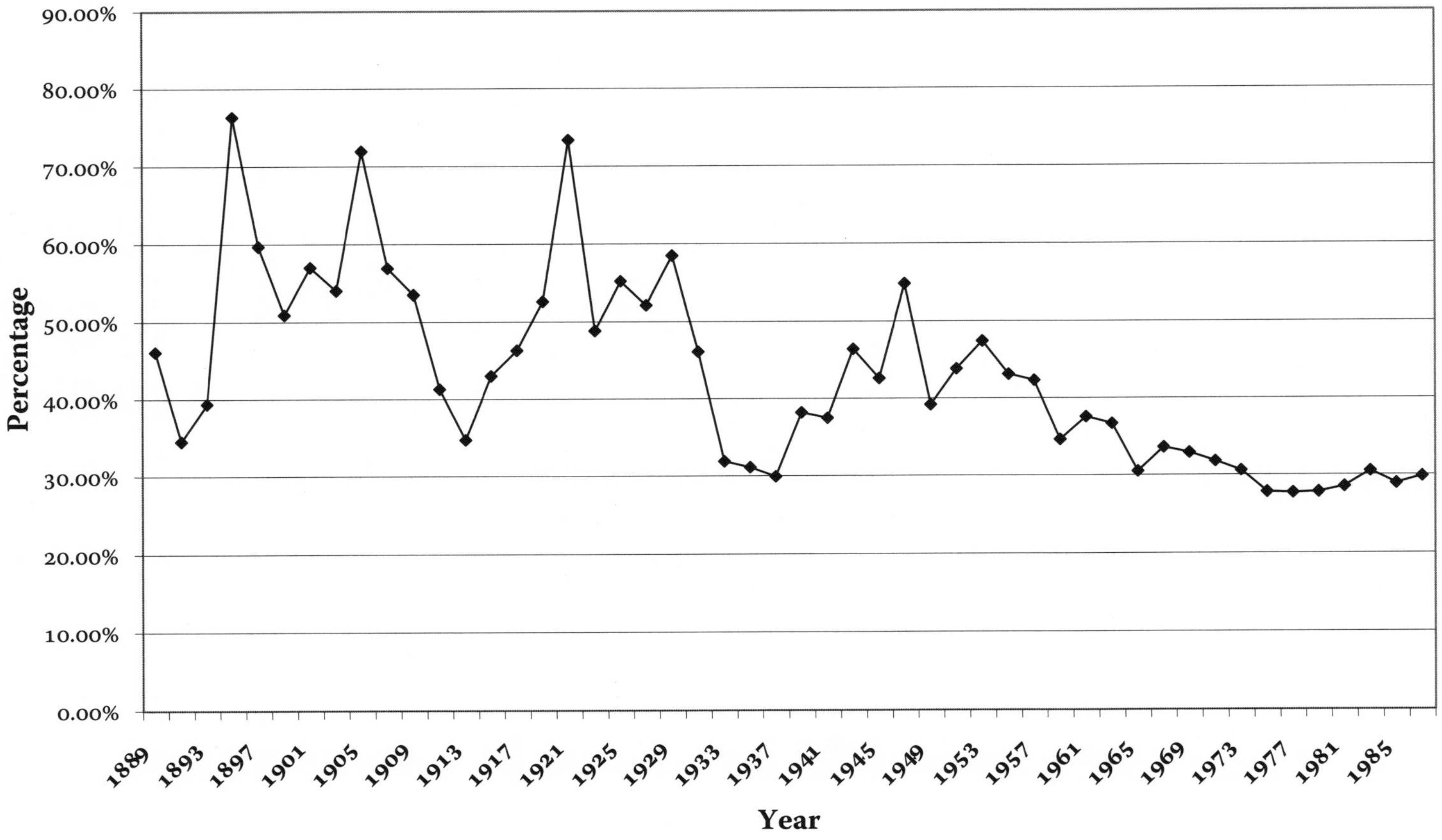

FIGURE 1-1. PERCENTAGE OF HOUSE DEMOCRATS FROM FORMER CONFEDERATE STATES, 1889–1987

from states of the former Confederacy, and, on three occasions, over 70 percent of the House Democratic membership was southern. Moreover, because the South was a one-party region that lacked competitive elections between the parties, southern congressmen often stayed in Congress a long time accruing seniority and institutional power.[3]

But if the states of the Old Confederacy were the "base" of the House Democratic Party prior to the New Deal, it was Republicans who typically had majority control of the House at the end of the nineteenth and beginning of the twentieth centuries. Republican Speakers presided over twenty-four of the thirty-six Congresses from December 1859 to March 1931 (see figure 1-2). During this time, Republican party leaders, particularly Speakers Thomas Brackett Reed of Maine and Joseph Cannon of Illinois — "Czars" Reed and Cannon — dominated the legislative process and House politics. Chief among the Speaker's procedural advantages were the ability to appoint the membership and chairs of the House's standing committees, the complete control over the House Committee on Rules (the Speaker was the chairman of the Rules Committee), and that committee's control over the flow of legislation to the floor of the House. This "Czar era" of the Speakership ended in 1910 when progressive Republicans joined forces with minority party Democrats in a revolt against Cannon, which resulted in a reduction of the Speaker's power, most notably stripping the Speaker of his chairmanship of and control over the Rules Committee.[4]

These post-revolt procedural changes and weakening of the Speakership were adopted by Democrats when they took control of the House in the aftermath of the 1910 elections. In 1911 Democrat Champ Clark of Missouri became Speaker, and the newly empowered Democratic majority reduced the powers of the Speaker even more. The Democratic members of the Ways and Means Committee became the House Democrats' Committee on Committees that assigned congressmen to committees. Moreover, one became chair of a committee through seniority rather than as a result of the whims of the Speaker. Because conservative southern Democratic members represented constituencies that were more safely Democratic, they tended to accumulate greater seniority than non-southern Democrats who were more likely to represent competitive districts. Compared to their northern colleagues, southern Democrats stayed in office for years and, in the process, built seniority and power. Thus, in addition to their sheer numerical advantage within the caucus, key aspects of House organization advantaged southern Democrats as

FIGURE 1-2. PERCENTAGE OF DEMOCRATS IN THE HOUSE OF REPRESENTATIVES,
1889–1987

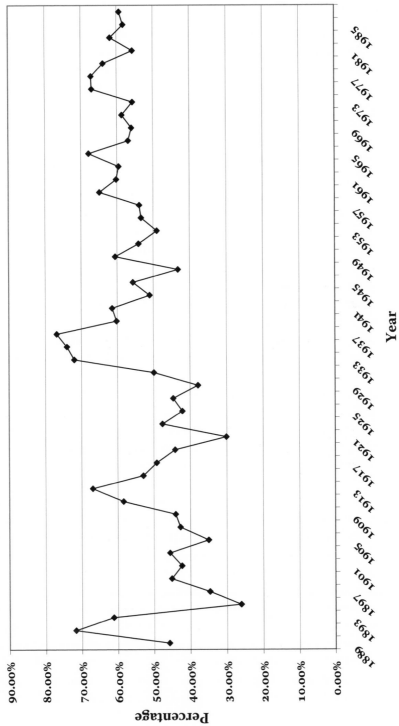

well. With the vast reduction in the powers of the Speaker from the revolt against Cannon, the House committee system, dominated by the more senior and conservative southern committee chairmen, filled the leadership vacuum in Congress.

The Regional Politics of the New Deal Coalition in Congress

The emergence of the New Deal coalition two decades after the revolt against Cannon challenged southern dominance of the House Democratic Party. With Franklin Roosevelt's 1932 victory and consequent Democratic gains in the Northeast, Midwest, and West, the Democratic Party in the House became a truly national party where the non-southern Democrats in the House significantly outnumbered the southern Democrats.[5] Still, the New Deal coalition was a fragile "strange bedfellows" alliance of, on the one hand, northern political interests, including organized labor and the cities, recent immigrants, Catholics, Jews, and eventually African Americans, grafted on top of a persistently conservative southern base that often included nativist and racist elements antipathetic to the party's newer, northern elements. Thus, the emergence of this national New Deal coalition meant, among many other things, that persistent sectional tensions in the United States no longer divided primarily along Democrat and Republican lines, but rather they were embodied in and, eventually, fought out within this broad Democratic majority.

At the New Deal's outset, traditional sectional divisions were muted by the general agreement among northern and southern Democrats that New Deal policies were necessary to alleviate the Great Depression. Moreover, the sheer size of the Democratic majorities in the 73d, 74th, and 75th Congresses (1933–38) rendered these divisions less important. Given that Democrats constituted over 70 percent of the House membership in each of these Congresses, whatever party defections there were provided only weak challenges to Democratic control and policy passage. Still, both the large majorities and intraparty tranquility were only temporary: Southerners retained their suspicions of national government, and increasingly frustrated northern Democrats grew resentful of the power senior southerners retained as chairs of the House's influential committees, particularly as southerners used their committee positions to apply the brakes to New Deal policies.

During Roosevelt's second term, many southern Democrats in the House and Senate balked at further expansions of the New Deal, joined in a "conservative coalition" with Republicans with increasing frequency and success, and turned their attentions (and considerable power as committee chairs) to investigation and oversight of the administration.[6] These intraparty fault lines revealed themselves as early as the 75th Congress (1937–38) when southern Democrats failed to support FDR on "court-packing" and other legislative efforts like the wages and hours bill, which historian James Patterson called the "clearest indication of sectional divisions of any vote to that time" and political scientist Richard Bensel claims "foreshadowed" the conservative coalition's emergence in subsequent Congresses.[7] Roosevelt's frustrations with these and other failures led him and his New Deal lieutenants to target the most conservative and obstructionist dissident congressional Democrats, chiefly southerners, for defeat in primary elections. This "purge effort," as it was derisively known, failed in all but one case (that of Tammany-affiliated Rules Committee Chairman John O'Connor of New York), thus exacerbating the tensions between the administration and its southern opponents within the Democratic Party who had survived Roosevelt's purge effort.

The purge effort was but the most famous of Roosevelt's efforts to wrest control of the Democratic Party from the South (and other conservatives) and to lead the party in a leftward, liberal direction. Even when first seeking the nomination in 1932, the Roosevelt forces sought to change the Democratic Party's rule that required that the presidential nominee win not only a majority but two-thirds of the convention delegates, a rule that had stood since the party's first conventions in the Jacksonian era and functioned to give the party's southern "base" an effective veto over the party nominee. Although FDR abandoned efforts to alter the "two-thirds rule" in 1932 when none other than Sam Rayburn "warned" that Roosevelt "would have to play according to the rules of the game," the rule was subsequently eliminated at the 1936 convention (a fact that paved the way for FDR's 1940 nomination and unprecedented third term).[8] These efforts to influence the ideological direction of the party extended to the traditionally internal politics of congressional party leadership selection. As Sidney M. Milkis notes, "Roosevelt worked quietly behind the scenes" in favor of Alben Barkley of Kentucky over Pat Harrison of Mississippi in the 1937 contest for Senate majority leader.[9] Less attention has been paid to FDR's similar efforts in the House that are one aspect of this book. Indeed, that same year that Roosevelt advanced Barkley's candidacy in the Senate, the White House successfully (though, again, behind the scenes) backed

Sam Rayburn for the majority leader's post over the same John O'Connor whom it would purge a year later. If such White House meddling might be thought of as taboo in these traditionally internal legislative leadership races, they nevertheless were consistent with FDR's overall efforts to transform the Democratic Party.

By the 76th Congress (1939–40), the "uneasy truce" between southerners and the administration gave way to the New Deal's "third stage," which "was characterized by a spirited battle between the New Deal Democrats and a bipartisan conservative coalition" of southern conservatives and Republicans.[10] As sectional differences became more salient (and were reinforced by personal animosities of "purge" survivors) on a range of policy issues and on matters regarding executive power and government control, FDR's New Deal party and policy management switched more generally from liberal, legislative expansionism to mere maintenance of the policy and administrative gains already made, primarily, according to Milkis, through executive leadership and administrative management rather than traditional party and legislative leadership.[11] FDR's hopes to further transform the Democratic Party were dashed with the failure of the purge and the emergence of the conservative coalition; as a fallback position, however, he could save the Party from southern conservative dominance.

Consistent with these broader efforts, managing the ideological and sectional divisions within the Democratic Party became a prime task of legislative organization as well. Committee organization and a "norm of committee deference" served to ameliorate and otherwise manage intraparty divisions by giving to the disparate elements of the party extraordinary influence over the policies most important to them.[12] But party organization was no less important. If the Democratic Party was, in some respects, an overarching logroll between disparate regional and sectional interests, maintaining such an arrangement required planning, coordination, and maintenance. More specifically, it required the selection of personally popular legislative leaders who enjoyed reasonably good relationships with many members of the party (especially committee chairs) and who were also ideological "middlemen" able to reach out to the disparate elements of the party in order to forge broad successful coalitions for policy passage. To the extent that prior studies are correct that intraparty balancing in the New Deal era's Democratic Congresses was accomplished, in part, through committee deference, the Austin-Boston alliance formalized and stabilized it in the legislative party leadership as well.

Why Austin and Why Boston?

If the need to bridge intraparty divisions suggested balancing northern and southern representation in the House Democratic leadership, the Austin-Boston alliance was, nevertheless, not preordained. A compelling question to consider is: What were the special qualities of Texas and Massachusetts members that made them particularly well-suited for such balancing?

To be sure, part of the answer is personal and has to do with the connections and special qualities that Sam Rayburn and John McCormack possessed as individuals, particularly compared to the most likely alternatives in the House. The leadership races that established Rayburn and McCormack as top Democratic leaders in the House were Rayburn's race against John O'Connor of New York for majority leader in 1937 and McCormack's against Clifton Woodrum of Virginia in 1940. Both Rayburn and McCormack were personal friends and protégés of Vice President Garner, and each had proven a valuable New Deal ally. For the New Dealers in the administration, both the 1937 and 1940 majority leader choices were clear, and the administration weighed in by providing support, albeit behind-the-scenes support, to loyal New Dealers Rayburn and McCormack over their more conservative, anti–New Deal challengers.

Still, it is also true that the Texas and Boston districts that produced these men were ideal constituencies for New Deal leaders. Rayburn was from a rural, small-farmer district that benefited greatly from New Deal farm programs, public works, and rural electrification. Most importantly, his district contained no oil — a resource whose owners were often rabidly anti–New Deal and whose views were often reflected by Texas politicians. McCormack's base was northern, urban, and Irish-Catholic. His constituency also benefited from the New Deal's public works and social welfare programs.

Second, and a more general and enduring factor, Texas and Boston were demographic outliers within their regions, particularly in terms of their racial composition. Subsequent history would prove that the great fracture in the New Deal coalition was race. The House's southern Democrats were overwhelmingly segregationists. White voters elected them, even though some of the southern states had very large African American populations. African Americans did not vote in much of the South, at least not in significant numbers. There were numerous formal restrictions on their voting such as literacy tests, poll taxes, character tests, and hostile voting registrars, not to mention violence and intimidation against potential African American voters. At the same time (and not coincidentally), a great many African Americans migrated to northern cities, where such voting restrictions were not in place. Compared to African Americans in the South, African Americans in northern cities could vote, had political influence, and, as time went by, became important politically. Given their new source of political support, northern Democrats (particularly those from cities) tended to be supporters of civil rights and increasingly opposed southern Democrats' efforts to thwart civil rights legislation.

Whereas the impact of race differed between the North and the South, it varied within regions as well. Long ago, political scientist V. O. Key Jr. pointed out that the politics of race in the South was related to the proportion of black citizens within geographical areas. According to this "black belt" hypothesis, the greater the proportion of blacks within an area, the greater the anxiety of local whites, and the greater the propensity of the whites to resort to suppression of black aspirations. Conversely, fewer blacks meant lower white anxiety and less racial suppression. It is in districts such as these that southern moderates could survive.[13] Thus, it is something of an irony that those southern Democratic congressmen who represented the most black constituents tended to be more conservative and segregationist whereas those members who represented fewer black constituents could be more moderate, having been elected without resorting to racist rhetoric. Southern politicians outside of the "black belt" could finesse the question of race without facing an electoral backlash in their districts, and they were more likely than their more segregationist and nativist counterparts to have friends and political allies in Congress who were Catholic, Jewish, liberal, northern, and even black.

Bridging the South and the West, Texas had been less dominated by slavery and subsequently had fewer African Americans than other former confederate states. For example, when Sam Rayburn became Speaker in 1940, his district contained only 13 percent African Americans. By the same token, in 1970, Speaker Carl Albert's Oklahoma district (adjacent to Rayburn's) contained only 5 percent African Americans. And, in 1980, Speaker Jim Wright's district had only 15 percent African Americans. In national Democratic Party politics, Texans and other moderate southerners were more acceptable to the more liberal, racially tolerant, northern wing of the Democratic Party. Interestingly, Boston was a northern, urban analogue of this phenomenon. Of the twelve largest standard metropolitan statistical areas (SMSA) in the country, Boston ranked twelfth in the

1950 census and eleventh in the 1970 census with regard to the proportion of blacks in the SMSA's "core city." In 1960, Boston's 9.1 percent proportion of blacks fell 15.5 points below the 24.6 percent median for these twelve urban places. In 1970, Boston's 16.3 percent was 16.9 points below that year's median for black populations in the core cities of the twelve largest SMSAs. In 1950, when he had been majority leader for a decade, John McCormack had only a 7 percent African American population in his district, though that population had grown to 27 percent by the time his Speakership ended. Tip O'Neill in 1980, however, had only a 4 percent African American population in his district.

Just as many Texans and moderate southerners could finesse race matters, without a sizeable number of blacks in their districts, McCormack, O'Neill, and other Boston-area representatives were not obliged to become spokesmen for civil rights demands. To be sure, Boston-area representatives did not vote against civil rights legislation, but neither did they place themselves in the forefront of civil rights conflicts or make the kinds of anti-segregationist speeches that might antagonize their southern colleagues. And, on a more personal level inside the House, the unique racial composition of their districts allowed Boston-area congressmen the flexibility to accommodate some of the more vocal and vehement racists that have sat in the House. One of John McCormack's best friends in the House was Eugene Cox of Georgia, a leading segregationist. It was also McCormack who made possible the return of segregationist William Colmer of Mississippi to the Rules Committee over the opposition of Speaker Rayburn. McCormack, O'Neill, and other urban congressmen with relatively small black populations in their districts were in a position to negotiate with (and, in many cases, befriend) southern hardliners without fear of electoral retribution back home.

Thus, at a time when the great emerging fault line in the Democratic Party was race, Texan and Bostonian leaders were unusually flexible and amenable to intraparty compromises on civil rights and related issues. In this crucial policy area and more generally, Texas and Boston representatives were uniquely well-situated "middlemen" who could bridge the intraparty divisions endemic in the New Deal coalition in the House.

The Personal Politics of House Leadership Selection

When focused on broad regional politics, it is easy to forget the personal side of congressional and party politics. If the House is a venue where the broad and disparate views and interests of the nation are represented, it is also an institution comprised of individuals who form friendships, alliances, and other personal relationships to fulfill both personal needs and political goals.[14] This was particularly the case in the more insular and slow-paced House of the "textbook" Congress (that is, prior to the 1970s reforms). House members, seldom having serious opposition for re-election, did not have to raise much money for campaigns or even have to campaign that much. Building a long-term career in the mid–twentieth century House, members focused much of their political and personal attention on building relationships — friendships and alliances — inside the House.

Moreover, nowhere are personal factors — friendships and rivalries alike — so pronounced in congressional politics as they are in intraparty leadership selection. Conducted by secret ballot, intraparty leadership races are somewhat insulated from outside interest group, press, or White House influences. Considered internal "family affairs," leadership races are dominated by highly personalized member-to-member campaigning where the House's friendships and rivalries are important considerations for candidates and their supporters alike.[15] Moreover, the fact that balloting in intraparty leadership races was conducted under a multiple-round single elimination method that ultimately required majority support for victory meant that strictly regional candidacies were unlikely to succeed. This voting process stressed the value of broad cross-regional alliances. These factors, when coupled with the House Democrats' tendency to develop "leadership ladders" of succession, meant that the ability of top legislative leaders to appoint allies and protégés to key committees (particularly Ways and Means and Rules) and lower-level leadership posts, especially the Whip post, made mentor-protégé relationships and individual preferment a recurring factor in party leadership selection. As Nelson W. Polsby observed long ago, the outcomes of such leadership elections and the trajectories of leadership careers more generally are significantly determined by "the mysteries of how men interact with one another, of what leads people into enmity, jealousy, friendship."[16]

Personal Politics in Congress

There are, of course, many different types of friendships in politics. As Ross Baker has pointed out, within a political environment, friendships can be personal ones where sociability is important, or friendships can be based on professional or political bonds. Personal friendships can include mentor-protégé relationships, social friendships, and pure friendships. Mentor-protégé relationships cross generations and involve mutual solicitude and assistance. Social friendships are based on compatible social styles and shared interests. Political agreement is often irrelevant to these friendships; rather, sociability, companionship, and leisure-time association are important. Pure friendships involve affection and mutual concern for the other's welfare. There is a strong emotional attachment that enables the relationship to survive serious policy disagreements. Professional friendships are based on institutional kinships or alliances. Institutional kinships are based upon the mutual experiences that come from being elected to the institution. It arises from professional pride, collegiality, and a satisfying business relationship. Alliances are the result of fairly consistent political agreement that leads to personal bonds as well as a sense of political solidarity.[17]

Unusual friendships have developed in Congress, such as the famous friendship between John Nance Garner, a crude, vulgar Democrat representing South Texas, and Nicholas Longworth, an educated, aristocratic Republican representing Cincinnati, Ohio. Still, it is more likely that friendships will develop between members who come from the same area of the country, who share similar life experiences, and have more opportunities to interact with one another. Moreover, members of the same political party and those who face similar political pressures given the region of the country they represent can develop close personal bonds that reinforce their common political and ideological predispositions.[18] This was particularly true for the old southern Democratic politicians who were in office for decades and accumulated vast networks of friends. When new members came to the House, they sought out (and were sought out by) senior congressmen who befriended and mentored them. To be sure, both benefited from such friendships. The senior member had a young ally in Congress who was useful in providing information, garnering votes, and in suggesting and developing political strategy. The younger member could rely on the power of the older member to advance his political interests in legislation, build a political career, and, especially, move up the hierarchy of the House of Representatives.[19]

Of course, in writing about the importance of friendship, we must also consider the impact of the absence of such personal relationships and even outright hostility among members. Writing of the importance of "foes" as well as friends in the Senate, Ross Baker argued that the potential sources of hostility included personal and political elements as well as ideological differences, personality conflicts, or feuds caused by conflicting ambitions, disputes over legislation, or a sense of betrayal and disloyalty.[20] All relationships — friendships and rivalries alike — have both political and personal elements, of course.[21] Reflecting the personal side of the deeper regional divisions in the House Democratic Party, these friendships, particularly mentor-protégé relationships, as well as numerous personal rivalries prove remarkably important in explaining why members move up into the leadership of the House of Representatives in the period studied in this research.

Mentors, Protégés, and Preferment Perpetuating the Alliance from FDR through Reagan

It is the strong personal and political ties that develop between senior leaders and younger members and their importance in intraparty leadership selection that, we believe, also explain the persistence of the patterns of leadership in the Democratic Party within the northern and southern wings. The hand of past friendships is fascinating to see in these leadership battles. Of course, it was more than just friendship that explains the advancement of these men up the leadership ladder. Obviously, they had other assets going for them as well — luck, ambition, ability, intelligence, and the right combination of key personal traits needed at their own particular moments. Moreover, each generally fit the needs of a Democratic Party that required well-liked middlemen to balance competing regional and ideological factions. Still, this system of mentor-protégé preferment and the ability to tap the vast political and personal networks aided them in their quest for leadership in the House and provided often determinative advantages in securing their leadership posts: Joseph Weldon Bailey's protégés were Sam Rayburn and John Nance Garner; Garner mentored and offered key assistance to Sam Rayburn and John McCormack; and Rayburn's and McCormack's protégés — Carl Albert, Hale Boggs, Tip O'Neill, and Jim Wright — advanced this alliance, begun prior to the New Deal, well into the Reagan era of U.S. politics. These mentor-protégé relationships dominated House politics and significantly affected U.S. history in the second half of the twentieth century.

It is the confluence of racial and regional politics, on the one hand, and friendships, especially mentor-protégé relationships, on the other hand, that explains much of this half century of struggles over leadership in the Democratic Party in the House. It is to an examination of these struggles that we now turn. We can not begin, however, with 1940 and the accession of Sam Rayburn of North Texas to the Speakership and John McCormack of Boston to the majority leadership. We must begin much earlier — in the nineteenth century — when events transpired that placed forces on track that led to this long-lasting House leadership pattern. In reality, the Austin-Boston connection has its origins with a nearly forgotten North Texas congressman and Texas senator who in his day was one of the most influential and controversial politicians in Texas and in the nation: It all began with Joe Bailey.

oseph Weldon Bailey was the first Texan to achieve a chamber leadership position in the U.S. House of Representatives, having become Democratic leader by the age of thirty-four in 1897. Because the Republicans controlled the House while he was the Democratic leader, Bailey never reached the Speakership. Bailey later moved to the Senate where he quickly became an influential figure. Through notable protégés (including future Speakers John Nance Garner and Sam Rayburn), Bailey left a lasting legacy on the House Democratic leadership. Indeed, ultimately, Bailey's influence over and preferment of Garner and Rayburn laid the groundwork for the Austin-Boston alliance.

Eloquence and Violence The Bailey Style

Joe Bailey's fast rise to congressional leadership reflected his remarkable talent, with notable figures in congressional history often singling Bailey out for acclaim. Missouri congressman Champ Clark, a Democrat who became the Speaker in 1911, described Bailey as "young, brilliant, able, enthusiastic, and aggressive." Clark later told Sam Rayburn, when asked who had been the ablest member of Congress with whom he had served, that "If I had to pick one, it would be Joe Bailey." Famed Republican Speaker Joe Cannon once made a similar observation. Cordell Hull, a congressman from Tennessee who later served as secretary of state, considered Bailey "a legal mind scarcely second to that of anyone in our history." Longtime New York Central Railroad executive and congressman Chauncey Depew considered Bailey to be one of "the most brilliant debaters of any legislative body" who "would have adorned and given distinction to any legislative body in the world."[1]

Oratory was Bailey's special talent. One writer, unfriendly to Bailey, nevertheless noted, "It is worth riding miles over a rough road to hear Bailey extract, with exquisite modulations and variations, the music concealed in those melodious works. He can cajole, caress, command and convince with that phrase; and he sprinkles it though his speeches almost as liberally as he sprinkles the pronoun 'I.'" Comparing Bailey to the great orator William Jennings Bryan, this author wrote that Bailey's "greatest attribute is his voice": "Bryan had a voice somewhat of the same quality as Bailey's when Bryan first began to speak; but the constant wear on Bryan's voice has roughened it somewhat — it is not so musical now as it was in 1896. Bailey's voice is a remarkable instrument. It is soft and melodious, but with a timbre that makes it at times sound like the deep tones of an organ. He is a master of it."[2] Claude Bowers, a historian of the era, wrote that "no man drew greater crowds to the gallery on the announcement that he would speak. His voice was melodious as a fine organ." Moreover, wrote Bowers, Bailey was "domineering, extraordinarily able and eloquent. . . . Tall, powerfully built, with a handsome head and features, he carried himself like a conqueror. His eloquence was both powerful and persuasive. . . . His voice was melodious, and when he finished his peroration his tones lingered in the chamber like the echo of chimes in a cathedral."[3]

To match his oratorical style and prowess in debate, Bailey had a colorful personal style. Adopting the dress of a post–Civil War southern gentleman, for over twenty-five years Bailey wore a broad-brimmed hat, a Prince Albert coat, and long hair. But his eloquence and colorful personality were but a thin veil for his burning intensity and hot temper. As Champ Clark described Bailey, "Nothing that ever wore the human form could bully Bailey. He would hold himself erect and express his honest convictions in any presence, however august." If Bailey was courageous in oratory, he also was sensitive and could nurse a grudge. For example, when Gov. O. B. Colquitt was considering appointing a man named Hall to an Amarillo, Texas, court, Bailey remembered that a few years earlier Hall had been the mayor of Vernon and refused to sit next to him on the stand when he spoke at a Fourth of July celebration in that town. Bailey wrote Colquitt, "Leaving aside the natural and just resentment which I feel against that conduct, I am absolutely certain that no man capable of it could be trusted to perform honestly and without prejudice the duties of any high position."[4]

Not surprisingly, Bailey's swashbuckling personality also had a violent dimension. He was accused once of going after a political opponent with a knife and, on another occasion, pulling a gun from a satchel to silence some critics on a train.[5] In 1902, Bailey, then a U.S. senator, displayed his famous violent temper. Bailey was involved in a controversy with W. L. Penfield, solicitor of the State Department. Bailey had become interested in a contract dispute between a constituent and Mexican interests. When his constituent lost the case in a Mexican court, Bailey insisted that the State Department intervene before the Mexican Supreme Court. When the State Department provided insufficient assistance to satisfy Bailey, he severely criticized Penfield. Indiana senator Albert Beveridge rose to defend his friend and fellow Indianan Penfield, referring to the Bailey speech as "an unwarranted attack." Taking offense, Bailey asked that the words be withdrawn. When Beveridge refused to withdraw them, Bailey became furious, jumped to his feet, and then either grabbed Beveridge around the throat or was caught by others just before doing so. Bailey was grabbed by the doorkeeper and several senators and taken into the cloakroom.[6]

Bailey often supported his words more with his oratorical skill than knowledge. As the years went by, his expertise was questioned. Bowers recalled a debate on the tariff in 1910, where Bailey asserted "with great force and confidence" that Democratic statesmen had never favored free imports of raw materials, challenging the Senate to produce a name of such a Democrat. Democrat John Sharp Williams of Mississippi, a well-educated man with a biting wit and a soft southern drawl, listed a string of Democrats who had favored free imports of raw materials. That frustrated Bailey so much that he responded, but Williams again politely replied with facts. Bailey became so angry that he was red in the face and said the opposite of what he meant only to be corrected again by Williams. Bowers believed it was at that point that Bailey lost his control of the Democratic minority in the Senate.[7]

Bailey's rise to prominence seems remarkable considering his background. Born in Crystal Springs, Mississippi, Bailey was never a good student. He attended a string of colleges, including Mississippi Baptist College, the University of Mississippi, Vanderbilt, the University of Virginia, and Lebanon Law School. He settled in Hazelhurst, Mississippi, was admitted to the bar, and quickly became involved in politics, an involvement that proved short-lived.[8] In 1883, an election riot took place in Copiah County, Mississippi, because Republicans were soliciting the votes of blacks in order to reestablish a majority. The riot became violent, and some people were killed. Bailey was implicated in the violence; when asked what should be done about those who opposed the views of the Democrats, Bailey apparently said that while he would not advise killing political enemies, he believed it would be done anyway. Thinking that this incident would hamper his career in Mississippi, Bailey moved to Gainesville, Texas, in 1885.

To Texas and to Congress

Just across the Red River from Indian Territory, Gainesville had good possibilities for trade and community growth. There, Bailey opened a law
office, got married, and began to hone his political skills, learning to spin
wonderful yarns and relate to the problems and feelings of others.[9] By
1887, he was making speeches in support of prohibition. In 1888, Bailey
could have been a serious candidate for Congress, but because he was
not yet of legal age to serve, he deferred to Silas Hare. By 1890, at the age
of twenty-seven, he successfully challenged Hare, becoming the youngest
member in the House. That year, Bailey allied himself with the beginnings of an agrarian uprising driven by the Farmer's Alliance and became
a spokesman for the Silver Democrats in the House and "a self-proclaimed
expert on the Constitution."[10]

Bailey would spend most of his congressional career in the minority,
though it did not start out that way. When he entered Congress in 1891,
Republicans controlled the Senate, but the Democrats overwhelmingly
controlled the House. However, Democrats lost control of the House in the
1894 elections, relegating Bailey to the minority for his final three terms.
When Bailey went to the Senate in 1901, the Republicans controlled both
House and Senate, a situation that continued until Bailey's last Congress,
the 62d. During that Congress, the Republicans controlled the Senate, but
Democrats had regained control of the House.

Even though Democrats controlled the House, Bailey started life in the
House majority supporting the losing side in an intraparty leadership race.
When Congress convened in December 1891, Bailey supported fellow
Texan Roger Q. Mills for the Speakership. Mills, notably the first Texan to
be a serious candidate for the Speakership, lost to Charles Crisp of Georgia.[11] Bailey's support of free silver, an essential goal of the agrarian rebellion, led him to request an appointment to the Committee on Coinage,
Weights, and Measures.[12] Instead, Speaker Crisp created an instant problem for Bailey by appointing him to the Committee on Public Lands, an
unimportant committee for the ambitious Texan. However, Bailey made a
mark even in his first term, being cited by future Speaker Champ Clark as
proof that a freshman could have an impact.[13]

In Congress, Bailey supported the continuation of the parliamentary
rules changes Republicans had instituted to empower the House majority party. Reed's Rules, created by the Republican Speaker Thomas Reed,
enabled the Speaker and the House majority party to facilitate business
while minimizing minority party efforts at obstruction. Among the most

important aspects of Reed's Rules were that the Speaker could count those members not voting as present for purposes of a quorum and could deny recognition to members proposing dilatory motions.[14]

When Democrats took back the White House in 1892, Bailey proved to be no friend of the Cleveland administration, breaking with Cleveland over policy and patronage. Cleveland supported repeal of the silver purchasing law, which caused many agrarians, including Bailey, to break with him.[15] Still, Bailey's support for free silver was not enough to forestall significant opposition from the Populists in 1894. Bailey differed with Populists on racial and economic issues. The Populists' efforts to capture the black vote rankled Bailey, a white supremacist. Additionally, the Populists wanted government ownership of railroads, direct aid to the farmer, and governmental intervention in the economy to improve conditions for labor. Never accepting that more fundamental changes were necessary to improve the conditions of the farmer, Bailey rejected these solutions, believing instead that regulation of the railroads and free silver were the solutions to the problems of agrarian society.

Bailey responded strongly to the Populist assault. When faced with personal attacks in a debate with the Populist candidate, Bailey flew into a rage, saying that before he would allow his opponent to continue speaking, he would cut the man's throat. Although Bailey won that election, his antipathy toward the Populists lingered. He opposed William Jennings Bryan as the Democratic nominee two years later, believing Bryan too close to the Populists. At first, an angry Bailey announced that he would not seek reelection, although four days later he changed his mind.

Bailey also quarreled with the Cleveland administration over Cleveland's uncooperativeness with the patronage needs of members of Congress and his support of civil service. On one occasion, Bailey and eleven of the thirteen representatives from Texas had supported Nat Gunter for the seat of collector of customs at El Paso, but Cleveland had given the position to someone else, causing bitterness among the Texans. Bailey's independence and temper exacerbated these patronage battles. Once, when Bailey returned to Washington after making speeches critical of Cleveland back home, Postmaster Gen. Wilson Bissell expressed reluctance to comply with Bailey's request about appointing a postmaster. Bailey replied, "It is none of your —— business what sort of speeches I made. I wasn't sent to Congress to represent you or Cleveland. I answer to nobody but my own constituents and my own conscience for my speeches. You can appoint this man or I will withdraw all my recommendations and will never set foot in this office again while you are here."[16] When Bailey did not get his appointment, he never again visited the Post Office Department until Bissell left office. Early in the new McKinley presidency, Bailey continued to oppose civil service reform, referring to it as "a colossal humbug" and as "'snivel-service' reform."[17]

By 1896, Bailey was a leader in the House with agrarian Democrats as the main source of his strength in a divided Democratic caucus. Speaker Crisp expressed his frustration to Bailey: "Nobody can lead this wrangling, quarrelsome, factionalized Democratic minority. I do not intend to return to the House. I am going home to stand for the Senate. If I lose that, I will quit public life forever."[18] When Crisp became a candidate for Senate, Bailey ran for minority leader. By March of 1897, Bailey had consolidated his position and became the minority party candidate for the Speakership, losing to Republican Thomas B. Reed by a vote of 200–114.

As head of his party, Bailey was among the most influential Democrats in Reed's Republican-dominated House, though his Democratic enemies thought him too close to Reed. Their charges were not without merit, for Reed did seem to favor Bailey, in part because of his anti-Bryan stance. Bailey served on the Rules Committee and the Ways and Means Committee. When reports circulated, beginning in 1897, that Bailey would seek a Senate seat, Bailey deflected these rumors, claiming that he had more power as minority leader in the House than he would have as a U.S. senator.[19]

Bailey would soon grow frustrated in the House, however, learning firsthand the truth of Crisp's sense of disgust with the Democratic minority. Clark recalled, "It is interesting to note that Bailey, young, brilliant, able, enthusiastic, and aggressive, became minority leader of the 55th Congress, and with all his splendid ability was so pestered by Democratic kickers that he followed Crisp's example, declined to stand for reelection, and went over to the Senate, where he developed into one of the most powerful debaters of this generation." Additionally, Bailey lost influence with Republican leaders. Once a close friend with "Czar" Reed, by the late 1890s, they became mortal enemies. Champ Clark thought the split occurred on the day that the United States declared war on Spain when it was rumored that Bailey had challenged Reed to a duel.[20]

Bailey's frustration came to a head when he insisted that Congressman Joe Wheeler of Alabama should not be able under the Constitution to hold seats both in the Congress and in the military. In 1899, Bailey introduced a resolution, referred to the House Judiciary Committee, that declared the seats of all congressmen holding both military and congressional positions be vacated. Bailey's fellow Democrats failed to support him, and Bailey announced that he would not seek reelection claiming he could no longer be the minority leader of "a large number of Democrats . . . unwilling to insist upon obedience to the perfectly plain provisions of the Constitution."[21]

Senator Bailey

Bailey's threat to resign his seat in the House allowed him to explain his decision to resign on constitutional principle instead of rejection of his leadership or mere ambition. But there was more than a little ambition in Bailey. One author suggests that Bailey decided to enter the Senate because he remembered Roger Mills's failure to become Speaker and concluded that a Texan could not attain the Speakership.[22] Also, Bailey did have plans to resign his seat in the House in order to run for Sen. Horace Chilton's seat in 1900. Writing of Bailey's increasingly frequent references to flag, Constitution, home, and mother, Chilton realized that soon Bailey would openly oppose him.[23]

Now focused on the U.S. Senate, Bailey canvassed the state in opposition to Chilton. On one significant issue, imperialism, Bailey showed his new ambition to move to the Senate. Prior to his Senate race, Bailey had argued that imperialism was inconsistent with American ideals. Under the Jeffersonian philosophy of social contract, there was no place for imperial subjects. But now that he was a candidate for Senate, the tone of his anti-imperialism argument changed. He now argued that in countries annexed by the United States, after a period of military control, they would eventually have to be given statehood. Inhabitants of these countries would be treated the way the South had been treated by the carpetbaggers, but statehood would come, meaning that the "lowest Spaniards and the meanest Negroes on earth" would become citizens of the United States.[24] Ultimately, the result of imperialism and annexation would be race equality.

On January 23, 1901, Bailey was overwhelmingly chosen U.S. senator by the Texas legislature, and, as senator, he continued his appeals to white supremacy. For example, after Booker T. Washington dined in the White House with Pres. Theodore Roosevelt, Bailey made a speech in Brownwood, Texas, in September 1904, saying, "No wonder Roosevelt eats with Booker. He wants the Negro vote in the North. I believe more in the purity of the Anglo-Saxon race than I do in the principles of democracy."[25]

One important political alliance Bailey formed as a candidate for the

Senate was with Col. Edward House, at that time a major political op-
erative in the state. Although House recognized Bailey's popularity and
significant political support, he was wary of Bailey. Given Bailey's vola-
tility and the difficult nature of his personality, House kept his distance
from Bailey, always approaching him through third parties and avoiding
familiarity with him.[26] But House also had an alliance with Jim Wells,
which gave Bailey the ability to build a relationship with the South Texas
political mogul.

Bailey changed in important respects as he moved from the House to
the Senate. In the House, Bailey had voted with southern Democrats and
agricultural interests, advocating lower tariffs and, while he supported
the Spanish-American War, opposing imperialism. In the Senate, Bailey
became more conservative and often voted with northern Democrats.
Perhaps more importantly, with his election to the Senate, he became increasingly involved in business schemes to gain personal wealth. One critical magazine article claimed that "Mr. Bailey spent money like water, as
men of fancy, appetite, and imagination ever do; and since his needs were
forever outrunning his resources, he was perennially 'hard up.'"[27] Previously, Bailey's income had been dependent on his House salary, but now
he sought wealth through investments and an expanding law practice. He
reasoned that he could do so without affecting his public responsibilities.
Another critic, Alfred Henry Lewis, wrote, "Once in the Senate, Bailey
began to think of and long for money. He had tastes, and while they were
not elevated, they were expensive. He liked horses, he liked cards; and
horses and cards are not within the wages of a senator."[28]

David Graham Phillips observed that Bailey had previously been "poor,"
but that he "suddenly struck 'pay-dirt' in quantity." Bailey had apparently
been insolvent as late as 1899, but he began to buy property in 1903. Soon
it was claimed he owned substantial property in Cooke and Dallas counties in Texas and also in Kentucky. He also purchased stock in a newspaper
worth $10,000, and earned a fabulous fee on the sale of Tennessee Railway
properties worth $500,000. In all, political opponents suggested that his
property was worth over $1,000,000. With his typical flair, Bailey claimed,
"In all the long and glorious history of our and of other Southern States,
there never lived and served a man whose record is as much above suspicion of unselfish men as mine."[29]

His rapid economic success came in part through controversial business deals. He became a good friend of John H. Kirby, owner and president
of the Houston Oil Company and the Kirby Lumber Company. In 1902,

the Houston Oil Company, a holding company for southeast Texas timberlands, was valued at more than $38,000,000. When the company got caught in a legal tangle over company stocks, Bailey recovered the stock for Kirby and earned legal fees of $149,000 between 1902 and 1906.

But it was Bailey's friendship with Pres. Henry Clay Pierce of the Waters-Pierce Oil Company, the major supplier of lighting fuel in Texas, which became the center of his political problems. In 1895, charges were filed against the company alleging it was in violation of the anti-trust laws of Texas. On March 17, 1900, the state won its suits, which required the company to forfeit its charter to do business in Texas. On the recommendation of David R. Francis, a former Democratic governor of Missouri, Pierce hired Bailey to assist the company's efforts to regain its license. Prior to returning to Texas, however, Bailey went to Kentucky to sell some racehorses he owned to settle a debt. When he was unable to make the sale, Bailey borrowed $3,300 from Pierce and executed a note payable to him.

In May 1900, Bailey went to Austin and met with Gov. Joseph Sayers about the relicensing of Waters-Pierce. While the governor was supportive, Atty. Gen. T. S. Smith denied the relicensing, saying that the company could not transact business in Texas again. The only way around the court ruling was to dissolve the company, reorganize, and apply for a new license, which the company did. The new Waters-Pierce Oil Company was soon doing business in Texas under a new charter.

Bailey's assistance in the relicensing of the Waters-Pierce Oil Company became controversial. In the midst of increasing criticism and rumors, Bailey erred in not admitting that he had, in fact, borrowed money from Pierce. Bailey had a lot to lose should things go wrong, and as questions arose, the legislature met in Austin in 1901 and undertook an investigation of the Waters-Pierce scandal. State Rep. David McFall of Travis County introduced a resolution charging that the Waters-Pierce relicensing had defrauded the state and constituted an evasion of the ruling of the Supreme Court punishable by law. Most importantly, McFall wished to investigate whether "Mr. Bailey is a proper man to send to the United States Senate."[30]

The McFall Resolution threatened Bailey's career. A group of Bailey's allies in the House, led by John Nance Garner of Uvalde, went to Bailey's apartment at the Driskill Hotel to develop a response strategy. Bailey told the group that the accusations should not be altered except to add the phrase "by David McFall" after the words "it is charged" so as to place Mc-

Fall in the roles both as complainant and as prosecutor.[31] This change was known as the "Garner substitute" to the McFall Resolutions.

The Texas House appointed a committee to investigate Bailey's role in the Waters-Pierce re-incorporation and relicensing. Tom Connally, then a state representative, recalled that Bailey lobbied the committee for a single report acquitting him while denouncing his accusers. Bailey asked Connally for his assistance. Connally had been told that "to refuse a Bailey request . . . was a capital political offense," but he refused to go along. Connally remembered, "Bailey became furious; he banged on the table; he shook his big fist in my face; and he gave off a barnful of upbraiding sarcasm. But I wouldn't let him talk me into changing my mind, and he stormed out of the room in deep anger."[32] During the hearings, Bailey testified that he had become convinced that Waters-Pierce was not a trust. Only then did he talk to the attorney general and the secretary of state to assist Pierce in getting a new permit.

What Bailey did not mention was the incestuous relationship between Waters-Pierce and the Standard Oil Trust. In September of 1899, Waters-Pierce had increased its capital stock from $100,000 to $400,000. Trustees of Standard Oil held $120,000 of these new shares. An additional $60,000 in shares was held by a subsidiary of Standard, the Chess-Carley Company. Thus, Standard Oil not only owned stock in Waters-Pierce but, in effect, had controlling interest. Bailey, however, claimed that Pierce had convinced him that Standard Oil trustees no longer held stock in Waters-Pierce, allowing Pierce to dissolve Waters-Pierce and organize a new corporation. Bailey denied that he was the paid attorney for the company and claimed that he helped Pierce because of his friendship with David Francis.

Bailey concluded his testimony by saying that through misrepresentation, his integrity had been questioned. He averred his innocence, stating that he had never accepted a fee from Pierce, although he saw nothing wrong with accepting employment from Pierce had he chosen to do so. He mentioned neither the $3,300 loan nor other transactions.

The investigation was quite limited, and the House, by a vote of 87 to 25, exonerated Bailey of all charges. In part, the majority report read as follows: "[We denounce] the malicious imputations and insinuations against the integrity of the Hon. J. W. Bailey, . . . as the most cruel, vindictive and unfounded attack ever made upon the character of a faithful public servant in Texas."[33] Forty minutes after he had been exonerated by the legislature, he was chosen U.S. senator by a vote of 110 to 4.

But these allegations would haunt Bailey's career, arising again at reelection time. Bailey had accepted several large cases in compliance with his belief that "a Senator had the right in his spare time to practice law with a view to laying up a competence in his old age." By May of 1906, Texas Atty. Gen. Robert Davidson and Asst. Atty. Gen. Jewell Lightfoot reopened an investigation of the connection between Bailey and Waters-Pierce. Although the loans made to Bailey had been personal loans, they were put on the books of the Waters-Pierce Oil Company as "Texas legal expenses." Bailey wrote the two officials assuring them that they had been falsely informed about his connection to Pierce and asserted his innocence. But rumors of the vouchers circulated, and Cosmopolitan Magazine published an article resurrecting the charges against Bailey in which it was claimed that "If he [Bailey] would love riches less and honest poverty more, he would be the man that nature intended him to be."[34]

During July, Bailey had again been nominated to the Senate, and the renewed allegations against him had divided the state into "Bailey men" who still supported the senator and "anti-Bailey men" who opposed him. Although it was optional, Bailey ran in the primary, where he was unopposed. At the state Democratic convention in August 1906, delegates voted to denounce the unjust attacks made upon Bailey's personal character.

Still, a lawsuit involving Pierce brought out Bailey's integral role in getting Waters-Pierce re-licensed in Texas. It also showed that Bailey had been employed to help Pierce with his investments worth $13,000,000 in the Briar Collieries, the Tennessee Construction Company, the Tennessee Central Railway, and the Cumberland Coal Company. The Houston Good Government League publicized the revelations, placing Bailey's political future in doubt. He returned home to defend himself, arguing that he had not tried to conceal his work as an attorney for the Tennessee interests.

Then, in September 1906, the state of Texas filed pleadings accusing Pierce of fraud in attempting to settle cases against him by offering large sums to secure the readmission of his oil company "through supposed political influence." Bailey saw this, quite correctly, as a political attack, and throughout October he toured the state and made numerous speeches. At the Texas State Fair in mid-October, Sen. "Pitchfork" Ben Tillman of South Carolina spoke in Bailey's behalf, telling the crowd, "If they don't give us any more corrupt men . . . any more cowardly men than the two Texas Senators, by the Eternal Gods we will be able to hold our own."[35]

As the Texas suit against Waters-Pierce progressed and documents showing that the Pierce loans to Bailey were legal fees emerged, Bailey once again returned to Texas. In December 1906, he declared that any documents that showed him being paid legal fees were forgeries. At this point, Bailey stated that in 1900 he had borrowed money from Pierce, adding that he had not attempted to conceal his actions. After all, he had stated in 1901 that "time permitting, [he] would have accepted employment from the oil company itself, for he was then convinced that it was no part of the Standard Oil combine" based on assurances to him by Pierce.[36] He had only discovered the connection between the two oil companies after the Missouri prosecution of Waters-Pierce.

However, the admission that he had borrowed money from Pierce at the same time as Waters-Pierce was having legal problems in Texas began a firestorm of criticism. The *Dallas News* withdrew its support of Bailey and wrote that "the Democracy of Texas should unite upon some other man for the high place [Bailey] now holds."[37]

The Bailey controversy reached its height as the 30th Texas Legislature convened on January 8, 1907. The following day, about seventy-five Bailey Men in the Texas House met to allow Bailey to tell his side. It was decided that specific charges should be made in the case and a general investigation should be opposed. In late January, both the state Senate and House appointed committees to conduct investigations. After only one month, the Senate discharged its committee and voted for an exoneration of Bailey, but the House proceedings dragged on. Bailey declared that "every Socialist in Texas is standing on the street corner reviling me day and night." Bailey promised to drive his enemies into the Gulf of Mexico for they were "anarchists, thieves, liars, hyenas, dogs, and hessians."[38]

One of the few anti-Bailey legislators demanding an investigation was Sam Johnson, the father of Lyndon Johnson. In a meeting in Bailey's Austin hotel room, Johnson told Bailey that his constituents wanted an investigation, and Bailey told Johnson he would make sure that anyone opposing him would never again hold office. Bailey denied threatening Sam Johnson. "Mr. Johnson," Bailey said, "is a brother-in-law of one of the best friends I have in this state. . . . [Johnson] seemed to think, that although these men stand upon street corners and denounce me as a traitor to my country, insinuate that I have not been an honest man, that I ought to draw my cloak around me, and with meekness and humility say, 'Pray, sirs, don't do that.' . . . I think I deserve great praise for not taking a shotgun and killing them, and if I could have gotten around, that is what I would have done."[39]

The anti-Baileys showed that since going to the Senate, Bailey's wealth had grown beyond any reason. He had received many loans from people who were seeking various favors from the government and had accumulated $1,029,251.18 and that in February 1908 Bailey was one of the thirty-two senators who had been listed as a millionaire. Bailey consistently defended himself: "I despise those public men who think they must remain poor in order to be considered honest. I am not one of them. If my constituents want a man who is willing to go to the poorhouse in his old age in order to stay in the Senate during his middle age, they will have to find another Senator. I intend to make every dollar that I can honestly make, without neglecting or interfering with my public duty; and there is no other man in this country who would not do the same, if he has sense enough to keep a churchyard."[40] Bailey admitted that the documents exhibited by the proponents of the charges were true documents. He also confirmed that on April 25, 1900, he had accepted a $3,300 personal loan from Pierce, though it had been listed on company books as "account of Texas cases." Any services he provided were friendly, not legal services. He added that he repaid the loan with interest, although the Waters-Pierce books did not show repayment. Other records showed more substantial financial transactions between Bailey and Pierce. Bailey testified that he received between $25,000 to $40,000 from Pierce between 1902 and 1907, but, in spite of such admissions, the committee voted 4–3 to exonerate Bailey, and the House voted 70–41 for Bailey. Even with the second exoneration, Bailey's opponents like M. M. Crane were unconvinced of his innocence. In 1912, Crane wrote that he had seen "the strongest evidence of a conspiracy to dominate not only the politics of Texas, but the politics of the Nation."[41]

A 1911 *Saturday Evening Post* echoed Crane's assessment:

Bailey came to Washington a raw Southern boy, with a great talent. He has developed that talent — public speaking — until there is no man who matches him, so far as the method goes. He has developed from the raw Southern boy, who boasted he was from and of the plain people, into the worldly-wise man, who, so far from refusing to wear evening clothes — as the story goes — now can be seen frequently in the New York hotels in most modish attire. He has grown rich, they say, and he has grown in many ways; but, eloquent as he is, able as he is, he never will be anything but a special pleader. He never will command a stable following because of his own utter instability, his sophomoric view of national problems and his exaggerated view of Bailey himself.[42]

Bailey chose not to seek his Senate seat again in 1912, seemingly in another fit of anger. He had attempted to resign over New Mexico and Arizona statehood. He had resigned from the Committee on Privileges and Elections and the National Monetary Commission. He had been denounced by fellow Democrats, and he had denounced them. Bailey's own explanation was that he quit politics because of the prohibition question. In 1928, he developed that theme, claiming that he concluded that prohibition would become a dominant issue for several years, and he thought any man running for the Senate who made prohibition an issue was unworthy of office.[43]

Bailey was uncomfortable in an increasingly progressive Democratic Party. On March 4, 1911, Bailey sent a telegram to Texas Gov. Oscar Colquitt attacking "those populistic heresies known as the initeave [sic] referendum."[44] He claimed that he would not remain in the Senate if a majority of those in his party supported them. When he interpreted a vote of the Democrats in the Senate that very morning as supporting those policies, he resigned. Only after he was assured that he had misconstrued the Democrats' votes and had received requests from his friends and from the governor did he decide to withdraw his resignation.

But the die was cast. Bailey had replaced his traditional trademark dress with a black derby hat and an ordinary suit and in July, 1911, he announced that he was building a home in Washington that would cost between $30,000 and $50,000. He was, in other words, detaching himself from the political scene. At the age of 49, Bailey would leave the U.S. Senate as he made clear in a September 5, 1911, speech. His official resignation came on January 3, 1913, apparently with the understanding that his friend Rienzi M. Johnston would fill the vacancy. While Johnston was appointed by the governor, twenty five days later the legislature elected Morris Sheppard to both the unexpired and the long term. It was claimed that eighteen legislators went back on their word to back Bailey-ally Johnston and instead supported Sheppard, a Woodrow Wilson man.[45]

Though personal controversy dominated Bailey's career, he also had legislative accomplishments. His greatest, which he shared with Theodore Roosevelt and Benjamin Tillman, was the Hepburn Rate Bill, which empowered the Interstate Commerce Commission to regulate the railroads in 1906. Additionally, he was an early advocate of the income tax by fighting for the corporate income tax in 1909, which was a precursor to the personal income tax. Bailey continued as a major advocate for the personal income tax until its implementation in 1914. Still many of his views seem archaic. He strongly advocated states' rights and opposed the franchise for women.[46]

Bailey Men

The relationships that Bailey fostered with younger politicians, however, would be more important to his legacy than his legislative successes. McKay and Faulk state, "For nearly three decades after 1900, Texas voters were inclined to judge the qualifications of all aspirants for public office on the basis of whether the candidates favored or opposed Senator Joseph Weldon Bailey."[47] That far-reaching legacy extended to the House where two central figures in twentieth-century Democratic politics, Speakers John Nance Garner and Sam Rayburn, first cut their political teeth as Bailey men.

Garner became a Bailey man because his political mentor, South Texas political boss Jim Wells, aligned with Bailey. Wells's support was essential for Garner to get to Congress and then to stay there. The Wells-Garner relationship lasted for twenty years. When Jim Wells's political power and health were in decline, Garner wrote him, "As I grow older I think I grow more appreciative, and I never think of myself or my service in Congress that I do not remember that it all would have been impossible had it not been for your goodness—I shall never cease to love you for it."[48]

Of the many political alliances Jim Wells entered into over his lengthy career, the alliance with Joe Bailey was one of the most persistent. Bailey supported Wells's campaigns to the Democratic state executive committee and for the chairmanship of the Democratic state party, and he supported Wells's man, Francis Seabury, in his effort to become Speaker of the Texas House of Representatives.[49] By the same token, Wells repeatedly threw his considerable support behind Bailey. Indeed, more than just a convenient political ally, Wells admired Bailey and considered him to be the most articulate and aggressive spokesman for conservatism in Texas. For Wells, Bailey was more than just a reliable friend in Washington; "he symbolized the Jeffersonian ideals of limited government and states rights—concepts Wells believed in."[50]

Bailey relied on Wells's support in South Texas for his statewide campaigns and Wells remained loyal throughout the Waters-Pierce scandal.

During the first legislative investigation of Waters-Pierce, Wells went to Austin and personally lobbied on Bailey's behalf. One ally, Garner, chaired the pro-Bailey caucus while another, Francis Seabury, served on the investigating committee.[51] And, in 1906, as attacks on Bailey mounted, Wells extracted pledges from legislators in the Rio Grande Valley to support Bailey, writing one legislator who had doubts about Bailey, "If you are making enemies by standing by dear old Joe Bailey, your friends, and all true Democrats, will love you better for the enemies you are thus making; please, for me, never falter in your defense of Bailey, and I shall never cease to feel grateful to you for it." And, in the 1907 Bailey investigation, Wells successfully pushed for Bailey's reelection to the Senate even before the investigation concluded. Wells worked in Bailey's behalf in 1908 to send only Bailey men to the Democratic convention.[52] Even at the end of Bailey's campaign career, when he ran for governor in 1920, Wells remained loyal.[53]

In a Texas politics divided between Bailey men and anti-Bailey men, Garner's closeness to Wells made Garner a Bailey man. In the 1901 investigation of Bailey, Garner took the lead role in building the coalition defending Bailey in the Texas House of Representatives. Then, when Garner faced a major political challenge in his run for Congress, Bailey came to his rescue and campaigned on his behalf.[54]

If the Bailey-Garner association formed through local Texas bosses, the Bailey-Rayburn connection was both a political alliance and a close personal bond. Rayburn traced his ties to Bailey to his youth, likely to 1897, when Rayburn was fifteen.[55] Rayburn explained that he rode for eleven miles on the back of a mule in a heavy rain in order to hear Bailey. He described the experience: "I'd never been to Bonham since we bought the farm, and I was scared of all the rich townsfolk in their store-bought clothes. But I found a flap in the canvas, and I stuck there like glue while old Joe Bailey made his speech. He went on for two solid hours, and I scarcely drew a breath the whole time. I can still feel the water dripping down my neck. I slipped around to the entrance again when he was through, saw him come out, and ran after him five or six blocks until he got on a streetcar. Then I went home, wondering whether I'd ever be as big a man as Joe Bailey." Rayburn described his excitement over the experience by saying, "This Adonis of a man with a massive brain captured my imagination and became my model." After hearing Joe Bailey, young Sam Rayburn would practice giving speeches to the animals on the Rayburn farm.[56]

Rayburn became one of Bailey's closest protégés. Early in Rayburn's political career, Bailey embraced the mentor role. Nineteen years older than Rayburn, Bailey was old enough to be Rayburn's father. Their personal ties were close enough that Bailey paid a condolence call on Rayburn's parents after their son Abner died in 1914. Rayburn's mother wrote Sam, "You don't have to be with him but a few minutes until you find out that he knows nearly everything. He certainly speaks in the highest terms of you. . . . He said there were great things in the future for you if you would study. He always puts that in, but he said you were studying."[57]

In addition to Rayburn's early admiration of Bailey and their close relationship, Rayburn also shared much of Bailey's old political base. The House districts they represented overlapped in Collin, Fannin, and Grayson counties.[58] In Fannin County, some of Rayburn's closest political supporters, such as Thomas Steger and Ed Steger, were also Bailey men. Thomas Steger, a lawyer with whom Rayburn practiced law, represented the Santa Fe Railroad, and Ed, also a lawyer, was on the state Democratic Executive Committee and was the president of a short-line railroad, the Denison, Bonham & New Orleans. Along with a brother, Gus, a flour mill operator, the Stegers were closely associated with Joe Bailey.

Indeed, Ed Steger was involved in an early Bailey scandal. Also a mule buyer (Bonham was a mule-trading center), Steger was involved in mule and cattle deals with Bailey. One allegation against Bailey was that Bailey had a financial interest in horse, mule, hay, and grain contracts with the U.S. government, held in part by Ed Steger. Another charge was that Steger had given Bailey five thousand dollars for his help with a contract to supply mules to the government during the Spanish-American War. Ed denied those allegations in a handwritten letter to Bailey, although his letter did state, "I proposed to remunerate you, but you indignantly refused to accept . . . and explained that you had steadfastly refused to make money out of any thing that came to you on account of your being a congressman, but that you were glad you had been of service to your district." Bailey and Steger were involved in a number of other business deals as well, though both always insisted that the deals had been on the up and up.[59]

Another political associate was W. A. Thomas, the brother-in-law of and advisor to Rayburn, who arranged an appointment of Thomas as regional director of the Internal Revenue Service. So close was Thomas to Bailey that Thomas spoke in Bailey's behalf in 1920 when Bailey attempted to restart his political career and unsuccessfully ran for governor of Texas.

By this point, Rayburn had come to see Bailey as a political liability, and, to Rayburn's dismay, Thomas became director of Bailey's campaign in Dallas. Believing that this association would be politically harmful, Rayburn wrote to his sister Kate, W. A.'s wife, that he was "very much grieved" since "everyone knows our relationship and can never be convinced that it has not at least my passive sanction."[60]

When Rayburn was elected to the Texas House of Representatives in 1906, he represented Fannin County, where he was from, in the heart of Bailey country. During Rayburn's first session in 1907, the anti-Bailey faction in the legislature sought to replace Bailey in the Senate, and Bailey declared that he was returning to the state to drive "into the Gulf of Mexico the peanut politicians" opposing him. Anyone who replaced him, Bailey argued, would "rattle around in his seat like a mustard seed in a gourd." Rayburn took a quiet, low-key role in the investigations but supported Bailey. Whereas the anti-Bailey men believed they had witnessed a great miscarriage of justice, his supporters, including Rayburn, joyously carried Bailey into the House chamber where a vindictive Bailey delivered a speech that Rayburn would talk about for decades, telling Jim Wright about it to the extent that Wright memorized parts of it.[61] Bailey's venomous speech shocked and sickened many of Bailey's friends. Said Bailey,

> My countrymen . . . they have drawn the line. These infidels who have waged war on me . . . have made their own graves. We are going to lay them gently in those newly made graves. We are going to bury them face down so that the harder they scratch to get out, the deeper they will go toward their eternal resting place. . . . My friends say this is a bitter speech. I intend it to be bitter. . . . I sometimes wish I might possess words of pure hate, words that would writhe and hiss like snakes, for only then could I express my opinion of the man who organized and conducted this conspiracy. . . . I will not forgive them this side of the grave. . . . I owe no grudges that I have not tried to pay to my enemies, and I owe no obligation that I have not tried to pay my friends. . . . In my home I intend to put the photograph of this Legislature. Two pictures will embrace that photograph. Over the one I am going to write, "The Roll of Honor" . . . over the other, "The Rogue's Gallery." . . . I am going to swear my children never to forget the one or forgive the other.[62]

Years later, Rayburn told Jim Wright that Bailey had later confessed to him that his bitter outcry was a mistake. In reality, Bailey was far less forgiving. In 1956, Edmond Travis, Bailey's publicity man for the 1920 campaign for governor, told D. B. Hardeman that Bailey was "defiant, arrogant, unrepentant to the end." Rayburn himself told Hardeman that he had said to Bailey long after Bailey had left politics, "Senator, if I had been one of your good friends that night you made the "Rogue's gallery" speech, I would have broken your leg or put you in jail or done anything to you to keep you from making it." "No, Sam," replied Bailey, "I had to make that speech."[63] Interestingly, Rayburn was one of Bailey's good friends that night but did not stop Bailey, perhaps because Bailey's anger could not be thwarted. Of course it is probably also the case that Rayburn could not have questioned his idol at that time.

Rayburn supported a Bailey man, A. M. Kennedy, for the Texas House Speakership in 1909.[64] As Speaker, Kennedy appointed Rayburn to the chairmanship of the Committee on Banks and Banking, and Rayburn remained on the Common Carriers Committee. Kennedy ran into trouble as Speaker when he was accused of inappropriate expenditures for furniture for the Speaker's office and for excusing absences and paying House employees in ways banned by House rules. Though Rayburn defended Kennedy, Kennedy was forced to resign, and John Marshall of Grayson County became Speaker.[65]

In 1911, in only his third term, Rayburn sought the Speakership of the Texas House. Although Rayburn and Bailey differed on some issues (for example, at this time Rayburn was a prohibitionist, and Bailey, by this point, had become an anti-prohibitionist), Rayburn remained loyal. Having already experienced two investigations, Bailey needed a friend as Speaker who might protect him in the future. Having Rayburn in the Speakership would be an insurance policy. In a House that Governor Colquitt thought had sixty-four pro-Bailey and sixty-nine anti-Bailey members, Rayburn was known to be a Bailey man.[66] Bailey used his influence to convince an opposing candidate's supporters to switch their votes to Rayburn. It is claimed that Bailey sent telegrams and letters to his closest friends in the House telling them to "Get right"; that is, switch to Rayburn. As Texas Speaker, Rayburn remained a loyal Bailey protégé to the point that job applicants might seek Senator Bailey's help to get a state job under Texas House Speaker Rayburn's patronage. Even notorious South Texas political boss Archer Parr asked Bailey to get Rayburn to help him with a political appointment.[67]

Still, for all of his admiration of and association with Bailey, a mainstay of Rayburn's image during his long political career was his personal integrity. Rayburn apparently had learned an important lesson from the

Bailey scandal: not to mix public office with personal financial gain. With the Bailey investigations in the legislature fresh in his mind, Rayburn returned home only to be offered one-sixth of the monthly retainer fee from the Santa Fe Railroad that Rayburn was entitled to as a partner with the Steger and Thurmond firm. Rayburn refused the money, telling Ed Steger that "men who represent the people should be as far removed as possible from concerns whose interests he is liable to be called to legislate on."[68] In future years, Rayburn would tout his simple integrity as a campaign theme. A 1932 election flyer pointed out that "Sam Rayburn owns no stocks or bonds, but that his savings are in a farm in Fannin County, Texas; that he was reared on a farm and that, therefore, he has the interests of the farmer at heart," and in 1948, a political advertisement noted that Rayburn had "served this district for thirty-six years without getting rich. He has had the power and the intelligence to have feathered his nest with millions, and today is no richer in this world's goods than the rest of us. You can name others who have not been up there over six years that have retired with a fabulous fortune, and they were men without the ability of Sam Rayburn."[69] Rayburn was rigid on ethical questions. He argued with friends that either a man was honest or he was not; there was no in-between. Rayburn praised the dismissal of students from the military academy, for he maintained that a student who cheated on an examination should not be allowed to wear the uniform of a U.S. military officer. Privately, in his later years, he criticized Senator Bailey's financial affairs.[70]

Just as Rayburn's career in Texas politics had benefited from Bailey's power, his advancement to Washington would benefit from Bailey's withdrawal from politics. Rayburn thought about running for the U.S. House as early as January 1911. His opponent might have been Choice B. Randell, long an anti-Bailey man who had replaced Bailey in the House when Bailey went to the Senate.[71] From Sherman in Grayson County, Randell had also served on the powerful Ways and Means Committee and gained a reputation as someone who could obtain funds for public buildings in the district. But Bailey detested Randell and threatened to endorse one of Randell's opponents in the 1900 congressional race even while campaigning against incumbent Sen. Horace Chilton. Randell sought Bailey's neutrality by promising to support no one in the Senate race if Bailey would remain neutral in the House race.[72]

Given his influence in the House, Randell would have been tough opposition for Rayburn, and a Rayburn-Randell race would clearly have been a referendum on Bailey in his old district. But Rayburn would not have to challenge Randell, who vacated his congressional seat in 1912 to run against Bailey for the Senate.[73] Anti-Bailey leaders had identified several potential opponents for Bailey, including Congressmen Albert Sydney Burleson and Morris Sheppard, though Sheppard had repudiated a published suggestion that he attempt to oust Bailey.[74]

Randell announced he would challenge Bailey in March 1911, far earlier than the other major candidates. Sheppard announced his candidacy on September 25, and another candidate, Jacob Wolters, did not declare until October 8. Only Randell had declared his candidacy before Bailey's September 5 announcement that he would not seek reelection. Bailey disparaged Randell, characterizing his challenge by telling others: "Ha, ha. Just say that I laughed" and "Who is Randell? He is my successor in Congress and that is about all he ever will be known as." Still, Randell's early attacks on Bailey made him popular with the anti-Bailey forces.[75]

Randell characterized himself as a Progressive against the old-style corrupt politician Bailey. As early as September 1909, Randell thought he might successfully challenge Bailey on the issue of accepting graft. As the author of the Anti-Graft Resolutions, designed to prevent congressmen from receiving gifts or fees from corporations or individuals interested in legislation before Congress, Randell could differentiate himself from Bailey.[76] The resolutions, of course, were a rather blatant attack on Bailey.[77] Still, some of Randell's views were themselves decidedly anti-Progressive. For example, he opposed women's suffrage because that would give black women the right to vote.[78]

A month after Randell announced his candidacy, Bailey forces in Congress attempted to retaliate. Randell ran for chairman of the Texas delegation, a group not surprisingly divided along Bailey lines. Of the fifteen representatives, seven, including Congressman John Nance Garner, were pro-Bailey, and eight were anti-Bailey. With the support of the other anti-Bailey congressmen Randell won, but the Bailey forces moved to reconsider the vote. The result was a tie, because Randell felt he could not vote on the issue. Ultimately, Randell remained as chair but only after a long battle. Morris Sheppard later described that time as "when Bailey and Randell were bitterest enemies," and when Sheppard was later accused of being a Bailey man, he cited his vote for Randell for chairman of the delegation as evidence that he was not.[79]

As the Senate race heated up, an event at the Texas State Fair in October 1911 occurred that would in retrospect prove quite significant in the 1916 Democratic primary in Rayburn's congressional district. Woodrow

Wilson came to Dallas to speak at the fair in recognition of the American Bible Society's tercentenary anniversary of the translation of the Bible. Earlier, under the leadership of Thomas Love, a number of Texans had met to organize support for Wilson at the 1912 Democratic convention.[80] As Wilson traveled to Dallas, several delegations joined his train entourage. In Parsons, Kansas, Congressman Randell's son Andrew joined the Wilson party. When Wilson arrived at his destination, Gov. Oscar Colquitt and Sen. Charles Culberson came to meet him. Later, two candidates for U.S. Senate, Morris Sheppard and Choice Randell, attended a luncheon for Wilson at the Oriental Hotel. Conspicuously absent was Joe Bailey.[81] The Randell-Wilson tie would create havoc for Bailey man Sam Rayburn five years later.

Congressman Sheppard won the Senate seat, partly because of a terrible performance by Randell. Randell spoke two to three times a day but did not inspire large crowds.[82] Randell and Jacob Wolters were both anti-prohibitionists while prohibitionist Sheppard tried to focus the election on the issue of "the organized liquor traffic." He argued that Randell's candidacy against Bailey diverted from the real issue in the campaign, which was prohibition. One might think that Randell's involvement in the race split the anti-prohibition vote between himself and Wolters to the benefit of Sheppard. However, Sheppard supporter Thomas Campbell thought that one of the "most important things right now is to get Randell out of this race," because he believed that Sheppard would get 95 percent of Randell's support. Similarly, Thomas Ball claimed that nine-tenths of Randell's followers would support Sheppard if Randell withdrew. But Randell stubbornly stayed in the race, receiving only 40,693 votes compared to Sheppard's 182,907 and Wolters's 146,214.[83]

In retrospect, Randell's choice to leave the House to run for Bailey's Senate seat seems to have been ill-advised, especially since he was on the Ways and Means Committee in the seat that John Nance Garner parleyed into the Speakership. But it was only in Randell's last term in the House that he was in the majority, and by then he seems to have made up his mind to run for Bailey's Senate seat. He did so without knowing how strong the opposition would be. Morris Sheppard, after all, had denied that he would challenge Bailey for the Senate seat and only announced after Bailey chose not to run for reelection. Finally, Randell knew that there was going to be a reapportionment of his district, making reelection more of a challenge. As a result, Randell may have thought that the timing was perfect for his run for the Senate.

With Randell running for the Senate, Rayburn could run for Congress in an open seat race. As Speaker of the Texas House, Rayburn could take advantage of redistricting to shape his future congressional run. Rayburn used his influence to insure that Lamar County was not included in the newly drawn district, thus preventing a strong potential opponent, state senator B. B. Sturgeon, from opposing him. It was, nevertheless, a tough race for Rayburn, who faced seven opponents. Out of a total of 21,336 votes, Rayburn had a plurality, polling 4,983 votes.

Now, just as Bailey was leaving the Senate, his talented protégé ascended to the U.S. House. Shortly after the November 1912 election, Bailey wrote Rayburn saying that he was receiving letters asking him to intercede with Rayburn on patronage issues but that he refused, claiming that Rayburn should only consider "the recommendations . . . [of] the patrons of the offices." He added, however, "wherever you can find one of your own friends qualified for the position, make it your absolute rule never to appoint one of your enemies." Rayburn promptly replied to Bailey with thanks and asked for a meeting to talk about "a great many things" and to obtain "a great deal of information."[84]

Under the Spell of Joseph Weldon Bailey

For all of his admiration of Bailey, Sam Rayburn later came to view his connection to Bailey as a political liability. As Speaker, he reflected on Bailey's influence on his early career. Rayburn aide D. B. Hardeman recalled a conversation in which Rayburn said, "When I came to Congress I was under the spell of Joseph Weldon Bailey. Bailey was very reactionary, but he was my hero. He was my boyhood hero, and I idolized Joe Bailey. He was about the biggest-brained man I ever knew. And about the vainest man I ever knew. It took me several years to get loose from his ideas. But I was very, very conservative when I came to Congress because I was following Joe Bailey's lead." Bailey became increasingly conservative as he aged. In January 1918 he argued against the vote for women, claiming that women should not be able to vote because they were "incapable of performing the three highest duties of citizenship — military service, posse comitatus service and jury service." He thought women's morals dictated their beliefs and that they would push those morals upon men as they voted for what they believed. Prohibition was the prime example; the right to vote for women would bring prohibition with it.[85]

In addition to being saddled with Bailey's conservatism, Rayburn was also saddled with Bailey's many enemies both in Washington and in Texas.

For example, when Texan Tom Connally was elected to the House in 1916, he became friendly with Sam Rayburn but not close because Rayburn was a Bailey man, whereas Connally was anti-Bailey. And, back home in Texas, the anti-Bailey forces geared up to challenge Rayburn. Most specifically, the Randell family would remain a thorn in Rayburn's side for years to come. After his unsuccessful Senate bid, Choice Randell practiced law in Sherman. Soon he began testing the waters for an election campaign against Rayburn. In the end, concluding he could not beat Rayburn, he chose to forgo the challenge.[86]

The more difficult challenge would come two years later from Randell's son Andrew. Andrew practiced law in Sherman with his father and was only two years older than Rayburn. When he decided to challenge Rayburn in 1916, Rayburn wrote, "I think it had just as well come now as any time, for the reason that I have known ever since I was elected to Congress that I was going to have to fight the Randells sooner or later." There were several major issues, but one was the old Bailey and anti-Bailey battle. Former Speaker of the Texas House, John Marshall, who had become Speaker after the pro-Bailey Speaker Kennedy had been ousted, managed Randell's campaign.[87] Kennedy had, of course, managed Rayburn's successful bid for the Texas House Speakership.

Rayburn understood that Andrew's "strength would come from his father's old political organization, but Rayburn was 'two campaigns ahead of Randell.'" That is, the senior Randell had not run a district-level campaign since 1910; Rayburn had run in 1912 and in 1914. Rayburn could also call on what was left of the Bailey organization. Rayburn even had the support of Silas Hare Jr., whose father had served in Congress from 1887–91 but who had then been defeated by Bailey. It was said that Bailey, for the only time in his life, had cultivated an opponent's friendship and Bailey and Hare became friends. That friendship spawned a friendship between Rayburn and Silas Jr.[88]

In the campaign, the Randells attempted to portray Rayburn as anti-prohibition. Although Rayburn was a prohibitionist, he supported local option on prohibition rather than statewide or national prohibition; he defended his prohibition record by claiming that he opposed national prohibition for the same reason that he opposed national woman's suffrage. That is, he was a supporter of states' rights. Given that Bailey was an anti-prohibitionist, Rayburn probably received both prohibition support and anti-prohibition support.

But the main issue in the campaign turned on Woodrow Wilson and which of the two candidates was the strongest Wilson man. It was more than mere association with Bailey that made Rayburn the conservative candidate in the 1916 contest with Randell. First, Rayburn ran into trouble because of his opposition to a federal child labor bill. That bill was central to Wilson's policies and to Progressive thought. Rayburn defended his position on the basis of states' rights, much as Bailey would have argued. Indeed, Rayburn argued that the Texas child labor law already in place was better than the federal law and that the state law had been strengthened with Rayburn's support when he was in the state legislature. He argued that he was a friend of labor, citing a bill for an eight-hour day for telegraphers about to be reported out of his congressional committee.[89]

Still Rayburn's opposition to the federal child labor law had the potential to hurt him. Like his mentor Bailey might have done, Rayburn personalized the issue. Rayburn pointed out that he had picked cotton fields as a youngster and knew what it was to work in the hot sun. In contrast, Andrew Randell was a city boy who had lived in Sherman, Texas, Washington, D.C., and Princeton, New Jersey, and "had silken palms that had never been soiled."[90] Rayburn told the voters that the federal legislation banned the interstate shipment of cotton produced by the labor of children under fifteen. He argued that farm families needed the help of their children in the cotton fields.

Progressives also proposed a reduction in the workday. At the time, the American Federation of Labor was proposing to reduce the length of the federal workday. Rayburn took on that policy as well: "I worked fourteen to sixteen hours a day in the hot sun on a Fannin County farm, and I voted to make these white-handed, bay windowed gentry work at least eight hours a day under an electric fan, and sitting on easy cushioned seats."[91] The appeal to his agrarian constituents worked. Rayburn was able to project the image of a hardworking farmer running against the Princeton-educated city slicker Andrew Randell. Andrew's elitist credentials were exaggerated, of course.

Rayburn claimed that, despite important policy differences, Wilson wanted him retained in Congress and cited a letter from Wilson praising his legislative work: "We have all looked on with admiration and genuine appreciation as your stock and bond bill has been put through the House. It seems to me you deserve a great deal of praise for your part in the matter, and I want to make my humble contribution to the congratulations which I am sure you must be receiving."[92] The letter was praise for Rayburn's work that would have given the Interstate Commerce Commission authority to review and approve all railroad stocks and bonds before they were issued. This would prevent the overcapitalization of railroads, a notorious problem that had led to the sale of enormous sums of over-valued railroad stocks and bonds. As a freshman congressman, Rayburn pushed strongly for the bill, but action was postponed as a result of the outbreak of war in Europe. By 1915, Wilson no longer enthusiastically sup-ported Rayburn's bill, since the administration was now inclined to culti-vate business. Rayburn met with Wilson and urged passage of the law. To his dismay, Wilson declared that the bill would have to be delayed until after the war, adding that his administration was already being accused of being anti-business, and that the bill would also need to wait until af-ter the election. Wilson's change of heart led to an angry confrontation between the two where Rayburn stood up, expressed disagreement with the president, insisted on continuing his efforts in behalf of the bill, and walked out of the president's office. Years later, Rayburn admitted that he had been "impudent" toward the president, and it damaged his relation-ship with Wilson.[93]

But in 1916, Wilson was quite popular in the district, and Rayburn used Wilson's congratulatory letter as the centerpiece of his campaign. Randell, on the other hand, emphasized his Princeton ties to Wilson and obtained a letter from him stating that he was neutral in the race and did not "feel at liberty to express a preference in any congressional fight and would cer-tainly take no such position when a friend like yourself was involved."[94]

Although Rayburn was to have closer elections, he looked back to the 1916 campaign as one of his most difficult, and he never could admit to himself that Woodrow Wilson, his onetime political idol, had tried to have him defeated. However, in his later years, he described Wilson as "a very cold, frigid individual." Bailey hated Wilson and almost everything Wilson stood for. The Wilsonians, in Bailey's mind, were "semi-socialists."[95]

Andrew Randell never again challenged Rayburn for office. Instead, he involved himself in civic causes, as a fundraiser for Austin College in Sher-man and as a Mason. As grand master of all Texas Masons, he used that position to speak against the Ku Klux Klan throughout the state. Masonic activities kept him out of politics. He developed a spinal infection and died at the age of 51 in 1931.[96]

Strangely, it was not the last of the Randells. In 1930 Choice Randell had run a weak campaign against Rayburn, and in 1932, at the age of 73, he challenged Rayburn again. By then his political organization was long gone, and the old Bailey and anti-Bailey alliances were past. His son's recent death had left him the last survivor in his family.[97] His 1932 race seemed more like the efforts of a lonely old man than a serious effort to wrest control from Rayburn. Though it was a tough race, it was not because of Randell but because of the combined opposition of Randell and Jess Morris, who exploited Depression conditions to the extent that Rayburn was almost forced into a run-off. Rayburn received 17,895 votes; Morris, 10,481; and Randell, 6,911.[98]

Joe Bailey, too, remained a presence in Rayburn's life and career. During the Wilson years, Bailey lived in Washington and was close to Rayburn. In March of 1915, as an act of friendship and affection, Bailey sponsored Rayburn for admission to the bar of the U.S. Supreme Court.[99] After Rayburn's 1916 win in the Democratic primary, Bailey wrote his protégé's parents, "I was very much gratified by Sam's reelection, and the ability that he displayed in the campaign gratified me even more than his success. I have known for years that he is a man of splendid ability, and if he will apply himself with diligence to the study of public questions, he will soon become one of the foremost men in Congress." Typically, Bailey enclosed his photograph for the Rayburns to display in their home.[100]

Bailey continued his involvement in Texas politics. Possibly because he perceived betrayal by the Texas Legislature in electing Morris Sheppard to his Senate seat, Bailey contemplated a return to politics in August of 1914, when he announced that he would run for Sen. Charles Culberson's seat but soon changed his mind.[101] Then, when Jim Wells's wife Tinie became the Texas representative to the National Association Opposed to Woman Suffrage and president of the Texas anti-suffragists, Wells contributed to her campaign, enlisted the assistance of wealthy landowners such as R. J. Kleberg, and helped persuade Bailey to return from Washington, D.C., to campaign against the suffragists. Texas defeated a suffrage amendment by twenty-five thousand votes, though soon the federal women's suffrage amendment was ratified by the Texas legislature without a popular vote.

Wells visited Bailey again in early 1920 when he traveled to Washington to persuade Bailey to run for governor, and Bailey clearly had a receptive ear. Moving to Dallas in 1920, he entered the race for governor and declared that he would "redeem Texas and Democracy" as an anti-Wilson, anti-Progressive candidate. Amazingly, given that he had not lived in Texas in years, he got a plurality of the vote. Large crowds gathered to hear the great orator promise to cut state appropriations in half and to promote an anti-labor agenda. He also wanted to improve education, separate church and state, and have less control from Washington. He also opposed national prohibition, woman's suffrage, the League of Nations, socialism, monopoly, and class legislation. He seemed unhappy with the modern world, preferring old church organs to pipe organs, square dancing to modern dances like the "fox trot," and old standards like "Swanee River" and "My Old Kentucky Home" to modern songs like "Oh, You Beautiful Doll" and "I Love My Wife, But Oh You Kid."[102] Pat Neff's attacks on Bailey seemed on target when he said of Bailey, "He is the only living statesman; all others are dead. He walks with his face to the past and his back to the future. He is satisfied with everything except the League of Nations, the national administration, the State administration, the Democratic Party, the President of the United States, Congress, the two Texas senators, the eighteen Texas congressmen, the State Legislature, prohibition, woman's suffrage, and the enforcement of prohibition laws. However, Joe is highly pleased with himself." In a run-off election, Pat Neff won. It was said that with the defeat Bailey "aged twenty years at one stroke."[103]

To illustrate how much Texas politics had changed, consider the story of the third candidate in the primary, Ewing Thomason. Thomason was Speaker of the Texas House and would later go to Congress and to a federal judgeship. As a youngster, he had lived in Cooke County, Bailey's home county, though now he lived in El Paso. He was contemplating a run for governor but would not run if Bailey ran, because he did not think he could win and he did not want to face stress and financial sacrifice for nothing. He visited Gainesville to speak with Bailey's allies who assured him that Bailey would not run and that he would get the Bailey vote. Thomason entered the race, but so did Bailey. Bailey's friends then urged Thomason to drop out but he refused, saying he "was not going to let him [Bailey] run me out." Thomason was angry about Bailey's late entry and endorsed Neff in the run-off, embittering Bailey. Thomason wrote, "Bailey pretended to admire me when I was a young man just starting out. He no longer even pretended." Bailey probably believed that Thomason cut into his vote and deprived him of the governorship. Indeed, with the exception of the precincts with voters of German origin, Thomason carried every precinct in Bailey's home county, including Bailey's home precinct. It was, as Thomason said, "the political death knell for Bailey."[104]

Bailey's reentry into Texas politics was discouraging for Rayburn, who was thinking about running for the Senate in 1922, as was Bailey, at least initially. Culberson had enjoyed a long career, serving as attorney general of Texas, governor of Texas, and senator. He had chaired the Committee on the Judiciary from 1913 to 1919 and had been Democratic minority leader from 1907 to 1910. However, alcoholism and other illnesses had rendered it difficult for him to speak. He had not visited Texas in ten years and was physically unable to return there and campaign for reelection. In other words, there was a good chance to defeat Culberson in the 1922 election.[105] Although Bailey ultimately decided not to run, Rayburn believed his old mentor had become a political liability. He wrote W. A. Thomas,

> Just as long as Bailey is everlastingly coming to the front as a candidate it will be practically impossible for me to become the state figure that I have reason to expect to become. You probably do not know that of all the men in Texas who followed his flag in his black hour that I am the only one who today holds an office. I am truly the last of the Mohicans. . . . The press of Texas is ninety-five percent anti-Bailey and every time he bobs up they are reminded that I am the last of the old crowd, and I am punished. As an example, when I was elected chairman of the Democratic Caucus here, the second highest honor that the Democrats in Congress can bestow, the nomination for Speaker being the only one higher, there was not a paper in Texas outside of my district that commented editorially on the fact. There must be a reason.[106]

By 1928, Rayburn intended to stay in the House and build seniority there. Tom Connally spoke to Rayburn as he had to Garner about challenging Earle Mayfield for the Senate, and Rayburn told Connally that his preference was to stay in the House and eventually become its Speaker.[107]

Even the loss of the governorship did not completely end Bailey's political career. In 1922, the KKK was very strong in Texas and helped elect Mayfield to the Senate over the four-term Senator Culberson. Bailey, along with Garner and Rayburn, was anti-Klan. In 1924, Bailey supported Miriam Ferguson for governor as an anti-Klan candidate over the KKK candidate, Felix Robertson. In 1928, Bailey's vindictiveness against anti-Bailey Tom Connally outweighed his hostility to the Klan, and Bailey supported the Klan-backed Sen. Earle Mayfield against Connally. But Bailey's days as a political powerhouse had ended. Even Bailey's speaking ability was diminished because he had gained an enormous amount of weight. In 1927, Rayburn wrote to his sister Kate, "When he is animated as he always is when he talks, he is something of the old Bailey, but in repose he is saggy and sad looking—He is a mighty old man for 63."[108]

Bailey died on April 13, 1929, while arguing a case in district court in Sherman, Texas. Perhaps the best assessment of Bailey was offered by historian Joe Frantz who wrote, "Although Bailey had the qualifications to become a national force and was later exonerated by a state legislative joint committee, the accusation terminated his effectiveness." Still, Bailey's name carried weight. In 1932, Joe Bailey Jr., known as "Little Joe," was elected to the U.S. House in a statewide race for congressman-at-large. In 1934, "Little Joe" unsuccessfully ran against incumbent Tom Connally for the Senate, though as a New Dealer rather than a conservative like his father.[109]

Of course, both Garner and Rayburn would successfully step out of the shadow of Bailey, and a first step was to "get loose from" Bailey's conservative ideas and avoid some political forces that, Rayburn believed, enforced those ideas. In 1953, there was an effort to redistrict Sam Rayburn, and, since Rayburn's district had a relatively small population compared to other districts in the state, it appeared likely that the district would have to be increased. Rayburn refused to consider adding Cooke County, Bailey's old political base to his district, arguing that Cooke "is a Republican County or near so."[110] Cooke County was, of course, years away from being Republican, but Rayburn must have remembered that it produced his reactionary idol, Joe Bailey.

Lone Star on the Rise The Bailey Legacy in the House

Despite Rayburn's eventual realization that Bailey had become a liability to him, clearly key elements of Garner's and Rayburn's rise in the House are attributable to Bailey's influence and place in Texas politics. When Choice Randell left the House in an attempt to unseat Bailey, he opened up a Texas seat on Ways and Means that would be filled by Bailey man John Nance Garner. Moving from the Committee on Foreign Affairs to Ways and Means, which was, in those days, also the Democrats' Committee on Committees, was Garner's path to power. Indeed, years later, Minority Leader Garner wrote Congressman Fred Vinson and offered his opinion about the importance of the Ways and Means Committee: "I know the Ways and Means Committee is the most important committee in the House of Representatives and always will be. It is the heart of the economic and political organization of the House of Representatives."[111]

Garner would, in turn, use his influence to the benefit of Rayburn. Both cut their political teeth as Bailey men, both had served in the Texas House before going to Congress, both men were sons of Confederate veterans, and both had lived much of their lives in North Texas. In fact, Garner was born in Blossom Prairie, not far from Rayburn's home. Although he had subsequently moved from North Texas to Uvalde due to a diagnosis of tuberculosis, the connections were clear. Rayburn now had a well-placed ally in the House to serve as his advocate and mentor. In determining committee assignments on Ways and Means, Garner argued that Rayburn did not come to Washington as a green congressman but more with the experience of a governor, citing Rayburn's experience in the Texas House, particularly his service as Speaker, as evidence that Rayburn was prepared for a top committee assignment. Rayburn's service on the Texas House's Committee on Common Carriers provided evidence concerning which committee that should be, and Garner tapped Rayburn for the powerful Committee on Interstate and Foreign Commerce, the only committee on which Rayburn ever served. Rayburn was to claim that he wanted to chair the committee because his hometown, Bonham, was a "hamlet on a branchline railroad," a railroad managed by Rayburn's friend and Bailey man Ed Steger.[112] But there was more to chairing the committee than that hometown tie. Denison, also in his district, held the Katy Railroad locomotive repair shops, which employed large numbers of workers. Most importantly, Rayburn's district was an agricultural district, mostly cotton farming, and depended on the railroads for the shipment of livestock and crops.

Garner welcomed his young colleague, even allowing him to move into his office in the House Office Building until he could have his own office in the addition to the House Office Building.[113] Bailey's career was in its twilight, but Garner was now the rising star in the Texas congressional delegation.

istory has not treated John Nance Garner favorably. He is best remembered as Franklin Roosevelt's two-term vice president who rebelled against Roosevelt's left-leaning tendencies and challenged Roosevelt's decision to seek a third term. Historian Joe Frantz questioned whether Garner "brought any affirmative qualities to either the speakership or the Vice Presidency except a certain wiliness and the ability to keep his mouth shut," and John L. Lewis described Garner as "a labor-baiting, poker-playing, whiskey-drinking, evil old man."[1]

Still, Garner's remarkable career in the House of Representatives spanned the first third of the twentieth century, from 1902 until he became vice president in 1933. During his House career, Garner rose to the Speakership in 1931 and left a strong legacy, helping to build the Austin-Boston alliance that would dominate the House long after he left. As a member of the Ways and Means Committee and Democratic leader, he sponsored Sam Rayburn's budding career; even as vice president, Garner pushed Rayburn's candidacy for majority leader. Garner's relationships with Rayburn and Massachusetts Democrat John McCormack facilitated the Austin-Boston alliance in the 1936 majority leader's race, an arrangement solidified when Rayburn became Speaker and McCormack his majority leader in 1940.

The Garner Style

Born in 1868 in a log cabin in Blossom Prairie, Texas, not far from the Red River in Northeast Texas, John Nance Garner came from a farming family. His father, a Confederate veteran, was illiterate, but he became prosperous by East Texas standards, giving his son greater opportunities than most farm boys in post–Civil War Texas. After an unsuccessful stint at Vanderbilt University, John Nance came home to study law in Clarksville, Texas. By 1893, Garner contracted tuberculosis and sought, as the cure for his disease, the drier climate of Uvalde, Texas, four hundred miles to the southwest. Deep in South Texas, Uvalde had a "wild west" tradition where many people still carried side arms when Garner arrived.[2] In that world of ranches, cattle, and cowboys, under heavy Hispanic influence, an amiable man who could hold his liquor and play a good game of poker could succeed. Garner fit right in.

Arthur Schlesinger Jr., described Garner as having a "bright, ruddy face, short-cropped white hair, cold blue eyes, and a tight small mouth," presenting the appearance of "an infinitely experienced sage and of a newborn baby." Prominently displayed above his blue eyes were bushy eyebrows, which one reporter claimed were two and one-half inches long, curly and turned up. He was often disheveled, frequently unshaven, and sometimes compared with Speaker Joe Cannon for his somewhat seedy appearance.[3]

His speaking manner in House debate also resembled Cannon's. When Garner spoke in the well of the House, he stood almost up against the first Republican row of seats. His face would get progressively redder as he would throw out both arms from his head. He would extend his arms full length with the palms facing one another; then raise and lower his body from the knees in violent contortions in a "camp-meeting" style.[4]

Garner amassed wealth with holdings that included two banks, numerous mortgages on homes in Uvalde, significant coffin company stock, and large amounts of South Texas farmland, ranchland, and pecan orchards, including a 23,000-acre ranch with the largest goat herd in the world. Yet Garner was notoriously thrifty, a characteristic that became a running joke among his companions. Garner's close friend John McDuffie recalled, for example, commenting to one of Garner's fishing partners that Garner had 90 cents out of every dollar he made. The reply? "You are wrong. . . . Because he has 99 cents out of every dollar he ever made."[5]

For years John Nance and Ettie Garner lived in the Washington Hotel where admirers would bring them food such as venison, bear meat, and beef because of Garner's well-known love of hunting and the outdoors. Much of the food spoiled in the hotel iceboxes because the Garners could not bear to give it away. A newspaperman once observed Ettie in Garner's office sorting a crate of pecans one by one into three piles. A friend had shipped Garner a crate of pecans to be shared with Sam Rayburn and Speaker Bankhead, and Ettie did not want to miss a pecan. Even as a vice presidential candidate, Garner wore inexpensive suits and ties. While Garner was vice president, Ettie spent no more than one hundred dollars a year on clothes. In 1938, Garner reluctantly provided his most battered souvenir gavel to the Speaker of a mock Congress. Six months later, the Speaker of the mock Congress received a request for the return of the gavel. Sam Rayburn loved to tell the story of a constituent who asked Garner to autograph a dollar bill as a souvenir. Garner, Rayburn claimed, replied, "You give me that dollar bill and I'll write you a check."[6]

Garner smoked cigars and drank Jack Daniels whiskey mixed with tap water.[7] One author claimed that Garner consumed a quart of whiskey each day, starting at 7:00 in the morning, and that the corners of his living room in Uvalde were stacked with cases of Jack Daniels given him by lobbyists. His Washington office had a large closet stocked "with many bottles, some in crock jars." House doorkeeper William "Fishbait" Miller described Garner as "one of the most determined boozers the Capitol has ever known." After reading a 1944 account in which Garner had claimed that he was going to live to be 93 and that his longevity would be due to drinking bonded Bourbon whisky, Garner's friend John McDuffie wrote Garner, "[You have] become much more fastidious or exclusive in your taste. I knew when you would drink most anything that had the least alcoholic content, and on one occasion in your intense desire to satisfy an overwhelming appetite you paid six brand-new ten-dollar bills for six quarts of pure Washington water, beautifully labeled as Scotch."[8] Garner felt that policy-making required a glass of whiskey, a game of poker, and good conversation, characteristics that suited the cultures both in Uvalde and early-twentieth-century congressional politics.

Though a Democrat, Garner frequently met during the Speakership of Republican Nicholas Longworth in what was called the "Bureau of Education" where he would "strike a blow for liberty" and arrange political compromises.[9] Carl Albert related that Parliamentarian Lew Deschler told him that "he never knew a congressman that drank as much as John Garner did. That he would go in his office, and he just kept — he kept a bottle in there all the time. Said he never did take a big drink and enjoy it. Said he'd just sip a couple of sips, put it down, fifteen minutes later he'd leave the chair to somebody and go in there and take a couple of sips and then go back. Said he did it all day long, every fifteen minutes."[10]

Though Garner had an enormous capacity for making friends, he had few intimate friends and tended to keep his own counsel.[11] He did not even tell his closest protégés, including Sam Rayburn, about his presidential plans until the last moment. He also enjoyed testing the mettle of men, pushing them to assess the strength of their characters. Once, when Lew Deschler was a new twenty-five-year-old clerk for Speaker Longworth,

Garner suddenly accosted him, "Why the hell did you tell Nick Longworth so and so?" Deschler replied that he had not done so, and Garner responded, "The hell you didn't! You sure as hell did!" When Deschler again denied telling that to Longworth, Garner shouted, "Goddamn it, don't you lie to me! I know you told him that!" Deschler got angry and slammed the desk in front of him shouting, "Goddamn you, don't you tell me I'm a liar! I didn't tell Nick Longworth that." With that reply, Garner leaned back and said, "Young man, you've got a lot of spunk." Deschler recalled, "Garner was my greatest supporter from that moment on."

In a similar vein, Texas Congressman John Lyle claimed that Garner had a system for testing new Congressmen as well: "He had two different types of whiskey. One was a good whiskey and one was a rather bad whiskey. He had nickel glasses like they used to use in the cafes and he would pour out a full glassful of bad whiskey and hand it to the Congressman and he would see what kind of reaction he had. He would always say, 'Bottoms up' to his good whiskey and he always judged them on whether or not they took it well. [He judged] their character that way."

The tough-talking Garner had a cruel, hard side and an acid tongue, which could be turned on foe and friend alike. Hardeman and Bacon saw a quality of the frontier about him, and he was "painfully truthful, even blunt, ambitious, and felt satisfaction in dealing with national problems." He was rough with people, telling Sam Rayburn, "You've got to bloody your knuckles." And anyone not on Garner's side risked being seen as an enemy, including some that he hated passionately, such as Tennessee Congressman Finis Garrett. Carl Albert claimed that Congressman Wright Patman had told him that after Patman made a motion to pay the World War I veterans their bonus, Garner thereafter refused to speak to him.[12]

Garner could be vicious in floor debate, violating the House's courtesy norm. After fellow Texas Congressman Tom Blanton criticized the $325 approved as a stationery allowance for members of Congress, Garner called Blanton "as common and base a liar as ever spoke a word of English in this country," "a miserable, cowardly creature," and an "individual would charge you with nepotism in order that he might parade his virtue in Texas, and at the same time have two of his children on the pay roll of the government." In short, "I would say what 430 men believe at this moment, that Thomas Blanton, of Texas, is a discredit to the House of Representatives and ought to be kicked out."[13]

Even those close to Garner were not spared. Sam Rayburn confessed, "I was Garner's lieutenant for fifteen years, and God, what a chore it was at times. But when the time came for him to throw his feet out for you, he went all the way."[14] Once during a near-fatal bout with pneumonia in the early part of 1925, Garner, a devoted reader of the *Congressional Record,* tried to read the *Record* while he was delirious with fever. After he held the *Record* upside down, John McDuffie took it from him. McDuffie claimed, "I never had a man to blaspheme and curse me as you did." Telling of the incident to Congressman Hatton Sumners, McDuffie explained the fever had driven Garner out of his head. Sumners disagreed, saying that Garner was "just being natural."[15]

Ideologically, some thought Garner an ultra-conservative while others claimed that he was "more or less a Bolshevik." Though Garner sometimes seemed out of control, he told Bascom Timmons that "my acts usually were done deliberately." He also understood, even in the early 1920s, that he was "no diplomat. I have to go at things in a rough and sometimes uncouth way. In politics as well as business I have adopted the old geometrical formula that the nearest distance between two points is a straight line."[16]

When an old friend told Garner that "I know you can be rough when you need to, but generally speaking you've relied on persuasion, it seems to me, more than anything else," Garner took another sip of bourbon and said, "I think I would have to attribute my success in having my own way in the House to the fact that I was always willing to take a beating in order to have my own way."[17]

South Texas Politics Jim Wells's Man in Washington

Not long after arriving in Uvalde, Garner was appointed county judge and, in 1894, was elected to that office. Four years later, he was elected to the first of two terms in the Texas House of Representatives. In 1902, with the backing of Sen. Joe Bailey, former governor Jim Hogg and South Texas political boss Jim Wells, Garner was elected to Congress. Garner's fast rise in Texas politics can not be understood merely because his personality fit well in Texas ranching country. Instead, he became the candidate of large ranchers, landowners, and the county political leaders who dominated South Texas politics, most importantly James B. Wells. In South Texas, no politician could hold office long without the support of Jim Wells.[18]

Wells served as Democratic chairman in Cameron County from 1882 until 1922. During that time, he also served stints on the State Democratic Executive Committee, as chair of the Democratic Party, and as a state district judge. Wells hobnobbed with statewide political leaders including E. M. House of Austin, delivering South Texas votes for House's preferred candidates. In addition to Wells, Garner gained the confidence of other Valley political bosses, including the notoriously corrupt Archer Parr of Duval County, Judge John Valls of Laredo, Robert Kleberg of Kingsville (who was the attorney for the King and Kennedy ranches), Manuel Guerra of Starr County, Tom Coleman of Dimmit, and Pat Dunn of Nueces County (who owned much of Padre Island). Along with Wells, these leaders were central to Garner's success. Although Wells supported other congressmen over the years, including W. H. Crain, Rudolph Kleberg, and Jeff McLemore, Garner was his most successful protégé.[19]

Garner and Wells forged a personal bond as well as a political one. Shortly before Garner announced for Congress, he wrote Wells, urging him "to treat me as you would your own boy." When Wells had problems with his daughter Zoe, whom he feared would marry a young man he disliked, and he banned her from Texas, she attended school and in the summers visited friends, including E. M. House and John Garner.[20]

In the Texas legislature, Garner worked to pass a bill, written by Wells, to help settle ownership of lands south of the Nueces River with unperfected titles, a critical issue for the big landowners in Garner's area. Although vetoed by the governor, an amended bill was later passed and signed by the governor in a special legislative session. Wells promised Garner that passage would allow the two of them "to go over Congressional races."[21]

In addition to gaining Wells's backing, Garner used his position as chair of the apportionment committee after the 1900 census to create a favorable district for himself.[22] Texas' 15th congressional district, an area largely unsettled at the time of the Civil War, encompassed a sprawling area larger than the state of Pennsylvania, including 150 miles of shoreline along the Gulf of Mexico and 400 miles along the Rio Grande, twenty-two counties, and the cities of Brownsville, Laredo, and Corpus Christi.[23] With a population of 160,694, it was the second smallest district in Texas, almost 30,000 people less than the average, had a population density of five per square mile, and a small 5.8 percent black population. Bordering Mexico, 27.2 percent of the population was foreign born, and perhaps twice that many were the children of foreign born. An agricultural district, the value of its livestock was nineteen times the value of its manufactured goods.[24]

Garner often had Democratic primary opposition and, unlike many southern congressmen, fairly significant Republican opposition. However, once he had established his value to the political bosses, he paid little attention to what most politicians would consider fundamental concerns:

building a personal campaign following for elections, public speaking, and dealing with the press.

Garner had little need to campaign: the bosses provided necessary campaign resources and votes. Though Wells raised money statewide for Garner's first campaign, the main source of support for Garner in the district was not money but votes.[25] The Wells organization could deliver largely Mexican American votes in large numbers, and some were also cast at the behest of Archer Parr.[26] Garner was once asked how he was able to get the votes of Mexican Americans. His simple explanation was, "I had as my campaign manager Judge James Wells of Brownsville. He knew the Mexicans well and they had great confidence in him." That "confidence" often came in the forms of threats, intimidation, personal influence, and any other technique imaginable to the South Texas bosses. Noncitizens often voted, and sometimes Mexican citizens were imported from Mexico to vote.[27] O. Douglas Weeks wrote that Mexican American votes often came through friendship or fear:

> Voting has little or no significance beyond returning a favor to somebody higher up to whom they owe employment, money, personal attention, or something else. They recognize some local politician as the political chief. When election time comes around, in many instances they receive poll-tax receipts by mail or otherwise. Some kind benefactor has paid the poll taxes. Carrying these receipts to the polling place, they are addressed in Spanish by an election judge who may be aware ahead of time how they have been advised to vote. The ballots are printed in English. Therefore the judge kindly offers to mark the ballot properly, if indeed he has not already done so to save time. . . . In former days it was not uncommon for the chief or some of his local henchmen literally to corral the voters several days before the election, keeping them together by providing a barbecue for them, and voting them en bloc at the proper time.[28]

Of all the bosses, Archer Parr was probably the most corrupt. He could assure that candidates opposed to his chosen candidates would fare poorly in his Duval County home.[29] For example, in the 1926 Democratic primary, Duval County reported 1,342 votes for Garner and 1 vote for Garner's opponent, Sid Hardin. Similarly lopsided figures were reported in Zapata, Starr, Kinney, Kenedy, Brooks, and Jim Hogg counties. Yet Hardin was a fairly significant opponent. Altogether in that election Garner won 18,546 votes to Hardin's 7,287. Hardin's tough campaign depressed and upset Ettie Garner, who wrote Alabama Congressman John McDuffie, a close Garner ally, that though Hardin was a schoolteacher, a pious Bible Class teacher, and a prohibitionist, he conducted the nastiest mud-slinging campaign Garner had ever faced: "God deliver all honest men from opposition of that kind. I believe it was Felix who said to the Apostle Paul 'Almost thou persuadest me to be a Christian.' Hardin ALMOST persuaded me that it was ignominy to pose as one. Thank God, however, that his kind are not many." Even prior to his first election, Garner wrote to Archer Parr, "[I h]ave no fears as to what column your county will be in. I leave the whole matter in your hands, and should we be successful you will always find me fighting just as I did at Austin for my friends."[30]

Indeed, Garner left so much of the home front to the South Texas bosses that he rarely campaigned or even visited major parts of his district. Biographers Bascom Timmons and Marquis James both wrote that over the thirty years Garner was in Congress, "he rarely canvassed his district or gave speeches to his constituents." By 1914, it was claimed Garner had never visited five counties in his district, that he had not visited Brownsville in two years, and that he had only sent two speeches home in ten years. In 1914, he did not even go home to vote for himself, although he won with ease. In his last ten years in Congress, his main campaign effort appears to have consisted of hosting huge barbecues with seating for up to a hundred people at his Uvalde home.[31] Throughout his career, Garner rarely even corresponded with constituents, either not writing them or leaving the task to his wife, Ettie.[32]

Though in Garner's first campaign he knew or made himself known to nearly every voter, he later told O. C. Fisher, "I didn't have to do much campaigning at home after I got established. I was very fortunate. After I had been there ten years I never had any trouble. I didn't have to pay any attention to my district after that. The people kept me in Congress voluntarily."[33] Because he saw little need to campaign, Garner also granted few formal interviews with the press, although he sometimes used the small number of correspondents he admitted into his personal circle for his political purposes. Although reporters Cecil Dickson, Marquis James, and especially Bascom Timmons became as close to him as any politician, Garner never developed good press-handling skills.[34] Famed journalist and author William S. White recalled that as a young man, he called on Vice President Garner. Garner was dismissive, telling him, "Son just go hereafter and talk to people like Bascom Timmons." White bristled at that suggestion and recalled replying to Garner, "I'll be damned if I'll do that."[35]

Garner's lack of attention to campaigning and the press meant that, for an elected official, he lacked experience in public speaking, a deficiency that would haunt him during his later campaigns for national office. In 1932, Garner worried about his ability to campaign in ways that would be acceptable to Roosevelt. Confessing his concerns to Sam Rayburn, he wrote that some of his views would not be appropriate for the campaign. Since Garner thought the election was won anyway, he saw no need to campaign. Ettie Garner wrote Rayburn, pleading with him to "do what you can to keep him from making speeches. He never opens his mouth, as you know, that the papers don't jump on him, and what is worse we get the nastiest letters, signed and unsigned. If he could just mix with people and not talk, his personality would carry, but something is wrong somewhere, when he talks." Ettie's fears were soon laid to rest when, a few days later, Garner reached an understanding with the Democratic National Committee and Roosevelt's advisors that he would confine his efforts to Texas and California, focusing on getting out the vote rather than "all this speaking and ballahoo."[36]

Garner fully understood that South Texas political bosses would assure his reelection over Democratic primary challengers and Republican opponents in exchange for patronage, help with constituent problems, and pork barrel projects to aid in the development of the Rio Grande Valley.[37] If he was no orator, Garner's style was well-suited to patronage politics. Garner sought Wells's advice on whom to appoint to West Point and to Annapolis.[38] Also, Wells asked Garner to intervene for military appointments for his friends and for pensions and pension increases.[39] He sought Agriculture Department publications from Garner, too; as Wells put it, "place them with people to some advantage." Garner delivered much desired legislation, further endearing himself to Wells. Wells wrote him regarding his desire for a deep-water port at Point Isabel: "John for MY sake, . . . do all you can to get us [a] deep water [port] . . . , as YOU, and YOU, alone, old friend, we must depend on. . . . No need to have apprehension as to your being a Member of Congress next year."[40]

At times Garner seems to have gotten frustrated with Wells, warning him that he needed to spread appointments to West Point or Annapolis around the district rather than giving them all to Cameron County, which was the base of Wells's political support. In 1916, Wells did not seem to be able to maintain a satisfactory correspondence with Garner, so he started writing to Ettie, Garner's wife.[41] In 1914, Wells had claimed that Garner must be the sole person responsible for a deep-water port at

Brazos Santiago. Garner wrote a frustrated letter to Wells, insisting that Wells and others in the district must work to secure the project as well. By 1916, Garner suggested to Wells that his age and health no longer permitted him to control the political situation as he once had. Garner even complained, in an angry letter to Joe K. Wells, James's son, that his interests were not being adequately served: "Some time ago I wrote your father, and then to you about the appointment of a Rural Carrier but did not receive a reply from either — later in writing to Judge Yates about another matter in which he was interested, I asked him for information concerning these applicants for the rural route and he gave it to me. . . . I simply must have some one in Cameron County on whom I can call for help in recommending appointments, and if you cannot give it to me I wish you would tell me who I can call on for just such dependable advice as you and your father can give me. . . . I wish you would let me know *immediately* if there is any objection to the reappointment of these men."[42]

Though tensions seemed to increase as Wells aged and Garner gained power in Congress, no break occurred. Wells, the other county bosses, and Garner needed each other too much. One news clipping reported that Garner had secured larger appropriations for public buildings and a greater number of items than any other congressman, including buildings for Del Rio, Eagle Pass, and Laredo and authorization for more at Uvalde, Corpus Christi, Beeville, and Seguin. He secured agricultural soil surveys of sixteen thousand square miles of the district and had gotten the Geological Division of the Interior Department to work there as well, the only district in Texas with such service. In addition, work had begun on an intercoastal canal and on improvements at Port Aransas, Corpus Christi, and Baffins Bay. Garner had aided in getting good roads and highways in the district. Finally, Garner worked to keep military bases in the district open and to move in additional federal troops to protect banks and cattle from raids from a Mexico undergoing revolution. When the War Department threatened to close a cavalry post near Brownsville, Garner successfully lobbied Secretary of War William Howard Taft to prevent closure. Wells was especially pleased that Garner had facilitated a Department of Agriculture laboratory in Cameron County that examined the feasibility of introducing certain plants to the region.[43]

Among Garner's most significant efforts were the beginnings of an intercoastal canal crucial to water transportation between the coastal parts of his district and the Mississippi River. He even accompanied the Corps of Engineers to his district when the canal was surveyed and rewarded the officer in charge of the survey by appointing his son to West Point. When a Corps of Engineers survey recommended against deepening the Corpus Christi harbor, Garner got the Corps headquarters to reverse the survey recommendation. Garner understood his role, recalling that "the first few years I was up there, except for working on my 'projects' [government projects in the district] I spent much of my time over in the office building after it was built, playing poker."[44]

By 1920, the Wells machine declined as a result of Wells's declining health and the growth and development of South Texas, but by then Garner's power base was well established, and the local political bosses continued in power. Garner remained loyal to the South Texas bosses, even unsuccessfully intervening while he was vice president to get a charge of income tax evasion dismissed against George Parr, the son of Archer Parr and Archer's successor as Duval County political boss.[45] But the direction of influence had reversed. When Garner's influence in the House was on the rise, Wells's role in Garner's career and his continued influence were clear to many. Wells became increasingly sought out by those who wanted his assistance because it was well known that Wells had Garner's ear. Late in his life, Wells, the mentor, would brag of his protégé, "I put him [Garner] in Congress."[46] Garner, however, had the dominant position later in his career.

Pork for Me; Economy for Others

When Garner first served in Congress, it was 1903, Theodore Roosevelt was president, and Joe Cannon was beginning his first term as Speaker. Democrats were in the minority, 178 to 208, remaining so until 1911, when Champ Clark of Missouri was elected Speaker. Cannon, working through key lieutenants such as Sereno Payne, John Dalzell, and Jim Tawney, who were known as Gentlemen of the Red Carnation because of the flower each wore in his lapel, thoroughly dominated the House, and Garner was inconspicuous.[47]

Like many minority party members, Garner received largely unimportant committee assignments: the Committee on Expenditures in the State Department and Railways and Canals. Luckily, Garner was able to use that latter assignment as a forum for pushing a proposal for the intercoastal canal. Garner spent his early years in Congress developing networks of friends and allies, not the least of which was Speaker Cannon. He became a regular at the Boar's Nest, Cannon's hideaway club on K Street where, it was said, Garner began building a personal fortune at the poker table.

Garner's relationship with Cannon, built across a poker table, helped convince Cannon to grant extraordinary last-minute approval for an amendment allowing the deepening of the harbor at Corpus Christi, an amendment very important to Garner's district. It also got Garner appointed to a committee in charge of the construction of the first House office building. After being in the House for two years, Garner was assigned to the Foreign Affairs Committee, still not among the House's most important committees but a useful appointment for a congressman whose district bordered Mexico. The assignment to Foreign Affairs led to an important friendship between Garner and Nicholas Longworth, who began on that committee on the same day. Although Longworth was in many ways Garner's opposite — Longworth was well educated, cosmopolitan, and cultured — they became fast friends and, during Longworth's Speakership, developed one of the most famous working relationships ever between two opposing party leaders.[48] Also on Foreign Affairs was Jim Curley of Boston, a political mentor for future House leader John McCormack.

Within the House, the rule of Cannon was not to last. Garner was a loyal Democrat who supported the revolt against Cannon's rule that ultimately led to the weakening of the Speaker's powers in 1910. In 1911, when Democrat Champ Clark became Speaker, Garner became a member of the majority. Under the new rules, the Rules Committee was no longer controlled by the Speaker, and the party caucus established party policy, binding members to support policy. Seniority was increasingly important as a method for managing diffuse power after the weakening of the Speakership. Importantly, there was an increasing trend toward longevity of service, one especially noticeable in the South where leadership in the Democratic Party was centered. Of the fifty-eight standing committees in the 63d Congress, thirty were chaired by southerners and eight by representatives of border states. Four of the seven Democrats on the Rules Committee hailed from the South, while one came from a border state.[49]

By 1909, Clark appointed Garner party whip, a position Garner retained under Majority Leader Oscar Underwood when Democrats took control of the House in 1911. Garner also was appointed to the three-member Committee on Organization that distributed patronage jobs in the newly Democratic House. In 1913, Garner passed up the chairmanship of Foreign Affairs to become a member of Ways and Means, which served as both the House's tax writing committee and the Democrats' Committee on Committees. A decade after his election, Garner was now a leader in the majority party and positioned on one of the most important committees in the House. He bragged to Jim Wells, "You will be happy to know that all hands seem to take more cognizance that I am a member of Congress, than they have heretofore."[50]

Garner, whose political base was built on pork barrel politics, ironically began to develop a reputation as a protector of the public purse. Herbert Hoover received intelligence reports from the Republican National Committee, gathered largely from materials in the *Congressional Record,* on Garner's congressional actions. Those reports portrayed Garner as developing a reputation for economy that "was picayunish economy. It was largely grandstand play to the public.... [It was] hypocritical ... when it came to a question of expenditures in his own District."[51]

Garner often objected to small expenditures, such as whether clerks should be paid $125 a month instead of $6 a day; whether canceling machines at the post office should be bought or rented; whether too much money was being spent on furniture in the House office building; and similar minor matters. Yet Garner strongly supported an appropriation of $35,795 for the purpose of promoting sugar cane and beets in his district. Garner also tried to vastly increase the appropriations for a government building in Corpus Christi.[52]

Noting Garner's strong interest in securing projects for home, President Hoover's secretary Theodore Joslin received a report from J. Bennett Gordon of the Republican National Committee quoting Garner in a 1916 speech to constituents: "Those fellows from New England and other northern states have plastered their country with unnecessary federal buildings. Now we Democrats are in charge of the House, and I'll tell you right now, every time one of those Yankees gets a ham, I am going to do my best to get a hog."[53] In explaining the relationship between Garner and his district, Michie and Ryhlick claimed, "The bosses took care of Cactus Jack; Cactus Jack took care of the bosses. The relationship was self-perpetuating. It required only a solicitous regard for the pork barrel." And Garner was quite solicitous, writing Nueces County boss and Padre Island owner Pat Dunn, "If you want a post office or some other public building on Padre Island, I'll be glad to get it for you."[54]

Garner and the Politics of the 1920s

With the Republican landslide of 1920, Garner seemed to be on the road to Democratic Party leadership. Champ Clark was defeated, as were Cordell Hull and Henry Rainey. Claude Kitchin became party leader, and Garner was second-ranking Democrat on Ways and Means behind Kitchin.

But when Kitchin's health failed him in 1921 and he left Washington for a rest, Kitchin chose Finis Garrett as floor leader rather than Garner. Perhaps Kitchin resented Garner's leadership role during the Wilson era when Kitchin's opposition to World War I limited his role as the spokesman for the administration in Congress. James Byrnes believed that Kitchin and Garner had angry words over whether Byrnes, who was backed by Kitchin, or Texan James Buchanan, who was backed by Garner, would be appointed to the Appropriations Committee. Garner won the battle because Postmaster General Burleson, also a Texan, used his patronage powers to forward Buchanan's interests. But, Byrnes believed, Kitchin resented the involvement of Burleson in the battle, was angry with Garner, and, until his illness, never spoke with Garner unless business required it. Another explanation is that Kitchin, a free trader, distrusted Garner's views, which favored a tariff on raw materials. In a letter to Kitchin in 1922, Garner did try to convey to him, "I don't believe our tariff views differ materially." But, of course, those views did differ. One press report regarded Kitchin's action as a rebuke to Garner because of Garner's vote in favor of the Emergency Tariff Bill, noting that Carl Hayden's vote for the Emergency Tariff clearly kept him off the Ways and Means Committee.[55]

In any event, Garner's rise to power in the House was temporarily frustrated by Garrett's selection. Garner had once told Bascom Timmons that when Speaker Cannon had let him take the Speaker's chair on the day when statues of Stephen F. Austin and Sam Houston were unveiled in the Capitol's Statuary Hall, February 25, 1905, Garner claimed, "When I left the Speaker's chair that day I had made up my mind I was going back as its elected occupant."[56]

At the time of Garrett's selection, Jim Wells was urging Garner to replace Charles Culberson in the U.S. Senate. Some of Garner's biographers believe he was even seriously considering retiring in 1922. He seems to have been overwhelmed by a mixture of feelings about his future during that time. In 1921, for example, perhaps responding to Wells's urging that he run for the Senate, Garner wrote, "Speaking confidentially, . . . if the Democrats carry the House next year and I am re-elected to Congress, I will be elected Speaker. . . . As I grow older I think I grow more appreciative, and I never think of myself or my service in Congress that I do not remember that it all would have been impossible had it not been for your goodness — I shall never cease to love you for it."[57] Not only was Garner overly optimistic about his prospects within the Democratic Party, but, despite gains, Democrats did not win control of Congress. Still, Pres.

Warren G. Harding's ineffectiveness plus an economic downturn put the Democrats within a dozen seats of a majority and gave them a gain of seventy-eight seats.[58]

Bascom Timmons, however, did not believe that it was Garner's ambition to be Speaker that kept him in the House in 1922. Rather, it was the challenge of the Ku Klux Klan, a powerful force in Texas opposed by and opposed to Garner. Though by the 1922 election the Wells organization was in disarray, the county bosses remained. Klan success would have harmed Hispanic voters, and the Klan's anti-immigrant and anti-Catholic views could have eroded the power of the South Texas bosses; they needed Garner. Although Garner did not actively campaign, he made his opposition to the Klan known, writing Claude Kitchin, for example: "We have an unfortunate state of affairs in Texas — Ku Klux and anti Ku Klux, which means Catholic and anti-Catholic. You know these differences are unhealthy for any State — I fear that it will develop throughout the country."[59]

In 1923, after his victory over his Klan-backed opponent, Garner wrote a heartfelt letter to Claude Kitchin, stating that there was likely to be a battle over the leadership and that to reduce friction in the party, Garner would eliminate himself as a candidate for leadership. Moreover, Garner wrote, stepping aside would "be a relief." Garner continued:

> I know as you do that the power of the Democratic organization is in the Ways and Means Committee, and I regret to leave it. I would hate intensely to see a single vote cast against you as Speaker on the Democratic side, but it is possible that a situation may develop where you would have opposition. This can be obviated, as above suggested. Now, it occurs to me that the thing for me to do in the interest of the Party, as well as your interest, is to announce that I will not be a candidate for Active-Floor Leader, in case of your continued illness. . . . Now, my dear Claude, do not think that I am making a sacrifice, because I frankly tell you in confidence that I desire to get out of public life. I want a little freedom in my declining years.

Soon thereafter, though, Kitchin died and Garner seemed to forget about retirement. Instead, he seriously considered opposing Finis Garrett for the leadership, in part because of a "keen personal rivalry, even hatred" between the two men. Sam Rayburn, a friend of both men, advised Garner, "You can't win, John," good advice that Garner heeded. Jimmy Byrnes, a supporter of Garrett's, claimed that a few days before the Democratic caucus, where the battle for leadership would occur, Garner dropped by Byrnes's office while Byrnes was meeting with Garrett. Garner said, "Finis, I have announced to the press my withdrawal and wish to extend to you my best wishes." While Garrett was trying to express his appreciation of Garner's action, the typically blunt Garner responded, "I want it clearly understood that I am withdrawing only because I know when I am licked."[60]

Garrett remained the barrier to Garner's advancement until 1928. That year, Garrett left the House to run for the U.S. Senate from Tennessee but lost in the Democratic primary.[61]

After Garrett's loss, Joe Tumulty proposed to Garner that they help Garrett find a job. He urged Garner to use his friendship with Nick Longworth to assist Garrett's nomination for the Court of Customs Appeals. Garner, did so, writing Tumulty that "I admire Garrett just as much as you do and will be glad to do anything I can to assist." It was a remarkably magnanimous act from a man often seen as cruel and cold. Garrett was appointed by President Coolidge, who looked favorably on Garrett's work as minority leader.[62]

During the 1920s, Garner made his reputation as a shrewd practitioner of legislative politics and a critic of Republican revenue policies. Although he rarely defeated Republicans, through modifications of their bills and through alliances with insurgent Republicans, he was able to moderate the strongly pro-business stance of Republican legislation. Since public speaking was not Garner's strength, he engaged in the art of vote trading and compromise, avoiding opposition to Republican policies in the open battleground of the House floor. As things developed, in the late 1920s, the Republicans also had a leader who was willing to deal and compromise, Garner's friend Nicholas Longworth of Ohio. Their friendship flourished though they were from different worlds. When Longworth died, John McDuffie of Alabama, a Garner protégé, gave a radio eulogy and sent a copy of the address to Garner who offered a heartfelt reply, praising Longworth's memory and McDuffie's eloquence: Longworth "may have been what the world would term our political enemy, but outside of politics he was our warm friend and we both loved him and won't forget him very soon. What you said about him was beautiful. I wish I had the gift of saying what I think."[63]

Often they were able to iron out issues and work out compromises in the privacy of the Board of Education where they and their allies would retire at the end of the legislative day for drinks and conversation. For

Garner these negotiation sessions allowed him to have a Democratic voice in policy-making without expending the political currency necessary to fight pitched battles in committees and on the floor. For Longworth, these sessions could reduce delay in legislating. He also could avoid the battles and Garner's continual probing of his forces in an effort to drive the progressive Republicans from the regulars.[64]

These negotiation sessions were remarkably confidential affairs. Bascom Timmons, who attended many of the sessions, claimed that all understandings between the two men were precise ones, with no ambiguity. However, Timmons did not divulge any negotiation other than a trivial one involving U.S. embassies.[65] Of course, there were limits to these negotiations. Many of the major issues of the 1920s, such as the tariff or tax reduction, had to be debated on the floor. While Garner and Longworth had great influence within their parties, neither were czars in the image of earlier congressional leaders.

Speaker Garner

After the elections of 1930, a series of deaths among Republicans (including Longworth's) gave the Democrats a tiny majority. Garner's seniority and Democratic leadership clearly put him in line for the Speakership. To obtain that position, he recognized the need to guarantee some northern power in the House.[66] He had a breakfast meeting with John Curry, the leader of Tammany, after which Curry announced his support for Garner as Speaker.[67] And Garner reluctantly accepted Henry Rainey of Illinois as majority leader. Had Garner not been able to win the Speakership, Joseph W. Byrns of Tennessee, incoming chair of the Appropriations Committee, was waiting in the wings.[68] If Garner did win, Byrns was ready to try for the majority leadership, with reports that he had obtained support from Tammany for that office. Ultimately, Byrns did not withdraw from consideration for majority leader until the day after Garner's ally John McDuffie withdrew his candidacy. Byrns announced that he thought being chair of Appropriations was second only to being Speaker, and he claimed that since Garner was from the South, the sentiment in the House was to recognize other sections of the country in the choice of floor leader.[69] The Democrats organized the House and elected Garner as Speaker. Garner's protégé Rayburn moved to the chairmanship of the Committee on Interstate and Foreign Commerce.

Garner's Speakership was held together by a bare majority with internal tensions. For years the party had been primarily a southern party, and that domination was based, in large part, on the seniority of southern Representatives. Thus, northern Democrats felt excluded from the leadership. And Garner, regardless of whatever promises he had made to Tammany boss John Curry and to the political requirements of greater northern representation, continued that practice of exclusion. For example, he backed Alabama Congressman McDuffie for the majority leadership against Byrns of Tennessee, John J. O'Connor of New York, and Illinois Congressman Henry Rainey. Though Rainey won the leadership position, Garner never included Rainey within his leadership circle. Believing Rainey to be "loose-lipped," Garner rarely invited him to the gossip and strategy sessions at the Board of Education meetings. Rather, Garner preferred to work with the southern committee chairmen to accomplish his goals; he opposed the concept of a party steering committee, which would have diffused power from the Speaker and the committee chairs.[70]

The battle over the steering committee was the first major challenge to Garner's leadership — and it was a threat led by Joseph Byrns, a man who had already been seen as a Garner alternative in the Speaker's chair. Byrns, Charles Crisp of Georgia, and William Ayres of Kansas, all of whom had been mentioned as majority leader possibilities, had proposed a steering committee days prior to Garner's election as Speaker.[71] They wanted a committee of eleven members, including the Speaker and the majority leader, to set party policy. Garner, of course, saw the steering committee as a threat to his Speakership and successfully opposed it (although the steering committee was implemented later during Henry Rainey's Speakership). In this struggle, Byrns was perhaps Garner's main rival, beginning a pattern that was to earn Byrns the enmity of Garner and his allies in the House.

Instead of relying on a steering committee, Garner worked through southern committee chairmen. Among his key allies were Texans Marvin Jones, James Buchanan, Sam Rayburn, Hatton Sumners, and Joseph Mansfield; North Carolinians Lindsay Warren and Dean of the House Edward Pou; John Collier of Mississippi, chair of the Ways and Means Committee; Charles Crisp of Georgia, second-ranking member of the Ways and Means Committee; John McDuffie, the Democratic whip, William Bankhead from Alabama; and Missourians Clarence Cannon and Jacob Milligan. All of these men were either committee chairs or relatively senior members; therefore, they were not willing to voluntarily relinquish power. When Bankhead, for example, picked up on a newspaper report that Edward Pou would relinquish his claim to the chairmanship of the

Rules Committee to a northern Democrat, he immediately wired Garner that he hoped the report was false and, if true, that he wanted the job.[72]

The challenge of leading a small majority required Garner to effectively plead for intraparty harmony and kept him from innovating too greatly. The narrowness of his majority also encouraged him to reach out to Progressive Republicans, as he had during the late 1920s. He often worked through Fiorello LaGuardia, whom he called "Frijole," and who was able to deliver about fifteen dissident Republicans to Garner's side.[73]

Garner's razor-thin majority and his conservative base of support in the House (coupled with his own conservative inclinations) made it difficult to initiate an alternative to the Hoover program. Garner's policies, however, as he expressed them in a letter to McDuffie, were remarkably orthodox. He wrote that his goals included:

1. reducing by 10 percent government salaries over $1800 a year;
2. increasing the income tax all along the line to help balance the budget; and
3. increasing the inheritance tax to address the deficit.

He continued, "Just how Mr. Mellon and Mr. Hoover and other international bankers, who control the government at the present time, can possibly insist that Germany and England and other countries where they have their money invested, should balance their budget and then continue to leave ours with a billion dollar deficit each year to be made up by borrowing is something I cannot understand. It is not logical, it is not sound economics; in fact, it is not good government business." Although his letter shows that he distrusted the "international bankers" in the Hoover administration and that he was opposed to the debt moratorium, it is clear that his primary goal was to balance the budget. Given that overpowering objective, there was not much difference between Garner's thoughts and those of Herbert Hoover. Indeed, Jordan Schwarz has stated, "Notwithstanding the desperate condition, the Democratic Party offered few alternatives to the policies of the party in power." Garner supported many of Hoover's policies, and Hoover would later write that Garner was "a man of real statesmanship when he took off his political pistols." The major focus of disagreement between Garner and Hoover was that Garner was somewhat more sensitive to the human needs resulting from the Depression and more aware that the 1930 elections were a demand by voters for greater governmental involvement in the economy.[74]

Though Garner backed somewhat more government action than did

Hoover, he was nevertheless a disappointment to liberals such as Rexford Tugwell, who saw Garner as a "confused Texan" who was "so conservative and so lacking in imagination that nothing had occurred to him that Hoover had not thought of first. . . . And anyway Garner was known to be more worried about balancing the budget than about unemployment. He was hopelessly sterile as a leader."[75] While Tugwell's evaluation of Garner was harsh, Garner did not offer — indeed could not offer — a clear alternative to Hoover's policies.

Nevertheless, Garner was the highest-ranking Democrat in the national government. With control of the Texas political apparatus and the support of publisher William Randolph Hearst, Garner became a presidential contender. The candidate to stop was Franklin Roosevelt, but if Roosevelt faltered, Garner had a good chance of getting the nomination. As his friend Joseph Tumulty assessed Garner's prospects, "Whether you believe it or not, it is becoming strikingly clear that, unless your own action prevents it, you are likely to be called to the headship of the Nation." To the "ordinary man," wrote Tumulty, John Garner is "plain, simple, forthright, courageous, and the very essence of candor."[76]

Even so, Roosevelt could not be stopped, at least not without a major conflict within the Democratic Party. Had Garner joined a "block FDR" movement, he would likely not have become a compromise candidate, and the alternate compromise candidate might not have the strength or ability to beat the Republicans. And Garner was, if anything, a devoted Democrat. He wanted a Democratic victory and chose to join the Roosevelt ticket. Not surprisingly, Sam Rayburn represented Garner at the convention and helped broker the deal that resulted in the Roosevelt-Garner ticket.

Garner continued to be quite intimidated by campaigning. Henry Rainey wrote Farley that Garner did not want to campaign in the North because "he is afraid he will make some mistake." Moreover, Garner wrote Farley that he preferred to remain in Texas because he was not in the best condition, and, Garner feared, his campaigning might do more harm than good.[77] Since he drank enormous quantities of whiskey, there was always the concern that he would not be fully in control of his faculties when he spoke. Additionally, when Garner spoke, often extemporaneously, what he said could be uncontrolled and inconsistent with the desires of the Roosevelt campaign.

To his credit, Garner was well aware of these problems. In his first speech in twenty-five years outside of the House, Garner gave an unrehearsed address to a crowd in Dallas that had turned out to see him on his way home to Uvalde. It was such a strong and demagogic attack that it startled editors and politicians. On July 23, 1932, Garner wrote Jim Farley, saying, "My idea is to punch the Administration in the nose, especially Hoover and Mills, at every opportunity. . . . A short sermon on Mellon, Mills, and Meyers, would be good for the people in all this western and southern country. I don't know how it would set in the East." However, the Roosevelt managers felt Garner's nose punching and "short sermon" would be negatively construed, and Charles Hand, a New York journalist, was dispatched to keep an eye on Garner.[78]

By Garner's reasoning, the Depression was Herbert Hoover's, and the country would not tolerate a second term for the hapless president. But the campaign was an early indication that Garner would not be the usual vice president. An independent and very stubborn man, Garner did not want to campaign. His idea was to stay in Uvalde, say as little as possible, and win the election. Garner explained, using his congressional experience as his guide, "Usually at election time, my friends would wire me that I could stay on at my work in Washington, that it wouldn't be necessary to come home and campaign. Maybe if I'd gone down and started talking, I might have lost votes. Now, today, in a wider field, the same situation seems to me to exist; I don't see any need to make speeches." Victory in November, he felt certain, was "in the bag."[79]

However, Garner was colorful — perhaps too colorful. This rough politician was frightening to the business community, so much so that Jim Farley gave a dinner at the Biltmore where Garner could visit with businessmen, bankers, and politicians. For twenty minutes, Garner spoke and reviewed his career, emphasizing that he supported the gold standard. Business-oriented Democrats like Jesse Jones also spoke, telling the audience, "[I]f you think Mr. Garner is reckless, all you've got to do is look at his financial statement." References were made to his control of two banks and to his considerable real estate holdings. Former Governor Harry F. Byrd of Virginia said that he thought it the most "amazing thing" for Garner to be labeled a radical.[80]

Garner was no radical, but he was impulsive in his public pronouncements, showing a continuing lack in campaign sophistication. In one interview (that got little publicity), Garner said, "You know, this depression may do us some good. We have been thinking of nothing but money. Why when I was a boy we ate breakfast by candlelight, and supper, too." Then to make matters worse, he told reporters, "You know Roosevelt doesn't have any legs. I mean that he has but little use of them. Roosevelt's legs are crippled. But he has them strengthened by steel." Then he gave a demonstration to the reporters of how Roosevelt got up from a chair and walked. His first radio address ever came on October 14, 1932, and that was enough for him. By then, he was ready to quit campaigning. When less than two weeks later he was accused of being a member of the Ku Klux Klan (an especially dangerous charge that was made by New Jersey state senator Emerson Richards), Garner simply let his secretary issue a denial, and the charge disappeared.[81] His campaigning days were over.

His reluctance to campaign did not lessen over time. In 1936, he wrote Joe Tumulty that he would do a radio broadcast the next night: "I hate like hell to do it," but, he noted, he had to be a good soldier even though he thought only Republican presidential candidate Alf Landon could make a worse radio address.[82] Furthermore, Vice President Garner would not speak for congressional friends if it required leaving the Capitol. Congressman William Colmer of Mississippi prevailed upon Sen. Pat Harrison of Mississippi to ask Garner to come to Colmer's district and dedicate a new federal building. Though Harrison was a great friend of Garner's, he could not persuade Garner to make the trip. Garner responded to the invitation, "Son, I'd like to do that for you. I'd like to go down there, say some nice things about you. But if I did, I'd be like a virtuous gal, having made a misstep once, and finding it hard to quit. I never make a speech outside the dome of the Capitol."[83]

Keeping Contact with the Senate and House
Garner's Congressional Influence

Garner could contribute little by way of campaign skills to Roosevelt, but he could assist the administration greatly with the Congress. He wrote Roosevelt in 1934 that he felt like a "cur dog" in campaigning but that he would offer great assistance with Congress: "I think my greatest contribution can be while the Congress is in session in keeping contact with the Senate and House. I have had some experience and I might add, what seems to be luck in that particular. As your messenger, I will try to hypnotize, mesmerize and otherwise get our friends to approach matters in a helpful way." And, as vice president, Garner proved good to his word. It was not until about 1937 that his disagreements with Roosevelt's policies turned him into a hindrance for the administration. Until that year, he was a useful legislative tactician in passing New Deal legislation. In his thirty years in Congress and two years as Speaker, Garner had developed a vast network of friends and great knowledge of the legislative process. He had enormous support within the powerful Texas delegation (Texans chaired nine standing committees and one special committee) and an especially close relationship with Sam Rayburn, chairman of the Interstate and Foreign Commerce Committee, a key committee for early New Deal legislation. Nineteen Senate members had served with Garner in the House, and almost every one was a personal friend. Although Garner did not agree with some policies of the early New Deal, he was loyal to the administration and became one of the most powerful vice presidents in history.[84]

The skills honed in the Board of Education in the 1920s benefited the New Deal. Lionel Patenaude wrote of Garner's early years as vice president: "Operating from his vice presidential room just off the Senate Lobby, Garner would gather his friends and spin a few yarns, which were highlighted by pertinent suggestions. The President regularly used him to pass the word to Congress on priority legislation. But he was not just a messenger; he was the New Deal's 'mid-wife.' In the process he 'worked wonders on law makers. . . .' In his inner sanctum, or in his Bureau of Education, over branch water and bourbon, many an important decision was made which affected New Deal legislation."[85]

Still, Garner was fundamentally conservative. When Raymond Moley visited him in Uvalde in September 1934, Moley asked Garner to tell him what he thought of New Deal policies. Garner told Moley he would cut "spendin [sic]," and that he would especially focus on cutting "relief." And there were hints of tension between Roosevelt and Garner as early as 1935, when Roosevelt became irritated over what he believed were Garner's discussions with Senators over the Veterans Bonus Bill, discussions, Roosevelt felt, that "got me in a spot where I can be accused of bad faith if the bonus is passed over my veto." In March 1935, Garner complained that cabinet meetings, which he attended, were not useful, and, like many southern Democrats, Garner was thinking that the economic emergency was over and that some of the policy experiments could be ended.[86]

Pressure also came from back home. In 1936, wealthy Texas lumberman John Kirby, a former business associate of Joe Bailey, wrote Garner, "How long are you going to tolerate the apostasy of the Roosevelt Administration to the cardinal principles of the Democratic Party and the notorious contempt for the plain terms of the Constitution?" Garner's reply became public and indicated frustration with the New Deal: "You can't do everything you want to and I can't do half what I would like to do. You can't control everybody you would like to and I am in a similar fix. I think that answers your question."[87]

In 1937, that fundamental conservatism began to create a break between Garner and FDR. At first, Garner denied that the break was anything more than disagreement. Writing Jim Farley, Garner issued a plea that he had not split with Roosevelt:

> When I see articles such as Mr. Stokes' story, especially those saying that there is a break between the "Boss" [Roosevelt] and myself, it peeves me, and yet I know that you and the "Boss" and the others who are acquainted with the facts know that there isn't any truth in it.
>
> I have never said a word touching the Administration that the "Boss," you and others could not have been present and heard. Frankly, Jim, I have almost gotten to love Roosevelt from a personal standpoint.

However, Garner then mentioned his concerns with Roosevelt's positions on the sit-down strikes and lawlessness that Garner said could not be sustained from the standpoint of statesmanship or patriotism. He added that he thought Roosevelt had also been talked into making exceptions to good economic policy.[88]

In spite of these protests to the contrary, it was not long until Garner set out to sabotage the New Deal. Garner and Roosevelt disagreed on the sit-down strikes, deficit spending, packing the Supreme Court, the battle on the majority leadership in the Senate between Pat Harrison and Alben Barkley, the wages and hours bill, and the effort to purge the Democratic Party of anti-Roosevelt members of Congress. In a three-hour legislative meeting dealing with the sit-down strikes, an angry argument between Garner and Roosevelt ultimately had to be silenced by Sen. Joe Robinson. Jim Farley ascribed the beginning of the split to the sit-down strikes. Said Farley, "At the time of the sit-down strike in Detroit Garner was "very vehement" in and out of the Cabinet. I think from that time on, and I say this very kindly, Garner began to not have as much confidence in Mr. Roosevelt as he'd had prior to that time." By 1938, Garner and Roosevelt were barely on speaking terms.[89]

When Roosevelt's court-packing plan was read in the Senate, Garner walked from the rostrum, making a "thumbs down" gesture. Moreover, in 1938, Garner was reported to be aiding southern Democrats in opposition to the wages and hours bill. By the end of 1937, conservative Democrats were thinking of Garner as a likely presidential candidate. Garner was opposed to a third term for Roosevelt, and by 1939, Garner, Farley, or Cordell Hull were seen as the three most likely successors to Roosevelt.[90]

Finally, on December 17, 1939, Garner officially announced his candidacy. Despite Garner's having tremendous financial backing for his campaign, Jim Farley noted that when "Garner's announcement was finally made, . . . it did not create any excitement because it was somewhat expected." Everything, Farley claimed, awaited the president's decision on what he would do. But Claude Bowers believed that Garner had misplayed his political hand. He wrote, "I noticed Garner's announcement but it had been practically announced long ago and I know as you know that he cannot be nominated as an out and out enemy of the New Deal. If he had played along outwardly at least as on the team it might have been different, but it was a fatal blunder to permit his friends to put him forward as an anti-Roosevelt candidate."[91]

With the declining international situation and Roosevelt's decision to seek a third term, Garner's presidential prospects ended. He returned to Uvalde where he was apparently content. Writing Lewis Schwellenbach of his retirement, Garner stated,

> I gather that life moves along about the same there, always with something of great importance happening or about to happen.
>
> I stay busy and have never in my life been more contented. I guess I am getting about as much fun out of living now as anyone can.

In 1942, after his son Tully volunteered for the military, Garner was willing to be called by Roosevelt to help with the war effort. Garner wrote to Sam Rayburn, "You can tell the Boss [FDR] that I am at his service. . . . I hope the Boss will not draft me since there are many who can do any job better than I can. I am selfish enough to want to stay in Uvalde and enjoy health and all that goes with it, but I repeat, I am subject to the call of the Commander-in-Chief." That call never came. With FDR's death, Garner had a good friend in the White House, and correspondence between Garner and Harry Truman contained friendly banter. Chief Justice Fred Vinson, who had been Truman's secretary of the treasury, apparently assisted Garner with some tax difficulties, and Truman appointed Tully Garner, John Nance's son, to be collector of customs in Laredo. Truman, however, was unwilling to accede to Ettie Garner's request to release her granddaughter's husband from active military duty until he met the minimum eligibility requirements for separation from the service. Nor did Truman take Garner's advice in 1950 that he should go to war with Russia: In Garner's words, "In re Russia — If it is to be, why not *now*" (Garner's emphasis). In 1952, Garner still had enough political influence in Texas that when he endorsed the Democratic nominee for president, Adlai Stevenson, liberal Texas Democratic leader Walter Hall wrote Sam Rayburn that it was "among the highly effective things" done in the campaign.[92] By then, however, power in the House had long been in the hands of another Texan, Garner's protégé Sam Rayburn.

1. Joseph Weldon Bailey, April 14, 1909. *Library of Congress Prints and Photographs Division, Washington, D.C.*

2. Joe Bailey with Texas businessman J. L. Wortham, undated. *Library of Congress Prints and Photographs Division, Washington, D.C.*

3. Speaker John Nance Garner, undated.
Library of Congress Prints and Photographs Division, Washington, D.C.

4. John McDuffie.
Library of Congress Prints and Photographs Division, Washington, D.C.

5. John O'Connor.
Center for American History, University of Texas–Austin. Used by permission.

6. John Nance Garner and FDR, 1934. *Center for American History, University of Texas–Austin. Used by permission.*

7. Majority Leader and future speaker Joe Byrns and Speaker Henry Rainey, 1934, preparing for the 1935 session. *Tennessee State Library and Archives.*

8.
Sam Rayburn
press conference
upon being
elected majority
leader, January
5, 1937. *Center
for American
History, University
of Texas–Austin.
Used by
permission.*

9. *From left:* Speaker William Bankhead, Vice Pres. John Nance Garner,
Sen. Alben Barkley, and Majority Leader Sam Rayburn, January 2, 1940.
Center for American History, University of Texas–Austin. Used by permission.

10. Majority Leader John McCormack (*center*) stoops to talk with Pres. Franklin Roosevelt (*bottom right*) while Speaker Sam Rayburn (*upper right*) and Vice Pres. Henry Wallace look on. *Franklin D. Roosevelt Presidential Library and Museum.*

11. Sam Rayburn and Jim Wright in Fort Worth, 1956. *Jim Wright Papers, Special Collections, Mary Couts Burnett Library, Texas Christian University. Used by permission.*

12. *From left:* Lyndon Johnson, Harry Truman, John Nance Garner,
and Sam Rayburn celebrate Garner's ninetieth birthday, 1959.
Center for American History, University of Texas–Austin. Used by permission.

13. Sam Rayburn with Hale Boggs, Mobile, Alabama, 1960.
Center for American History, University of Texas–Austin. Used by permission.

14. *From left:* Jim Wright, Carl Albert, Tip O'Neill, unknown, and John McCormack. Picture taken at a tree planting ceremony in December 1976 just before Albert left Washington. *Carl Albert Collection, University of Oklahoma, Norman, Oklahoma. Used by permission.*

15. Morris Udall (*left*) shakes hands with Majority Leader Carl Albert during his challenge of Speaker John McCormack (*center*). *Carl Albert Collection, University of Oklahoma, Norman, Oklahoma. Used by permission.*

16. Candidates for majority leader appear on "Meet the Press,"
December 5, 1976. *From left,* Richard Bolling, Phil Burton, John McFall,
and Jim Wright. *Jim Wright Papers, Special Collections,*
Mary Couts Burnett Library, Texas Christian University. Used by permission.

17. Majority Leader Wright and Speaker O'Neill.
Jim Wright Papers, Special Collections, Mary Couts Burnett Library,
Texas Christian University. Used by permission.

hen John Nance Garner ascended to the vice presidency with the landslide 1932 election, it opened a vacancy in the Speaker's chair. In the House, as in the nation as a whole, the Democratic Party had become a national one. The "New Deal coalition" included large numbers of both conservative southerners and liberal northerners, both groups seeking leadership in the House. The nation was in the midst of a Great Depression, the stakes were high, and the competition within the House was fierce.

The Failed Effort John McDuffie of Alabama

In the early days of the New Deal, Garner was still viewing the Democratic Party as a southern party. Garner's choice for his replacement was John McDuffie of Alabama, clearly a man centered in the southern wing of the party. In spite of Garner's best efforts, however, McDuffie could not succeed his mentor in the House leadership.

Garner had never been close to Henry Rainey of Illinois, but he counted party whip John McDuffie of Alabama a dear friend. When McDuffie first went to Washington in 1919, he had considered Oscar Underwood of Alabama to be his political mentor, but he lived in the same Congress Hall Hotel where Garner lived, and by 1924, Garner had become his "political daddy." McDuffie's office was on the fifth floor of the old House Office Building, directly above Garner's, and the two of them visited every day after the adjournment of the House. In 1929, after Garrett left the House, Garner was chosen minority floor leader, and he appointed McDuffie as minority whip. McDuffie was a regular at the Garner-Longworth Board of Education meetings and even had a key to the room.[1] Like Garner, McDuffie had a taste for good bourbon.

McDuffie's friendship with Garner was perhaps the major factor in his selection as minority whip, but he also was "pleasant, energetic and capable." According to one report, if McDuffie had been an actor, "he wouldn't have been a leading man during the era when the movie magnates decreed that pretty men should be starred as the heroes of celluloid romances; rather he belongs to the Wallace Beery era, the era of the he-looking men who look and act as if they might quite capably do the things in real life that they are supposed to do in reel life." McDuffie was "of medium stature, muscular but not heavy, quick moving and springy, thinning brown hair, blue eyes, large nose and plenty of chin, with an air of pugnacity and a make-up which decries hypocrisy." He had a "reputation for straightforwardness and keeping his word to the point that some called him 'Honest John.'" However, McDuffie was chary about giving his word.[2]

Although he had a "rather bluff exterior," he was also "sensitive to a degree," and he had "many friends and a considerable number who might be described as intense friends." His conservatism led him to oppose public power, a key element of the New Deal, which caused some colleagues to have qualms about his leadership. John O'Connor, one of McDuffie's rivals, offered a negative private assessment, portraying McDuffie as "Garner's closest friend. He was little known in the House and did not participate until last session, when Garner started to push him. Garner appointed him whip. [McDuffie is] not so popular as [the] press says." Sam Rayburn, Garner's campaign manager at the Chicago convention, also managed McDuffie's Speakership campaign, showing McDuffie's alignment with the Garner faction. Further, said the memo, McDuffie was thought to know "practically nothing about Rules or procedure." Still another concern about McDuffie's candidacy for Speaker was that Alabama might gain too much influence. Though Edward Pou of North Carolina had the title of chairman of Rules, his poor health meant that William Bankhead of Alabama served as Rules chair. Thus, the Speaker and the *de facto* Rules chair would come from the same state.[3]

As the Representative from Mobile, a port city, McDuffie was a spokesman for river and harbor development and for a national merchant marine, but he held views similar to Herbert Hoover on the economy, believing the appropriate response to the Depression was to cut government spending and to sacrifice until there was an upturn in the economic cycle. Consequently, McDuffie opposed Garner's public works bill, saying that spending on public works would open "a Pandora's box." Garner responded by accusing his friend of being "like Marie Antonienette [*sic*], who allegedly suggested that her subjects eat cake." Such arguments between McDuffie and Garner were apparently not unusual, but normally took place behind closed doors.[4]

McDuffie was a skilled orator, but his leadership style as whip involved quiet negotiation, moving around the Capitol and having private conversations with members as the opportunities presented themselves.[5] When the Democrats had gained control of the House in 1931, with Garner in line to become Speaker, McDuffie became a candidate for the majority leadership. Regional tensions soon broke out, with eastern and western Democrats claiming that southern Democrats would monopolize the House.

Though Garner delayed the party caucus on House organization, the controversy remained. The new Speaker was a Texan, and southern Democrats would get three-fourths of the committee chairmanships, including most all of the important committees.[6]

As early as December of 1930, Sen. James Hamilton Lewis of Illinois urged Henry Rainey to try for the leadership, even the Speakership, noting that had the southerner Underwood gotten the Speakership rather than Missouri's Clark, it would have "embarrassed us in the House and greatly interfered with what followed in 1912." In a clear attack on Garner, Lewis then added that "our southerners must see this situation, and I am compelled to say to you that the memory of the day when the cry was 'Texas — everything for Texas,' under the Wilson administration, ought not now to be revived." Rainey replied positively to Lewis's letter, noting that before his defeat in the 1920 election, he was the ranking minority member, next to Claude Kitchin, the Democratic leader. With Kitchin's poor health, Rainey often acted as leader. Unfortunately, his two-year gap in service had cost him seniority, even though he was re-elected by the largest majority he had ever received. He added that the pro-Texas bias had caused harm in the North. To Rainey, the Democratic Party needed to expand in the North because "We can gain no more seats in the South and we can gain no more states in the South. If our party is restored to the position where it can again function we would have an opportunity to make effective the principles for which we stand." Rainey believed that he might be able to attract some progressive Republicans and others who would allow him to organize the House if southern Democrats did not reach out to the North.[7]

Of course, it soon became evident that the Democrats could and would organize the House when a series of deaths moved the House slightly into Democratic control. Rainey understood that Garner would be unopposed for the Speakership, although he believed he might have won had it not been for his 1920 defeat. As a result, Rainey turned his attention to the majority leadership. With the Speakership and the chairs of all the important committees in the hands of southerners, he sought balance in the leadership, especially since the majority of Democrats in the House would be from the North. Given that even some southern members had spoken to him about being a candidate for leader and that he thought he could get almost all the votes from the North, Rainey was confident about his chances. His biggest challenge might come from New Yorker John J. O'Connor, the ranking Tammany Hall machine member of Congress. But Rainey felt that O'Connor could not get other northern votes and would not get southern votes. Additionally, Rainey noted he had far more seniority than did O'Connor.[8]

Rainey's calculations regarding O'Connor proved correct. Even the New York delegation was split when Tom Cullen, another New Yorker, became busy making his own deals with Garner.[9] The rivalry between O'Connor and Cullen had broken out shortly after O'Connor arrived in Washington. As a new congressman with the support of Tammany boss Charles Murphy, O'Connor had been appointed to the Rules Committee, a position also coveted by Cullen. Brooklyn leader John McCovey apparently backed Cullen's opposition to O'Connor because he believed O'Connor's brother Basil had prevented a friend from being appointed superintendent of insurance by Gov. Franklin Roosevelt. Three years later, when John Carew was appointed by Governor Roosevelt to the Supreme Court in New York, Cullen and O'Connor battled again, this time for the leadership of the Tammany delegation. This time Cullen got the leadership designation, but the feud between the two continued. When O'Connor was first proposed for majority leader, Cullen swore he would stop him, calling O'Connor, whose law degree was from Harvard, the "Harvard stuck-up," and even declaring himself a candidate. The Cullen-O'Connor feud was to have a vast impact on O'Connor's future in the House. As O'Connor's ally John Cochran explained the effects of the split in the New York delegation, "I do not think it is doing you or anyone else much good." An O'Connor ally noted that Cullen was trying to cut his own deal with Garner, and O'Connor needed to find out what the deal was: "whether that means you as Floor Leader or whether he intends to go along with someone from the South."[10]

The split New York delegation required O'Connor to withdraw in favor of Rainey. Thus, Rainey's regional calculations made sense; he had a chance. Rainey's path was not completely clear, however, because Tammany seemed, for awhile, supportive of Joseph Byrns of Tennessee, the ranking member of Appropriations. Byrns formally withdrew the day after McDuffie, claiming that he never had been a candidate for majority leader. Tellingly, though, when a reporter mentioned that Byrns could not have beaten Rainey for majority leader, Byrns's secretary became indignant.[11]

Realistically, the major battle was between McDuffie and Rainey. Rainey was over seventy and held the ranking seat on Ways and Means. Only two representatives were more senior than Rainey, Pou of North Carolina and Garner. Rainey had come to the House with Garner in 1903, but his loss in the Harding landslide took him from the House in 1921–23. The sectional divisions forced McDuffie to withdraw from the leadership race, though he retained the position of whip.[12]

Although Rainey was officially second in the leadership, the Democratic Party power structure did not change. McDuffie was considered the man next to Garner; Rainey was never made a member of Garner's Bureau of Education. Instead, the regulars during Garner's Speakership were James Collier of Mississippi, Charles Crisp of Georgia, Joseph Byrns of Tennessee, Lindsay Warren of North Carolina, Jacob Milligan of Missouri, Clifton Woodrum of Virginia, Anning Prall of New York, Sam Rayburn of Texas, William Bankhead of Alabama, and John McDuffie.[13]

Two years later, though, when Garner received the vice presidential nomination, the House became abuzz with speculation about his successor as Speaker. Candidates mentioned prominently included Majority Leader Rainey, Appropriations Chairman Byrns, John O'Connor, John Rankin of Mississippi, William Bankhead of Alabama, John McCormack of Massachusetts, Dean of the House Edward Pou of North Carolina, Lindsay Warren of North Carolina, Heartsill Ragon of Arkansas, and Fritz Lanham of Texas. Byrns was seen as the frontrunner, though Rainey was the logical choice since he was majority leader. Speculation was that Rainey might stay as majority leader but more likely would take the chair of the Ways and Means Committee. McDuffie was seen as Garner's choice for the job, but since Bankhead also was a candidate, the two Alabamians would cancel each other out. O'Connor was defined as a Garner critic. John McCormack was seen as a northern candidate who would likely be majority leader if Rainey gave up that position for Ways and Means.[14]

Rankin claimed the support of the Mississippi delegation and ran as a "progressive Democrat." He endorsed inflation, public power, and support for veterans. He criticized McDuffie and Rainey's support of the previous year's sales tax bill, which would fall most heavily on "people who are least able to pay" and "destroy what little commercial intercourse we now have."

He hoped for support of the incoming members of Congress and feared an effort to organize the House on March 2, prior to the arrival of many of the new members. In an indirect attack on Garner's leadership, he, like many of the other candidates for Speaker, supported a steering committee elected by the caucus and representing every section of the country. Claiming that he had tried to have a steering committee two years ago but was "blocked by the very forces that are now attempting to organize the House," Rankin promised, "If I am elected Speaker, there will be no 'Cannonism' practiced."[15]

The campaign seemed to begin with a slap at Garner's attempt to move McDuffie into the Speakership over Rainey so that the Garner allies would maintain control in the House. Adolph Sabath of Illinois believed that Garner's forces bypassed Byrns, who was then chairman of the congressional caucus and in line for running the Speakers' Bureau of the National Democratic Campaign Committee. Instead, McDuffie was installed as vice chairman and then as chairman, because, argued Sabath, he "could talk to the candidates for Congress . . . and help them with $200 or $300 or $500 here and there and at the same time would have a chance to talk to them and get, in many instances, their promises to support and vote for him for the Speaker." Furthermore, Sabath believed that Democratic National Committee Chairman Jim Farley was in on the plot to promote McDuffie.[16]

Rainey actually wrote Farley to complain about Robert Jackson, who was head of the Speaker's bureau when McDuffie was vice chair. As secretary of the Democratic National Committee and a committeeman from New Hampshire, Jackson was considered a mouthpiece for Roosevelt. Rainey complained that Jackson was pro-McDuffie and that close friends of FDR were pro-McDuffie. After reminding Farley that he would still be majority leader and chair of Ways and Means, Rainey claimed that his loyalty to FDR "entitled" him to the Speakership. He emphasized that he was "one of the original Roosevelt-for-President men" and that his "close relations with Speaker Garner" would allow him to work well with the presiding officer of the Senate. He made the regional argument as well. As a result of the election, the number of Democratic members from the North had increased, yet Garner and the chairs of all major committees were from the South. Clearly, the North needed representation, and "I am the only Democratic Member of Congress from the North who has ever attained a ranking position on a major Committee in this century, and I have done that twice." Finally, he made a personal argument. If McDuffie did leapfrog over him for the Speakership, "It would be a distinct demotion for me." In response to his plea, Farley apparently promised to rein in Jackson's pro-McDuffie behavior, because Rainey later wrote to thank Farley for efforts to "correct the situation created by Mr. Jackson." About two weeks after his thank you letter to Farley, Rainey claimed that Farley had written him that Jackson "had no authority whatever to say that Mr. Roosevelt favored Mr. McDuffie's candidacy."[17]

Rainey had not been alone in complaining about Jackson's activities. John O'Connor wrote his brother Basil, FDR's former law partner, complaining that Jackson was "very active, I understand in advocating McDuffie for Speaker." In addition, Byrns had phoned the president-elect on December 8 to complain about rumors that "you and your close friends were interested in the candidacy of Mr. McDuffie for Speaker." After the phone call, Byrns remained unhappy and checked with several newspapermen who told him that Jackson had left the impression that "national headquarters was interested in Mr. McDuffie's campaign and anxious to see him elected Speaker." Byrns proposed that Roosevelt issue a statement announcing his neutrality in the Speaker's race. Most interestingly, in view of the support John Garner was giving McDuffie, Byrns also proposed to Roosevelt that a statement from Garner would stop rumors that Garner was supporting McDuffie. Byrns sent two newspaper clippings. One claimed that while FDR was not involved, the men around Roosevelt wanted McDuffie as Speaker. It also noted that Byrns's chances were hurt when he visited Tammany leader Curry to ask for his support and that Roosevelt had resented Byrns's trip because of Roosevelt's "cool relationship" with Curry, and Roosevelt did not want a Speaker indebted to Curry. The article predicted that McDuffie would be elected Speaker, and Rainey would remain as majority leader and chair of Ways and Means. The second article reported that Byrns, seeking Tammany support, had called on Curry, as had McDuffie. Adding that Curry had backed Garner in his run for Speaker, the article also claimed that Curry would vote with Frank Hague and other eastern Democratic bosses but that John O'Connor was counting on the support of FDR's intimates. Garner, in contrast, supported McDuffie.[18]

Byrns's efforts to block stories of Roosevelt's involvement in the Speaker's case ultimately got a response from FDR himself, though it took nineteen days. FDR insisted that he believed in "complete separation of legislative and executive functions," and therefore "[t]he last thing in the world I should do as President would be to interfere by 'thought, word or deed' in the matter of the organization of the House." All the candidates were "old friends of mine, and all of you have my blessing." Roosevelt copied the letter to Garner with a note that he wanted to "set at rest any silly stories about my preference or interference in the Speakership matter." He told Garner that "You can make it abundantly clear that I am not interfering and will not interfere in any shape, manner or form nor shall I express any preference publicly or privately!"[19] However, there was no effort to persuade Garner to lay off his activities.

Even laying aside Roosevelt's claimed neutrality, he may not have been favorable to McDuffie. Jouett Shouse, chair of the Democratic National Executive Committee, had tried to organize anti-Roosevelt forces at the 1932 convention; he backed McDuffie. In fact, McDuffie sought Shouse's aid in getting support from the Missouri, Ohio, and Indiana House delegations. McDuffie was Garner's man, but he had no reason to be devoted to Roosevelt. Indeed, O'Connor wrote that McDuffie "has no real support except Garner—and would be impossible [as Speaker]." Further, McDuffie's reputed ties to large corporate and utility interests in Alabama would have troubled Roosevelt.[20]

By December the Speaker's race, according to Garner, was between Rainey and McDuffie. Garner had also told Roosevelt that Byrns would make a deal with Rainey. Roosevelt "spoke well" of Byrns and had told John O'Connor that Rainey was popular and that he had hoped for the sake of party harmony that there would be no fuss [about Rainey becoming Speaker.][21]

O'Connor talked to Roosevelt about Roosevelt's sense of the race. FDR told him that Rainey was popular, and he spoke highly of Byrns. Roosevelt inquired if O'Connor could broaden his support beyond Tammany since O'Connor's Tammany ties were "poison." Roosevelt understood that the battle "might [get] so tangled up that I [O'Connor] might have a chance, but," noted O'Connor, Roosevelt "wasn't very encouraging about it." O'Connor thought Roosevelt had in fact stayed out of the race, with the result was that "people are lining up, and unless something is done soon, we'll be out of the picture." Farley visited with O'Connor as well, telling him that Roosevelt had "told him it would be bad policy to show his hand now." Thus, at least according to O'Connor, Roosevelt had chosen to let the candidates fight it out without his involvement. Mostly, FDR hoped to maintain party harmony.[22]

Roosevelt's sense of Rainey's popularity was instructive. At seventy-four, Rainey had a massive head of white hair and "dressed like a cartoonist's version of a congressman." A newspaper account noted that while Rainey had mellowed with age, he had been caustic and "poison-tongued" in earlier years. One reporter stressed Rainey's liberal ideology, quoting Rainey as saying that "the trouble with a lot of Democrats is that they don't know Thomas Jefferson is dead." He had spent the summer of 1931 in Russia, actively seeking a resumption of relations with that country, even speaking of the Soviet Union's "intelligent planning." He maintained a passion for the traditional Democratic doctrine of low tariffs. But, the reporter noted, Rainey lacked leadership skills such as "an intimate knowledge of individual members" and "just what concessions have to be made . . . to keep [congressmen] in line."[23]

Still, Roosevelt knew Rainey would be a loyalist. Rainey was a man who had "expanded his devotion to William Jennings Bryan to encompass Roosevelt." A memorandum in the John O'Connor papers, however, was hostile to Rainey, describing him as "slow, inaudible," and not participating "in debate on an average of more than once a year before last session. Knows few members. He has always been radical on the Tariff, Taxation and Russia, etc. He knows little about the Rules or procedure." If Rainey became Speaker, the assessment continued, McDuffie or Bankhead will serve as majority leader "and run the show." Additionally, if Rainey became Speaker, he would leave Ways and Means leaving Robert Doughton of North Carolina as chair. The memorandum concluded, "No one in the House wants that."[24]

As a result, the need to keep Rainey to chair Ways and Means became one argument for McDuffie as Speaker. Also, Joe Byrns, it was claimed, was needed on Appropriations to keep Buchanan of Texas from becoming chair. The argument would have left only Rankin, Bankhead, and McDuffie as candidates. Rankin was not viewed seriously, and Bankhead was handicapped by the Alabama legislature's endorsement of McDuffie. Following this logic, McDuffie was the only viable candidate for Speaker. Still, it was hard to argue against the idea that the South had too much power in the House. Southerners chaired twenty-nine committees, including Ways and Means, Appropriations, and Rules. Texans alone chaired six committees — Agriculture, Interstate and Foreign Commerce, Judiciary, Public Buildings, Rivers and Harbors, and Territories. McDuffie's mere fourteen years of consecutive service also weakened his campaign.[25]

McDuffie's efforts to gain the Speakership were hurt by the ambitions of other Garner allies. Initially, Sam Rayburn expressed interest in the

Speakership. Rayburn wrote his friend Jacob Le Roy ("Tuck") Milligan, a congressman from Missouri:

> As to the Speakership, I am extremely embarrassed as you know my devotion to John McDuffie and Will Bankhead both. On top of that these people down here in Texas are urging and expecting that I be a candidate. It is not my intention at this time to become an active candidate for the present I feel that I should hold myself as an available candidate. Of course, I understand that talk that Texas has got a great deal and that they may have the Vice-Presidency but it will be remembered that Coolidge was Vice-President and Gillett was Speaker of the House at one time. I do not intend to become active and embarrass any of my friends or friends of any other candidate, and it is entirely possible that when the time comes I will not be a candidate.

Rayburn ultimately decided to support McDuffie, especially after Garner advised Rayburn that there would be resentment against another Texan attempting to succeed a Texas Speaker.[26] Perhaps most damaging to McDuffie was the ambition of McDuffie's fellow Alabamian William Bankhead for the Speakership. Bankhead had told McDuffie he would run for Speaker, but several events led Bankhead to eliminate himself. Gov. Benjamin Miller, the Alabama legislature, other prominent Alabamians, the Mobile *Register,* and the Birmingham *News* all supported McDuffie. The *News* also noted McDuffie's loyalty to the party in 1930 in withdrawing from the leadership fight; arguing that the Bankhead family had already received its share of honors from the state, it called upon the Alabama delegation to unite behind McDuffie.[27]

Trying to show that he would not be a sectional Speaker, McDuffie promised that he would create a steering committee that would represent every section of the country and would shape the legislative programs of the House Democratic majority. He also pointed out that his support of Boulder Dam showed his concern for the West and let it be known that he would support a northerner for the floor leadership.[28] Bankhead actively campaigned for McDuffie, leading McDuffie to believe he could win Byrns's supporters' votes and the Tammany votes of John O'Connor.[29]

The air in the capitol was full of rumors of "deals" and candidates making promises to members in exchange for their support. For example, O'Connor claimed that Rainey, McDuffie, and Byrns had wanted to orchestrate a deal with him where in exchange for his support, he would become majority leader. Optimistically, he believed that if McDuffie and

Byrns lost their chances at the Speakership, he would get their support over Rainey. He thought it a real possibility since he believed Cordell Hull would go to the cabinet and Byrns would get a Senate seat. If that happened, Byrns and the Tennessee delegation had assured him that they would support O'Connor. Rainey, he thought, was ahead, and if McDuffie gave up, the McDuffie supporters would back him over Rainey. O'Connor thought he had the support of Louisiana, Pennsylvania, and New England. He also believed he had big city support from Ohio and Chicago, some western support, and possible support in Maryland and Virginia. Though he had opposition in New York from his enemy and rival, Tom Cullen, and Tammany political boss John Curry was quiet, he had other New York delegation support. He communicated with an unidentified person and referred to "your friend" (almost certainly a reference to President-Elect Roosevelt) where he angled for support and suggested that Jim Farley could also help him. Finally, O'Connor wondered if a patronage deal could be made with John Curry and Brooklyn boss John McCooey to get their support. Curry could help get backing from political bosses in New Jersey, Chicago, Indiana, and from the Pendergast machine in Kansas City. He also suggested the value of support from Jimmie Byrnes in South Carolina, along with supporters from Maryland and Nebraska. It was an ambitious strategy, but he was not the only one talking of deals.[30]

With his political machine ties, O'Connor was able to contact political bosses to generate support. He wrote to ask for Jersey City's Frank Hague's support, but Hague would not commit until he knew "what the attitude of the President Elect is going to be, because after all he is the boss of the party and if I am to call myself an organization democrat I shall be expected to obey orders." From Mayor James Curley of Boston, O'Connor asked for help in getting the support of John McCormack. Curley offered to speak to McCormack and to meet with O'Connor and "to do anything I can in your behalf." However, he later claimed that his attempts to sway McCormack were futile. Curley said that McCormack "seems to have definitely committed himself to McDuffie."[31] Garner had supported McCormack for a spot on Ways and Means, and it was clearly time, in McCormack's mind, to reciprocate the favor.

Rainey's fellow Illinoisan Adolph Sabath emerged as his campaign manager. He went to Joe Byrns, who was also seeking the Speakership, and found him angry that he had been denied the chairmanship of the Congressional Campaign Committee. Sabath told Byrns that he did not think Byrns could win because the North would support Rainey and the

South would split its votes between Byrns and McDuffie. Sabath therefore offered Byrns a deal. If he would support Rainey, Rainey forces would support Byrns for the majority leadership. Byrns delayed agreeing to the deal, however, and Sabath went to William Bankhead to offer similar terms. Sabath believed that Bankhead would not only divide the Alabama delegation but that he was personally more popular than McDuffie. Like Byrns, Bankhead asked for time to think about the deal.[32]

Later, Bankhead approached Sabath and said, "Adolph, they might defeat me for Congress [if I enter into this arrangement]. So you better select someone else." Sabath then went back to Byrns, and the deal was struck. Meanwhile, Sabath was talking to western and northern Democrats as well, pitching the argument that the North needed the Speakership and that the South had too much power. Tammany Hall, however, backed McDuffie, and McDuffie's forces were claiming not only the support of Jim Farley, but also of President Roosevelt. Sabath then contacted Louis Howe, Roosevelt's closest political advisor, and reminded Howe that the president should not involve himself in House business. Furthermore, Rainey, as majority leader, was entitled to the Speakership. According to Sabath, he received a call from Howe, who told him, "Judge, I read your letter, I think you're right. I think the north is entitled to consideration. I think you're right that the President should not be used aiding McDuffie. . . . I feel that . . . McDuffie, a reactionary, he might be able to hold up progressive and liberal legislation." Sabath was reassured that the president would not allow anyone to use his name in the Speakership race.[33]

Still, though Garner said he would not get involved, he clearly backed McDuffie, which caused ruffled feelings between Rainey and Garner. John Rankin, one of the minor candidates for Speaker, recognized that the position of FDR might prove the determining factor in the race. He wrote Governor Roosevelt, asking that the president-elect "continue to maintain a neutral attitude" since the race would prove "interesting" and possibly "bitter" and that neither Rainey nor McDuffie seemed strong enough to win. In response, Roosevelt wrote Rankin that he would remain neutral. Despite that promise, conflicting reports emerged. The Washington *Times* reported that "it is as secret as if it had been told at a woman's bridge club that the White House would like to have seen John McDuffie of Alabama in the speaker's chair" while other press reports claimed that Roosevelt was supporting Rainey.[34]

In early December, McDuffie was very optimistic about his chances, writing that it looked as if "things are taking such a shape that this high place will fall to me." He believed that he was seen as "the lesser of all the evils" and had the support of "the newspaper men in Washington." By the end of December 1932, with the caucus about two months away, Rayburn claimed that eighty-seven congressmen were pledged to vote for McDuffie, far more than those pledged to any other candidate. McDuffie was more than halfway to victory. Additionally, McDuffie was wooing the North and West by promising that a northerner or westerner would become majority leader.[35]

Things slowly began to fall apart for McDuffie. McDuffie supporter Charles Hand had met with Tammany leader Curry in December and had received positive news. Expressing a desire to talk with McDuffie, Curry had claimed that Brooklyn boss McCooey would go along with his decision. Hand reported that Curry still felt angry about Chicago Mayor Anton Cermak who he felt had deserted him at the 1932 Democratic convention and that he did not feel positive about anyone from Illinois. Hand said, "Naturally, Curry didn't say, 'I am for McDuffie.' The leaders of Tammany never talk that way three months in advance of an event. But I am quite convinced from his attitude that he strongly inclines to you." In the meantime, Hand wrote, he would continue to try to get support from Brooklyn's McCooey and from Jersey City's Frank Hague.[36]

But good feelings are not firm promises, and soon the tide shifted. At the end of December, Adolph Sabath announced that Roosevelt had authorized him to "say unequivocally [sic] that reports were unfounded and spread without approval that he favored McDuffie."[37] Representatives from Tammany met with Sabath in the privacy of a taxi, and they promised support for Rainey if they could get the patronage chairmanship and if one of their members could become assistant majority leader. The deal was made.

In January, McDuffie asked Huey Long for the Louisiana delegation's endorsement, but Long refused because he believed McDuffie too conservative. In spite of that setback, however, McDuffie remained optimistic, claiming strength from all over the country and over one hundred pledged votes, more than all the other candidates combined. He thought Byrns would get out of the race and support McDuffie. Besides, he had strong southern support — listing a majority of the Georgia delegation, nine of the eleven-member North Carolina delegation, seven of the nine-member Virginia delegation, and at least fourteen members of the twenty-one-member Texas delegation. In mid-February, McDuffie was claiming support from Maine to California with a majority of the Ohio, West Virginia, and Iowa delegations. While he realized that Byrns would prefer Rainey over him, he did not think Byrns had substantial support and did not think he would be able to carry more than two or three votes to Rainey after Byrns pulled out of the race.[38]

However, in late February 1933, McDuffie sent a telegram to Robert Jackson seeking confirmation on a story he had heard. Supposedly, Joe Guffey had met with the Pennsylvania delegation and had spoken of a visit with Roosevelt and Jim Farley. Guffey then told the delegation, "We want Rainey Speaker."[39]

Until March 1, 1933, McDuffie's forces continued to lobby Tammany leader Curry and Brooklyn boss McCooey (who had both moved into the Shoreham Hotel in Washington) for their candidate, but it was too late. The caucus was on March 2, 1933. Rainey was nominated by Byrns with seconding speeches by Robert Crosser of Ohio and by Tom Cullen, a Tammany leader. Bankhead nominated McDuffie with seconding speeches by William Connery of Massachusetts and Hart of Michigan. The caucus vote was 166 for Rainey, 112 for McDuffie, 20 for John Rankin of Mississippi, 2 for Marvin Jones of Texas, and 1 for Bankhead. Evidently, the Rainey-Byrns deal even drew some Texas votes away from McDuffie. Byrns was chairman of the Appropriations Committee. If Byrns moved to floor leader, Texan James Buchanan would gain the committee chairmanship, an enticing deal for some of the Texas delegation.[40] Rainey was Speaker.

McDuffie claimed he had "no sore spots" as a result of his unsuccessful campaign for the Speakership, but he also noted that he felt betrayed by Tammany. No other southerner "had spent more time than I had in defending Tammany," and their lack of support "was something of a surprise to me."[41]

Until Tammany's abandonment, McDuffie had been so confident of victory that he had ordered a new tailored overcoat. McDuffie believed that he had won "until twelve hours before the caucus when Tammany turned the trick."[42] The advance announcement of the Rainey-Byrns deal led McDuffie to consult with Garner, but generally the McDuffie forces believed that a negative reaction to the deal would assure McDuffie's victory.

That reaction never happened, and the Rainey-Byrns deal in the caucus was well choreographed. Oddly, it may have been John Garner's blunt honesty that doomed McDuffie. According to Arthur Krock, Tammany chieftain John Curry approached Garner and guaranteed McDuffie 29 votes if Garner could assure a McDuffie victory. When Garner responded that he could not give such a guarantee, Tammany began to negotiate with the Rainey forces. Ultimately, Krock stated, Representative Ed Crump of Tennessee, the manager of Joe Byrns's effort to get the majority leadership, got Tammany to vote for Rainey and to give the majority leadership to Byrns. Crump was crucial in engineering the deal that created the Rainey-Byrns ticket. He convinced the Byrns forces that McDuffie would win if Byrns stayed in the race for Speaker. He then put together a series of conferences between Sam McReynolds of Tennessee, Byrns's campaign manager, and Adolph Sabath of the Rainey campaign. Crump brought about the agreement for Byrns's support for Rainey in exchange for Rainey's support of Byrns. Apparently, it was not an easy sell — there were doubts among Rainey's backers that Byrns could deliver. However, Crump persisted and the deal was struck.[43]

Even McDuffie recognized that his defeat signaled a broader lesson. He wrote, "Byrns never had the slightest chance and so stated more than a month ago, however he got even with Garner and myself." There was enough hostility to Garner in the caucus that even several House officers brought in by Garner two years previously were challenged. There were plans to replace the sergeant-at-arms, the doorkeeper, and the House postmaster, though these plans eventually crumbled. Yet the clerk was renominated only after a hard fight, and even the House chaplain faced a renomination battle.[44]

Had the Tammany votes gone for McDuffie, he would have earned a narrow victory. Krock added that Garner's hesitation was "a fact which he deplores to this day." It may be that Tammany was also using the Speakership race to strike back at John Garner for throwing his support to FDR at the Democratic convention, thus ending Al Smith's chances for the nomination.[45]

While Krock's interpretation of the outcome of the race is intriguing, there was probably a more fundamental political reason for McDuffie's loss. Of the 435 members, 150 were freshmen washed into office on the Roosevelt tide. Because the freshmen were from the North, they supported the first northern Democrat as Speaker in more than fifty years.[46]

With the loss of the Speakership — "In desperation," Sabath claimed — the Garner forces put up William Bankhead for majority leader against Joe Byrns, but Bankhead's support seems to have been limited regionally. Representative Clifton Woodrum of Virginia nominated Bankhead, and Edward Pou of North Carolina seconded the nomination, hardly the geographical balance usually demonstrated in such choices.[47] Byrns was elected.[48] Byrns's victory, however, was close. There were 301 Democrats in the caucus and Byrns was elected by a majority of only one vote. He received 151 votes to Bankhead's 140.[49]

It was a major defeat for the Garner forces, argued Sabath, because not only did they keep Garner allies out of the Speakership and the majority leadership, but they were also able to fill four vacancies on the Ways and Means Committee with Rainey's allies. Sabath argued that it was far better for the president to have Rainey in the Speaker's chair than McDuffie as Speaker and Garner as president of the Senate. Nor was it just Sabath who saw the vote as a repudiation of the Garner forces. *The New York Times* reported that Garner's supporters had been "unhorsed by a group of liberals."[50]

Just how much the caucus was an attack on Garner was clear in an announcement that Rainey made about the creation of a Democratic steering committee: "It is a long step forward, and it takes from the Speaker powers he has arbitrarily exercised and gives it back to the House. Failures in the last Congress have been due to the fact that the determination of policies has come entirely from the Speaker's chair; it will now come from the party. We will put over Mr. Roosevelt's program." Salvaging what they could, the Garner forces tried to strategically place allies on key committees. That is how Howard W. Smith of Virginia was able to obtain a seat on the Rules Committee after only two years in the House.[51] Years later, of course, Rayburn was to regret helping to get Smith appointed.

But one person the Garner forces could not salvage was McDuffie. As McDuffie admitted, "The outcome of the Speakership race in 1933 had left me without official status in party councils among the House leadership."[52]

The Garner Forces Continue to Fail Sam Rayburn of Texas

When Rainey died on August 19, 1934, Roosevelt made plans to attend Rainey's funeral back in Illinois and wired John Garner in Uvalde expressing hope that Garner would be able to attend as well. The funeral was at 4:00 P.M. on August 22. On August 21, Garner wired Roosevelt that he had gotten Roosevelt's telegram "yesterday too late for me to reach Carrollton [Illinois] in time for the funeral. I am very glad that you found the situation so you could attend. Owing to our thirty years service together, I had a very warm spot in my heart for him." It seems likely that Garner's efforts to arrange to attend the funeral were minimal and the "warm spot" hardly one of affection. Rainey's death presented another chance for Garner's southern conservatives to take the leadership, but it was also seen as opening an opportunity by John O'Connor. O'Connor wrote Tom O'Brien, a leader of the Chicago delegation, that he would attend Rainey's funeral and might stop to meet with Patrick Nash, the Democratic boss of Chicago. He asked Brooklyn congressmen Loring M. Black Jr. and George W. Lindsay to talk with "your friend Kelly" — Frank Kelly, Brooklyn political boss — "and especially your friend, Mr. Guffey" — Joe Guffey, Pennsylvania's political boss — "in reference to my possibilities in the reorganization of the House." O'Connor's friend Jim (James J.) Dooling, Tammany leader and successor to John Curry, lobbied Kelly on several occasions. Seeking to line up Louisiana, O'Connor wrote Huey P. Long: "Knowing your interest in me in the past I would appreciate it if you would talk to your delegation about me. I know some of them have a friendly feeling toward me, but of course they naturally hold back waiting your counsel." However, O'Connor's major obstacle was that he could not hold his own delegation. James Mead of Buffalo wanted a leadership post and had the support of the two Buffalo members, and the eight Brooklyn members were backing Brooklyn's Tom Cullen. O'Connor believed, "If I could get those eight members to stop their idle jesters and come out for me, I'm quite sure the matter would be settled."[53]

William Bankhead met with O'Connor in early December 1, 1934, to confer "about . . . matters in which you and I are interested." No doubt they discussed the Speakership and leadership. Perhaps they mentioned the subject of endorsements if one of their ambitions faltered. Bankhead chaired Rules at that time, and O'Connor was ranking member, so they would have known one another well.[54]

By December 1934, O'Connor had determined that Joe Byrns of Tennessee would be Speaker. On the day after Christmas, he wrote, "Of course the Speakership has been definitely settled. Joe Byrns is practically the unanimous choice. I am a candidate for Floor Leader and I have a real chance to win." He saw Bankhead as his major opponent but thought he could get enough votes from the North to win. Adolph Sabath of Illinois was also a candidate, but O'Connor did not believe he was a serious contender. To O'Connor, his real threat was the potential candidacy of John McCormack of Massachusetts. A "capable and likeable fellow," McCormack might siphon enough northern votes to prevent either O'Connor or McCormack from winning, leaving the floor leadership to Bankhead. O'Connor backer James Dulligan believed that to prevent a Bankhead win,

O'Connor would need the entire New England delegation, where McCormack had strong support. As Dulligan put it, "Let the best man win but make damn sure that it is a McCormack or an O'Connor."[55]

O'Connor continued his efforts to win the majority leadership. He had not counted on much support from the South, but he thought he had some serious support there, especially in Virginia. And Gene Cox of Georgia had told him that he would either support O'Connor or McCormack. O'Connor had tried to get the support of McDuffie, but McDuffie was loyal to Bankhead. He wrote O'Connor that he supported Bankhead even though he considered O'Connor to be a friend. Making sure that O'Connor knew he could not sway him, McDuffie added that he had not considered a second choice.[56] O'Connor would be unable even to claim McDuffie's support as a back-up candidate.

Though support did not seem forthcoming from McDuffie, O'Connor hired a public relations man, Sam Jones, to work in his behalf.[57] He also sought newspaper articles favorable to his candidacy.[58] Ultimately, however, Bankhead cinched the majority leader position when Joe Guffey of Pennsylvania abandoned O'Connor for Bankhead.[59] O'Connor's disappointment was tempered by the fact that he would replace Bankhead as chair of the Rules Committee, giving him an important role in the leadership.[60]

Bankhead's success effectively shut fellow Alabaman McDuffie out of the possibility of moving up in the leadership. McDuffie felt that he could not oppose Bankhead, who had stepped aside for him in the earlier Speakership election. Privately, McDuffie preferred Rayburn, his most effective supporter in his campaigns for the leadership. He thought Rayburn had qualities of effective leadership such as political courage and an ability to say no. Ideally, an alliance between Rayburn and Bankhead would stop Byrns who McDuffie felt was "wholly unfit" for leadership and "essentially a political coward."[61]

At the time of McDuffie's withdrawal, *The New York Times* reported that in "a private discussion," President Roosevelt indicated that he would not interfere in the selection of a Speaker but that he wanted the House to help him extend the Democrats' hold on the western states that went Democratic in 1932. That meant, the *Times* argued, that the majority leader would have to come from the North. The seniority rule put southerners in charge of the major committee assignments, so the North could only hope for an elected position. With Byrns moving up to Speaker, the

Times speculated that the northerners most likely to become majority leader would be James Mead of New York or John McCormack of Massachusetts. Mead, the article added, had greater seniority and the backing of the powerful New York Democratic delegation.[62]

Initially, McDuffie seems to have laid some groundwork for another bid for the Speakership. He had a long-standing friendship with African American politician Arthur Wergs Mitchell, whom he had met in Alabama in 1914. McDuffie may have found employment for Mitchell and his wife in the federal government in 1919. In 1932, he got Mitchell a job with the Democratic National Committee to follow Oscar DePriest, the African American Republican congressman, and refute DePriest's pro-Republican speeches. And in 1934, he urged Mitchell to run against DePriest. DePriest attacked Mitchell for his secret southern backing — his friendship with McDuffie — but Mitchell won. McDuffie helped Mitchell settle in Washington and adjust to congressional life. Mitchell was grateful to McDuffie to the point of describing both McDuffie and FDR as "his idols."[63] It was, to say the least, unusual for an Alabama Democratic congressman to have such a relationship with a black congressman representing Chicago. But the relationship would have been very useful to McDuffie had he run for the Speakership again, showing he had national vision and was not bound by southern tradition.

Upon reflection, though, McDuffie concluded his work in Congress was finished. Ideologically, he wrote. "I had gone as far as possible with the New Deal." He went to his mentor, John Garner, and to Jim Farley and expressed interest in the federal bench; shortly thereafter he received a federal district judgeship in Mobile. Roosevelt's good-bye to McDuffie was an unwarm two-sentence note, "I am happy to sign this [document appointing McDuffie a federal judge]," Roosevelt wrote, "— but I do and will miss you in Washington. Best of luck to you and my very warm regards." Nor was McDuffie's return to Alabama pleasant. The day after he took the oath as federal judge, his beloved wife Cornelia died. Judge McDuffie became increasingly alienated from the New Deal, writing John Rankin of Mississippi in 1944 that New Deal "destruction of Democratic ideals is a tragedy. Our gradual, sure and onward march to National Socialism is more than I ever thought I would live to see."[64]

The congenial Joe Byrns had aided many congressmen as chair of Appropriations and in 1934 as chair of the Democratic Congressional Campaign Committee. A "tall, lanky, friendly" man with a "Southern, drawly voice," he was a strong candidate for Speaker. Though by national standards Byrns was conservative, he considered himself progressive. One reporter portrayed him in this way:

> If persons were given descriptive names after they were grown, Mr. Byrns would have been named Long. His legs are long. His body is long. His arms are long. His fingers are long. His neck is long. His nose is long. Underneath the nose is a comparatively short but tough chin which closes his mouth with something approaching the closing of a powerfully springed steel trap when occasion demands.
>
> When he draws his long, white, bushy eyebrows down over his gleaming brown eyes you don't quite know what to expect. He looks something like a fierce old, bald-headed eagle whose pre-eminence has been challenged. Some one said he was ugly enough to be compared to Lincoln.

In the previous session, Byrns had launched a fight for a party steering committee that was comprised of committee chairs. That, of course, would give him a greater voice in policy and yet would maintain the South's control of the party in the House. However, he modified that stance to support a more general steering committee and to have committee appointments removed from the Ways and Means Committee.[65]

Believing in governmental economy, he thought that veterans were getting too much money from the Treasury. Some opposed him because they perceived him as too closely supportive of business interests who wanted a free hand in development of water power and use of natural resources. Most interestingly, the author of the profile on Byrns wrote, "His legislative career has been devoid of history making incidents of the spectacular kind." He had an informal style, never forgetting a name or a face, and maintained a strong personal interest in the people in his district. He maintained a simple lifestyle; the social life of Washington did not appeal to him.[66]

Byrns came to the House in 1909 after service in the Tennessee legislature. Over the years, however, he had moved to a position of real power in the House — the Appropriations Committee. He enjoyed a good fight, but unlike John Garner, he had "no venoms in his veins." During an interview, he told a reporter, "Well, now, it seems to me that there's not a bit of sense in staying mad. A lot of the boys here on the Hill can't go along with me on everything. And when they can't, I don't write it down in the little book. No, sir, I just tell 'em I'm awful sorry that they can't go along, but maybe we can get together the next time. Seems sorta sensible to me."[67] As Speaker, Garner had been tough and iron-willed in his effort to maintain the party line, while in contrast, Byrns was much more gentle and easygoing. Of course, Byrns had a 3–1 Democratic majority in the House in contrast to Garner's razor-thin majority. But these were vastly contrasting personalities.

Personality differences were but the beginning of the contrast between Byrns and Garner. Vice President Garner was not fond of Byrns. Quietly waiting to see if Garner's strength would hold when the Democrats gained control of the House in 1931, Byrns had kept himself available until the late stages of Garner's efforts to become Speaker. Then, in the days before Garner was officially elected Speaker, Byrns had been the spokesman in the Byrns-Crisp-Ayres proposal for a steering committee that would take power away from the Speaker. Moreover, it was Byrns who had made the deal that made Rainey Speaker and Byrns majority leader, defeating Garner's candidate, McDuffie. Byrns also had differed from Garner on major policy issues, including Garner's position on unemployment. Even worse, he had opposed Garner on a national sales tax in such a way as to embarrass Garner. In the debate over the sales tax, from the rear of the House Chamber, Byrns arose, demanded recognition, and with chin jutting out strode down the aisle to chastise Democrats for abandoning "the traditions and principles" of the party. "Inferentially, he hurled scorn at Rainey . . . and at Garner, who had said he was willing to 'abandon every one of my economic principles' in order to balance a budget." Garner's defeat on the sales tax was thought to destroy his chances for the presidency and caused talk of a revolt against Garner as Speaker — one that would install Byrns in his place. While Byrns apparently discouraged such plans, Garner did not forget them.[68]

Byrns's "soft-spoken, mild-mannered, and congenial" presence made him well-liked in the House, but he had been somewhat inept as a leader for the administration, in part because he tried to please people — a flaw that tough-minded Garner would have detested. He had been tripped up by Republican parliamentary tricks from time to time, making it necessary to adjourn the House in order to sort things out.[69] Garner was not about to let someone like Byrns become Speaker without a fight.

Still, Byrns had certain advantages. He was senior in the House, having served thirteen consecutive terms. There was the tradition of the House leader being promoted to the Speakership. And he did have great personal popularity. In addition, as chair of the Democratic Congressional

Campaign Committee, he could help congressional candidates and perhaps put them under obligation to him.[70]

Initially, Garner's candidate to oppose Byrns was Rayburn, though his support was later withdrawn, either when Byrns threatened to oppose Garner's renomination for the vice presidency in 1936 or simply because Rayburn's strength was uncertain. Prior to Garner's reversal, Texan Marvin Jones, Agriculture Committee chair, withdrew from the Speaker's race in Rayburn's favor. If Rayburn failed in his effort, Rayburn was to support Jones in the next Speakership race. However, Jones's Speakership ambitions seemed half-hearted. As early as 1935, he had talked to the attorney general about a federal judgeship, a position he took in 1940 with the U.S. Court of Claims. More than three weeks after Rainey's funeral, Jones issued a press release that demonstrated indecisiveness. Not wanting to make a definite statement on the Speakership at that time, he wrote, "Naturally I should like to be Speaker. Who wouldn't? Whoever is elected, I hope he will show a sympathetic attitude toward this vital problem [agriculture]."[71]

Though Rayburn was away from Washington in early October of 1934, his friend Cecil B. Dickson, a news reporter, was keeping an eye on things for him, including the plans of Jones. Dickson noted that while Jones had interest in the Speakership, he doubted he could get sufficient support. He was particularly concerned over a conversation he had had with Byrns, who had told him that "he had more pledges than Rainey had before the deal was made in 1932." Dickson described Byrns as being "very jittery on one hand and apparently very confident on the other." Byrns and one of his supporters were writing letters asking for support and were talking with all the congressmen who were in Washington during the congressional recess. Dickson reported that the big problem for Byrns would come if the administration backed Rayburn: "Byrns is scared of the White House angle as far as it affects you. A lot of the people around here say that it is in the bag for Byrns. . . . I understand he put Farley on the spot about the White House attitude and that Farley assured him that the White House was not going to interfere. I asked Farley the other day about the speakership and he said that he was not going to get into that because he was having enough trouble on his own." Dickson wanted Garner to return to Washington and get behind Rayburn. He reported that Congressman "Tuck" Milligan had been talking to administration officials, urging Rayburn for the Speakership. Dickson thought it likely that Byrns was "running scared" and was working hard to sew up victory. Without Garner's assistance and White House timely support, Rayburn would lose to Byrns.[72]

Dickson was right that Byrns feared White House involvement. Secretary of Commerce Daniel Roper wrote Marvin McIntyre, the president's secretary, "Rep. Joe Byrns is very anxious that the President and those close to him shall express no preference with regard to the Speakership." Louis Howe, Roosevelt's top political advisor, wrote Jim Farley that Byrns had discovered a confidential newspaper sheet prepared by the McClure newspaper syndicate that said that Howe was leading the fight against Byrns. Howe was alarmed enough to want to know how these reports had been leaked.[73] Even Adolph Sabath of Illinois wrote Roosevelt claiming that he had heard stories that Garner and some cabinet members were trying to get the president to support Sam Rayburn, but, argued Sabath, that was a mistake. Sabath saw Rayburn as a southern conservative who "is not the man to carry out your progressive policies. I know that all the vested interests who have been antagonistic to you in the past, and will be more so in the future, are building him up so as to hold the House in rein." Adding that Texas already had the vice presidency and five chairmanships, Sabath thought it would be wrong to add a Texan as Speaker. In reply, Roosevelt wrote Sabath that he would not take sides in the race and had warned every member of the cabinet to stay out of the race. In response to Josh Lee, Democratic nominee from Oklahoma — who sought guidance from Louis Howe about how he should vote in the Speakership race as "a red-hot New Dealer" — Howe wrote that the "president can express no opinion nor make any suggestion." FDR advisor Raymond Moley, however, actively supported Rayburn for the Speakership. He saw Rayburn as young, vigorous, and supportive of FDR in contrast to Byrns, who at sixty-five was a somewhat feeble leader and not a strong New Dealer.[74]

Byrns was not the only one who feared administration support for Sam Rayburn. William Bankhead also worried about the role of the administration. He wrote Jim Farley that he appreciated the administration's neutrality in the race but that they owed him support:

I feel that in view of my service to the party in the House for a number of years, and especially in view of the fact that as Chairman of the Committee on Rules, I was very largely responsible for the promotion of the Administration's program in the last Congress, that I am entitled to every fair consideration at the hands of the Administration and know that I shall receive it. There have been some whisperings not only in the press but by grapevine channels that Sam Rayburn would receive the favor of the Administration in this contest. I have no warmer friend in Congress than Sam Rayburn and he and I thoroughly understand each other in our aspirations to be Speaker of the House, but am sure that he would not receive any marks of favoritism over me from the Administration and from you in this contest and I would be glad to have your assurance along that line.

Bankhead had deferred to McDuffie's ambitions in the previous Speaker's race, perhaps because McDuffie had received so many state endorsements and perhaps because of some political threats.[75] However, Bankhead had also believed that Rainey was unbeatable and that a southerner could not win in 1933. Five days before receiving a letter from McDuffie seeking his support for the McDuffie campaign, Bankhead wrote to Eugene Cox of Georgia, "It begins to appear to me confidentially that with the great number of new members from the north, east and west it will be impossible for any one to defeat Mr. Rainey for Speaker." On December 2, 1932, Bankhead even went to McDuffie's office to tell him he was surprised at how strong McDuffie was in the race for Speaker.[76]

Now, however, it was Bankhead's turn. Bankhead planned to announce for Speaker right after Rainey's funeral, and, even at that point, he was certain that McDuffie would support him. Still, he worried about other candidates from the South, especially Sam Rayburn and John Rankin of Mississippi. Of the two, Rayburn was clearly the biggest threat. Prior to announcing his candidacy, Bankhead received a telegram from Missouri congressman "Tuck" Milligan that stated, "Sam Rayburn should be next Speaker. Get on the Job." Though Bankhead believed Rayburn and Rankin would hurt his candidacy, he realized that "Joe Byrns has the inside track at this time." Byrns had been majority leader under Rainey and was chair of the Democratic Congressional Campaign Committee. In spite of Byrns's advantages, there were rumors that Roosevelt had been unhappy with the leadership of Rainey-Byrns, and there were stories that Byrns had been offered jobs to get him out of the way. One rumor was that he had been offered the budget director's job — potentially an attractive position for a former Appropriations Committee chair; another story claimed that Byrns would be offered a judgeship. Such rumors forced Byrns to issue a denial: "There isn't any federal appointment that I would take and I am sure that it will not be offered."[77]

McDuffie did defer to Bankhead, a *quid pro quo* for Bankhead's earlier support of him. C&O Railroad lobbyist Walter Chamblin also warned McDuffie that he really had no chance for the Speakership in 1934 and that Chamblin would support Bankhead. Also, Chamblin noted that McDuffie had not maintained close relationships with New Dealers such as Farley, Emil Hurja, and Dr. Ross McIntyre: "to be very blunt, they are not talking about you." Chamblin added that McDuffie could not be a compromise candidate, because no one was talking about compromise — if Byrns did not get out of the picture, there would be a fight. That fight would be between Byrns and Rayburn, who would, Chamblin thought, ally himself with John McCormack as candidate for majority leader.[78] And Garner — McDuffie's mentor — was backing Rayburn.[79]

Chamblin went on and assessed Bankhead's chances. He thought Bankhead was unpopular with the administration, in part because his brother, Sen. John Bankhead, had pushed cotton legislation against the desires of the administration. And Will Bankhead, Chamblin noted, had even fewer New Deal credentials than did McDuffie; also, Bankhead lacked support from John Garner and in the press. Chamblin also suggested that Bankhead's poor health would keep him from performing effectively. Finally, Bankhead was valuable as chair of the Rules Committee. If he became Speaker or majority leader, John O'Connor would chair the committee, to the dismay of the Administration.[80]

Rayburn, in Chamblin's mind, had the best chance against Byrns with the support of Garner and many New Dealers. The press "is almost one hundred percent for him." Rayburn had seniority and he was "on the ground making a strong, sensibly conducted campaign."[81]

To all this, McDuffie replied that he had no "ambitions or hopes that I might become a dark horse candidate." He stressed that he was not an administration man and had "never entertained the slightest inclination to believe that those in control of the New Deal thought enough of me to become interested in me. As a matter of fact, I have gotten nothing out of the New Deal except the pleasure of trying to serve it." McDuffie heartily disliked Byrns: "Byrns will be hard to handle if he remains in the picture" and "he is to be feared by all other candidates for Speaker."[82]

Meanwhile, Chamblin was in Washington acting on his belief that Rayburn was a viable candidate. Chamblin felt that the Virginia delegation would be uncommitted on the Speakership until Harry F. Byrd made a decision about who the delegation should support. But then Chamblin reported the bad news that Byrns had the "inside track."

> My agents tell me that he is promising everything possible in the way of campaign assistance and that he also is promising what probably isn't even possible in regard to taking care of members with favored spots in the House. From what I hear, the Administration seems to feel that they have no need to worry about Byrns in the Speaker's chair, providing they get a satisfactory floor leader. I know that you and myself both feel that this is a mistake, as a strong Speaker could be much more effective than the combination of a weak Speaker and a good leader. However, from what comes from the White House, via the grapevine, they do not seem to think that way. I do not know how you would feel about accepting the leadership, and I just want to mention something that you already have thought over many times — namely, that Mr. Byrns' health is not too good and that the worries of the Speakership may overtax his heart. There is every reason in the world to believe, from the way things look now, that the Democrats will continue to control the House for quite a few sessions to come and it would not surprise me in the least bit if the House would find itself called upon to choose another Democratic Speaker.

Both Cecil Dickson's and Chamblin's letters were sent to Garner in Uvalde, but the responses from Garner offered Rayburn little encouragement. Garner's wife and secretary, Ettie, responded to Dickson's letter with, "Don't become discouraged. Fight to the last ditch." But she also wrote that the president had approved Garner's delaying his return to Washington until Congress convened. Rayburn must have known that this would hurt his chances. Three days later, Ettie wrote that Garner had read Chamblin's letter "with interest." Rayburn must have concluded that his prospects for the Speakership were seen as dim even in faraway Uvalde. When Garner returned to Washington, he met with Roosevelt and then publicly announced that the president would take no part in the race.[83]

Within days of Garner's announcement of administration neutrality in the race, Pennsylvania, led by Senator Guffey, announced in favor of Byrns. Rayburn lost hope for the leadership. Though there was talk that Sam Rayburn would join in a coalition with John W. McCormack, with Rayburn running for Speaker and McCormack for majority leader, he withdrew from the race, saying, "Under the circumstances I cannot be elected." Rayburn could not even hold the support of the Texas delegation. Thomas L. Blanton of Abilene declared for Byrns, claiming that Texas already had enough positions of power, and James Buchanan of Austin, chairman of the Appropriations Committee, also supported Byrns. However, Byrns did make overtures to Rayburn, offering him the majority leadership. Robert T. Bartley, Rayburn's nephew and a member of his staff, thought that Byrns offered him the leadership as a deal in order to get Rayburn out of the Speakership race. Rayburn, however, would not deal with Byrns. It has been suggested that Rayburn preferred his committee chairmanship and the forthcoming battle over the Public Utility Holding Company Act to the number-two leadership position. However, there were also personal tensions between the two men that made Rayburn reluctant to serve as Byrns's floor leader. There had also been hostility between Byrns and Garner. Additionally, until 1936, Rayburn's attitude toward party leadership was, as he told his friend Cecil Dickson, "The Speakership or nothing. By Gosh, the Speakership or nothing."[84]

When Byrns offered the majority leadership to both Rayburn and Bankhead, suggesting that the first of them to endorse him would get the job, Rayburn told Bankhead of his lack of interest and returned to Texas. Bankhead, on the other hand, met with Byrns. After that meeting, Bankhead wrote Ed Crump, Memphis political boss and Byrns supporter: "I feel sure that he [Byrns] would have no objection to my being elected Majority Leader. As a matter of fact I feel assured that we could cooperate in every way in carrying forward the Party interest." Bankhead asked Crump to talk to the newly elected congressman from Memphis about supporting him for majority leader, support which soon came. Clearly, Bankhead was willing to work with Byrns. He wrote to John Miller, "I am sure that Byrns would be entirely satisfied with my selection. He is taking no part for any other candidate." In August there was a report of an arrangement where "a Tennesseean [sic] becomes Speaker" — certainly Byrns — and "an Alabaman" would be floor leader. The problem with this arrangement, it was claimed, was that it gave too much power to the South. Then in October, an article reported that Tammany was attracted to the deal, because with Bankhead as majority leader, John O'Connor became chairman of Rules. While such a deal ultimately occurred, it seems more likely that it did not happen until mid-December, 1934. Indeed, Bankhead wrote about meeting Byrns on the morning of December 13, 1934, where he assured Byrns of a desire to cooperate and where, Bankhead wrote, Byrns "expressed kindly sentiments toward me." The previous day Bankhead had assessed his chances against Byrns and had spoken with Sam Rayburn. He concluded that in the caucus, he would only receive twenty-five to thirty votes for Speaker. He believed that the only hope of defeating Byrns was by an alliance of Bankhead, Rayburn, and Rankin on the first ballot, something that could not happen. He never believed he had a chance to get the support of the Pennsylvania delegation, but he thought Rayburn did. In fact, Byrns had Pennsylvania and considerable support in New York, Oklahoma, South Carolina, North Carolina, and Florida. Bankhead was certain he had no chance and thought Sam Rayburn would withdraw as well.[85]

Remarkably, Bankhead and Rayburn remained friendly competitors even while they campaigned seriously for the post. The two met in St. Louis, likely while making train connections between Washington, D.C., and their homes, and exchanged ideas on the Speaker's race. Bankhead told Rayburn that of the 130–140 replies to a request for support that he had mailed, 90–95 percent were noncommittal. He asked Rayburn for his assessment of Byrns's strength and the possible candidacies of Mead and McCormack. He even promised not to infringe on Rayburn's support by seeking support within the Texas delegation. Bankhead wrote, "Although we are trying to beat each other out, nevertheless, I feel that a candid and frank interchange of information upon this subject might be helpful to both of us regardless of what the ultimate outcome may be." Rayburn responded with an optimistic account of the chances to beat Byrns. He wrote, "When I reached here the Burns [sic] crowd was very 'cocky.' Claiming all was over, that pledges were rolling in so fast. I understand they do not feel so well now. Constant pounding by some of the press that Burns is not satisfactory to administration is having its effect." Rayburn had received about 50 replies to his solicitations of support in Washington and an unknown number back in Bonham. Like Bankhead, Rayburn had a high percentage of noncommittal replies. Rayburn's assessment was that Byrns had "tried to flush them at the start." Byrns had several pledges, but with many members waiting until after the election, there were still opportunities for the Rayburn and Bankhead forces.[86]

Then Rayburn wrote Bankhead that Lindsay Warren of North Carolina was considering running, that Mead had sent up a trial balloon, and that he had not heard from McCormack. The real campaign would come after the election, at which time, "I'll be here for keeps." Rayburn, however, insisted, "I think Burns [sic] can be stopped."[87]

In early November, Rayburn wrote Bankhead, confirming their friendship: "We are in opposition at present but I want you to know that my affection is now as always and shall remain. It matters not what may happen." Bankhead responded in kind that Rayburn's note "touched me very deeply and that I appreciate in the fullest measure the sentiments expressed in it."[88] Their ability to maintain a friendship served them well for the future.

Still, they were vigorous competitors. Bankhead tried to counter Rayburn's influence with the administration by writing Jim Farley to point out his own loyalty to the administration. He wrote McDuffie that while Rayburn hoped for administration support, the president and Jim Farley could not overlook Bankhead's own work. And from Interstate and Foreign Commerce Committee member George Huddleston of Alabama, he learned that several members thought Rayburn "too conservative" and might support Bankhead. Very few committee members felt an obligation to Rayburn, who, Huddleston claimed, had granted few favors and ran the committee without consulting associates. John McDuffie thought that Francis Maloney of Connecticut, a member of Rayburn's committee, might support Bankhead. McDuffie also thought that an alliance with New Englander McCormack, a sort of "Alabama-Boston alliance," might help Bankhead. He advised Bankhead that Rankin was not a serious threat — that he would get less than 20 votes — and that John O'Connor might help since he would chair Rules and since presumably he realized that "no Tammany man can be Speaker." Moreover, McDuffie shrewdly realized that Bankhead needed not only Tammany but Pennsylvania's Joe Guffey and Jim Farley representing the administration. He tried to talk in behalf of Bankhead to Farley, who insisted he was "hands-off" in the race.[89]

As things unfolded, Cecil Dickson spoke with Bankhead. Like Walter Chamblin, Dickson was aware of Byrns's fragile health, caused in part by a battle with influenza in 1930 that had damaged his heart. Byrns had started to run for the Democratic nomination for the U.S. Senate in 1930 when heart trouble forced him to quit the race, and he had suffered two heart attacks about that time. Dr. George Calver, the physician for the House, had told Dickson that Byrns would not live two years. Dickson, in turn, told Bankhead that if he served as Byrns's majority leader, he would be in line for the Speakership, and the wait would not be long.[90]

Bankhead's decision to team with Byrns and wait for his opportunity for the Speakership proved a good one. When Byrns was selected as Speaker and Bankhead as majority leader, the blocks were set in place for an eventual Bankhead Speakership. The job as Speaker apparently took its toll on Byrns's health. An article written prior to Byrns's selection as Speaker mentioned that Byrns "had been warned both by his personal physician and the House physician against undue exertion." Byrns's son claimed that Byrns had decided he would retire after one more term in Congress and that he had planned to announce his plans after he was renominated for his seat in August. If he had served one more term, Byrns would have served thirty years in Congress.[91] His death came suddenly. He presided over the House on June 3, 1936, took ill that evening, and died at 12:15 A.M. on June 4. Bankhead's decision to become majority leader seemed well-timed, but like Byrns, Bankhead had serious heart problems.

The Re-Emergence of Texas in the Leadership
Becoming Majority Leader

Rayburn's success in obtaining the Speakership was not merely winning election to that post in 1940, rather it was placing himself in position for that office by winning the job of majority leader in 1937. Six of the previous seven Speakers, beginning with Champ Clark, had served as floor leader first. Becoming majority leader was one of Rayburn's greatest political achievements. To win the job, he had to overcome the strong North-South division in the Democratic Party that had led to efforts to provide regional balance within congressional leadership positions. Garner, a Texan, was vice president, and Bankhead, an Alabamian, was Speaker. Rayburn's selection as majority leader would give the leadership in Congress an even stronger southern tinge. Additionally, Texans chaired the Appropriations, Judiciary, Agriculture, Interstate and Foreign Commerce, Rivers and Harbors, and Public Buildings and Grounds Committees.

Bankhead was a "quiet and efficient" leader. As chair of the Rules Committee, he was very proficient in the procedures of the House. In spite of the lack of regional balance in a Tennessee-Alabama leadership, he seemed a good person for the leadership. However, the day before he became majority leader, Bankhead suffered a heart attack from which he never fully recovered. In November 1935, Rayburn urged him to continue in the leadership and thus prevent a fight in the party prior to the 1936 election; he feared that any leadership struggle would be bitter. Bankhead reported that his health was better and that he would stay as leader, but he would "take things easy." Then, in June 1936, Byrns died, and Bankhead moved to the Speaker's chair. John O'Connor of New York, chairman of the Rules Committee, became the acting majority leader for the remainder of the session.[92] O'Connor began campaigning for the majority leader's job on the way to Byrns's funeral; Rayburn, who was fishing in the Ozarks and could not immediately be reached at the time of Byrns's death, did not board the funeral train. On the train back to Washington, he vacillated about whether he would run. Cecil Dickson wrote a story the day after Byrns's death that Bankhead would be Speaker and Rayburn the majority leader. Rayburn called Dickson and cursed him saying that he would repudiate the story: "I told you for years that it is the Speakership or nothing. I don't want the Leadership."[93] Rayburn, however, changed his mind, both about Dickson's article and about the majority leadership.

At the close of the session, there was some doubt as to whether Bankhead would return to the Speaker's chair in 1937, owing to the poor state of his health. Even if Bankhead did not step down immediately, however, his health indicated a brief tenure. In 1935, for example, Bankhead's health kept him from performing as majority leader during a session of Congress, and, though he claimed in a letter to his colleagues that "his progress toward full recovery is most favorable," his doctors told him that he needed to return to Alabama for further recuperation. Bankhead never came close to the "full recovery" that he mentioned in his letter. After he was sworn in as Speaker on June 4, 1936, he left the floor immediately after the session and had to lie on a couch to recuperate from the brief session's excitement.[94] O'Connor was healthy and only fifty-one years old. If Rayburn did not successfully become majority leader, he likely would never be Speaker.

Bankhead wrote Jim Farley that he expected "a rather bitter fight over Majority Leadership." Bankhead believed that in light of the likely battle, it was best for him to remain neutral, but he feared that the result might damage the harmony of the House. "We are," noted Bankhead, "going to have a most important session of Congress and it will require considerable diplomacy to keep things running in smooth order."[95]

O'Connor had the advantage of having had the position on an interim basis. He was also chairman of the Rules Committee, the position Bankhead had held when he became majority leader. O'Connor had long-standing ambitions for chamber leadership, having run for majority leader twice previously, in 1931 and in 1935. Although O'Connor was a Tammany man from New York at a time when leadership in the House was heavily southern, and his New Deal credentials were questionable at a time when Roosevelt's powers were at their peak, he was viewed by the business community as a "brake" on New Deal liberalism, and the utility companies were especially grateful to O'Connor for his covert support in the Holding Company Act battle.[96]

Rayburn, now having decided to challenge for the leadership, went to Marvin Jones and asked to be released from his promise to support Jones for the Speakership. Jones relented, although he was hurt by Rayburn's request. In addition to O'Connor and Rayburn, John E. Rankin of Mississippi became an active candidate. However, Rankin's difficult personality, hostility to some programs of the New Deal, and lack of support from his own state made him a weak candidate.[97] *Houston Post* correspondent George W. Stimpson noted that Rankin could probably only count on a scattering of votes and that most of those votes would eventually go to Rayburn.

James M. Mead of Buffalo also joined the race. Primarily seen as a compromise candidate should Rayburn and O'Connor deadlock, Mead also cut into O'Connor's support in his home state. Democrats in the Pennsylvania delegation had endorsed Patrick J. Boland of Pennsylvania, the Democratic whip, for the leadership. Boland, however, was hindered by only five years of service, and press reports indicated that he would probably throw his support to Rayburn. In case of deadlock, other Democratic congressmen who commanded a following were John McCormack of Massachusetts; Fred Vinson of Kentucky, who was managing Rayburn's race for the leadership; Clifton A. Woodrum of Virginia; Robert Crosser of Ohio; and Adolph J. Sabath of Illinois. Press reports suggest that Rayburn was a strong candidate because of his New Deal record and chairmanship of the Interstate and Foreign Commerce Committee. Additionally, he ranked fourth (with four others) in the House in terms of seniority, although he was only fifty four.[98]

The race quickly boiled down to a Rayburn-O'Connor struggle described by *The New York Times* as "a spirited contest," "not without virulence." House members began to choose sides. Alfred F. Beiter of New York, who had put forth James Mead's name for the leadership, wired O'Connor that Mead's name would be withdrawn and that upstate New York would unite behind O'Connor. Edward T. Taylor of Colorado, chair of the Democratic caucus, backed Rayburn. Shortly before the caucus, Rankin withdrew, saying he favored either a dark horse or a "liberal" candidate. Rayburn's supporters believed they would get every Mississippi vote except possibly Rankin's. McCormack and Crosser both announced that they were not candidates and declared for Rayburn.[99]

By 1936, Rayburn had built a strong reputation as a New Dealer. Such legislation as the Securities Act, the Securities Exchange Act, the Public Utility Holding Company Act, the Communications Act, and transportation legislation had gone through his committee. O'Connor, in contrast, had opposed some New Deal programs, particularly the Holding Company Act. To O'Connor's dismay, since he believed the appointment was a "deliberate build up planned by Garner," Rayburn had been appointed to head the Speakers' Bureau for the Democratic National Committee in the 1936 campaign, facilitating a great deal of contact with House members. Roosevelt never openly supported Rayburn, and the O'Connor forces claimed that O'Connor was actually the president's choice, but Garner's strong and open support helped put the administration's seal of approval on Rayburn. Garner stated, "I am for Sam Rayburn 200%. . . . My guess is he will win, and I will contribute all I can for that purpose." James MacGregor Burns suggests that Roosevelt seems to have made a number of commitments to Garner in 1932 in order to gain the nomination: "Garner's willingness to accept the vice presidential nomination was due in part to Roosevelt's willingness to recognize southern, and especially Texas, power in Congress. The most important understanding was that Rayburn would be in line for the majority leadership and later the Speakership of the House. It was the president's recognition of Rayburn's claim that accounted in part for the desertion of the New Deal by rival aspirant, Representative John O'Connor of New York." Many years later, in a 1959 interview, Garner offered a simple explanation of his support for Rayburn: "I was always for Texas and Sam was a much better man than O'Connor. O'Connor would have had to ask Tammany if he could take a ⸻ in the morning. We didn't want that." Rep. Thomas Ford of California even claimed that the battle was not between Rayburn and O'Connor, "but rather it is a contest between Vice-President Garner and John O'Connor." News reports indicated that Garner's return to Washington and endorsement of Rayburn was preceded by consultation with FDR. Shortly thereafter Gov. Richard W. Leche, a leader of the Long faction in Louisiana, coaxed his state's delegation to become the first to endorse Rayburn. This group had gained the enmity of the Roosevelt administration as Huey P. Long pressed his presidential ambitions and became critical of the New Deal. After Long's assassination, Leche wished to make peace with Roosevelt. On several occasions, O'Connor had claimed promises of support from several Louisiana representatives. Congressman "Bathtub" Joe Fernandez of Louisiana had even written O'Connor that from conversations in the House it seemed clear that O'Connor would be elected majority leader "without any great deal of trouble." Fernandez wrote that he was "gratified" at this news and added, "I wish it were the Speakership."[100] But this support evaporated when Leche presided at the delegation's meeting. Sen. Joseph Guffey held a luncheon for his Pennsylvania delegation at which Rayburn was endorsed by a vote of eighteen to six. Guffey was not only the Democratic boss of Pennsylvania, but he was described as being, "next to Postmaster General James A. Farley[,] . . . the most important of President Roosevelt's political managers."[101] Rep. Michael Stack of Pennsylvania wrote the president that at the caucus of the Pennsylvania delegation the members were "led to believe that the Administration wanted Rep. Rayburn."[102]

The Pennsylvania support for Rayburn jeopardized O'Connor's strategy of emphasizing northern representation in the leadership. It also suggested that O'Connor would not receive unified support from Catholics, a group that O'Connor hoped would lend him assistance. In 1936, O'Connor compiled a list of all the Catholics in Congress and found that there were ten Catholics in the Senate and seventy-three Catholics in the House, excluding O'Connor.[103] Getting their support would have been a boon.

Other indications of administration support for Rayburn were present as well. For example, Charles West in the Interior Department campaigned for Rayburn; so much so that O'Connor wrote him an angry letter criticizing him and emphasizing that his work was being interpreted as an official endorsement of Rayburn by the president. O'Connor was also angry that Emil Hurja, executive director of the Democratic National Committee, campaigned for Rayburn.[104]

O'Connor, however, was not above relying on political party machinery himself. In July 1936, O'Connor wrote Patrick Drewry, a congressman from Virginia and chair of the Congressional Campaign Committee. He suggested the possibility of working through the Campaign Committee to contact congressmen and possibly develop a way by which he could use the committee to provide financial help to members. To some extent, Drewry went along. Drewry wrote Martin F. Smith of Washington State about $250 that he had received from the Congressional Campaign Committee in which he mentioned that John O'Connor "came in to see me concerning your campaign and I am writing to tell you of his interest." O'Connor rented a suite at the Bellevue Stratford during the 1936 Democratic convention in Philadelphia and lobbied members on his own behalf.[105]

Northern political bosses, some of them Irish Catholics — such as Tammany leader Tom Cullen and Chicago's Edward J. Kelly and Jersey City's Frank Hague—endorsed Rayburn, a sign of FDR's hidden-hand support.[106] Roosevelt's support became more visible when Tom Corcoran met a ship carrying Postmaster General Jim Farley home from a European trip. Farley had planned to endorse O'Connor once he returned to the United States, but Corcoran instructed Farley to remain silent. Corcoran remembered that "all the Tammany bunch was waiting for him on the dock to see what he was going to tell them about this [House] leadership business. I got a friend connected with the Coast Guard to give me a launch and went out to meet Farley's ship. I climbed a ladder up the side of the ship and found Farley. 'Rayburn's our man,' I told him. Then I beat it back to the dock. When Farley met the Tammany bunch, he knew what to say." There is some dispute between Farley and Corcoran over this incident. Farley did arrive in New York on December 10 on the SS *Washington,* and he claimed Corcoran did meet the boat to tell him not to endorse O'Connor until he first spoke with Roosevelt. But Farley claims he was hardly compliant, telling Corcoran, "What right have you got to tell me that? I'm for O'Connor. I'm his friend. He was Mr. Roosevelt's friend. Don't you be telling me what to do. Mr. Roosevelt knows I'm for Mr. O'Connor." But, claims Farley, his efforts came to no good because "Well, of course Mr. Roosevelt came out for Rayburn." Corcoran's biographer, David McKean, claims that because Roosevelt thought it politically unwise to openly support any candidate for the leadership, he enlisted Corcoran to provide behind-the-scenes support for Rayburn. McKean believes Corcoran got Bronx political boss Ed Flynn and Tammany Leader Tom Cullen to back Rayburn. Eventually, eight members of the New York delegation supported Rayburn over O'Connor.[107]

Like O'Connor, Farley was a New Yorker, Irish, and Catholic, and he continued to work for O'Connor. For example, O'Connor asked Farley to help him with the New Orleans, Chicago, and Kansas City congressmen. Also, Adolph Sabath, who had opposed McDuffie and supported Rainey in an earlier leadership battle and who was a leader of the Chicago delegation, wrote Farley that he would support O'Connor because of FDR's declaration of neutrality and O'Connor's promise that he had Farley's and the New York delegation's support. Sabath added, "I fear that it would be a great mistake to side-track him just because he is a New Yorker and a 'C' [Catholic]." Still, in early January, when O'Connor realized that he did not control the Chicago delegation, he begged for Farley's help: "Chicago not straightened out. Please telephone Sabath in Washington at once."[108]

Though Roosevelt remained neutral, the press noted that Garner openly backed Rayburn and that Louisiana had joined the Rayburn forces shortly after Garner visited New Orleans, when the Louisiana state organization was seeking to return to the New Deal fold. Additionally, the press noted that Guffey's support showed the administration was backing Rayburn. Prior to June 1935, James T. Patterson observed, O'Connor had generally supported FDR. But he had opposed the president in the Rules Committee on the "death sentence" in the Public Utility Holding Company Act of 1935, helping make certain that "the House Rules Committee emerged on the scene to play a role it would later perform with abandon: the 'villain' in an otherwise pro-New Deal drama."[109]

Not only did Rayburn have Garner lobbying in his behalf and the reputation of being a strong New Dealer, he had, unlike in the 1934 race, a unified and powerful Texas delegation behind him. He also had a more pleasant personality than the aggressive O'Connor. Patterson described O'Connor as a "red-headed, aggressive Tammany Democrat, [who] was 'one of the most unpopular members of a supposedly popular House.'"[110]

Richard W. Bolling, a Rayburn protégé, compared the two. Rayburn was "short, stocky, erect, and shiny bald. . . . He knew more about the ins and outs of the legislative process in the House than any member. . . . He was kind and helpful to all new members and to all old members, too, unlike most House seniors. He took a personal interest in their families, their private and public problems, and their careers in the House. He could be remarkably persuasive. He seemed simple but was complex; he seemed open and frank but kept his own counsel." O'Connor, on the other hand, "combined a quarrelsome nature, frustration over successive leadership defeats, and opposition to substantive economic alterations proposed by Roosevelt. . . . In explosive exasperation, Roosevelt placed O'Connor's name on a list of House and Senate members to be 'purged' at the 1938 fall elections. Only O'Connor lost. . . . Until then, he had helped hobble the New Deal."[111] As the election came near, Rayburn left nothing to chance. He began an outside lobbying campaign through Texas and Washington friends, who contacted influential men in various congressional districts in an effort to secure votes for Rayburn. For example, Ira P. DeLoache, a real-estate developer in Dallas, suggested that Walter Chamblin get in touch with C. B. Kincaid of the C&O Railroad, who could in turn pressure Cincinnati and Kentucky congressmen in Rayburn's behalf. Additionally, DeLoache offered to contact John H. Kerr and Lindsay R. Warren of North Carolina and Cliff Woodrum of Virginia. To these suggestions Rayburn responded that they were "very fine and I hope that you will follow them up." He was particularly anxious to learn the attitude of Cliff Woodrum. Rayburn noted that his Washington friend Mr. Kornhauser "did untiring work in my behalf." Kornhauser called his brother-in-law, J. J. Kurlander, in Cleveland, Ohio, who contacted Congressman-at-large Harold G. Mosier and obtained his pledge for Rayburn. Mosier also promised to lobby Congressman John McSweeney and others. In addition, Kurlander lobbied Ohio congressman Robert Crosser, and his letters to the editor supporting Rayburn were published in both the *Cleveland Press* and the *Cleveland Plain Dealer*.[112] Interestingly, Kurlander seemed to think that Rayburn's campaign was being directed from the White House. He wrote Marvin McIntyre, Roosevelt's secretary, that he had learned from Cleveland congressmen that Catholic and Jewish congressmen were being urged to vote for O'Connor and that he believed it to be at the urging of Father Charles Coughlin, a radio priest who had become an important political force. He asked McIntyre to "please advise Congressman Rayburn to act accordingly."[113] Walter L. Hensley, a St. Louis attorney and friend of Rayburn's, lobbied his congressman, Charles Arthur Anderson.[114]

Furthermore, Rayburn's brother-in-law W. A. Thomas, collector of Internal Revenue in Dallas, suggested that Rayburn write a Kansas congressman who had been supportive of his quest for the leadership. He then offered to supplement some of Rayburn's lobbying efforts by contacting the collector of Internal Revenue in New Orleans, who was influential with at least two Louisiana congressmen and collectors and one or more prominent friends in Kansas City, Little Rock, Chicago, Salt Lake City, Denver, San Francisco, and all the southern states. Thomas wrote that he was "personal friends" with collectors in Mississippi, North Carolina, South Carolina, Oklahoma, and Tennessee.[115]

On his own behalf, Rayburn sent a most unsubtle plea for support to Congressman Clarence F. Lea of California, who was next in line for the chairmanship of the Interstate and Foreign Commerce Committee. Rayburn wrote Lea that if he were elected, Lea was "certain to become Chairman of that Committee, which is, in my opinion, the most important legislative Committee in the Congress. You have risen to the top of the Committee by virtue of hard work and long service."[116]

Press reports later indicated that Lea and eleven other members of the California delegation were supporting Rayburn. Jerry Voorhis of California, for example, noted that since California had no important chairmanships, Lea's elevation to the chair of Interstate and Foreign Commerce was an important consideration. Additionally, Rayburn was considered the more progressive of the two candidates.[117]

Enlisting the support of the large crop of newly elected Democratic congressmen with little tie to either Rayburn or O'Connor, whose votes were therefore particularly unpredictable, was a final task. Eighty-eight of the 331 Democrats were newcomers in 1936. Luckily, Rayburn's job as head of the Speaker's Bureau had enabled him to aid their election battles, since it entailed the scheduling of speakers to assist Democratic congressional campaigns. Reporter Kirke Simpson saw the job as a way in which the administration sought to gain support for Rayburn's race in the following session, either for the leadership or the Speakership. Newly elected Oklahoma congressman Lyle H. Boren, whose family was friendly to Garner, was enlisted to campaign for Rayburn among the new members. Additionally, Boren became the spokesman for Rayburn in the Oklahoma delegation against John C. Nichols, the Oklahoman who was one of O'Connor's campaign managers.[118]

With 101 of the 331 Democratic members coming from the eleven states of the old Confederacy, O'Connor had to make inroads in the South to be successful in his bid. As part of that strategy, at the 1936 Democratic convention, O'Connor backed the two-thirds rule, which required that the presidential nominee receive the vote of at least two-thirds of the convention delegates. The South cherished the rule as a major weapon in making its influence felt in the National Democratic Party. Additionally, O'Connor made a deal with Jack Nichols of Oklahoma, promising Nichols the majority whip position if he could move Oklahoma into the O'Connor camp and influence other southern votes as well. Nichols became a campaign manager for O'Connor, but he could not sway the bulk of the Oklahoma delegation to a New York, Irish Catholic, and Tammany Hall Democrat.[119] Nichols did send out a letter to members that generated several favorable replies, including John Lesinski and John Dingell of Michigan and Benjamin Whelchel of Georgia. Francis "Tad" Walter of Pennsylvania even offered to take a leading role in O'Connor's campaign.[120]

One O'Connor supporter caused considerable concern, as O'Connor concluded he was a spy for the Rayburn camp. Martin Dies of Texas had claimed he was enthusiastic for O'Connor and even sought to make O'Connor's nominating speech. But O'Connor declared, "I have reason to believe he is on the other side. He has just been up to New York and has come back here to stay. He was most anxious to see me and I had a long talk with him last night in which he did a lot of pumping. I painted a rosey [*sic*] picture for him and was interested in watching him work in his usual way." He wrote to his ally Kenneth Romney, the sergeant at arms of the House, "I beg to warn you I believe he is on the ground working for my opponent." "If I am not mistaken," wrote O'Connor, "from long experience with him, you can take anything he says in reverse."[121]

While Rayburn had significant support, O'Connor chaired the powerful Rules Committee, and he had a strong sectional argument: sectional balance required a northern majority leader. Though the Rayburn forces claimed that Texas was part of the West, not the South, their argument was patently weak. O'Connor was banking on the attitude that Texas had enough power. Although the Pennsylvania delegation decided to vote as a unit, Rep. Charles Faddis refused to honor the delegation's decision and endorsed O'Connor. His argument in behalf of O'Connor had an explicit sectional appeal: Democrats could not remain a national party "by permitting its leadership in the House to become sectional."[122]

At times, the O'Connor forces claimed that Roosevelt's real candidate was O'Connor and, at other times, that Roosevelt was neutral in the race. O'Connor had some ties to FDR since his brother Basil had been FDR's law partner in New York and ran the Warm Springs Foundation. Roosevelt had found the waters of Warm Springs to be soothing to his polio. However, O'Connor was not a New Dealer, having tried to block the Holding Company Act. Additionally, James Roosevelt thought that both Basil O'Connor and FDR "looked upon John O'Connor as someone they wished they didn't have to deal with," adding that he "would be amazed if there was any real evidence that father ever preferred to have John O'Connor as Leader."[123]

In reality, however, Basil did come to John O'Connor's support when he heard stories circulating that suggested that FDR supported Rayburn. He wrote the president in support of his brother, claiming that his brother's election was assured unless the political bosses thought Roosevelt opposed him, something that Basil could not believe was true. He continued, "If John should fail to be elected Majority Leader because it is believed that you are against him, when in fact you are not, it would seem to me to be a sad commentary on public life in this country."[124]

Not surprisingly, at a presidential press conference on December 18, 1936, the first since his return from South America, Roosevelt stated that he had never interfered with Speakership or leadership contests. Roosevelt was asked if he had any preference in the leadership race. The press corps laughed at the question, but Roosevelt offered a lengthy response: "Since 1933, the fourth of March, there have been three different speakers elected by the House. In two cases, as I remember it, there were contests, and the White House took absolutely no part, directly or indirectly, in those elections. There have been one or two majority leaders elected since the fourth of March 1933, and again the White House took no part, directly or indirectly, in those elections. It has been the rule and will continue to be the rule." The refusal of the president to express a preference led O'Connor to remark:

> As I have stated confidently right along what would happen when the President returned, he has blown into thin air the built-up propaganda emanating from both high and low places that the White House is taking sides in the contest for majority leader, either by preferring any one candidate or opposing another candidate. The statement of the President is consistent with the Executive's unvaried policy of not attempting to interfere with the legislative branch of the Government and no thinking person — let alone any member of the House of Representatives — even for a moment thought he would pursue any policy other than that which he so clearly and emphatically stated today. And any attempt at this time to place any other interpretation on the President's statement will be to impugn the frankness and honesty of the President.

O'Connor also sent an editorial to Margaret (Missy) LeHand, Roosevelt's secretary, who was very close to Roosevelt personally. The editorial noted that Rayburn forces had been claiming Roosevelt's support, but Roosevelt was neutral. It added that the battle between Rayburn and O'Connor was a clash between northern, western, and southern factions in the Democratic Party and a skirmish in a conflict of political and economic interests.[125]

Privately, however, O'Connor wrote, "The Rayburn group are still winking their eyes and saying the President's statement doesn't go and that Sam is still the white-haired boy." He urged Farley to announce that the administration was indeed neutral and added, "I have the votes and the other side has the 'ballyhoo.'"[126] O'Connor was not trying to mislead Farley. He genuinely believed that he had the votes. On December 29, 1936, less than a week before the Democratic caucus, O'Connor made separate lists of the congressmen committed and leaning toward him and those toward Rayburn. He counted 147 congressmen committed to him and another 22 congressmen leaning toward him; he estimated that he would get at least 155 votes. His tally even showed significant support in the South, with 24 of the pro-O'Connor congressmen from states in the former Confederacy. Rayburn, in contrast, only had 57 firm votes and 22 more leaning in his direction. O'Connor thought Rayburn would get at least 70 votes, 38 from the South, including 15 from Texas. The remaining members were uncommitted or undecided, though O'Connor thought one congressman might persist in supporting John Rankin of Mississippi. Many of the new congressmen's views were unknown to O'Connor, but, presumably, that was also the case for Rayburn. By O'Connor's count, Rayburn looked weak. After putting together his list, O'Connor scribbled a confident note in pencil, ". . . it's a landslide."

Careful examination of O'Connor's list discloses some problems. Wright Patman, a Rayburn friend representing an adjoining district, and Marvin Jones, Rayburn's former brother-in-law and fishing buddy, are listed as unknown votes. Incoming Oklahoma congressman Lyle Boren is also unknown. O'Connor and his campaign manager, Oklahoman Jack Nichols, may not have known that Boren was working the incoming congressmen in Rayburn's behalf.[127] In addition, there were other hints of problems for O'Connor on the list. Ultra-conservative Georgian and Rules Committee member Eugene "Goober" Cox was backing Rayburn. Brooklyn political leader Tom Cullen was listed as the only New Yorker backing Rayburn. Cullen was never friendly to O'Connor, but O'Connor must have wondered if Cullen could bring along other New Yorkers. And in Illinois, only Tom O'Brien and Kent Keller were listed as pro-Rayburn, but O'Brien had vast influence with the Chicago delegation. Could this bode poorly for O'Connor's Chicago support? In Massachusetts, John McCormack was listed as the only Rayburn supporter. O'Connor might well have asked why urban, northern, Irish Catholics like Cullen, O'Brien, and McCormack were not going along with a fellow urban, northern, Irish Catholic. And "Goober" Cox had considerable influence among southerners and was on O'Connor's Rules Committee. There was room for O'Connor to be concerned. Perhaps a touch of concern is why O'Connor scribbled over his "it's a landslide" notation.[128] The only comment from Rayburn's forces was that of Rayburn's campaign manager, Kentucky representative Fred Vinson, who responded, "Everything's lovely."[129]

A few days after Garner urged that Rayburn be chosen majority leader, a press report claimed that Senate Majority Leader Joseph Robinson of Arkansas endorsed O'Connor. According to the article, Robinson said that while he would not take part in the battle between O'Connor and Rayburn, "he would be glad to commend O'Connor to anyone interested in knowing his attitude." The next day, Robinson wired O'Connor that this report was in error, and he expected "you to correct if your office is responsible for the publicity." He telegrammed Rayburn that the "only expression I have made on the subject is in a letter written in reply to one from O'Connor in which I stated I did not believe it was proper for me to interfere in the matter but if anyone was interested in my viewpoint would commend him as qualified." Robinson's secretary then wrote Rayburn on Robinson's instructions that "either Mr. O'Connor's office or some reporter took an unfair advantage of Senator Robinson in the matter and the telegram to Mr. O'Connor and the correspondence will clearly show you his position." In addition, Garner also received a letter explaining that the report that "Senator Robinson had endorsed Mr. O'Connor . . . is untrue."[130] O'Connor's effort to get an endorsement from a major administration figure had failed. There was, of course, a vast gap between someone of Robinson's stature considering O'Connor qualified and endorsing him.

Likewise, the O'Connor forces had begun hammering away during the previous week: Senator Guffey of Pennsylvania was accused of breaking a promise of support to O'Connor, given in return for O'Connor's work on behalf of the Guffey Coal Bill. Franklin W. Hancock of North Carolina and Byron B. Harlan of Ohio claimed that the South would have too much with both the Speakership and the leadership and that Texas had enough power with six major chairmanships and the presiding officer of the Senate. Harlan noted that he believed Rayburn's forces were trying to stampede his election prior to Roosevelt's return from South America and that the tactic of claiming Roosevelt's favor had been used by Rayburn in an earlier Speaker's race: "When Speaker Joseph Byrns was seeking the Speakership, the friends of Sam Rayburn were handing out the same propaganda, as to their monopoly of Presidential favor, that they are disseminating now. Its absurdity at that time was no greater than is the same contention today. If President Roosevelt has any preference in this contest, he does not need any spokesman to advocate this preference during his absence." Yet Roosevelt could not openly back Rayburn; to do so would be to plainly interfere with the organization of the House. Nor would Speaker Bankhead back Rayburn openly, although Rayburn requested him to do so. Claimed Bankhead, "No, sir-e-e-e! I'm ab-so-lutely neutral in this contest. I'll accept the man elected by the caucus of the House Democrats." In response, Rayburn wrote Bankhead that his neutrality was a proper position in such a circumstance. Bankhead was close to Rayburn, but, claimed reporter Robert C. Albright, he owed O'Connor for his immediate succession to the Speakership upon the death of Speaker Byrns.[131]

To combat Rayburn's endorsement by such men as Garner and Guffey, the O'Connor camp tried to undermine Rayburn for seeking help from party bosses and those outside the House. That strategy failed when it became known that Sen. Joel Bennett Clark, the son of Speaker Champ Clark, of Missouri had been asked by the O'Connor forces for his assistance in obtaining the support of the Missouri delegation. Senator Clark stated, no doubt to the embarrassment of the O'Connor forces, that he had not lobbied the Missouri delegation. Rather, he said, "If I could do anything for my very good friend, Sam Rayburn, I would — but I haven't."[132]

Election of the majority leader, given the pattern of succession and Bankhead's health, would likely determine the next Speaker as well. In addition, based on Bankhead's health, the majority leader would be greatly depended upon by the Speaker. The race was thus a crucial leadership contest that raised fundamental questions for the Democratic Party in the House: would the party maintain sectional balance in its leadership, or would it choose a majority leader in harmony with the president? John McCormack, a northern Irish Catholic, put the issue clearly in a statement endorsing Rayburn for the leadership: "The main issue involved in the election of the Floor Leader is not what section of the country a candidate comes from, but what type of leadership a candidate stands for and represents. It appears to me to be essential, and in the best interest of the Nation and of Party that a Floor Leader be elected who will, without question or uncertainty in the minds of the Democratic members, follow the policies of President Roosevelt and fearlessly fight to have those policies enacted into law. All other issues, all of the candidates being able and experienced, are to me of a minor nature, and not worthy of consideration in the present contest." Long part of the Garner-Rayburn-McDuffie faction in the House, McCormack was the first New Englander to declare for Rayburn. In 1934, journalist Will Kennedy wrote that if Rayburn or Bankhead could not get the majority leadership, the faction would back McCormack for the job. McCormack had proven his loyalty to the faction in his dogged support of McDuffie in the bitter fight between Rainey and McDuffie, standing with McDuffie even when it was clear that Rainey was going to win. The Garner-Rayburn-McDuffie faction considered that they had a "debt of honor" to McCormack for that effort. Just as he had supported McDuffie, McCormack backed Rayburn because both men had been key allies of Garner. Having been influential in winning admittance for McCormack to the Garner group, Rayburn had also aided him in getting a seat on the coveted Ways and Means Committee. As McCormack stated, "I don't go back on my friends; if I did, I would be an ingrate." With McCormack's support, one writer argued, ten other New England Democrats entered the Rayburn camp. And it seemed that a majority of the Democratic caucus agreed with McCormack, for sectional balance was sacrificed, and on January 4, 1937, Rayburn won, 184–127. After the result was announced, Rayburn hurried to Vice President Garner's rooms to receive congratulations.[133] The Garner faction again controlled the House.

Columnist Robert Allen wrote O'Connor a few days after the vote: "I should like to take this opportunity, however, to tell you that I think you are a damn swell sport and that you took it and gave it like a man. May I also wish you better luck next time." But O'Connor was a very sore loser. He was angry with many who he felt had betrayed him, especially Tammany Representative Cullen, who rose in the caucus to second Rayburn's nomination, an act of treason according to O'Connor. Of Cullen, O'Connor wrote only days after his defeat, "If I thought he would attend my funeral, I just wouldn't be there." Other machine Democrats had failed him too; he wrote his brother, Basil: "I got the foot in the Bronx, Brooklyn, Philadelphia, Chicago and New Orleans." Writing Memphis political boss Ed Crump, O'Connor claimed that the Tennessee delegation "was a great disappointment to me, especially in view of their former association with Joe Byrns. Jere Cooper made a nominating speech against me and the story still persists that your new governor was a most active manager for my opponent." To Sidney Hillman, who sent him a labor pamphlet titled "Carpetbaggers of Industry," O'Connor indicated his surprise at receiving the pamphlet once he had gotten reports that Hillman had opposed him for majority leader — something that he claimed had surprised both him and Jim Farley, given his support for labor legislation. This opposition by Hillman, O'Connor wrote, suggested that "you were undoubtedly misled in jumping into the political bed with strange bedfellows."[134]

Initially, it was believed O'Connor would retreat to New York and accept a state judgeship, which paid a much higher salary than that of a congressman. However, he had gotten a substantial vote in his race with Rayburn, and, Arthur Krock noted, O'Connor was "the first Eastern city Democrat in years to loom so large in the House of Representatives." Rayburn initially thought that the close vote was beneficial since "that will make for a better feeling all around." He was wrong. O'Connor stayed in

Congress and proved to be a thorn in the side of Roosevelt, Bankhead, and Rayburn. O'Connor's Rules Committee became a major barrier for New Deal legislation. Harold Ickes, who often used his diary entries to vent his anger rather than to accurately record events, claimed that O'Connor held a grudge against the administration because Rayburn became majority leader. Ickes observed that O'Connor did as he pleased on Rules, that Bankhead was an ill man who could not control the House, and that Rayburn was neither strong nor effective, since he desired not to offend anyone so that he could become the next Speaker.[135]

However, O'Connor seemed to understand that he lacked real power and was more of a hindrance than anything else. When he was asked by Joseph W. Byrns Jr., the son of former Speaker Byrns, to intercede with Congressman James M. Mead and get him appointed counsel to an investigatory committee, O'Connor wrote on Byrns's letter, "Am doing all I can to help but fear I am not influential — now!"[136]

Not surprisingly, O'Connor was one of the Democrats singled out by Roosevelt to be purged from Congress in 1938.[137] Rayburn opposed the purge, fearing that "our trouble of last session with him would be a small affair compared to what we would have next session . . . if O'Connor returned to Congress." O'Connor embraced his opposition from FDR, writing that "all the Communists, Radicals and their ilk are making a dead set for me." He predicted that he would "lick the stuffing out of all of them," but he was successfully purged by his defeat in the Democratic primary. O'Connor subsequently received the Republican nomination. Bankhead feared that O'Connor would be elected and expressed "great anxiety" over the prospect. However, O'Connor lost the general election, thus ending his threat to the New Deal. When O'Connor went down, Rayburn wrote Bankhead, "Of course, I shed no tears at the result of the 16th New York district."[138]

However, not everyone was overjoyed by O'Connor's demise. James F. Byrnes of South Carolina, a key figure in Congress and later in the Roosevelt and Truman administrations, wrote bitterly to Garner, "Where were you when little Sherman started marching through the South? I did not hear from you but I knew you were active in the purge and I cannot refrain from saying I regret that you and the other leaders of the administration interfered in the Primary Elections in the States. . . . I think you treated John O'Connor wrong. You first beat him for leadership, then drove him out of the House and into the Republican Party. When I see you I certainly want to learn who inspired this purge." And Jim Farley, an O'Connor supporter, wrote that Roosevelt should never have opposed O'Connor. After all, O'Connor had supported FDR in 1932 when Curry and other Tammany leaders had opposed him, and O'Connor's brother had been a loyal law partner to Roosevelt. Farley remembered: "It was one of those things that I never could understand. It was quite unfair. I made known my position at that time."[139]

Roosevelt actually tried to get Farley to lead the primary campaign against O'Connor, but Farley refused. Roosevelt then got Tom Corcoran to try, and Corcoran recruited James H. Fay to run against O'Connor, but Corcoran botched the campaign. Finally FDR persuaded Bronx political boss Ed Flynn to take over the campaign against O'Connor. Though Flynn was also hostile to the purge, he disliked O'Connor and so, unlike Farley, was willing to take him on.[140]

O'Connor, as might be expected, remained bitter about his defeat. In 1940, he wrote former classmates from Harvard, "For some years, long before the 'purge,' and not based on any 'sour grapes,' I have been outspoken against many of the trends toward radicalism, and under the name of the 'New Deal,' or otherwise, which I sincerely felt were injurious to our form of government and our nation's welfare. In this year 1940, we face a 'front line,' and party labels mean little in comparison to the continuance of our republican and democratic form of government. We just cannot stand four years more of all that has been going on. If our leading citizens, such as you, do not take the lead, we are headed for a greater dictatorship than we now have or toward the rocks of communism." In another letter, O'Connor wrote, "I believe Mr. Roosevelt to be the greatest menace to our form of Government."[141]

When Congress went back to work, Bankhead's health remained poor. He never was able to provide vigorous leadership, and he died September 15, 1940. After three years as majority leader, Rayburn succeeded him without difficulty and served as Speaker for seventeen years, longer than anyone in U.S. history. Interestingly, O'Connor wrote a congratulatory letter to Rayburn, who responded in kind.[142] When Rayburn became Speaker, John McCormack, Rayburn's Irish Catholic northern ally, was elected majority leader. His election marked a return to maintaining sectional balance in the House leadership and marked the beginning of the emerging Austin-Boston connection, which was to dominate Democratic politics in the House for nearly fifty years.

ew, if any, congressmen had the wealth of political experience in the House that John McCormack had prior to becoming Speaker. Although McCormack completed nine consecutive years as Speaker, at that time a record, he faced open rebellions against his leadership from members of his own party. McCormack, unlike his friend and predecessor Sam Rayburn, could not maintain the universal respect of his colleagues and seemed unable to control divisions within his party. McCormack as majority leader had been "very feisty . . . and an able, gifted debater." As Speaker, although he was generally liked, he was "rarely feared." Some saw him as lacking forceful leadership, especially in reference to liberal legislation, and he "seemed to represent the old order of conducting House business."[1] Perhaps the circumstances of the 1960s would have made the going rough for any leader in the House as the civil rights era came to its culmination and the Vietnam War began to divide the nation; both hampered McCormack's leadership. Despite the problems, McCormack presided over some of the most productive legislative years in U.S. history as the Great Society and civil rights agendas moved through Congress. For almost forty years, McCormack was near the epicenter of political power. His life was a "rags-to-riches" rise from the Boston Irish tenements to one of the most powerful offices in the United States. In those positions of power, he was "in the room" for many of the political events in the second third of the twentieth century that altered the course of American life.

In spite of a remarkable career, McCormack never gained the stature of his predecessor, Sam Rayburn, or of his protégé, Tip O'Neill. Instead, to some younger members, represented by his challenger Morris Udall, he seemed old-fashioned, out-of-touch, and lacking skillful political judgment.[2]

McCormack the Man

McCormack led an admirable life. A lifelong teetotaler in a Congress rife with excessive alcohol use, he was a devout Roman Catholic who placed great value on loyalty. He did not revel in press attention. His devoted marriage of fifty-one years seemed to provide him all of the emotional sustenance he needed. His background of poverty helped frame his modest, frugal, and simple lifestyle. In spite of a scandal involving a staff member that was to mar the end of his career, he was known for his personal integrity.[3]

Like so many Speakers, McCormack was "a poor boy who had made good." Sam Rayburn came from a small farmer background; Republican leader Joe Martin's blacksmith father made too little money to educate his oldest son; Carl Albert's coal miner father raised him in a community only large enough to support a one-room schoolhouse; Tip O'Neill grew up the motherless son of a Boston Irish bricklayer; and Jim Wright's itinerant father roamed the Southwest as a traveling salesman. The shared hardships of their early lives united these men and gave them empathy for the deprivations from which some Americans suffered and the role that the federal government could play in alleviating them.[4]

McCormack's life hardships were genuine, but he altered his life story in order to gain public office in Boston. McCormack claimed to be the son of a poor Irish-born immigrant father who died young, leaving the thirteen-year-old McCormack to care for his mother and two younger siblings. It was a powerful tale reminiscent of the stories of the greatest Boston Irish politicians of McCormack's era, four-time Boston mayor James Michael Curley, John F. "Honey Fitz" Fitzgerald, and Patrick "P. J." Kennedy. The problem was that McCormack's story was not true and seemed cast to ease his entry into the Boston Irish political scene. His father did not die when he was thirteen, but rather not until McCormack was thirty-seven and serving his first term in the U.S. House. Joe McCormack had abandoned the family and lived in Maine where he worked in the granite quarries. Nor was McCormack's father from Ireland but was the son of a Scotswoman from Prince Edward Island. McCormack's mother did not emigrate from Ireland either. She was born in the United States, the daughter of Irish parents. Nor did his three oldest siblings die in infancy as McCormack claimed. But the story was politically useful as McCormack became a lawyer and entered the Boston political scene.[5]

In 1919, McCormack successfully ran for state representative. That same year, McCormack met Harriet Joyce, a professional singer and local celebrity. Marriage to Harriet in 1920 may have been the defining alliance in McCormack's life. His devotion to her in their fifty-one-year marriage took on legendary proportions. Even McCormack's enemies positively noted their successful marriage. After gaining election to the state Senate, McCormack rose to the position of minority floor leader, and in 1926 he challenged six-term incumbent Rep. James A. Gallivan for a seat in the U.S. House of Representatives. Defeated by Gallivan, he returned to the practice of law. However, with Gallivan's death in 1928, McCormack won the special election to fill the vacancy, and he and Harriet moved into the Washington Hotel in Washington, D.C., where they remained for the next forty-two years.

During their marriage, Harriet and John dined together every night, ordering room service from the hotel. Harriet occasionally shopped and went for walks, but most of her day was spent in anticipation of John's return from Capitol Hill. It was a childless marriage though an emotionally fulfilling one. And while their social life was quite reclusive, John could concentrate on legislative business and advancing his career in the House.[6]

McCormack Moves Up in the House

In 1930 the Democrats regained control of the House, and McCormack defeated his Republican opponent with 76.7 percent of the vote. McCormack had been serving on the Territories and Elections No. 3 Committee and in 1929 was added to the Civil Service Committee. He wanted to move up in the committee hierarchy when he met with Speaker John Nance Garner, who said, "John, where the hell have you been? We wanted you for chairman of the caucus. Bill Arnold [of Illinois] came in and I gave it to him but I wanted you." Arnold, in his ninth year in the House, clearly had stronger claims to that position than the third-year McCormack. Garner, however, told McCormack, "We want you for Ways and Means, but you have to be elected to it. Go and tell Billy Connery [the senior Massachusetts Democrat] to send a letter for you. Just get him to blow his nose at you and we'll get you elected." This committee was a prized position since it was both the tax-writing committee of the House and the Democratic Committee on Committees. With Garner's backing, McCormack became its youngest member.[7]

Several factors influenced Garner's decision to put McCormack on the committee. Both men were avid poker players who lived in the same hotel, came from humble origins, and had limited formal educations. Most importantly, however, McCormack was from Massachusetts, the only major industrial state to cast its electoral votes for Al Smith in the 1928 election. Garner could use a politically secure Democrat from a Democratic state in the North, especially an urban Irish Catholic Democrat. McCormack could be a useful ally if Garner ran for president in 1932 or if he did not run, a valuable protégé in the House where it seemed likely in 1932 that the northern wing of the Democratic Party would increase significantly.[8] Once he became part of the Garner faction in the House, it fell to McCormack to back Sam Rayburn in his race for majority leader in 1937. McCormack proved capable in bringing New England Democrats to Rayburn's side.

With Rayburn as majority leader, the leadership of the House was notably southern, rural and Protestant. Speaker Bankhead was a Methodist from Jasper, Alabama, and Rayburn was a Primitive Baptist from Bonham, Texas.[9] When Rayburn moved to the Speakership upon Bankhead's death, it clearly would be useful to have a northern, urban, ethnic Catholic as majority leader, especially since the issue of balance in the leadership had already been raised in 1937, when Rayburn ran for majority leader. Thus, Rayburn backed McCormack over his major competitor, Clifton Woodrum of Virginia.[10]

Woodrum was not a lightweight opponent. Born in Roanoke, Virginia, in 1887 into a financially modest but socially prestigious family, he had practiced law and served as a judge prior to his election to Congress in 1922. He was tall, handsome, and cultured, and possessed a talented singing voice. A member of the Appropriations Committee since 1929, he held a position of power in the House and, like McCormack, was personally close to John Nance Garner. Woodrum had been a moderate fiscal conservative who had moved considerably to the right by 1940. It was not surprising that McCormack was seen as the Roosevelt administration candidate for leader. FDR's secretary of the interior, Harold Ickes, for example, claimed to speak for the president in backing McCormack. Ickes told one influential Democratic congressman that "if he was going to support Woodrum, in order to be consistent he should also vote against the President for reelection." Richard Bolling called Woodrum a "recruiter for anti–New Deal majorities." Chairing an appropriations subcommittee that proposed to "slash $500 million" from the Works Progress Administration (WPA) bill, Woodrum had also tried to limit FDR's discretion on running the WPA. In 1939, Woodrum helped lead a movement to investigate the WPA and chaired an investigation that publicized a series of disclosures harmful to the agency. James T. Patterson pointed out that

FDR "had to suffer the discomforts of unfriendly House investigations by Woodrum, Martin Dies Jr. of Texas, and Howard W. Smith of Virginia, and he was denied so much as a shadow of his spending and housing programs." Woodrum was considered by Patterson to be one of the most conservative Democrats.[11]

Still, Woodrum and the other candidates for majority leader did not make it an easy victory for McCormack. Lindsay Warren of North Carolina was made "temporary leader," a move that facilitated a delay in the election of a permanent leader until the January organizing caucus. To challenge the delay, on September 19, 1940, McCormack forces circulated a petition to get the sixty House Democrats' signatures necessary to call an immediate meeting of the caucus and ballot for majority leader. Carl Vinson of Georgia moved to postpone the vote until the beginning of the 77th Congress, reasoning that the newly elected Congress ought to be able to select its majority leader. Richard Bolling offered two explanations for Vinson's motion: first, that Vinson wanted to prevent "a party row before the fall elections" and second, that "if the Democrats kept control as a result of the coming elections, one type of majority leader would be needed. If not, then a different type of man would be needed as minority leader." Close examination of the politics of the time reveals several additional reasons that delay would have helped Woodrum and McCormack's other challengers. At the time of Vinson's motion, it seemed McCormack had the votes to win. Delay might allow hope for others. Indeed, "all prospective candidates except McCormack voted in favor of delaying action."[12] A related reason the delay would aid Woodrum had to do with the expectations regarding the outcome of the 1940 elections, with some members of Congress thinking it would be a bad year for congressional Democrats. Franklin Roosevelt himself had long expected the same thing. In light of this, Roosevelt had asked young Lyndon Johnson of Texas to raise and distribute significant amounts of campaign money to help Democrats hold on to their majority.[13] If 1940 was to be a difficult year, there would likely be Democratic losses outside of the South. The increased importance of southern interests in the House Democratic Party might tip the balance toward Woodrum. Also, if the 1940 elections were a decidedly negative referendum on FDR in many congressional districts, the perceived White House's support of McCormack might actually hurt rather than help the Boston representative.

There is no way to be sure who supported the motion to delay, but the record does contain broad evidence of support and opposition from the members who spoke in favor and opposition to the motion. Supporting the motion were Clarence Lea of California and Henry Steagall of Alabama. Opposing the motion, and presumably supporting McCormack, were Joseph E. Casey of Massachusetts, John J. Cochran of Missouri, E. E. Cox of Georgia, James G. Scrugham of Nevada, and John D. Dingell of Michigan. The Vinson motion narrowly lost 108–91 by secret ballot.[14]

With this last effort narrowly defeated, the caucus proceeded to vote. Rep. Arthur D. Healey of Massachusetts nominated McCormack, and Rep. Schuyler Otis Bland of Virginia spoke for Woodrum. On the final vote, McCormack beat Woodrum by more than a two-to-one margin, 141 to 67, with a sole vote cast for Rep. Patrick Boland of Pennsylvania. Graciously, Woodrum moved to make McCormack's election unanimous.[15] It is hardly surprising that the candidate who offered regional, ethnic, and religious balance to the leadership of the House and had far more sympathy for the New Deal than his opponent would be elected majority leader.

The election had long-lasting consequences; for the next 21 years (1940–61), Sam Rayburn and McCormack served as the House's top two Democrats, never facing opposition in the Democratic caucus. The team's impact upon House politics and the national agenda was profound. McCormack, however, would time and again face opposition as he aspired to the final rung in the House leadership ladder — the Speakership.

1946 Who Will Be Minority Leader?

When the results of the 1946 congressional elections revealed an overwhelming Democratic defeat with a party line-up of 246 Republicans to 188 Democrats, Rayburn lost the Speakership to Republican Joe Martin of Massachusetts. Not wanting to serve as minority leader, Rayburn sent a wire to McCormack telling him that he would back him for that post in the 80th Congress. But when McCormack related this to John Sparkman of Alabama, whom Rayburn had appointed majority whip in 1946, Sparkman found that southern Democrats opposed McCormack, and northern Democrats would not accept any southerner except Rayburn. So Sparkman pressured Rayburn to take on the minority leadership. Truman, appalled at the thought that Rayburn might not be his right hand in Congress, also lobbied Rayburn.[16]

When J. Percy Priest of Tennessee was quoted in a newspaper saying that the party without Rayburn would "be torn apart internally," Rayburn replied that "I can be of more service to the country and the party by being free of the minority leadership, and taking the Floor when I feel it necessary on the larger issues. I feel this very deeply." Rayburn encouraged Priest to support McCormack for Democratic floor leader, writing, "I think John McCormack should be elected and I hope you and others of my friends from the South will go along with me in this." Similarly, Rayburn wrote to John H. Kerr, "I agree with you that it would be a mistake to attempt to defeat McCormack simply because he is a northerner as we cannot allow our party to be a sectional party. If we ever come into power again, we must have a great many northern votes."[17]

Still, other important party leaders thought it essential that Rayburn continue to lead the House Democrats. According to Hardeman and Bacon, "Truman weighed in . . . arguing that McCormack could not win and that Rayburn's refusal to serve would allow a reactionary southerner to step into a House leadership vacuum."[18] Indeed, the southerners continued in their efforts to stop McCormack's rise to leadership. Perhaps in an effort to induce Rayburn to accept a draft, southerners floated the name of fellow Texan Ewing Thomason of El Paso as leader. Thomason, who was first elected to the House in 1930, had run against Joe Bailey in a race for governor of Texas. Even with Democratic losses in the north shifting the balance of power to the south and the overall ideology of the House Democratic Party to the right, Thomason was probably too conservative to lead the Democrats of the 80th Congress.

At the beginning of 1947, Rayburn "prevailed upon my old friend and co-worker" McCormack "to accept the place of whip." Rayburn said that since "the majority passed to the other side and my colleagues on this side have imposed upon me the duty of the leadership, I am proud that I will have him as my consultant and co-worker in the leadership of the minority."[19]

Rayburn's acquiescence to the draft effort kept McCormack on the leadership ladder. Had Rayburn not accepted the minority leadership, McCormack would have had to compete against a southerner and would likely have lost. Upon losing, his claim to any party leadership position in the future might well have been diminished. As a result, one consequence of Rayburn's acceptance of the floor leader post might have been to preserve McCormack's career in the House leadership. Another, according to Rayburn's first biographer, was that Rayburn came to understand that "he had become, during his thirty-four years, a symbol of leadership for his Party in Congress, and as long as he was a member of the House of Representatives . . . he could not walk away from responsibility." It was symbolic

of Rayburn's role as a bridge between North and South that John Mc-
Cormack nominated Rayburn for Speaker in the caucus, and ultra-racists
Eugene Cox of Georgia and John Rankin of Mississippi made his second-
ing speeches.[20]

This may have been a wake-up call to McCormack that he needed to
have even better relationships with the South if he were ever to succeed
Rayburn as Speaker. Of course, McCormack already had forged ties with
southerners through the Garner faction and had previously backed John
McDuffie of Alabama for Speaker over Henry Rainey of Illinois, William
Bankhead of Alabama over Joseph Byrns of Tennessee, and Bankhead for
majority leader over John O'Connor of New York, a fellow Irish Catholic. Then McCormack was crucial in Rayburn's victory as majority leader
in 1936 over O'Connor. When he ran for majority leader in 1940 against
Woodrum, McCormack received strong southern support. Eugene Cox of
Georgia, a key southerner on the Rules Committee and considered by the
Republican floor leader, Joe Martin, to be "the real leader of the southerners in the House," placed McCormack's name in nomination for majority
leader. McCormack even attributed his victory to his southern friends.
McCormack said he won because "I had a lot of friends in the south. You
needed sixty to seventy votes from the South to win." Furthermore, "Gene
Cox and I were great pals. We voted just the opposite of each other. But
he handled my fight in the caucus. Gene Cox was a poker pal of mine. If
you're a poker pal, you're a goddam good pal."[21]

However, it was one thing to be the number two man in the leadership;
it was quite another matter to be the number one leader. Because of the
losses in the 1946 elections, the Democrats had to reduce their number
of members on the Rules Committee. One Democrat who lost his position on that panel was conservative William Colmer of Mississippi. When
Democrats regained control of the House after 1948, Colmer sought to
be reappointed and "asked McCormack for assistance in regaining a seat
on Rules. McCormack, without thinking, agreed. Rayburn felt that he
had to abide by the commitment." Richard Bolling viewed this as a "big
mistake" by McCormack that "changed the history of many subsequent
Congresses."[22] Colmer became a thorn in the side of House leadership
for years, especially in blocking civil rights legislation. But McCormack's
action helped build a powerful bond with the southerners. One day, that
act would help McCormack if the opportunity to become Speaker presented itself.

Minority Leader — 83d Congress

When the issue of Rayburn's retirement from the leadership came up again after Republicans took control of the House after the 1952 elections, the situation was somewhat different in that the balance of northerners and southerners in the party had not changed as significantly as it had from the 79th to the 80th Congress. Republicans had only an eight-vote advantage over Democrats (221 Republicans and 213 Democrats).

Even prior to the 1952 election, Rayburn had given up on the thought of retiring from the leadership. In a 1951 conversation, Rayburn spoke of his 1946 retirement wishes and his plans for the 1952 elections: "I did want to go back to the farm and take it easy for a while, but I was afraid that my action would have been a public confession that I believed Truman would be defeated. If I should open this issue with myself in 1952, it would also have a bad effect. I have just reached the point where I have to consider the welfare of others and forget about the ranch and farm. A good soldier does not question. There is so much yet to be done in these troubled times. Love and duty take the matter entirely out of my hands." Not long after the election, Rayburn wrote McCormack a letter informing him that he would be a candidate for minority leader.[23]

The Death of Rayburn and the McCormack Speakership

When Thomas J. Lane of Massachusetts nominated McCormack for majority leader on January 2, 1961, he emphasized the importance of Rayburn and McCormack binding the North-South division in the Democratic Party: "Sam and John will continue to unite the South and the North but this time under the new national leadership of the Democratic Party. By a happy coincidence, Massachusetts and Texas will 'team' up in the persons of President-elect Kennedy and Vice President–elect Johnson, to emulate a similar relationship of effective leadership that prevails in this House."[24] In a matter of months, however, Rayburn began suffering severe back pain and dramatic weight loss. Finally, he was diagnosed with incurable pancreatic cancer and returned home to die. His death in November 1961 cost the Democrats the only leader most members had known, raising the question of who would be Rayburn's successor. Although Rayburn and McCormack were close, Rayburn had been the senior partner, and his long tenure had blocked McCormack's ascension to the top. That was most notable in 1946 when Rayburn was seen as the preferred alternative to McCormack for the top post. Now, with Rayburn gone, the man who had loyally served for over two decades in the number two position among House Democrats had strong claims to the office.

Still, there were problems. McCormack's poker-playing pal Gene Cox, who was his major arm to the southern wing of the party, was long dead. There was a younger generation of northern liberals in the House, most notably Richard Bolling, who were strong critics of McCormack. Bolling had emerged as a young, brilliant, and vigorous Rayburn protégé with close ties to the media, northern liberals, and to the Kennedy administration. McCormack, in contrast, was seventy years old and looked much older. He had feuded with the Kennedy administration. He avoided media attention — even described by a longtime assistant as "the most secretive man I have ever met." Further, his formality with other members, simple lifestyle, refusal to drink alcohol, devout Catholicism, and quiet home life made him seem out-of-touch, old-fashioned, and unsociable in the glamorous Washington of the Kennedy years.[25]

Even his protégé, Tip O'Neill, saw McCormack as an "odd duck." McCormack had firmly fixed habits — for example, always breakfasting with Harriet, always arriving at the Capitol at 8:25 A.M. and having coffee in the House dining room. He had the same lunch every day — a grilled cheese sandwich, tea, and a dish of melted chocolate ice cream. He refused to use nicknames, always referring to Tip O'Neill not by his universally used nickname but by his given name, Tom. Some younger members thought him out of touch, and his style seemed to provoke hostility from liberal, anti-clerical Roman Catholics. While Rayburn had engendered deep personal loyalty from members, there seemed a lack of enthusiasm for McCormack as Speaker. Many felt that he lacked Rayburn's "power, prestige, or popularity." Because Rayburn had become almost legendary for his love of the House and his colleagues, McCormack suffered badly by comparison. Some even thought him to be someone who promised one thing while arranging the opposite to happen. The southerners seemed troubled by McCormack's Catholicism, but his core came from the twenty to twenty-five Catholic members from Catholic, urban constituencies.[26]

In a 1962 interview, Morris Udall, who would later challenge McCormack for the Speakership, reflected the criticisms of some of the younger members: "It's easy to see why he's so unpopular in spite of the fact that he has a progressive record, is fairly able, and works like hell. He's stand-offish, high-handed, not warm at all. He's blunt and brusque, doesn't mix with the boys or go out and get drunk with them. I suppose the main thing people have against him is his total lack of tact and finesse. Just about everybody I have talked with, especially among the younger men, said they'd have voted for anybody running against McCormack." Udall's assessment, of course, was not universally held. Future Speakers Tip O'Neill and Jim Wright both had great admiration for "Mr. McCormack." He was such a formal man that neither ever called him by his given name. But both supported him. O'Neill remembered that McCormack "was tall and lean, with yellowish white hair, and he always wore a dark suit and a white shirt." But despite the fact that he was "so conservative that he didn't even burn the candle at one end," O'Neill felt that McCormack had earned his position of power in the House: "John was a great talker and the finest debater I ever heard." Nor did Wright think that his frail appearance was a fair indication of his vigor as leader: "Mr. McCormack always had a spring in his step."[27] O'Neill and Wright had internalized the lessons that McCormack taught them. As McCormack had been loyal to Rayburn, they would be loyal to him. And such loyalty would serve them well too as they rose through the ranks.

Acting as Speaker during Rayburn's final illness, McCormack had substantial support for the position. In an era when seniority meant a great deal and committee chairs held extraordinary power, McCormack was very senior. When Rayburn died, the House was in recess, and, because communications were more difficult, it was daunting for the opposition to McCormack to organize. Additionally, southern Democrats considered him the best candidate for Speaker they would likely be able to get, even if he did have a liberal voting record and was a Catholic. At least he supported agriculture subsidies, and he was not an especially able antagonist. Northern liberals recognized that McCormack, for all his personal flaws, was a liberal. These factors taken together indicated McCormack was the obvious choice to replace Rayburn. Harry Truman, for one, understood the problem of replacing someone like Rayburn; he had a somewhat similar experience when he replaced Franklin Roosevelt. He wrote McCormack kind words of encouragement but emphasized that he should not focus on filling Rayburn's shoes or worry about the critics:

> Don't you let these damned columnists bother you. Do the job as you see it and let 'em go to hell. I'm your friend and always will be come hell or high water. Your greatest asset is Mrs. John McCormick [sic] as Mrs. Truman was mine.
>
> Best of luck to you and you can be sure of at least one friend!

Despite Truman's warm wishes, McCormack's Speakership was far from a peaceful one. During an appropriations battle between Sen. Carl Hayden and House Appropriations Committee Chair Clarence Cannon, Cannon denounced the new Speaker by saying, "I have sat under ten Speakers, but I have never seen such biased and inept leadership." Such criticism may have been going through McCormack's mind when he wrote a touching postscript to a letter to H. G. Dulaney, Rayburn's former secretary. McCormack wrote six years after Rayburn's death, "I miss very much our late friend, Speaker Sam Rayburn. I wish he was here — he as Speaker and I as Majority Leader."[28] Soon, McCormack was to face a rare open challenge to his Speakership from Arizona's Morris Udall.

The Udall Challenge

By the late 1960s, McCormack's critics wondered whether the Speaker had the energy, inclination, and skill to fashion liberal legislation given the Democrats' diminished numbers. Many worried that McCormack's ties to conservative southern Democrats were too strong, while other criticisms focused on McCormack's age. One reporter wrote that McCormack "runs the U.S. House of Representatives with a venerated but shaky hand." Another said that McCormack was "so pallid and gaunt that he looks as though a strong point of order would topple him over."[29]

By January 17, 1967, a *Washington Post* editorial called on McCormack to "step down gracefully." The *Post*'s criticisms of McCormack ranged from general complaints about his leadership to more specific charges that he was too close to southerners. The *Post* specifically mentioned William Colmer, whom McCormack had put back on the Rules Committee many years before. McCormack's defenders, including Majority Leader Albert and Majority Whip Hale Boggs, took to the House floor that morning to denounce the editorial. Albert pointed to McCormack's many *recent* accomplishments, noting that "the achievements of the 89th Congress are among the greatest of any Congress in all the history of the United States. If any proof is needed, they are proof of his legislative leadership." He continued, reminding House members that McCormack was "a kind man, a Christian, a gentleman, and a personal friend who loves us all and whom we all love from the bottom of our hearts."[30]

Following Albert, a parade of supporters took to the floor to praise McCormack and condemn *The Washington Post.* Missouri's Paul Jones called the *Post* an "uptown edition of the *Daily Worker*," while John Monagan of Connecticut said that the paper "does not speak for me, does not express my opinions, nor, I know, the opinions of many other Members of the majority party with whom I have spoken this morning."[31]

Perhaps the staunchest of McCormack's defenders was South Carolina's Mendel Rivers. Citing the editorial "in which the Speaker is needlessly but very lavishly and gratuitously libeled and slandered," Rivers sought "an hour on a point of personal privilege." When told by the chair that his request did not meet the criteria to be considered "personal privilege," Rivers asked to be recognized for a "long minute."[32] Rivers defended McCormack and lavishly condemned the *Post*: "Mr. Speaker, when they undertake to vilify the Speaker of the House of Representatives of the United States, they undermine the war effort of America, they undermine the fighting man on the battlefront and the most anti-Communist man in America, and they offend the dignity and the sensibilities of each one of us. Mr. Speaker you should have recognized me on a point of personal privilege." This would not be the only storm McCormack had to weather in 1967. Younger, more liberal members continued to criticize the Speaker. But rather than responding to the criticism by being more solicitous of his colleagues, McCormack often returned fire. When one liberal member complained to McCormack about the way he was running the House, McCormack reportedly replied, "Ah, what the hell are ya' crying about?"[33]

McCormack's harshest critic was Richard Bolling. On October 27, 1967, Bolling called on McCormack to resign from the Speakership effective at the beginning of the 91st Congress. Although both Bolling and McCormack had been close Rayburn associates, they did not get along. Bolling had written, "Unlike Garner and Rayburn, there seem to be no recognizable high points, or high point, in the Congressional career of John McCormack." Bolling and many other liberal Democrats believed that McCormack was a chief impediment to important House reforms; Bolling once said that McCormack was the "greatest defender of the status quo because it made him Speaker." Appearing on a Washington, D.C., local television program, Bolling claimed that Congress lacked "very effective leadership" with McCormack at the helm and that McCormack did not have "the skill to anticipate trouble" in the House.[34]

In response to Bolling's criticism and call for resignation, McCormack counter-attacked. The following day, McCormack's office issued a press release on "Speaker's Rooms Stationery" that read: "All members have known for a long time of Mr. Bolling's keen disappointment in not being elected to a leadership position in the House. I am not going to lower the dignity of the office of Speaker by noticing his presumptuous remarks."[35]

McCormack's defenders again took to the House floor. Just as Mendel Rivers had demonstrated strong southern support for McCormack in

January, on October 30, Florida's Bob Sikes took to the floor to defend Mc-Cormack: "He is Speaker because the House trusts him, because he understands the problems of its Members, because he is tolerant, because he believes in democratic principles of Government, because by experience and ability he is the best man for the job. I am certain that if there were an election today, the Florida delegation and the House would vote solidly for him, just as it did on the day he was first elected Speaker. His is proven leadership." The challenges to McCormack waned through the remainder of the 90th Congress, but the discontent did not disappear. In April of 1968, *Business Week* quoted an unnamed Democratic member of Congress who predicted that "a strong move to unseat Speaker John McCormack will take place in the first House Democratic Caucus after the 91st Congress convenes next January." Again, contending that McCormack was out of touch with the mood of the House, this particular member cited the move to strip Adam Clayton Powell of his committee chairmanship: "When the Adam Clayton Powell thing came up last year, there were only two men who hadn't judged the temper of the House. One was Powell, and he was off some place. The other was McCormack and he was right here."[36]

If McCormack had successfully beaten back these calls for his resignation in the 90th Congress, those who sought to topple the Speaker had foreshadowed potential future opposition. At the conclusion of 1968, McCormack began to seek expressions of support for his reelection as Speaker in the 91st Congress. Although regular solicitations of the Speaker for continued support were rare in contemporary congressional politics, Rep. Kika de la Garza reminded Speaker McCormack that it was commonplace in some legislatures, trumpeting the tradition in the Texas legislature where "At the start of each session we used to have each member of the legislature sign a card pledging his support of a specific gentleman as Speaker of the Texas House of Representatives." Garza attached a sample card affirming his support: "I hereby pledge my vote and support to John W. McCormack, Member of Congress for Speaker of the 91st Congress of the U.S. House of Representatives Signed this 21st day of November, 1968."[37]

Although he did not use the pledge cards, McCormack did ask explicitly for support. To do so, McCormack put his considerable talents at counting votes, talents honed in over three decades in the House, to use. As many leadership candidates whose vote totals never approached the amount they thought were pledged to them have found, it is sometimes difficult to pin down members of Congress on clear expressions of support. Some members have a way, for instance, of saying many good things about a candidate's leadership abilities or their "affection" for a candidate without ever committing to support the candidate in a race. Here, McCormack's experience was an asset.

A look at his correspondence reveals that McCormack had two general replies to his favorable responses. First, if a member offered a clear and specific expression of support for McCormack for the Speakership of the 91st Congress, then McCormack sent them simply a general reply of gratitude. For example, Rep. Mike Kirwan wrote: "To me, John, you are tops. . . . True, like the rest of us you are putting on a few years, but that in no manner disqualifies you for the continuance of your duties as Speaker of the House. This lies only in the minds of a few who perhaps should not have been sent to Congress in the first place." And Representative John Flynt wrote, "Of course, it will be my pleasure to support you for reelection as Speaker of the 91st Congress, and I shall do so enthusiastically and without reservation." If, however, a member sent McCormack a generally worded expression of support or a vaguely positive response, he sent them a reply that clarified that he took their letter as a specific commitment to vote for him for Speaker in the January 2 caucus. For example, when Wisconsin's Clem Zablocki responded affirmatively but only made a vague reference to a "continued association" with McCormack, McCormack's "thank you" response was specific on the subject of Speakership support. He wrote, "I appreciate very much your letter of November 26 conveying your support of me for Speaker of the coming Congress." Even Congressman-elect Mario Biaggi's (D-NY) statement that "you may be sure that I shall miss no opportunity to give you my full support in advancing our great national goals, and I am looking forward to working with you in the 91st Congress" was not quite specific enough for McCormack. In response, the Speaker wrote, "Dear Mr. Biaggi: I appreciate very much your letter of Dec 6th conveying to me your support of me for Speaker of the 91st Congress." This way, there could be no mistaking the new member's commitment to McCormack in the caucus.[38]

Even among the accumulating letters of support, there were signs that some members were, at least, unenthusiastic about the prospect of "status quo" leadership. Writing to pledge his support to McCormack, California's Richard T. Hanna suggested that it "would be very helpful in unifying the elements of the House" if McCormack were to broaden the leadership to include "one or two of the medium term (8–14) Congressmen in the liberal block such as O'Hara of Michigan, Blatnik of Minnesota, Reuss of

Wisconsin, or Udall of Arizona." In his response, McCormack made no such concession, offering only that he held those members "in very high regard." Similarly, Colorado's Wayne Aspinall registered his fear that Mc-Cormack would be too accommodating to incoming president Richard Nixon. He wrote, "I would be more pleased if you could see fit to be a little bit more representative of the legislative operation—independent, that is, of the Executive position." Another member confirmed his loyalty but with a caveat. California's Jerome Waldie wrote the following: "Dear Mr. Speaker: As I have counted on you for the past 2 ½ years, you can count on me." Still, Waldie's complaint that "I would, however, like to see a greater role for the younger Members" foreshadowed his call for a vote of "no confidence" in McCormack a little over a year later.[39]

McCormack seems to have regarded obtaining such commitments as key to his maintaining the Speakership. By the end of the month, Carl Albert wrote to McCormack, saying, "I will be looking forward to working with you again" and affirming that he would again be a candidate for majority leader. Believing that Albert was perhaps his strongest potential competitor, McCormack seems to have arranged with Albert for the majority leader to send the letter. At the bottom of the letter, Albert said, "P.S. John, this is the letter I talked to you about. I have sent it out in varying forms to all members." McCormack telephoned and then wrote Albert to let him know that the Speaker considered the letter "a masterpiece."[40]

Thus, McCormack's early action at the end of the session—making clear that he had Albert's support and his continuing accumulation of pledges of support—seemed to convince the Speaker and his allies that his reelection was secure. Writing at the end of November to express "full support" for the Speaker, Jim Wright observed, "I cannot imagine that any serious effort would be pursued to elect any other person than you as Speaker. If any such effort should develop, you may certainly count upon my active and energetic help in any way you see fit to call upon me." Wright handwrote at the bottom, "P.S. I think we may already have discouraged any precipitate action in this regard."[41]

The criticism of McCormack continued, however, probably led by Richard Bolling. This is evident in Rep. William Randall's (D-MO) offer of "complete and whole-hearted support" for McCormack's reelection as Speaker "notwithstanding any possible effort to the contrary by my neighbor to the west, the gentleman from Missouri, Mr. Bolling." But according to Patrick J. Maney, even Majority Whip Hale Boggs considered a challenge to McCormack in mid-November 1968.[42]

If Bolling or even Boggs were contemplating a run, the next action against McCormack's Speakership would be taken by another member. On December 19, Washington State's Brock Adams, a second-term liberal member, sent all Democratic colleagues a letter, a copy of a recent *Washington Post* editorial hostile to McCormack, and an internal poll asking for members' anonymous feelings concerning a referendum on McCormack's reselection as Speaker and potential candidates to replace him. The card read simply:

1. There should be a new Speaker of the House of Representatives for the 91st Congress. Yes ___ No___
2. The best candidate for Speaker is _____.

Adams told colleagues that he was "personally very fond" of the Speaker and that this did not "involve a clash of personalities." Arguing that *The Washington Post* editorial he enclosed was "typical of the national reaction to the choosing of a new Speaker," Adams was seeking nominees in the event that no individual candidate chose to run against McCormack. He planned to make a caucus resolution to remove McCormack and then use the poll responses to begin the discussion of who might succeed the ousted Speaker.[43]

That same day both Kentucky's Carl Perkins and Texas' Ray Roberts sent Adams's letter to McCormack. Roberts simply wrote, "Dear Mr. Speaker: Attached is correspondence which I have received from one of your fine liberal friends." In the face of this potential challenge, Perkins offered the Speaker encouragement: "This group will be able to muster so few votes, it will just be pitiful against your outstanding leadership. . . . I would tell them that I am not only a candidate in 1968 but that I intend to be a candidate in 1970, 1972, and all through the years in the foreseeable future."[44]

Inasmuch as the Adams effort may have been the seed for the Udall challenge that would follow, it was also another opportunity for McCormack's friends to rally to his support. When Adams's Washington State colleague Rep. Edith Green wrote to McCormack of her support for his continued reelection, she expressed disapproval of Adams's tactics: "One John McCormack is worth 50 Brock Adamses (as I see it) and I hope that you know he does not represent my views or the views of a great many of my close friends in the House."[45]

McCormack quickly rallied southern members. In the end, his support was particularly strong from that region, where some members expressed their tolerance of differences with him and their admiration of him as a presiding officer. Texas' Bob Poage wrote: "My office has been sending me clippings from the Washington press. I gather that some of our extreme liberal brethren, liberal with other's rights and properties, that is, have been starting their old refrain about kicking out the Speaker. Of course, I realize that nothing is going to come of their malicious campaign but I just want you to know that while I sometimes get irritated and sometimes disagree with you as well as all other Presiding Officers I ever knew and as some of my committeemen do with their chairman, I think we have a fine and outstanding Speaker. I haven't any intention of lining up with this group of critics." Texan Jack Brooks volunteered to second McCormack's nomination for Speaker.[46]

Even if Patrick Maney is correct that Hale Boggs considered a run against McCormack, by the second week of December, the ever-mercurial Boggs was firmly in the McCormack camp, even delivering the support of the Louisiana delegation to the Speaker. Along with Edward Hébert, Boggs wrote to McCormack on December 11 on behalf of the Louisiana delegation assuring him of their unanimous support.[47]

However, concern that Dick Bolling might turn the Adams effort into an opportunity to challenge McCormack spread even to his home-state delegation. Bolling's Missouri colleague, Rep. Richard Ichord, wrote to McCormack to "assure" him of support and appended this comment: "P.S. I am assuming, of course, that you are making no concessions to my colleague, Dick Bolling." Of course, there was little chance that McCormack would succumb to any such pressure, and he assured Ichord that no deal had been made: "I noted your handwritten postscript. You need not worry about me along the lines indicated in your postscript message."[48]

As it turned out, however, neither Brock Adams nor Dick Bolling became McCormack's greatest worry. Instead, it was Arizona representative Morris K. Udall who would challenge McCormack in the Democrats' organizing caucus. Frank Thompson of New Jersey, who had handled Bolling's unsuccessful campaign for the majority leadership in 1961, managed Udall's efforts. In an extraordinary move to defeat McCormack, he called Arkansas representative and Ways and Means Committee chair Wilbur Mills, one of the real powers in the House, to enlist his assistance. Mills demurred; he explicitly did not want to see McCormack mistreated like he believed Republican floor leader Joe Martin had been when he had been displaced by Charles Halleck (R-Indiana) in 1959. He also feared that Bolling had instituted the dump McCormack effort and had to be reassured that Bolling was not involved. When Thompson suggested that a Mills-Udall ticket could be successful, Mills seemed willing but stressed that he had no ambitions to be Speaker and that he was contemplating retirement in a term or two. Mills thought Albert should be included, and though Albert had had a recent heart attack, Thompson agreed that Albert should be given a chance to run and should be supported if he did. But if Albert did not run, Thompson said the liberals would put together their own slate.[49]

Later Thompson spoke to Phil Landrum of Georgia, telling him that Mills was the only southerner who could be sold to the North. There seemed to be a belief that if Mills sought the Speakership, he would win and would take national positions on issues such as civil rights. Again, Thompson stressed that Albert should be given a chance to run, but Landrum thought Albert's health would prevent him from doing so. Rostenkowski of Chicago, Landrum then noted, would also like a role in the leadership. Thompson, however, told Landrum that if Mills refused to run, Udall would run.[50]

Prior to declaring against McCormack, Udall called Mills, who refused a deal where he would be the candidate for Speaker. He told Udall that he was not ambitious for the job; moreover, in return for his support of McCormack as majority leader over a southern challenger many years earlier, McCormack had helped Mills get on Ways and Means. He was, Mills told Udall, close to McCormack, and they had fought many battles together. When Udall called Albert, Albert was quick to list McCormack's shortcomings: how he had prevented Albert from reforming the House and McCormack had overruled his decisions when Albert had tried to work out scheduling issues. Albert complained about Majority Whip Boggs and his drinking and laziness, seeming to suggest that Udall should challenge Boggs instead of McCormack. And Albert tried to talk Udall out of sending the letter announcing his candidacy but also told Udall that he understood.[51] Albert, however, was certainly not going to challenge McCormack.

McCormack should not have been caught off guard by Udall's challenge. Udall sent a lengthy response to his solicitation of support on November 27. Udall wrote that whereas "the easy and painless answer for me to write would be a short one, pledging my full and unqualified support for this term and as many more as you might want . . . honesty with you and myself compels me to say that I cannot make the unqualified statement that I will vote for you in all circumstances which might possibly arise."

Reading on, McCormack should have perceived something of a warning that a potential challenge was in the offing; Udall wrote:

> You will make a serious mistake if you conclude that the talk of new leadership in the House comes only from Dick Bolling and a few others of his point of view. I have been surprised at the kind and number of members who have privately expressed the same conclusion I have stated for myself above. These members come from all levels of seniority, and all sections of the country, and all different political philosophies. There are members who like and respect you, but who believe that for the good of the party in the new situation it faces, you ought to retire as Speaker, and yet remain in the House as a senior and most influential Member as long as you wish.
>
> This is probably not the answer you wanted or expected to receive from me. If it sounds presumptuous, I apologize. I hope you accept it in the spirit in which it is offered.

And McCormack's reply to Udall dripped with sarcasm:

> Dear Morris: I received your letter of Nov 27, which I have read not only with interest, but with special interest. Being human, I appreciate very much the very nice things you said about me in your letter. In your letter you made a suggestion and you said, "If it sounds presumptuous, I apologize." Having the high regard for you that I do, I would not consider any letter from you to be "presumptuous," but in all frankness, I must say that if such a suggestion came from almost anyone else, I would consider it to be "presumptuous."
>
> I note what you have to say about some Members speaking to you in private. That is naturally to be expected, because none of us are perfect. As you are frank in this respect, now I know you will respect my frankness in the following observation that on a number of occasions quite a few Members have criticized you in my presence, but I have always defended you. It is impossible for you, Morris, to please everyone, and I recognize the fact that it is impossible for me to please everyone.

New York representative Jack Bingham wrote McCormack urging him to retire, a suggestion McCormack called "most rotten, arrogant and disrespectful" and, more than that, "cheap." McCormack still had plenty of fight, refusing, for example, to shake hands with Frank Thompson. When Udall called to inform McCormack that he was going to challenge the Speaker, Udall wrote that they talked of flood control and electric power.

But when the topic turned to Udall's challenge, McCormack told him that he would "hardly expect that from you — very sorry to hear [it]."[52]

Larry L. King wrote of Udall's phone conversation as if McCormack was so out of touch that he could scarcely comprehend that he was being challenged: "On Christmas Eve day, 1968, Mo Udall telephoned old John McCormack in South Boston to announce that . . . he would run against him. . . . It was difficult because the old man kept hoo-hawing season's greetings." Of Udall's letter that formally announced his challenge, King said, "Old John McCormack may not have bothered to read it all." And, of the challenge itself, King wrote, "The old man could no more comprehend Mo Udall's 'symbolic' candidacy than an orangutan would be capable of grasping the concept of infinity."[53]

Udall's contention (and King's reporting thereof) that McCormack was caught off guard by the challenge is probably not correct.[54] Only two weeks before their phone conversation, McCormack sent his biting response to Udall. It may be that McCormack could not appreciate the "new politics" coalition that Udall was trying to put together to run the House, but similarly Udall and other reformers had difficulty understanding the importance and difficulty of maintaining the broad alliance that McCormack sought to protect. More than likely, Udall's implication that McCormack was out of touch was more a justification of his challenge than an accurate assessment of McCormack's understanding of their conversation.

After informing McCormack of his intent, Udall composed an announcement of his candidacy on December 26, 1968. As an additional courtesy, Udall sent McCormack a copy of the letter in which he handwrote at the end, "Dear John — As per our phone conversation this is the letter and memorandum I'm sending to each Democrat. I wanted you to have your copy before any one else. Sincerely, Mo." Udall's six-page letter would soon be sent to the rest of the House Democratic caucus. It announced Udall's candidacy, explained his reasons for making the challenge, and promised a series of changes should he be elected, such as combating the executive branch more effectively, increasing meetings of the Democratic caucus, and running a more service-oriented leadership. Emphasizing his "genuine respect and affection for Speaker McCormack," Udall offered, "For me there is no joy in making this challenge to a fine man who has treated me with every courtesy. I do so only because I deeply believe there is an overriding need for new directions and new leadership."[55]

Udall first argued that Democrats had to revitalize their leadership to compete with a reinvigorated Republican Party that had just won the White House, had revamped its internal congressional leadership structures, and was cutting into Democratic strength in the South. Udall wrote: "Old political alignments and loyalties are changing in every section of the country; the Republicans are moving strongly and often effectively to appeal to traditional Democratic voters and to the millions of new and younger voters."

Secondly, Udall claimed that his challenge resulted from a democratizing impulse within the House for members who sought greater control of their leadership. Noting that a "wide spectrum" of members "privately and sincerely want a change," he observed many of the norms of House leadership races by emphasizing that he merely wanted the will of the caucus to be reflected in the outcome of the balloting. Always promising to accept the will of the caucus should they choose to continue with McCormack as Speaker, Udall also, possibly as a swipe at Bolling's 1967 televised comments challenging McCormack, promised to "limit" his campaign "to personal contacts with . . . my colleagues" and to "refrain from any press releases or interviews, public statements or the like dealing with this matter."

And, third, Udall defended his challenge to McCormack against the charge that it would serve to weaken the national Democratic Party precisely at the time that it was already reeling from the November 1968 electoral defeats:

> I am told by some that a challenge to existing leadership at this time will weaken us as a party; that those who want change should wait, refrain from rocking the boat, etc. I have heard and heeded this counsel before, but no significant changes have occurred. I really cannot accept the idea that constructive, rational, responsible airing of differences in Caucus is bad for a political party. . . . If a majority chooses to continue our leadership, any grumbling is put in proper focus and laid to rest as the kind of ordinary complaining that every leader has to face. With any doubts cleared away, our elected Speaker will be strengthened in representing all of us, and will have the kind of clearcut mandate he needs. If, on the other hand, a majority of our number really wants a change of leadership, that change will occur. Either way, the Democratic party will be stronger and can go forward united.

In the letter, Udall also laid the groundwork for a few tactical maneuvers. First, he wanted to emphasize that he did not represent merely the liberal Brock Adams group; he mentioned that he had "consulted" only "a very few trusted colleagues" before deciding to run and that he was "the candidate of no individual Member or group of Members." Secondly, Udall stressed the importance of continuing the recent caucus tradition of having the election conducted by secret ballot. Wisely, Udall surmised that his long-shot chance to topple the sitting Speaker was improved if members felt insulated by a secret ballot to vote without fear of retribution from the top leadership. Third, he made the extraordinary "solemn pledge" that should he defeat McCormack in the caucus, he would open a new round of balloting for any other Speakership candidate.

To be sure, Udall hoped to win the Speakership, but he knew that the chances of toppling McCormack were improved by making the first vote an "anti-McCormack" vote rather than a "pro-Udall" vote. Indeed, even if after the first balloting Carl Albert decided to run for the now-vacant Speakership, Udall would be in a strong position to succeed Albert as majority leader and/or to be appointed or elected whip.

From the beginning, Udall thought he had a solid base of support. To be sure, McCormack dominated the House establishment, but in addition to younger liberal members, at least a few more established House members, frustrated with McCormack's leadership, supported the Arizonan. Frank Thompson, for example, sent a belated reply to McCormack's November solicitation of support by telegram: "Attempted to reach you by telephone today in order to inform you of my intention to nominate Morris Udall to be Speaker of the 91st Congress. Will try to reach you by phone tomorrow. I wish it clearly understood that my participation in no way detracts from my admiration or respect or friendship for you. You have assisted me in many ways over many years it is my feeling that a great many members desire at least an opportunity in Caucus to have their preferences expressed and to resolve the question of leadership in the New Congress. Whatever the outcome may be I shall continue to support the elected leadership as I have always done in the past, Respectfully, FT." Though Udall felt he had broad support, the McCormack forces remained confident of victory but wary of unforeseen last-minute tricks. William Colmer of Mississippi chaired the caucus. Perhaps fearing a liberal attempt to gain an advantage over McCormack, he refused to recognize Thomas Rees (D-CA), who sought to propose an amendment to caucus rules. Many liberals likely saw this as a serious abridgement of their right to participate in the caucus. Indeed, Rees's fellow California liberal representative Don Edwards observed, "Two years ago I was allowed to offer an amendment in caucus, but this year they wouldn't allow it unless we made prearrangement with the Establishment!" Edwards saw this as an ominous sign "that the conservative coalition is hardening and the McCormack-Boggs-Albert arrangement with the Southern Democrats is pumping along better than ever."[56]

In the caucus, Udall received only 58 votes to McCormack's 178. Udall's effort was probably harmed by the early threats of Bolling and Adams in that when Udall finally entered the race and began the process of obtaining commitments, McCormack had been soliciting expressions of support for over a month. Thus, even if Udall potentially had the strength to compete, by the time he got in the race, most members probably considered themselves "honorably pledged" to support McCormack.

The emerging liberal strength in the Democratic caucus in the late 1960s ultimately did not have the ability to provide a successful challenge to the establishment leadership. The McCormack team had sufficient liberal leanings for most members but still maintained its ties to the southern committee establishment. As Florida's Charles Bennett wrote to reassure McCormack, "I have found no opposition except among extreme liberals — and they are in a tiny minority. Have no fear!" Udall's challenge did not expand beyond a committed but small core of younger liberals. One observer noted that Udall was "leery of getting too close to the Adams group." In the end, Udall's support never expanded beyond the Adams group. Indeed, just before the caucus met, the Adams group scheduled a strategy meeting; the number of organizers (fifteen) and attendees (forty) is extraordinarily close to Udall's total votes.[57]

Ultimately, Udall's challenge to McCormack increased his visibility as an emerging potential leader and likely reinforced his support among younger House liberals. But there were costs too. When Udall would make his run against Hale Boggs for majority leader in 1971, he would encounter three key roadblocks. First, the potential liberal coalition that might support him against the southerner Boggs was split between Udall's "new politics" wing of liberals and the more traditional labor-backed liberals who would support James O'Hara. Udall had cast a key vote in 1965 against repeal of the "right to work" provisions (section 14b) of the Taft-Hartley Act. Since then, labor had been poised to oppose him on those grounds. Among McCormack's planning papers prepared when Udall challenged him was a brief note written in McCormack's hand on "Speaker's Rooms" stationery pointing to the weakness: "Udall votes against repeal of 14 B, July 28, 1965. . . . Udall voted to recommit; voted no passage of Bill." The second, and perhaps more detrimental, roadblock was that a number of northeastern liberals (Tip O'Neill among them) refused to support Udall out of loyalty to McCormack. His challenge to McCormack made Udall something of a hero to some of the press and House liberals, but it also reinforced opposition against any future Udall run for the leadership. Third, Udall expended some of his credibility in counting votes on this contest. Central to Udall's end-game strategy was to generate a sense he was likely to win, creating a bandwagon effect among uncommitted members. Accordingly, Udall claimed he had 85 "absolutely solid votes" against McCormack. When he asserted broad support in 1971, many House members questioned his numbers.[58]

In fact, Udall's private count was more out of whack than his public claims. In a January 1969 head count, Udall thought he had 102 favorable votes and 96 negative votes with six additional votes leaning in his direction. The remaining votes were unknown. When the quick-witted Udall actually got only 58 votes, he quipped that he must not be able to count. The only two explanations for the vote, claimed Udall, were either that his colleagues were liars or that he could not count. Since he knew that his colleagues would not lie, the only possible explanation was that Udall had poor math skills.[59]

In the aftermath of the Speaker's contest, Udall contemplated what had gone wrong in his campaign and about who had betrayed him. He concluded that the House was filled with ambition and jealousy. Key members such as Mills, Albert, and Rostenkowski had ambitions for leadership, thought Udall, and they feared Udall would "leap-frog" ahead of them to power. Thus, they opposed Udall. Illustratively, Mills concluded that Udall's campaign might hurt the South. Further, Udall concluded that Mills thought that Udall's key young liberal supporters such as Brock Adams were out to destroy the seniority system, something that was bound to displease a committee baron like Mills. Additionally, Udall thought he was hurt by McCormack's early effort to obtain written pledges of support for the Speakership. Despite his quip to the contrary, Udall clearly believed numerous members had lied to him. The secret ballot prevented him from identifying the culprits. He also noted that he had learned that liberals such as Dingell of Michigan and Charlie Wilson of California were not necessarily interested in reforming the House. Thus, although he counted on universal liberal support, liberal non-reformers supported McCormack. Pres. Lyndon Johnson had also supported McCormack, in part because of Udall's opposition to the Vietnam War. Wrote Udall: "LBJ sent word, especially to the Texas delegation to shoot me down because of my stand on Vietnam." Texas Democrat Ray Roberts, a close personal friend of LBJ's, told Udall that the administration felt that Udall "had run out on the President on Vietnam. This is confirmed by Dick Bolling apparently on information through Jim Symington." Finally, Udall noted that in reference to the Speakership, "An office like this is not just on popularity but deals with other sections and groups." And McCormack's supporters were quite good on the deals and alliances.[60]

Udall also offered a broad explanation for his defeat, one central to the theme of this book: "Speaker McCormack gained his strength through a particular alignment of forces — mainly the big city congressmen and the Southerners. Because of that alignment he has to perform in a certain way, taking into consideration his power base. . . . Meanwhile, we will continue with the majority Speaker McCormack put together — a majority that really goes back to the New Deal period." But could that New Deal coalition of southerners and northern big city congressmen survive in the House of the 1970s? Even as Udall was losing the Speakership race, he recognized that McCormack was near retirement. "There was talk," he wrote, "that McCormack will retire in two years." The next Speaker, he thought, would be Carl Albert, a man who reflected the old Austin-Boston connection. Though from Oklahoma, his district was adjacent to the north edge of Rayburn's old district, and he was a Rayburn ally. But in Albert, Udall saw a different type of leader. He would be the first Speaker born in the twentieth century, and, thought Udall, he had lots of drive, ideas, and considerable ability. To replace McCormack, Albert was "the obvious man to step up to Speaker and I would like to see this happen."[61]

If the Udall challenge was not enough to encourage McCormack to retire, the liberal-reform wing of the Democrats kept up the pressure. At a meeting between the Speaker and the House Education and Labor Committee members, William Clay of Missouri, forty-one years junior to McCormack, spoke to the Speaker: "Look, I'm not interested in what you did before I was born." When McCormack replied, "I think some of you want to run the House," Frank Thompson of New Jersey responded, "That's perfectly true, some of us do." When Jerome Waldie of California accused McCormack of failing in his leadership role, McCormack replied, "You have no right to criticize me." In response, Jerome Waldie wrote to McCormack and told him that he would ask the Democratic caucus for a vote of no confidence in the House leadership. In April 1970, Bolling continued his call for McCormack's retirement, characterizing McCormack as "a sad, tired, shaken shadow of a man who has outlived his time and his competence" who was "no fit symbol of leadership for a party that must appeal to the young and the vigorous middle-aged as well as to our older citizens." Bolling suggested several possible replacements including himself, Carl Albert, Wilbur Mills, James O'Hara, Morris Udall, and Dan Rostenkowski.[62]

Perhaps in part because of the vocal opposition in the House, McCormack had election opposition in 1970, thirty-year-old Daniel Houton. It appears that Richard Bolling may have offered encouragement to Houton. Bolling had three folders of news clippings on McCormack, and on the back of an unrelated clipping photocopy in the McCormack file is an address for Houton and Houton's phone number with the notation that he could be reached after 6:30 P.M. The pressure began to show on McCormack. For instance, at a press conference in March, 1970, as Carl Albert shook his head in disbelief, the normally composed McCormack called one reporter "a no good" and another "a mouthpiece."[63]

McCormack in 1970 — The Waldie Resolution

On February 2, 1970, halfway through the 91st Congress, Jerome Waldie wrote to McCormack advising him that he would offer a resolution in the February 18 Democratic caucus that expressed "no confidence" in McCormack and the rest of the top House Democratic leadership. Waldie complained that the current leadership offered "no challenge or opportunity for many concerned Members in their understandable zeal to have some role of significance in shaping legislation." Waldie's resolution had capped a series of media statements he made critical of the leadership.[64]

In response to Waldie's media campaign and in anticipation of the February 18 caucus vote, McCormack issued a statement to the press that said:

I received a letter from Congressman Waldie, and I read with interest the statements he and another member of the House [Bolling], who is not considered a fan of mine, gave to the press.

The synopsis of the situation seems to be as follows:

1) Waldie is very grateful to me for all that I have done for him;

2) Waldie wants to remove Carl Albert, Hale Boggs and myself because, in part at least, he is unhappy that the United States House of Representatives passed a resolution with which he did not agree;

3) Waldie states that he cannot win the fight that he is waging; and

4) At least one member of Congress, who is in sympathy with

Waldie's objectives, has criticized Waldie for waging a contest at the wrong time.

Mr. Waldie's criticism of our leadership in the House is apparently made more for personal publicity than for the improvement of our party. I am not interested in contributing to a dialogue that renders a disservice to the Democratic Party, so any comments I have to make on this matter will be made to the Caucus.

I will say that I share Mr. Waldie's view that the Members of the House will demonstrate their confidence in the leadership of Mr. Albert, Mr. Boggs and myself by their vote on February 18th.

In an article entitled "Such Ingratitude," *The Nation* wrote, "That statement alone should disqualify him [McCormack] for further tenure. He seems to regard politics as a succession of *quid pro quos*." Still, Waldie also regarded the relationship as one of *"quid pro quos"*; one need only recall Waldie's offer of support for McCormack at the end of 1968 when he wrote, "Dear Mr. Speaker: As I have counted on you for the past 2½ years, you can count on me."[65]

The Waldie resolution received a great deal of coverage, but it had no chance of success. In the February 18 caucus, the Waldie resolution was tabled by a vote of 192 to 23. To be sure, the votes in support of the Waldie resolution are difficult to interpret and clearly underestimate the discontent with Speaker McCormack. Indeed, the resolution to table the Waldie resolution was introduced by McCormack's longtime foe, Richard Bolling, who claimed that he offered the motion to table because he did not want the Waldie resolution, which would clearly fail, to be taken as a "phony" vote of confidence.

Less than a month after the failure of the Waldie resolution, House insiders were contemplating the Speakership of the 92d Congress. A scandal involving his staff was hounding McCormack as he was contemplating another term. It was likely that yet another challenge would emerge. As one close observer, Jack Beidler, wrote, "John McCormack is still in the race to succeed himself. . . . He may eventually decide to quit; it is almost a sure thing that the Speakership will be contested whether he does or not. Those who are most likely to run for the office have sufficient political support of their own to make his defeat a probability. His traditional support comes form the Southern-big city coalition which has dominated House Democrats since New Deal days. The two parts of the coalition each have a candidate, Mills for the Southerners and Rostenkowski for the big city Democrats." Championing James G. O'Hara of Michigan as the one candidate who would "make the most able and effective liberal Speaker," Beidler claimed that "McCormack's continued tenure as Speaker is a disaster for the country and the Democratic Party."[66]

On May 20, 1970, McCormack announced that he would not seek re-election to the House or the Speakership. It was no wonder that one of the reasons McCormack gave for his retirement was that he was "tired."[67]

In a career that dated from before the New Deal, McCormack shows the transformation in the House Democratic Party during his forty years of service. While McCormack remained steadfast to his version of liberalism, the southern-dominated party he entered in the late 1920s steadily moved in a northern and western direction, all the while becoming more liberal. Considered a liberal early in his career, by the late 1960s and early 1970s, the House's liberals were McCormack's challengers and detractors.

Indeed, McCormack's place in the party had shifted considerably since he first entered the leadership in 1940. Whereas southerners were an impediment to McCormack's accepting the minority leadership after the 1946 elections, by the end of the 1960s, *The Nation* reported that outside of New England, they were his primary support and that he had "smoother relations with the Southern wing of the party than did his Texas predecessor, Sam Rayburn."[68]

Although McCormack's closeness to southerners was obviously overstated by *The Nation* for political effect, it does point out an ironic development in McCormack's career: McCormack had entered the leadership as a key representative of the emerging liberal part of the coalition from the Northeast, and he would leave it a relic of the past, considered too conservative for the developing "new politics" of the 1960s and 1970s. Perhaps that characterization was a bit unfair, for though there was a constant drumbeat of criticism, McCormack had presided over the New Frontier of John Kennedy and the Great Society of Lyndon Johnson.

In McCormack's retirement announcement, he also declared his support for Carl Albert as the next Speaker. "While I will not be a member of the next Congress," McCormack said, "if I were I would have great pleasure in voting for Carl Albert for speaker."[69]

**W**ith Rayburn's death, a great void was left in the leadership of the House Democrats. At issue was not only who would replace Rayburn, but how the fragile coalition could be maintained through the Kennedy years. A relevant issue was which member might most closely bring Rayburn's skills to bear on the Congress. Although Richard Bolling of Missouri often claimed to be Sam Rayburn's protégé, many other leaders in the House also felt entitled to that label, including Carl Albert, Hale Boggs, and Wilbur Mills.[1] All were men who would become contestants for leadership in the House of Representatives in the 1960s and 1970s.

Carl Albert

The great battle — the public battle — over which one of Sam Rayburn's boys would become his political heir was fought in late 1961 and early 1962 over the majority leadership. Bolling had been close to Rayburn and had served as his chief voice on the Rules Committee and his envoy within the liberal wing of the Democratic Party for years. Of the many talented young men that Rayburn took under wing, Bolling was one of the brightest and certainly the most scholarly. In his later years, Bolling claimed that when he and Rayburn had talked about the succession to the Speakership, Rayburn had told him that to be elected, one had to be well-liked. The message for Bolling was, of course, that he would have to overcome his image as the Speaker's "hatchet-man" and that he would need to improve on his far from lovable personality. While Rayburn held him in high esteem and considered him a dear friend, others were put off by Bolling's personality. Carl Albert, the Rayburn protégé that Bolling opposed for the majority leadership in 1962, described Bolling's personality: "Bolling has a to-hell-with-you, you-son-of-a-bitch, you-don't-know-anything attitude about him." Without that "gruff and abrasive" style, Albert thought Bolling would have become Speaker.[2]

Rayburn kept an eye out for bright, hardworking congressmen who could work with him. Wright Patman, a Texas congressman from an adjoining district and a close friend to Rayburn, noticed Bolling's work on the Banking Committee and brought him to one of Rayburn's Board of Education meetings — drinking, talking, and political strategy sessions that Rayburn held at the end of each day of Congress. Just as John Nance Garner had, Rayburn used these sessions to judge the character and quality of his young colleagues. Soon, Rayburn issued Bolling a standing invitation to the board meetings, and over time, a real affection developed between the two men. In turn, Bolling earned Rayburn's respect and became a major leadership strategist.[3]

The battle for proximity to Rayburn was a relevant concern throughout the period after the 1946 elections, when the Republicans earned control of the House, relegating Rayburn to minority leader status. As previously noted, Rayburn was reluctant to take the reduced leadership role, feeling that he would be "freer and more effective to take the Floor on the larger questions . . . if I were not in the position of minority leader. I feel this very deeply." Ultimately, Rayburn took the job despite his reluctance. Again after the 1952 election, some believed that Rayburn would retire from the leadership. Actually Rayburn was far more willing to undertake minority leadership after the 1952 elections than he had been in 1946, but that was unclear to many House members and other top Democrats. At the request of Adlai Stevenson and Harry Truman, Bolling visited Rayburn in Bonham to convince him to remain as Democratic leader. In the course of the conversation, Rayburn mentioned that he thought Francis Walter of Pennsylvania would be a good successor, but Walter had badly damaged his credibility with non-southern Democrats through his service on the Un-American Activities Committee. Bolling emphasized Walter's weakness. Another likely successor was John McCormack, Rayburn's longtime majority leader. Bolling, however, had never gotten along with McCormack.[4]

The discussion proved irrelevant since Rayburn remained in the leadership until his death in November 1961. By that time McCormack was a logical successor and was selected for the Speaker post easily. Some thought that McCormack would serve only a short time because of his advanced age. After a short service as Speaker, he might leave the office to a younger and more able person. Though McCormack had broad support, he also had vocal critics among younger members, especially Richard Bolling. Indeed, for a short time, Bolling considered challenging McCormack for the Speakership.[5] It quickly became clear, however, that such a challenge would be futile. Instead, Bolling chose to run for majority leader.

Bolling would find that race difficult as well, because he would be challenging the majority whip, Carl Albert of Oklahoma. Unlike the arrogant Bolling, Albert was well liked. Albert had come to the House in 1947 and became whip in 1955 when Percy Priest of Tennessee left that post to become chair of the Interstate and Foreign Commerce Committee. At the time of Albert's selection, Hale Boggs and Wilbur Mills, both allies of Rayburn, seemed the favorites for Priest's replacement, but Rayburn and McCormack chose Albert. Albert had not known he was in the running, but Rayburn said he had long had leadership potential "since you sat there on the floor every day and listened to every speech and watched every vote. Since you showed us that you loved the House of Representatives." Then Rayburn told him, "We believe you have enough sense not to make people think you can drive them anywhere, but we think you have finesse enough to lead them part of the way."[6] At the same time Albert became whip, a new position of deputy whip was created for Hale Boggs of Louisiana.

From the beginning, Boggs supported Albert for majority leader. Although Albert did not announce for the position until November 19, 1961, the day after Rayburn's funeral, the campaign kicked off even before Rayburn's death.[7] Boggs, for example, wrote Albert on November 13 that he had had "a very nice talk" with McCormack and that he had "talked to a great many people and everything is okay." Boggs also included an article by respected reporter Doris Fleeson noting that McCormack was not equal to the task of being Speaker. Furthermore, the tension between McCormack and Kennedy had grown when McCormack backed the Catholic bishops and helped kill Kennedy's education bill. It also noted the potential problem of having a Catholic president (Kennedy), a Catholic Senate leader (Mike Mansfield), and a Catholic Speaker (McCormack). Fleeson thought it unlikely that JFK would intervene in the Speakership race, but if he did, she claimed Kennedy would favor Richard Bolling.[8]

Bolling had cultivated support within the Kennedy administration. He had told Robert Kennedy of his plans to challenge Albert. Bolling said that he told Kennedy, "I do not expect to have any help from anybody unless I am sure I can win, and two or three votes might make the difference." But, said Bolling, "I never got that close. So I asked for no help and I got no help." Brooklyn congressman Emmanuel Celler told the New York Democratic delegation that President Kennedy had told him he had no plans to interfere in the majority leader race. Bolling also tried unsuccessfully to get the support of Mayor Wagner of New York City. He did get the backing of his close friend, former president Harry Truman, who phoned some old friends to solicit support for Bolling.⁹

Stewart Udall, Kennedy's secretary of interior and a former member of Congress, tried to prevent McCormack's accession to the Speakership and, when that failed, backed Bolling for majority leader. But Udall's actions did not come with Kennedy's blessing; Albert received assurance from Kennedy Congressional Liaison Larry O'Brien that the administration would not get involved. Albert met with President Kennedy and O'Brien on December 14. Though he claimed the majority leader's race was not discussed, that meeting may have been when he received assurance that the administration would stay neutral.¹⁰

Regardless of whether Bolling or Albert won, the spirit of Sam Rayburn would be present. Rayburn felt fondness for Bolling but also for Albert, telling Tom Steed of Oklahoma that Albert had excellent speaking skills and was the brightest young member of the House. Invited as a regular to the Board of Education meetings from his first term, Albert, a Rhodes Scholar, thought that Rayburn liked him because of his education, oratory ability, scholarly accomplishment, voting record, and leadership abilities. Rayburn also had an affinity for Albert's district, "comfort with this part of the country." That district proximity — their districts were separated only by the Red River — was one key to Rayburn's support:

My mother and her father were born in that district [Rayburn's], and I had dozens of relatives living there. One of Mr. Rayburn's brothers lived for a while in my own district. His home in Bonham was only six miles from the Oklahoma border. I made it a point to visit Mr. Rayburn in Bonham as soon as I had won my first primary. During the next few years, I returned often. We took to fishing together once in a while — Mr. Rayburn used to say that he would rather catch a two-inch fish than spend two days playing golf — in Lake Texoma, which lapped across our districts' lines. He bought his alfalfa down in Yuba, in my district, and we would talk for hours, leaning against a truck.... Sam Rayburn loved the people with honest dirt under their fingernails. The men and women who toiled in the cotton patches, cornfields, and peanut rows of the southwest and the Red River valley — these were the ones he called the real people. He looked unblinkingly for one who might represent them as well and as powerfully as he did.

When Rayburn and McCormack named Albert whip, Rayburn knew the potential consequences. He told Albert, "You can be Speaker of this House if you play your cards right. You and I come from the best part of the United States to equate with the whole country."[11]

To be Speaker, however, Albert would have to first become majority leader. Though a few members had reservations about McCormack as Speaker, one unnamed Democrat summarized a common feeling saying, "I don't think John will be a great Speaker in any sense of the word, but I just don't think you can slap him in the face by naming someone else." Albert Rains of Alabama contemplated a race against McCormack for the Speakership but never formally announced. Congressman Frank Boykin of Alabama wrote McCormack and assured him, "I am sure that Albert Rains, who is a cousin of mine, will not oppose you. I think what he wants is to get some publicity." On the other hand, Boykin thought, Bolling really did want to be Speaker.[12]

As might be expected, press reports speculated about several potential rivals to McCormack. Doris Fleeson wrote that Rayburn might have tapped Francis Walter as his successor before Walter had become the embittered chair of the House Un-American Activities Committee. She also noted that Rayburn had been close to Carl Albert, Hale Boggs, Richard Bolling, and Wilbur Mills. Had the Speakership become vacant in 1958, an article in *Time* noted, Mills might have become the successor, but a redistricting under segregationist governor Orval Faubus in Arkansas, an inept performance as chair of Ways and Means in 1959 on several issues, and his being overcautious in dealing with Republicans had hurt his chances. An Associated Press report added Albert Rains to the list but claimed that Bolling was widely regarded as Rayburn's personal choice.[13]

On October 11, Kennedy mentioned at his press conference that he would not interfere in the selection of a Speaker. But one article noted, "To experienced observers here, however, it is inconceivable that the President's lieutenants will not deeply — but discreetly — concern themselves in the affair on the President's behalf.... There are reports they already have begun to do so." McCormack, however, would probably get the job. Though McCormack had good qualities, he was "pedestrian," and there were doubts about his leadership capacity. Moreover, he was not preferred by the administration. One article noted that while McCormack had a "large personal following in the House, particularly among older leaders," he lacked the force and political instincts that would make a good leader, and, it seemed, he would be no match for Republican leader Charles Halleck of Indiana.[14]

Even Albert received some encouragement to try for the Speakership.

U.S. News and World Report noted that Albert was mentioned as the likely Speaker if Rayburn did not return. Additionally, federal judge Stephen Chandler wrote to Carl Albert that he hoped Albert would get the Speakership if he wanted it. Ada, Oklahoma, oilman W. A. "Gus" Delaney wrote Albert that he had influential friends and would support him for the Speakership. But if Bolling were nominated by the Democratic caucus, he would work to elect Republican Charles Halleck as Speaker. Douglas Kiker wrote that McCormack was not a shoo-in for the Speakership, because he was opposed by a coalition of liberal Democrats and conservative southern Democrats. The logical compromise candidate, Kiker wrote, was Albert, "a man who gets along with everybody."[15]

McCormack, in contrast, had difficulty with southern Democrats because of his Catholicism and his lack of diplomacy among members. Some liberals disliked him because he killed the federal school aid bill and because of his failure to promote the financing of the foreign aid bill. McCormack was not close to Kennedy whereas Albert would be more effective in delivering votes for the administration. However, McCormack had long experience in the leadership, leading Hale Boggs to explain that seniority and previous position made his election virtually automatic. To deny McCormack would require something very unusual, such as strong and effective administration opposition to him. Boggs noted that neither Kennedy nor Johnson did anything to prevent McCormack's ascending to the Speakership. They regarded the election as a matter of the House handling its own affairs.[16]

But Albert was a political realist. For example, Charles V. Gilmore wrote that he would like to help get Albert elected as Speaker and offered to contact James A. Farley, Roosevelt's former postmaster-general, on Albert's behalf. In response, Albert wrote that "I think I shall go for Majority Leader, because I think McCormack will pretty well have the Speakership sewed up; but I have hesitated to do anything in view of the fact that the Speaker [Rayburn] is still with us."[17]

Albert had correctly calculated the odds. He could not beat McCormack and would have to settle for majority leader. He was further hampered because he could not overtly campaign while Rayburn was alive. That would be unbecoming and politically costly.

Even Albert's selection as majority leader would not be automatic. Briefly, even the exceptionally abrasive Wayne Hays of Ohio considered being a candidate. The chairs of the Columbiana County Democratic Committee solicited Congressman Burr Harrison's vote to support Hays.

A note clipped on the solicitation probably best described the general feeling about Hays's candidacy, "In the name of God, what next?"[18] Though Hays might have liked to run, the battle quickly turned into an Albert-Bolling race.

As soon as Rayburn left for Texas during his final illness, Albert claimed 50–60 members encouraged him to start running for Speaker or majority leader. When Rayburn had only been gone from Washington for two weeks, two weeks before he was admitted to Baylor Hospital in Dallas, a surprise party was given for Albert. Vice President Lyndon Johnson went to the party and waited forty minutes for Albert to show up. John Kennedy sent a message. John McCormack attended along with the assistant whips. Things were obviously lining up well for Albert. Some of the regional whips reportedly told him, "[J]ust say the word and we'll begin the campaign to make you Speaker," but Albert told them that McCormack was the obvious choice as Rayburn's successor. Albert rebuffed those who encouraged him to oppose McCormack: "I would never do that against John McCormack. Mr. Rayburn and Mr. McCormack picked me and made me whip, and to run against Mr. McCormack would have been the act of an ingrate."[19]

Even the ailing Sam Rayburn sent a praise-filled message: "I am proud that you are honoring Carl Albert, who is one of the greatest whips the House has ever known and one of the most capable legislators and finest gentlemen that anybody ever knew." It was not an endorsement, but it seemed a blessing from the old man. Albert promptly wrote Rayburn his gratitude for his remarks and added, "Everybody is hoping you are getting a very much needed rest and all are confident that you will be fit and back with us in January."[20] But just in case, of course, the members were beginning to line up behind those they believed would comprise the new leadership of the House.

Albert believed that Bolling "didn't have a chance. His very tactics were anathema to the House. He announced a platform and program to the press and he didn't call a member. He was already out of it when he started calling members." Rayburn's own Texas delegation immediately got behind Albert. Robert Kerr, the influential Oklahoma senator and oil man and a friend of Albert's, supported McCormack for Speaker and Albert for majority leader. Kerr provided funds to Albert to assist him in his race.[21] With Albert having such influential support, Bolling fell out of the game early, although he did not formally withdraw until January 3, 1962.

Originally, it was believed that President Kennedy supported Bolling for Speaker over McCormack, for whom there was longtime antipathy from Massachusetts political squabbles. But Bolling was unable to mount a challenge to McCormack. Though Bolling was a more reliable New Frontiersman than Albert, Kennedy could not easily support Bolling over Albert. For one thing, Albert was close to eleven southern House committee chairmen. He was also close to Sen. Robert Kerr through whose Finance Committee Kennedy's trade expansion, tax revision, and Medicare must go. There was, of course, the added danger of a president openly interfering in House prerogatives.[22]

Still, Bolling saw himself as the choice of the administration. Said Bolling, "I think the Administration generally would have been all for me. They would have been pleased if I'd won." Yet Bolling realized Albert's strength with Kennedy too, saying "they couldn't really have anything against Albert because Albert had been very cooperative as Whip. They were in a very awkward position."[23]

Nevertheless, when Kerr tried to get Kennedy to endorse the package of McCormack and Albert, Kennedy refused. Leslie Carpenter, a reporter well connected with members of Congress, saw good politics in a McCormack-Albert ticket. The well liked Albert had leadership experience as whip and was a border-state moderate. Though McCormack had previously had an agreement with Wilbur Mills where if Mills would back McCormack for Speaker, in return, McCormack would back Mills for majority leader. But circumstances had changed. Arkansas had redistricted, leaving Mills with a more conservative district. Mills might be in trouble at home if he were floor leader and had to support JFK's program. Perhaps Mills, Carpenter argued, could be Speaker, where he could be more discreet, but being floor leader was no longer good politics for Mills. Albert was a logical alternative. Mills might be more of a threat to McCormack's ambitions for the Speakership, especially if JFK backed him. Carpenter, however, speculated that the administration would prefer a non-southerner such as Richard Bolling of Missouri, Chet Holifield of California, or Francis Walter of Pennsylvania.[24]

However, Kennedy did do something for Albert that was almost as good as endorsing a McCormack-Albert leadership ticket. On October 30, 1961, only one day before Rayburn left Baylor Hospital in Dallas to return to Bonham to die, Kennedy went to Big Cedar, Oklahoma (population 2), to dedicate a nine-mile stretch of scenic highway through the Ouachita National Forest. It was described as "a mountain road that starts nowhere in particular and goes to a suburb of the same place." Kennedy told Gov.

J. Howard Edmondson, "Why Howard, I'm going to Oklahoma to kiss Bob Kerr's ass." However, Kennedy did more than that. He praised Carl Albert, helping Albert advance from whip to majority leader. Kerr claimed Kennedy's comments about Albert to an audience of sixty thousand people in Big Cedar "reverberated not only through the mountains of Southeast Oklahoma and the third congressional district, but reached the halls of Congress." In his remarks, Kennedy lauded Albert and noted his "regard for him." Moreover, "in fight after fight for the development of the interests of the people of this country this year — Congressman Albert was in front always leading, and always fighting for this country."[25]

On November 19, 1961, the day after Rayburn's funeral, Richard Bolling announced that he would seek the majority leadership. That forced Carl Albert to announce as well, about three days before he intended to do so. Bolling, however, then waited until November 28 to mail out letters advising members of Congress of his candidacy and seeking support. He boldly informed Albert on the same day that he was seeking the position of Democratic floor leader and that he had received encouraging reports about his candidacy. Bolling added, "I am in this contest all the way."[26]

Bolling ran an "outsider" campaign, seeking help from interest groups and the press. In contrast, Albert relied on personal contacts and friendships. Bolling had the active support of the NAACP and the Americans for Democratic Action. Roy Wilkins sent telegrams to NAACP branches noting, "Strictly on their voting records on civil rights issues since 1949, Representative Albert has voted wrong 26 times and Representative Bolling has voted right 26 times." Albert was impressed with Bolling's press coverage, writing, "I am fascinated and a little annoyed by the press coverage Dick is getting." He guessed that Bolling had employed a public relations firm.[27]

Indeed, Bolling's press coverage was remarkable. Initially there was support for Bolling to challenge McCormack. Wilkins also suggested that since both Kennedy and Senate Leader Mike Mansfield of Montana were Catholics, opposition might develop to McCormack's Catholicism and support could spin to Bolling, an Episcopalian. Paul Duke of the *Wall Street Journal* wrote that there were two groups of Kennedy advisors. One wanted to avoid a battle over the Speakership that they might not be able to win; the other thought that under McCormack the House would be chaotic and McCormack would prove only a "figurehead" Speaker. Furthermore, Arthur Krock of the *New York Times* argued that party liberals were a majority of the majority and that they would prefer Bolling for Speaker. Jack Williams of the *Kansas City Times* wrote that Bolling had strong liberal support for Speaker and that he was "very close to the Kennedys." But an October *Roll Call* poll showed McCormack highly favored over Bolling. Of 260 Democrats, 162 responded to the poll and 65 favored McCormack, 27 Wilbur Mills. Bolling came in third with 19 votes. Though Rayburn was dying, 11 members expressed support for Mr. Sam. On October 29, Kennedy told White House assistants that they were not to express a preference for Speaker. By then the election of McCormack was conceded.[28]

On November 19, when Bolling announced he would run against Albert, he claimed that the decision was "unilateral" and that he had not polled the liberal Democratic Study Group of the House or anyone else. Quickly, *The New York Times* ran two editorials in support of Bolling. One suggested that McCormack would be a weak Speaker who would require a strong majority leader. Albert, the editorial claimed, had "been a whipless whip overly disposed to compromise and conciliate." Bolling, on the other hand, was described as "a resourceful tactician with aggressiveness and constancy of conviction." The second editorial emphasized that Bolling was supported by civil rights advocates because of the "vigor and consistency he has exhibited over a twelve-year period in championing more effective civil rights measures." Albert, however, "has generally lined up with the Southern bloc in its efforts to defeat or emasculate bills to safeguard the rights of Negroes." In addition to Bolling's support from *The New York Times,* he also had favorable publicity in the *New York Post* and *St. Louis Post Dispatch.* But as early as four days after Bolling's announcement, Albert ally Tom Steed was publicly stating that Albert had enough firm votes to be elected.[29]

By November 30, 1961, Albert was writing that he had "more than enough Democratic Congressmen pledged to support me now." Always cautious, however, Albert added that it is "one thing to get them 'up the pole' and another to keep them there. I really feel good about the prospects but am trying to leave no stone un-turned and everybody has responded beautifully." By the time Bolling had sent out his letter, Albert had commitments from the vast majority of Democrats in the House. On November 27, 1961, he wrote Homer Thornberry and provided him with a list of members who had committed to him, who were probably going to support him, and who had not yet made a final decision. One hundred fifty eight members were committed to him; another nineteen members were listed as probably for him; and nine members were listed as not ready to commit. That meant that about 60 percent of the Democrats in the House had committed to vote for Albert for majority leader less than ten days after Sam Rayburn's funeral. Albert noted that fewer than ten people on the list were committed based on information other than personal contacts.

Why did Albert send the letter to Thornberry on the day prior to Bolling's mail solicitation of votes? Perhaps Albert simply was responding to Thornberry's interest. However, Albert's files provided no list of supporters addressed to anyone except Thornberry and surely there were many others who were interested and wished to help. Of course, Thornberry was very close to Lyndon Johnson, who may have wanted the list, but most Texas representatives — where Johnson would have had the greatest influence — were already committed to Albert. Jim Wright believed that Albert would not have needed Johnson's help and that involvement by Johnson in Albert's behalf might have brought charges of the vice president interfering with the internal business of the House. Instead, Wright speculated that Albert was trying to warn off Bolling. Thornberry and Bolling were both close to Rayburn, they both were regulars at the Board of Education, they both served on the Rules Committee where their seats were side-by-side. Mrs. Nona Bolling recalled that Bolling liked Thornberry and that the Thornberrys and the Bollings were social friends. Wright believed this memo was Albert's ploy to have Thornberry give Bolling a look at the list, hopefully preventing a contest that Bolling would surely lose. Wright added that this would have been Albert's subtle way of warning off Bolling. Thornberry wrote Bolling on December 1 explaining that he had just received Bolling's November 28 notice of candidacy. Interestingly, Bolling had not even personally contacted a close friend like Thornberry. While Thornberry considered both Albert and Bolling good friends, Albert had contacted him nearly two weeks earlier, and he had promised Albert his support.[30]

Albert's list of supporters demonstrated the breadth of his coalition. On the list was James Roosevelt, FDR's oldest son and a liberal from California, and John Bell Williams, a conservative from Mississippi. Powers in the House such as Howard Smith, Bernie Sisk, Bob Poage, Wright Patman, Tom O'Brien, John McCormack, Bill Colmer, Thomas O'Neill, Julia Hansen, Chet Holifield, Edward Hébert, Hale Boggs, and Dan Rostenkowski were on the list. Even four of the nine representatives from Bolling's home state of Missouri were on the list. It is no wonder that Joe O'Connell was able to write Albert about a conversation he had with John McCormack. O'Connell wrote, "John W. McC says you are 'in.'"[31] The support for Albert by Howard Smith, arch-conservative leader of the southerners and chairman of the Rules Committee, was used against Albert by the Bolling forces. It was argued that Smith believed he could control Albert but feared Bolling in the Speaker's chair. Albert supporters, on the other hand, claimed that Albert had not solicited Smith's support. Perhaps the Albert forces felt the Smith endorsement could be used to show that Bolling was preferable to the administration as the more liberal candidate. Smith, after all, had done everything he could to hinder the administration's objectives. But the Albert forces had in fact solicited Smith's support. Smith was listed by Albert as a supporter in the Thornberry letter. A week before Rayburn's death, Albert wrote Smith that he was unsure whether Bolling would seek the majority leadership, but he had checked with the administration and had been assured that the president would not intervene in Bolling's behalf. Then, before sending a telegram to all the members announcing his candidacy for majority leader, Albert consulted with Smith.[32] Clearly, Smith's endorsement keyed support from conservative southerners.

In contrast, Bolling's support, according to Nelson Polsby, never amounted to more than 65–70 members. Bolling realized that other members would join the bandwagon if he looked like a winner, but he was never close. Withdrawal was necessary, if for no other reason than to protect his supporters from retribution by the victors. Just before New Year's, Bolling met with his friend and campaign manager, Frank Thompson of New Jersey. As they lunched at the Occidental Restaurant, they concluded that the fight was hopeless, and Bolling decided to withdraw.[33]

Bolling had been optimistic from the beginning, so his decision to withdraw was difficult. But the math made his decision easier. At one point, Bolling thought he had as many as 110 votes, but even that would have fallen far short of the 128 that would have been necessary to win. More likely, his support never was never above about 75 votes.[34] Three years after his campaign for majority leadership, Bolling offered a dual explanation for the race. He claimed that while he had wanted to get elected to the leadership, he saw the "main purpose" of his race as a way "to protest what I thought was going to be weak leadership." Rayburn had been able to run the House as majority leader from 1936 to 1940 under Speaker William Bankhead, who was weakened by illness. Bolling may well have thought that he would be able to do the same under the aging McCormack.[35]

After his withdrawal, there was some press speculation that Bolling would try to become majority whip.[36] However, even if Albert had been willing to offer Bolling that position, McCormack, who was not favorable toward Bolling, might have blocked such an appointment. Neither Mrs. Nona Bolling nor Larry Bodinson, Bolling's longtime staff member and close friend, could imagine that Bolling would have considered the whip position and its subordinate role in the leadership. A man of the House, he seemed to have no desire for other posts, having even turned down an appointment to the U.S. Senate a few years earlier.[37] Instead, Hale Boggs was named to the whip post.

Unquestioningly, Bolling was unhappy with the liberal interest groups that he believed had not sufficiently supported him, including the AFL-CIO, the Americans for Democratic Action, and the National Committee for an Effective Congress. Though he called Albert a lip-service liberal who was weak on civil rights and beholden to oil interests, he came to regret running against Albert. After Albert moved on to the Speakership and to retirement, Bolling believed that Albert had been a good Speaker who had been greatly underestimated. Calling on Bolling not long after the majority leader's race, Albert asked for his help, and Bolling freely gave it. Thus, Albert's peace-making gesture enlisted the support of a man who could have turned into a long-term enemy but instead proved to be an exceptionally able ally. Indeed, columnist Kevin Phillips thought that early in Albert's speakership, Albert wished to replace Boggs with Bolling, in part because "Boggs is also reported to be physically ill." A month after the Phillips article, another report claimed that Boggs was under a doctor's care, and rumors persisted that the real problem was alcohol abuse, a charge Boggs denied. He was quoted as saying, "Frankly, I really don't drink very much. I've never been late for an appointment or missed a meeting because of any alcohol."[38] In any case, Albert turned to Bolling for tasks ordinarily left to the whip.

The Speakership

Albert was now the number two man in the House Democratic Party and heir apparent to the Speakership. However, in spite of McCormack's age, he served as Speaker for a then-record nine consecutive years. When McCormack retired, Albert had the job sewed up. Even McCormack's nemesis, Morris Udall, declined to oppose him saying, "It would be hard to find anyone who dislikes Carl Albert, and that's something to say for anyone in this jungle. It's because of his integrity, fairness and basic decency as a human being." There were press forecasts that Wilbur Mills, Ways and

Means chair, was a likely opponent, but Mills too demurred, writing to Albert, "If you are campaigning for the position of Speaker, quit it. You have already got it!" Explaining his decision to abstain from a race for Speaker, Mills said that he had never wanted to be a presiding officer. In contrast, "I like to legislate. I like to apply my mind against the minds of others. I like to get up on that floor and handle a bill and be ready for the questions of 430 other members." Of course, Mills' support for Albert would come with a legislator's desire for quid pro quo.[39]

Still, Mills seems to have considered challenging Albert, even after Albert was already Speaker. Mills told Sam Gibbons of Florida that Rayburn, McCormack, and he had been the ones who put Albert "on the escalator" to the leadership, and Mills did not want to be Speaker. Yet Mills thought Albert a weak leader, saying, "All of us have to reelect Carl . . . [H]e can't do it for himself — he has no platform, etc." Additionally, Mills told Gibbons that "he had a lot of people urging him to run against Carl, [but] he couldn't do that" because "[u]nder Rayburn Carl began to take on a halo." Within a few days, however, Mills seemed more inclined to oppose Albert saying, "We haven't had leadership. . . . Carl hasn't produced as we thought he would." Carl Albert seemed to sense a threat from Mills. Bob Sikes of Florida reported to Gibbons that "Carl is apprehensive about Wilbur." Sikes and Gibbons, however, both thought, perhaps echoing Dick Bolling's assessment of Mills's prospects for the Speakership, that "Mills has alienated himself with some groups." Richard Bolling wrote that what prevented Mills from being Speaker was the race issue. As he put it, "No House Member from the Old South, excepting Southwestern states (including Texas), could survive at home by taking a position on the race issue that would make him acceptable to the northern Democrats."[40] On race, Mills had to be very southern, even signing the segregationist Southern Manifesto in the 1950s.

Even so, Albert did have symbolic opposition. African American congressman John Conyers opposed Albert and got 20 votes to Albert's 220. It was a symbolic challenge but one Albert never forgot; years later he described Conyers as "erratic," "selfish," and "anti-white."[41]

Hale Boggs and the Race for Majority Leader

Hale Boggs, who had become whip when Albert moved to the majority leadership, was not to have it so easy. Boggs had been very close to Speaker Rayburn and was able and ambitious. His greatest asset was probably his wife, Lindy, an intelligent, attractive, charming, and politically astute woman. Like Lyndon and Lady Bird Johnson, Hale and Lindy Boggs were a formidable political couple. And Sam Rayburn loved them. He frequently visited their home, played with their children, and asked Lindy to speak at Democratic events where a female speaker seemed appropriate. Rayburn and Boggs even fished together, an activity Rayburn limited to those closest to him. Boggs described his relationship with Rayburn much like Lyndon Johnson also described the Rayburn-Johnson relationship, "Yes, I was very close to Mr. Rayburn, very close to him. I felt this father-son relationship with him."[42]

Ironically, Rayburn had initially felt hostility toward Boggs. Boggs had defeated a Huey Long–faction congressman, Paul Maloney, a member of the Ways and Means Committee and a friend of Rayburn's. Rayburn complained to the anti-Long faction governor, Sam Jones, about Boggs's opposition to Maloney. After Maloney left, F. Edward Hébert became Rayburn's key contact in the Louisiana delegation, but Hébert proved an obstinate personality, and Boggs's persistence in cultivating Rayburn paid off. Boggs became part of Rayburn's inner circle. Hébert described his decline by claiming that Rayburn expected his young associates to "yes Mr. Rayburn to death. Similarly, he is supposed to be awed whenever the President of the United States talks to him." Hébert believed that had he been a sycophant, he "probably would have become majority leader. It was all so easy, so effortless. But I had to be my own man." In contrast, Hébert claimed, "Hale Boggs did become the majority leader, despite Rayburn's early dislike of him, because Hale was an ingratiating person. He was always there when Rayburn wanted him. If I had played the game like Hale played it — well, I would have been available at all times. As much as Rayburn originally opposed Boggs, Hale ingratiated himself with Rayburn and became one of Rayburn's most trusted lieutenants."[43]

Boggs had first defeated Maloney in 1940 as a young reformer, but Maloney had come back in 1942 and defeated Boggs. Boggs gained back his seat in 1946 and held it for the remainder of his life. Boggs sought the governorship in 1951, though he finished third in the race. During the 1960s, he faced increasingly difficult challenges, such as defeating Republican challenger David Treen with only 51 percent of the vote in 1968. But redistricting later saved Boggs politically, and he regained political security at home.[44]

But political security hid other demons. By the 1970s Boggs was described as being ruddy-faced and a dandy dresser with a 1930s bandleader look. He could sometimes be wild and foolish while also being sly, tough, intelligent, and hard-core. In about 1968, Boggs seemed to exhibit unusual personality characteristics, alternately showing a glacial appearance and then, in turn, exuberance. Sometimes he would not seem to recognize friends. At times, he would tremble with energy and give long-winded speeches. Once he heckled his Ways and Means Committee chairman, Wilbur Mills. On another occasion, he held a strange two-hour press conference in which he read from news clippings, the Democratic platform, his personal appointment book, and the Bible. Another time, he gave a forty-minute monologue at a White House conference and then told President Nixon that he had to leave for an important appointment. Given his erratic behavior, when Boggs spoke of an effort to become majority leader, Wayne Hays of Ohio said that "Boggs was drinking and making a horse's ass of himself." Tiger Teague of Texas, one of the best liked members of the House, confessed to Morris Udall that he was concerned about Boggs's "irrational behavior" and "some of the other things he'd done." Even President Nixon called Minority Leader Gerald Ford in April of 1971 to find out what was going on with Boggs. Ford told the president that Boggs was "nuts" and added that "he's either drinking too much or he's taking some pills that are upsetting him mentally." Albert recalled in 1979 that "Boggs was one of the really brilliant members of the House, but he was conceited and he was — he got on a dope binge for awhile."[45]

Columnist Jack Anderson wrote about Boggs's behavior in his column. Attacking J. Edgar Hoover of the FBI at a time when Hoover was still held in considerable esteem, Boggs had complained of telephone wiretaps but had not been able to prove his charges. Anderson claimed the attack on Hoover was brought on by alcohol. Anderson also wrote that Boggs had fought a former congressman at the Gridiron Club dinner and that he had had a fight at a Baton Rouge restaurant. At a Florida congressman's fundraiser, Boggs was so out-of-control that friends locked him in a room, but he escaped and mounted the rostrum, engaging in what Anderson described as a "free-wheeling discourse." Anderson claimed that Albert was afraid to leave the chair to Boggs and had cancelled trips to prevent Boggs from being left in control.[46]

Other serious problems came to light. Boggs had allowed a builder who had significant problems with the federal government to do $40,000 worth of work on his Bethesda home at a fraction of the normal costs, placed his wife and son both on the congressional payroll, and seemed emotionally unstable and prone to crack under pressure. Younger members criticized Boggs as "old style," and others complained that he was abusing his authority, was aggressive toward members, and was "super-cilious" and "overbearing." Carl Albert thought Boggs "opinionated," and some faulted him for not working hard enough as whip. A critical article authored by an old friend of Carl Albert's claimed that Morris Udall or Dan Rostenkowski was more likely than Boggs to become majority leader. To make matters worse, the article was sent by Willie Morris, the editor of *Harper's* and one-time editor of *Texas Monthly,* to every Democratic member of the House. Though Boggs laughed and denied that he had ever suffered great emotional strain in thirty years in politics, his emotional stability had become an issue.[47]

Professor Robert Peabody noted that prior to the majority leader's race, Boggs was under great stress, having taken the difficult job of being chair of the platform committee at the 1968 Democratic convention. His nor-mal career path toward power was stymied, since he would never become chair of Ways and Means as long as Wilbur Mills was in office. His whip position was appointive and dependent on the largesse of the Speaker. At that point, he had not stood for election by his peers, and McCormack's retirement was imminent. And in 1968 he encountered his most difficult reelection race. Unless he could become politically secure at home, he would probably be eliminated from further leadership positions. Boggs, however, was fiercely ambitious for the Speakership. Peabody suggested that all of these stresses may have come together with an urge to drink too much, possibly leading to Boggs's strange behavior in 1968–69.[48]

In spite of Boggs's flaws, however, he was quite exceptional. Albert considered him "one of the really brilliant members of the House." Gary Hymel, who worked for Tip O'Neill as well as Boggs, called Boggs the "smartest man he had ever worked for." Albert thought Boggs had a special instinct to see potential problems. Said Albert, he "could smell a rat pretty good."[49] Boggs was also a man with considerable political courage. He had supported Rayburn's enlargement of the Rules Committee, getting four others from the Louisiana delegation to vote for it. He had backed Adlai Stevenson in 1956, JFK in 1960, and LBJ in 1964. He voted for the Voting Rights Act. These acts had made him one of the leading Deep South na-tional Democrats.[50] It was said of Sam Rayburn's protégés, "The old man never selected a dummy in his life, and was better than most in judging men for their organizational potential."[51] Like Bolling and Albert, Boggs was one of Mr. Sam's smart choices as a protégé.

Nonetheless, Boggs's flaws opened considerable opportunities for op-position to his becoming majority leader. Boggs was different from Albert. While both had been Rayburn's protégés, Albert was cautious and a worrier; Boggs was forceful and aggressive — even impulsive.[52] Albert's district was, like Rayburn's, a rural agricultural district with few big towns and few blacks. Boggs's New Orleans district, with a heavily black and urban population, was in a state that was much more a part of the South than was Texas. Instead of the Austin-Boston connection, with Albert as Speaker and Boggs as majority leader, it would be a rural southwestern-urban south alliance. And, as the politics of the majority leadership race worked itself out, Boggs reached out for an even more different alliance, one with the Chicago Democratic political machine.

While Boggs was making his plans, Morris Udall again decided to run for the leadership, appealing primarily to the liberal wing of the Democrats in the House. But James O'Hara of Michigan, a Democratic Study Group leader, party activist in the National Committee, and extraordinarily effective builder of legislative coalitions, had more reliable liberal credentials even than Udall and soon became a candidate too. He understood that his support among southern members was likely to be limited. As a close observer of the leadership race and O'Hara supporter acknowledged, "O'Hara will not seek Southern votes, and . . . probably could not get any, because he has defeated them too often in gut issues on the floor."[53]

At the same time, O'Hara was running into trouble garnering support from even the House liberals with whom he shared, more than any other candidate for majority leader, policy views and political support. Although he announced for majority leader only a day after Udall, O'Hara was in a difficult position. In many ways, Udall's campaign began when he challenged John McCormack in 1968–69, making him a rallying point for "new politics" liberals. Thus, when O'Hara tried to line up support, he often found that he was an acceptable second choice to many members who had already committed to Udall. Udall's early lead led even some of O'Hara's most likely supporters to question his viability. For example, Frank Thompson of New Jersey, a fellow DSG Democrat and influential leader of urban liberals, was a likely Udall supporter. An O'Hara staffer reported, "I'm told that Thompy cut you up at a meeting of around 15 legislators. O'Hara's ok he said but he has no chance of winning."[54]

Nonetheless, O'Hara's candidacy would have been a significant departure from the North-South leadership alliance. Offering a mix of midwestern-urban-labor support with the considerable support his Civil Rights advocacy had earned him among African American House members, his election would mean a different type of Democratic leadership coalition. As O'Hara's supporter (and eventually the member who nominated him in the caucus) Rep. Charles C. Diggs Jr. (D-MI) wrote, "The Congress and the Nation has been well served by the progressive leadership of the Rayburn-McCormack period which is drawing to a close. We now stand on the threshold of a new era that demands a different commitment for change and our support will be channeled behind that candidate for Majority Leader whom we feel can best build upon the foundation of the liberal tradition."[55]

In his search for a whip candidate, O'Hara looked South, likely in the hopes of shoring up his weakness in a region where his long and hard-fought battles in favor of expansive civil rights legislation were viewed with trepidation. Still, the O'Hara campaign faced the difficult task of trying to find a southerner to promote who would not compromise support among O'Hara's liberal base. It was then that his office examined Texan Jack Brooks's voting record on issues from federal aid to education and unemployment compensation to civil rights. They noted that "prior to Johnson administration . . . on tough votes for a southerner, he usually voted Dixie." However, there had been a transition in Brooks's record, from conservative southerner to national Democrat, particularly on civil rights: "In his early years [Brooks] also voted wrong on civil rights issues. . . . But in 1964 he voted for the major civil rights bill and has voted for most civil rights measures since." They also observed that Brooks was "hawkish" on defense and Vietnam, but he had high COPE (AFL-CIO) ratings and relatively high ADA ratings ("quite high for a southerner"). Though his ADA ratings had "slipped" from 73 in 1967 to 33 in "both 1968 and 1969, reflecting increased number of index votes on Viet Nam and defense issues," they enlisted Brooks in the campaign, having him make a seconding speech and holding out the possibility that O'Hara would offer Brooks the majority whip post.[56] Even so, it is unclear the extent to which Brooks could help O'Hara in the South. After years of leading positions in the House, the expectation of a whip choice would probably not make southerners vote against a Boggs, a Sisk, or even a Udall. It was also the case that Brooks, like other liberal southerners in the 1970s, was seen as too southern for the liberals and too liberal for the southerners.

O'Hara hoped that support from outside the House would help overcome some of his difficulties, a strategy similar to Bolling's in 1962. Party notables, recognizing O'Hara's broader contributions to party politics and reform, supported him. Former vice president and 1968 Democratic presidential nominee Hubert Humphrey wrote to a DNC official of O'Hara,

"I shall be in his corner in every way I can." In addition, organized labor was an important component of the O'Hara campaign. His campaign sent Cesar Chavez, director of the United Farm Workers Organizing Committee, a list of 128 House Democrats with whom Chavez's support would prove "helpful"; Chavez wrote the members on O'Hara's behalf from jail in Las Salinas, California. A list of O'Hara's "Majority Leader Lobby Group" included representatives from over a dozen unions (including the AFL-CIO and the UAW), House staff members from the Education and Labor Committee and the Democratic Study Group, and core supporters from among the House membership including Jack Brooks of Texas, Jim Scheuer of New York, Don Fraser of Minnesota, William Clay of Missouri, Jim Corman of California, and Charles Diggs, Bill Ford, and Lucien Nedzi, all O'Hara's Michigan colleagues.[57]

Though Udall had a head start, the O'Hara camp regarded Udall's campaign as the more quixotic and futile effort to win the leadership. Just days before the caucus vote, O'Hara's office examined the race. Writing that "the battle is not yet won — by anybody," the O'Hara forces estimated Boggs's strength on the first ballot as 70–80 votes, Udall 50–60, and O'Hara an optimistic third with "42 hard commitments and 5–6 possibilities," with Sisk and Hays with "30 votes between them," and 50 undecided members "mostly in the northern, big-city delegations." Having overestimated his own first-ballot support by almost 100 percent, O'Hara hoped not only to gain among the 50 undecided members but also to pick up votes from the Sisk and Hays supporters once they were eliminated. However, there were some in O'Hara's campaign who recognized that this, too, was an optimistic assessment of where the Hays and Sisk voters might go. Inasmuch as Hays would himself endorse Boggs, it was doubtful that the conservative supporters of Sisk (many from the South) would consider O'Hara as an acceptable second choice. And when *Congressional Quarterly* released the results of its "straw poll" for the majority leader's race, analysis within the O'Hara camp raised doubts about his viability as the poll revealed that "Sisk votes on second ballot go primarily to Boggs and Udall, not O'Hara." Moreover, although the O'Hara group believed that the new members of the class of 1970 were "strongly pro-O'Hara," this too was obviously optimistic in that even among these "strong" supporters, "some of them are obligated to honor first-ballot commitments they have made to Mo and/or Boggs."[58]

O'Hara thought Boggs's support was "soft" and that "ninety to 100 votes is his peak." O'Hara also observed that the whip had "made some enemies in public, more in private, and his 'temperament' bothers some of the Southerners who feel committed to him on the first ballot." Another memorandum outlined Boggs's weaknesses in greater detail: "First, he is not well-liked. Members complain of his high-handed, imperious manner. He had frequently lashed out at other members, often publicly insulting them on the House floor. Second, there are those who feel that his temperament is too erratic for such heavy party responsibilities. And, third, many northerners feel that Boggs is too heavily mortgaged to the Southern bloc to be an effective spokesman for their interests." Believing that "Mo can't get most of the uncommitted or most of the Hays-Sisk strength," O'Hara identified Udall's key weakness: "We keep finding that the 'regulars' have never forgiven him for running against McCormack in 1969 and are turned off by Mo's image. We have identified 50 or more of these 80 votes who simply will not go Udall under any circumstances." A similar memorandum put it more bluntly, "Udall's chances of getting these votes is rated about zero." This piece of intelligence led O'Hara to conclude that the race was really between Boggs and himself and that if he could hold on to later ballots, among the liberal candidates, only he could beat Boggs: "if it boils down to Boggs vs. Mo, it will be Boggs who will win. . . . You[r] job then is to let the hard-core O'Hara vote know where the hard counts leave everyone and urge them to hang tough until it boils down to Boggs vs. O'Hara. At that point, O'Hara will win." His camp believed that this would be true also of new members who were "pro-O'Hara" despite some being "obligated to honor first ballot commitments" to other candidates. After the first ballot, these members would be free to support other candidates, and, as the O'Hara campaign believed, "By the time it's fish or cut bait, they will be fishing in O'Hara waters."[59]

However, contained in these last week memos was one point of caution. The O'Hara camp worried that if Udall successfully created a sense of inevitability for his being the liberal alternative to Boggs, would-be O'Hara supporters among the "uncommitted regulars [might] get behind Boggs for an early round victory in order to 'stop Udall.'" Indeed, Udall was engaging in bandwagon politics. When *Congressional Quarterly* conducted a straw poll of the House majority leader's race, Udall encouraged supporters to respond and, as a result, enjoyed a 46 to 30 advantage over Boggs in first choice responses.[60] So convinced was the O'Hara camp that Udall could not win and that the only chance for a liberal to win the majority leader's race was an O'Hara victory on later ballots, that O'Hara saw Udall's efforts as the primary impediment to a liberal victory.

As Udall and O'Hara vied for the liberal vote, Bernie Sisk of California staked a claim to the moderate faction. He was on the Rules Committee and had Texas roots. Suspicious of Boggs's credentials, Mississippi's Bill Colmer, Florida's Bob Sikes, and Texas' Omar Burleson had recruited Sisk into the race. Before he could become a candidate, though, Sisk had to get the support from his own delegation. Another Californian, John Moss, also wished to run. Chet Holifield, dean of the California delegation, persuaded the two to compete within the delegation; the winner would be the "California candidate for majority leader," and the loser would "withdraw and support the winning candidate." Sisk won 9 votes to 7. Sisk's increasingly conservative voting record and Texas roots might be seen as threatening to Boggs, but the Boggs camp actually regarded Sisk's entry into the race as a decisive factor in their favor. According to one account, "When Boggs heard the news of Sisk's candidacy, he was jubilant. 'It's over, I've won,' he told aides. His reasoning was this: Although he and Sisk had comparable voting records, the Californian had a reputation of being more conservative. Certainly he lacked Boggs's personal identification with the Great Society. No longer the most conservative candidate in the race, Boggs now found himself more palatable to northern liberals." There were other candidates, such as Ed Boland of Massachusetts and Dan Rostenkowski from Illinois, who would not announce but seemed to be thinking about the race or wanting to be called upon if announced candidacies went bad. Wayne Hays of Ohio was the most difficult personality in the race, but he had made his Administration Committee a fiefdom and his base of support. Udall considered Hays a "shill" for Boggs who would take a few Udall votes with him on the first ballot. O'Hara, on the other hand, pulled liberals with strong organized labor constituencies since Udall had opposed the repeal of the right-to-work provision of the Taft-Hartley Act.[61]

Boggs was on the Ways and Means Committee, not only an important committee because of its revenue-raising function, but also important because the Democratic members of Ways and Means assigned Democrats to their committees. Since Boggs was backed by the influential chairman of the committee, Wilbur Mills, he gained considerable influence with the entering freshman Democrats seeking prime committee assignments as well as with veteran members wishing to improve their assignments.[62] For example, it was claimed that Congresswoman Shirley Chisholm, unhappy with her Veterans Committee assignment, traded her vote for Boggs for a promise that she would be appointed to the Education and Labor Committee.⁶³ Boggs also had the trappings of the whip's office and easy access to both John McCormack and Carl Albert, all of which he used to cultivate freshmen congressmen.⁶⁴

Still, though Boggs had been closely associated with Albert since the 1950s when Albert was whip and Boggs was deputy whip and though Albert claimed that Boggs was his choice for majority leader, he did not assist Boggs. Tension had developed between Albert and Boggs, and Albert did not wish to antagonize the competing groups in the House. He felt he could work with any of the candidates except Wayne Hays. But Albert's neutrality led Udall to believe that he opposed Boggs. Claiming that Albert's public silence spoke volumes, Udall noted that even though they had worked together in the leadership for ten years, Albert did not endorse Boggs. Privately, Boggs thought Albert could have quietly indicated a preference and avoided a contest but that "the liberals got to Albert." Also, there was a sense in the Boggs camp that "the price of a free ride for Albert was noninvolvement in the selection of a successor." The view was that if Albert stayed neutral, the Democratic Study Group would not oppose him, but if he endorsed Boggs, DSG would challenge him for the Speakership. And while the DSG indicated that they had not ever considered opposing Albert, DSG had overwhelmingly supported Bolling when he ran against Albert for majority leader in 1961. There were also reports that Albert had lunched with the DSG and implied that Boggs had not worked very hard as whip and had let him down.⁶⁵

Back in 1968 when Udall was about to run for Speaker against John McCormack, Albert and he had had a wide-ranging conversation that included Boggs. They had discussed Boggs's heavy drinking and his general inactivity as whip. He had not been on the floor enough and did not reliably respond to calls. They agreed that the Speaker should confront the issue and make a change in the whip if Boggs were unwilling to do a better job. In the course of the conversation, Udall believed that Albert wanted him to be in the leadership and that he would be preferred to Boggs. In an election in the caucus, Albert said, he thought Udall would beat Boggs.⁶⁶

Udall thought that irritation with Boggs extended beyond Albert. In seeking an opponent to McCormack, Udall had proposed that Wilbur Mills run for Speaker. Mills refused to challenge McCormack, but in the process of the conversation, Mills let it be known that he was unhappy with Boggs. Mills said Boggs rarely attended Ways and Means meetings and consequentially would be unable to chair the committee if something happened to Mills. Mills also complained that Boggs was never on the floor to assist Albert and that members resented his pressure tactics as whip. Yet, in spite of Mills's unhappiness with Boggs, he backed him over Udall. One suggestion was that with Boggs as majority leader, Mills would be able to get him off Ways and Means.[67] Whatever shortcomings Boggs had, he had the advantage of understanding the problems of southern Democrats, unlike Udall. Also, unlike the reformer Udall, Boggs was a traditionalist in his understanding of House politics. For committee barons like Mills, nonreform would clearly be preferable to reform.

Another sign of Boggs's slipping stature came when McCormack announced his retirement at a press conference on May 20, 1970. He did not notify Boggs of the meeting. Boggs only heard about the meeting from reporters, and he had to "elbow his way into the Speaker's rooms to get his customary chair near the right side of the Speaker's desk." To make matters worse, Boggs received only lukewarm praise from McCormack. It was only after Boggs was strongly challenged by perennial McCormack nemesis Morris Udall that McCormack gave Boggs strong support. At that point, though McCormack officially disavowed taking sides, he would "place Hale Boggs on display as presiding officer," would greet Boggs "with glad cries at social functions," and would select "him from the masses to park him in receiving lines."[68]

McCormack, always a betting man, actually left the Capitol betting that Boggs would win. And when Louise Day Hicks asked McCormack how she should vote in the majority leader race, McCormack said he hoped not for Udall. Though Ed Boland of Massachusetts nominated Udall for majority leader, in general, the Massachusetts delegation was cool to Udall. Tip O'Neill, for example, though slow to endorse Boggs, had never forgiven Udall for challenging McCormack.[69]

In the early stages of Boggs's race, he foundered a bit and turned to the powerful Dan Rostenkowski as a leading ally. Rostenkowski could deliver the votes of the Chicago delegation. In early December, Rostenkowski told Udall that he would probably not run for majority leader and might not even run for caucus chair again. In mid-December, he disavowed a run for majority leader, but Udall believed Rostenkowski had interest in being whip, an ambition that turned out to be true. Rostenkowski made a deal with Boggs to support him for the majority leadership in exchange for the whip's position. The Boggs-Rostenkowski alliance was appropriately described by Udall as being a "bombshell." He learned from a Chicago reporter that Rostenkowski would confirm that he was supporting Boggs and that he would be whip. But with the typical over-optimism that was characteristic of Udall's race against John McCormack for Speaker, Udall concluded that the Boggs-Rostenkowski alliance would actually hurt Boggs. That was because, Udall thought, several people wanting to be whip would be upset with the deal. Moreover, Rostenkowski was Mayor Daley's man, a person unpopular among southern members. Finally, given bad feelings between Rostenkowski and Carl Albert, Udall concluded that Albert's friends would not like the arrangement.

Continuing in his optimistic mode, on the evening of January 16, Udall calculated that in the worst scenario, he had 77 votes, Boggs had 95, O'Hara had 40, Sisk had 20, and Hays had 20. On the other hand, if things went as well as expected, Udall thought he had 85-90 votes to Boggs's 75-80. O'Hara would have 30 votes, Sisk would have 45 and Hays would have 15. On the second ballot, he believed he would receive 105 votes and Boggs would only have 90. In other words, Udall thought he would win the majority leadership. Actually, Udall's worst-case scenario was not quite bad enough, and his second ballot calculations were far afield. Instead of turning toward Udall, the election fell to Boggs on the second ballot. On the first ballot, the vote was Boggs 95, Udall 69, Sisk 31, Hays 28, and O'Hara 25. On the second ballot, Boggs received 140 votes to Udall's 88 and Sisk's 17.[70]

Boggs wanted to reward Rostenkowski with the whip's position as he had promised, but Albert balked. Rostenkowski had been on the Commerce Committee, but when the dean of the Chicago delegation and old Rayburn ally Tom O'Brien died in 1964, Rostenkowski got O'Brien's seat on Ways and Means. Rostenkowski had been appointed by Boggs as assistant whip in 1963 and in 1967 was chosen chairman of the House Democratic caucus. As a Ways and Means member, a part of the whip organization, chairman of the Democratic caucus, a major voice of the Chicago Democratic machine in Congress, and a protégé of Hale Boggs, Rostenkowski was a major player in Congress with ambitions to move even higher in the House leadership.

Sometimes, the big, burly Rostenkowski showed more ambition than good sense. For example, using his ties with Mayor Daley, Rostenkowski tried to engineer a team of Boggs as Speaker and Rostenkowski as majority leader in 1970, holding on to that hope far longer than was politically expedient. By the time McCormack retired, every large state except Illinois endorsed Albert for Speaker. Albert, of course, quickly found out why Illinois was holding out, and as a result, began to view Rostenkowski with suspicion. Rostenkowski then contemplated challenging Boggs for the leadership even with his numerous liabilities. First, he was a Tuesday to Thursday man which meant that he was only in Washington part-time. Second, he did not have experience managing floor debate. Third, liberals disliked his support for the Vietnam War. Perhaps most importantly, as a product of the Chicago Democratic machine he was regarded by many as Mayor Daley's stooge.

Only after realizing election as majority leader was hopeless did he arrange the deal with Boggs. He would deliver at least eighteen votes for Boggs for majority leader if Boggs would make him the whip. However, Albert needed to approve his choice as whip, and Albert had other grievances against Rostenkowski. At the 1968 Democratic convention, a chaotic one with demonstrations, violence, and major conflicts between delegates who supported and those who opposed the Vietnam War, Albert claimed that he had done Rostenkowski a favor when he gave the gavel to Rostenkowski to preside briefly over the delegates in his hometown. But an alternate story, one that Albert believed was being told by Rostenkowski, also circulated. That story held that the convention was in disorder and that Rostenkowski had taken the gavel from Albert's hands to bring order to a convention that Albert could not control. Mayor Daley considered Albert "that little guy who couldn't control the convention," and he was "surprised and disappointed" that Albert might become Speaker. Rostenkowski told Morris Udall that he considered Carl Albert a weak man.[71]

Because Albert had reservations about Rostenkowski, and because he was in charge, he would now get his revenge. Rostenkowski should have had a hint of retaliation when Albert failed to show up for a dinner meeting with Rostenkowski prior to the January 19 caucus. Then at the caucus, after Boggs was elected on the second ballot, there was an election for caucus chair. Rostenkowski was up for reelection to the position he had held since 1967. To his surprise, he faced an unusually popular opponent, Olin "Tiger" Teague, who was put up as a candidate by the Texas delegation. Jim Wright recalled that Teague had not been present at a meeting of the Texas delegation when he was nominated by Omar Burleson. Since the death of Rayburn, Texas had been out of the leadership, and the delegation believed that it could return to the leadership through the caucus chair position. He also recalled that at that time the position of caucus chair was not considered particularly powerful and that there was opposition to Rostenkowski serving a third term. Teague, who announced publicly his support for Rostenkowski, won overwhelmingly, by a vote of

155-91. Wright, for one, was surprised that Rostenkowski took his defeat as caucus chair so hard, and, claimed Wright, he saw no evidence of Albert conspiring against Rostenkowski's ambition to remain chair.[72]

Robert Peabody supports Wright's opinion that there was strong sentiment for a two-term limit for caucus chair and that the Texas delegation wished to regain its lost place in the leadership. The chair of the caucus was, indeed, the least powerful leadership position, yet there was more to it than that. Peabody noted that, "Enthusiasm for Teague . . . spread too quickly to be a strictly spontaneous ouster." He ascribed Rostenkowski's defeat to his divisive personality and his ties to Daley as well as Teague's great personal popularity. Rostenkowski's biographer saw the defeat as payback to Mayor Daley for the disastrous 1968 Chicago Democratic convention and a comeback for oil-producing states that had just suffered a reduction in the oil depletion tax break. There may well have been more to Rostenkowski's defeat. Albert had, along with Boggs, encouraged Rostenkowski to run for a third term as caucus chair, but in discussing Rostenkowski's defeat, he claimed that "enough of my friends shared enough of my wonder about Rostenkowski's attitude and sense to do something about it." Rostenkowski was surprised enough about his defeat that he claimed, "I got my brains beat out," but Albert "was not surprised at all." The tradition was that the majority leader chose the whip, subject to the veto of the Speaker. Boggs nominated Rostenkowski three times to Albert, but Albert refused, claiming that a person who had been rejected for caucus chairman could not be made whip and adding, "He insulted and humiliated me at the convention. I won't have him." The meeting between Boggs and Albert was described in one account as "a stormy private session." Though Albert had earlier endorsed the idea that the whip should be elected by the caucus, Boggs opposed the plan out of concern that he would be saddled with Udall as his whip. Others worried that election of the whip might deny representation in the leadership to the Northeast, especially since Udall was a likely victor.[73]

After Rostenkowski was excluded, discussions between Albert and Boggs turned to Tip O'Neill of Massachusetts or Hugh Carey of New York. When unexpected opposition to Carey surfaced from a fellow New Yorker, Tip O'Neill, a Boston anti–Vietnam War member of the Rules Committee and a McCormack protégé, became the compromise choice. Boggs and Albert knew his appointment would please McCormack.[74]

Though Boggs won the majority leader's race, in some minds there was another victor — a silent winner. Columnist Kevin Phillips noted that

Richard Bolling had stayed out of the majority leader's race, something of a surprise. And yet, Phillips noted, Bolling's most likely competition for power in the House, Udall, had been weakened by the race. The competitor to Bolling who still remained standing was Boggs — the erratic Boggs — and he was weakened by his failure to deliver the whip position to Rostenkowski. Interestingly, Peabody reported to Udall that Bolling had voted for Boggs for majority leader, and Udall clearly believed the allegation.[75] In a private tirade, Udall vented more hostility against Bolling than he ever had against Boggs, accusing Bolling of sacrificing his support of reform to his own ambition. To Udall, the best chance for reform in a generation had been sacrificed by Bolling to "some wild scenario to become Speaker in 1980." "If Bolling couldn't mount a serious candidacy in this one golden opportunity when there was no obvious establishment candidate or a very weak one, when O'Hara and Udall were junior, when he had done all the lecturing and writing in the prime years of his life, what reasonable substantial hope is there that the mere passage of time and his ascendancy to the Chairman of the Rules Committee under the seniority system would make him a serious threat against Boggs, for example, who would then be the sitting Majority Leader and heir-presumptive to the throne." Udall was right. Bolling made one more move toward power, though it would come four years earlier than predicted by Udall, and it would be a race for majority leader rather than for the Speakership.

In the meantime, however, by 1972 Boggs seemed secure, and it was believed that it would be simply a matter of time before Boggs became Speaker. He was seen as a role model for a new generation of southern white moderate politicians. In a guest appearance on Boggs's bi-weekly broadcast report to his district, Albert predicted that Boggs would be the next Speaker. Boggs had done numerous favors for members of Congress, favors that built IOUs for his future candidacy, including giving campaign speeches for Democratic candidates. First-term Democratic congressman Nick Begich of Alaska sought such assistance from Boggs. Boggs flew to Anchorage to speak for Begich on a commercial airliner. Then, with Begich, he boarded a small chartered plane to Juneau. On October 16, 1972, the plane disappeared and has never been found.[76] A week after the disappearance, Carl Albert wrote John McCormack, "Ugly rumors of people trying to replace him have already come to my attention. This is almost beneath the lowest limits of decency. The Air Force still thinks there is a good chance he may be living."[77] The search for Boggs would prove futile, and majority leadership was again in play. Ultimately, Tip O'Neill would take the position, helping preserve the Austin-Boston connection for one more generation.

Maintaining the Alliance Challenges from Within

As Albert assumed the Speakership, the regional distribution of the House Democratic Party was changing. The Austin-Boston alliance was forged in the 1930s and 1940s in recognition that if the Democratic Party was to grow, it could only grow to the North. As Democratic strength in the solid South waned, and the Party's regional basis expanded westward, a new House coalition became inevitable.

When the Austin-Boston alliance began, California had minor importance to the House Democratic caucus. During the 77th Congress, there were eleven California Democrats in the House, which was little more than half of Texas' twenty-one House Democrats. California had only four more Democratic congressmen than Massachusetts. But by the 1970s, California sent the largest single Democratic delegation to the House, generally constituting about one-tenth of the entire Democratic membership. Figure 6-1 below plots the growth of the importance of the California, Texas, and Massachusetts delegations from the first New Deal Congress (73d) until the end of the O'Neill Speakership (99th Congress). Although the importance of Massachusetts steadily increased over the time period, the big changes were in the importance of Texas and California. Increasing Republican strength in Texas eroded the role of Texas Democrats in the House Democratic caucus while the increased size of California and the competitiveness of California's Democratic Party increased its importance. Simply put, after 1962, California Democrats outnumbered Texas Democrats in the House and, at least in raw numbers, California came to occupy as powerful a place in the Democratic caucus of the 1960s and 1970s as Texas had in the caucus of the 1940s and 1950s.

California Democrats were increasingly aware of their newfound importance, and there was no shortage of Californians who were considered to be potential leaders. In the late 1960s and early 1970s, Californians Rees, Moss, and Waldie were high-profile critics of Speaker McCormack and Majority Leader Albert. More conservative Californians like John Mc-Fall and Bernie Sisk had leadership ambitions as well.

Californians and other westerners recognized their increased numbers and strength in the caucus and hoped to break into the top House leadership. Still, westerners' hopes were repeatedly thwarted by the leadership ladder that benefited the Austin-Boston connection. Among the key

FIGURE 6-1. PERCENTAGE OF DEMOCRATIC CAUCUS FROM TEXAS, MASSACHUSETTS,
AND CALIFORNIA, 73RD–99TH CONGRESSES

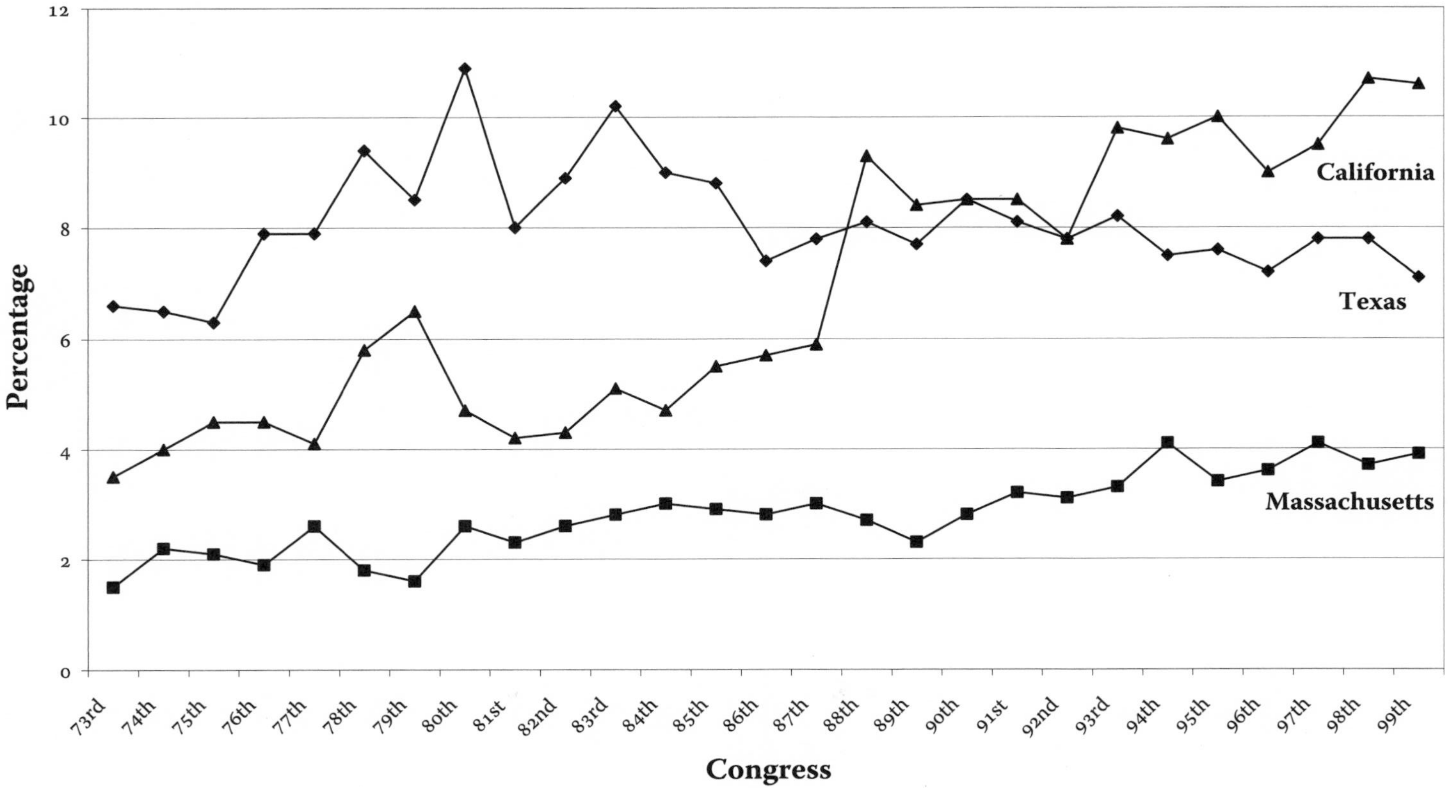

organizational structures that had helped maintain the alliance from the 1940s to the 1980s was the system of appointment of members to influential posts on committees and especially in the party leadership. Indeed, without a system in which highly placed leaders could appoint their protégés to key committees and other influential positions, such an informal alliance could have not been maintained for so long. New members coming to the House with each successive election (particularly those between 1964 and 1974) increasingly pressed for a more egalitarian, democratized House system.[78] Of course, their main target for much of this time was the system that elevated the most senior members of a committee (generally southern conservatives) to its chairmanship. In addition to overcoming the seniority rule and toppling committee chairs, this egalitarian spirit was aimed also at the tradition of appointing the whip.

Important as the whip position was becoming, what made the appointive whip such a point of contention was that a pattern of succession seemed to have taken hold: the whip would be elevated to majority leadership and then eventually become Speaker. Not only could top leaders continue to reward their friends and punish their enemies, but keeping the post appointive allowed the Speaker and the majority leader the ability to compensate for any ideological or regional imbalance in the leadership. Rather than leaving valuable regional balance to chance emergence in a series of leadership elections, appointment allowed leaders to hand pick the remainder of the leadership team to ensure such balance. For these reasons, the appointive whip post was perhaps the most important of the Austin-Boston alliance's structure of preferment.

Throughout the 1970s, younger, more liberal House members (and older members seeking to appeal to them) repeatedly sought to make the whip post elective. A perpetual issue in the organizational caucus meetings of the 1970s, the movement was frequently tied up with one or another leadership aspirant's effort to become the first elective whip. Tip O'Neill would be a chief defender of the appointive whip in both 1971 and 1973. Whereas in 1971, it was in O'Neill's interest to maintain the appointive post because he was in line for a possible appointment; in 1973 his direct interest resulted from the fact that, as the newly elected majority leader, he would make the appointment.

After bowing out of the 1971 majority leader's race after earning only twenty-eight votes on the first ballot earlier in the day, Representative Wayne Hays offered an amendment to the report of the Committee on Organization, Study, and Review (which was examining caucus rules and procedures) that read: "1) The position of Majority Whip shall be elective instead of appointive. 2) Each candidate desiring to have his name placed in nomination shall be entitled to one nominating speech not to exceed five minutes and no more than two seconding speeches not to exceed two minutes."[79]

In support of his own candidacy, Hays said, "I will be candid and outspoken. Twenty members have asked me to run for Majority Whip. I have been told that if I was elected Whip, I would not have to resign as Chairman of the Committee on House Administration, but Wayne Hays would resign as Chairman." Furthermore, Hays promised to accept the position only if it were elective because "rumors would fly that it was a deal, because of my vote for the Majority Leader, Mr. Boggs." In addition to the claim that the twenty members had prevailed upon him to run, Hays's pitch for making the whip post elective and his campaign for that post was almost too clever. His promise to step down as chairman of the House Administration Committee was really a tacit acknowledgement of just how unpopular he was with many House Democrats who disliked the way he used the position to build his own power base and punish colleagues he disliked. For some, making Hays whip might be taken as a demotion from his position as chairman of HAC where he had come to be known as the "second Speaker."

Moreover, his denial that he had arranged a deal with Boggs probably introduced the possibility of a deal to many House Democrats for the first time. Denial may have been a clever way to feed false speculation that there was a deal between Hays and Boggs and Albert. Any hopes that members might take Hays's denial of a deal with Boggs as evidence of such an agreement was quashed when both Albert and Boggs spoke out against Hays's amendment and in favor of maintaining the appointive whip. Arguing that the "Whip does not make floor policy" but, rather, "does the hard, tough, monotonous jobs," Boggs made the case that the "new leadership would be allowed the same privilege as former leaders" that would, in turn, produce "cohesive leadership."[80]

Perhaps in his haste to keep Rostenkowski from the leadership, Albert expressed to a reporter lukewarm support for the reform proposal, fueling speculation that the whip post would become elective. However, Boggs and other top House Democrats quickly persuaded Albert that such an arrangement might prove troublesome for the Speaker and the majority leader, who needed to be able to trust the loyalty of their whip. More to the point, some of the likely contenders for the whip position might not remain loyal to Boggs or Albert. Democrats such as Udall and Hays might make a successful run for the post and be in position to challenge the existing leadership team.

If there were many members whose ambitions for leadership might be met under the elective system, the appointive method had its interested defenders too. When both of them anticipated that they, in fact, might be appointed whip, O'Neill and Hugh Carey of New York made a strong case for maintaining the appointive whip by arguing that it alone could ensure regional diversity and unity in the top leadership. O'Neill told Albert, "This is absolutely ridiculous. . . . How do you know who's going to win? You have to have a man for whip from your own team. . . . He's got to be handpicked." Along with Carey, O'Neill argued that, in addition to ensuring the loyalty of the whip to the party's top two leaders, maintaining it as an appointed position would allow the Speaker and majority leader the ability to provide regional balance; in this case, the Bostonian and New Yorker were arguing that the leaders could and should appoint a northeastern member. This argument seems to have carried the day with a vacillating Albert. When the Speaker addressed the caucus as he had only days before, he once again sounded a conciliatory tone toward elective whips, saying, "I don't believe that this House would elect a Majority Whip that I or the Majority Leader could not work with." But in the end, the newly elected Speaker argued in favor of keeping the post appointive for a number of "considerations," including the "geographical balance and representation" argument that O'Neill and Carey had presented him.[81]

Two years later, O'Neill, the primary beneficiary of the maintenance of the appointive whip in 1971, would be the decisive defender of the practice immediately after having become majority leader in 1973. But should the whip post go elective in 1973, the potential field of candidates was large indeed. When defeated majority leadership candidate Sam Gibbons sought to be the first elected whip in the House Democratic Party, he kept running into potential rivals. Mentioning that Phil Burton, Jack Brooks, and Wayne Hays might be running for whip in 1973, Mo Udall himself told Gibbons that "I value your friendship, but I may be getting into this myself. . . . the reason I was going for the Senate was because I didn't think Boggs would be out and the leadership would never open up." Without Udall's endorsement, Gibbons pinned his hopes on garnering the support of his most important ally, as he planned to "corner Wilbur Mills on nominating you for Elected Whip." Mills told Gibbons that "Tip had been good—but we shouldn't follow the practice of elevating whips—whips ought to be elected. . . . 'If you want to win as whip, I would support you on making the whip elected.'" Indeed, Gibbons's announcement that he would drop out of the majority leader's race was both an acknowledgement that he could not win and a new effort to run for the whip post should it become elective. The "up side" of several withdrawal scenarios was that Gibbons "drop out and not allow vote to take place — In this way, you will not show weakness. Sympathy factor might be prevalent which would allow members to vote for you for elected Whip if this comes to pass."[82]

A month later, Mills and Gibbons had a "discussion of South being left out" where Mills told Gibbons that he "thinks South should definitely be in some spot." Mills's point was somewhat ironic in that the appointive nature of the position had maintained such regional balance for so long, and it was unlikely that a southerner would win the first whip election. In addition to this, there were many arguments in favor of maintaining the post as appointive. The general argument against election was that the whip worked for the elected leaders and, thus, should be responsive to them and them alone. Rostenkowski argued that the whip post should remain an appointed post reasoning that "if elective, then it is a popularity contest."[83]

Since the appointive whip was important to the survival of the Austin-Boston alliance, it is ironic that the 1973 resolution to change caucus rules to make the whip post elective came from a member of the Texas delegation, Bob Eckhardt of Houston. Rejecting the notion that an elective whip would divide the caucus, the liberal Eckhardt said, "I do not believe it would elect a whip that would not be a loyal supporter to the leadership. The whip should have the ultimate respect of this body, come from this body, and be elected by this body and I believe this would dissolve the possibility of schism in this body."

In contrast, Richard Bolling argued that internal divisiveness was "the reason that Congress is weak" and that an appointive whip was essential to a strong and unified House Democratic Party; he said,

We have just nominated a Speaker to wield strong effective power in dealing with the problems of the country, and a majority leader who indicates the same, and the first thing we want to do is to take some of that power away, what in fact we are saying is 'we do not trust you to wield this power.' I do not believe the Caucus wants that. We have to organize the power of each of us into the power of all of us. We must build a real team of power or we will go down in history as the Congress that gave away its power. The Executive branch has made it clear it wants all the power, we have to organize to compete with the President in the budget, foreign and domestic affairs, if we do not, historians will say we failed. I urge you to defeat this resolution and give the leadership the tools to effectively lead this House of Representatives.

After Bolling's motion to table the resolution electing the whip was defeated by a narrow 115 to 110 vote, the caucus broke for lunch. According to O'Neill biographer John Farrell, three O'Neill deputies, McFall, Brademas, and Wright (notably, all of whom would benefit personally from whip or deputy whip appointment), canvassed the caucus trying to change enough votes to keep the post appointive.[84] In its afternoon session, the caucus heard four speeches — two for each side — on the issue. John Moss of California joined Wayne Hays, who had originally made the motion in the previous Congress, speaking for an elective post. Considering the growing importance of California in the House Democratic caucus, an elective whip might do well to enhance a Californian's prospects for attaining a top leadership position.[85]

Besides Bolling (the House's informal institutional historian), the other two speeches arguing in favor of maintaining the system of appointment were, not surprisingly, a House member from Boston and one from Texas. Tip O'Neill addressed the caucus and acknowledged that he had had "the inside track" and "a tremendous advantage over other Members" for the majority leadership and that it was "probably unfair," O'Neill's plea for the right to select "his" whip was characteristically of a personal nature; he said, "it would be weakness on my part if I did not demand the same prerogative and right every other majority leader had, the right to name the majority whip." Although many observers of the event noted that the argument was selfish, few took note that O'Neill also paid homage to the success and stability of the intraparty alliances the appointive whip sustained. He concluded, "We have had control of Congress 38 out of 42 years that is ample enough reason to go along with the system. Let us vote down this resolution."[86]

Jake Pickle was the last member to address the caucus prior to the vote. Asking his colleagues to reject the motion made by fellow Texan Eckhardt, Pickle appealed the principles of unity and effectiveness. Similar to O'Neill's plea, Pickle said, "In the past appointing the whips has worked. I think we should be looking for ways to keep us all together, we divide ourselves, I think it is important we do not disrupt ourselves, not to have this division, the procedure of appointment has served us well."[87]

There is good reason to believe that the crucial votes in support of O'Neill and Pickle's viewpoint came from fellow members from their regions. According to Peabody, Phil Burton of California believed that O'Neill's speech turned around at least five votes, and Farrell claims that O'Neill's speech "was particularly effective among O'Neill's closest allies in New England and the South." And, to be sure, Pickle's speech "may have changed several votes within the large Texas delegation."[88] In the final vote, 125 Democrats stood with O'Neill in maintaining the appointive nature of the whip position whereas 114 voted to make the whip elective.

However, O'Neill's speech to the caucus was not only influential and possibly decisive, it was more than a little risky as well. Peabody quotes an "activist" who "saw it as a major gamble."[89] To be sure, something had changed from the morning vote against Bolling's motion tabling the resolution and the afternoon where O'Neill's side carried the day. If it was a gamble, a close look at the potential whip race if O'Neill had lost reveals that he had much to gain from his gamble. It appears as if the whip race that would have taken shape would have included Deputy Whips Brademas and McFall, Caucus Chairman Phil Burton, the freshly defeated Sam Gibbons, Wayne Hays, and possibly Mo Udall. Whereas two of the candidates, Brademas and McFall, were both personally acceptable and helped to bring greater geographic balance to the leadership, the other potential whips were unsuitable to O'Neill.

Gibbons was O'Neill's rival for the majority leadership who, from O'Neill's perspective, should not be rewarded with the whip post as a consolation prize. Moreover, in the majority leader's race, Gibbons had been characterized as "too southern" for the liberals and too liberal for the southerners; thus, he brought little to the leadership team. Similarly, Udall was unacceptable because the Arizonan's representation of the southwestern wing of the Democratic Party offered little in terms of numbers and was not all that different from Speaker Albert's Oklahoma strengths. Moreover, although he personally liked Udall, O'Neill's continued loyalty to McCormack meant the same animus that kept him from supporting Udall in the majority leader's race against Boggs in 1971 would keep him from wanting Udall as his whip.

But perhaps the stakes were highest when it came to Phil Burton. Indeed, the motion to elect the whip had this time been propelled by Burton's potential candidacy. As early as November 10, rumors were circulating that Burton would run for elective whip. Much as this excited Burton's core supporters, it also roused his legion of enemies. Not only were potential competitors like O'Neill aware of the challenge Burton posed, but even many of Burton's California colleagues resisted his rise into the leadership. Thomas Rees of California told Sam Gibbons, "if you don't make it [Majority Leader], what about the Whip—Phil's race disturbs me.... Brademas and McFall not good—I am very much interested in your getting a second alternative." Even the dean of the California delegation, Chet Holifield, viewed the whole issue of appointive versus elective whip in light of the specific candidates. Favoring fellow Californian John McFall over Burton, Holifield said, "Because ... [the] whip should have confidence of Speaker, be able to count noses for him, I won't go for the elective whip—I don't think Phil has what it takes to be whip at any rate."[90]

If the post had become elective in 1973, O'Neill faced the possibility of a competing power center within the leadership. Phil Burton, Sam Gibbons, Wayne Hays, or any other leader that he did not handpick might pose a challenge to him for the Speakership upon Albert's retirement. This was perhaps the most important consideration in defending the practice of appointing the whip.

To blunt the force of Burton's claim that California deserved greater representation in the leadership, the O'Neill forces had let word slip that should the whip post remain appointive, the new majority leader would appoint Californian John McFall to the post. The leak of a likely McFall appointment hurt Gibbons's efforts to push for electing the whip as well. When Wilbur Mills suggested to Gibbons that he should ask "someone— perhaps Chet Holifield," to introduce the resolution, Gibbons, who had already thought of the possibility, "responded that Chet wants it appointed and apparently will be for McFall—too, he had heard about a deal that had been made with California for McFall."[91]

O'Neill's personal efforts worked, and whip appointment was maintained until 1987 when Californian Tony Coelho became the first elected whip. The appointive whip, so crucial to the Austin-Boston alliance, was preserved despite the democratizing spirit of the early 1970s House Democrats. In addition to all of these strategic reasons for maintaining the appointive status of the whip, O'Neill's experience in and benefit from the Austin-Boston alliance also made him protective of the process of appointment. Indeed, Sam Gibbons's forces recognized this as a possible inroad into O'Neill's support in 1973: "[Gibbons] confirmed support of elected whip issue. O'Neill against it. SMG [Sam Gibbons] says many members don't like escalator system. O'Neill feels sorry for guys who want to get in another way but won't buck a system that he has ridden in on."[92]

Having defended the appointive whip as a means of maintaining regional balance, if not the Austin-Boston alliance specifically, O'Neill made his appointments with an eye toward the same geographical balance from which he had benefited. By naming McFall whip and Brademas chief deputy whip in 1973, O'Neill used his appointment powers to reflect diversity among House Democrats. According to a *Congressional Quarterly* reporter, "O'Neill's aims by selecting these deputies were to establish closer ties with the Western congressmen through McFall and with the younger activists through Brademas."[93] Indeed, the addition of McFall to the top leadership helped blunt the claims to leadership of other ambitious Californians like Phil Burton; now California had a high place at the leadership table.

With Albert as Speaker, O'Neill as majority leader, and McFall and Brademas waiting in the wings, southerners began to complain that they had no representation in the leadership.[94] Recognizing that he needed to maintain the South, O'Neill looked to expand the leadership team as he had done for California with McFall's appointment and the Midwest with Brademas's appointment. More specifically, pressure to reassert presence in the leadership was also coming from the Texas delegation. With Olin "Tiger" Teague nearing completion of his second term as caucus chairman, some expected that he might make a bid for whip; indeed, there was even early speculation that he might have emerged as the southern alternative to O'Neill in the race for majority leader. Teague instead opted to become chairman of the Science and Astronautics Committee and forgo his opportunity to advance up the leadership ladder.

Although other Texans, like Jack Brooks, had their eyes on leadership positions, much of the Texas delegation decided to push Jim Wright for a leadership post. Talk about Wright's moving into a leadership post emerged during the Gibbons-O'Neill campaign for majority leader. When asked about whether he could support Gibbons's campaign for majority leader, Jake Pickle revealed "that Jim Wright might be pushed by them [the Texas delegation] for whip or assistant whip." This was confirmed by other Texas Democrats in conversations with Gibbons. Expressing his dissatisfaction with O'Neill and Gibbons ("the hell with both of you"), Texan Kika de la Garza wondered to Gibbons "if Jim Wright is interested."[95] O'Neill would accommodate Texas' desire for a leadership position by appointing Wright as one of three deputy whips under McFall and Chief Deputy

John Brademas.[96] Indeed, according to O'Neill, it was a direct appeal from John McCormack, referencing his relationship with Sam Rayburn, that led to Wright's appointment. McCormack telephoned O'Neill saying, "The party has always had a special Boston-Austin connection. There was Rayburn and myself. There was Kennedy and Johnson. Now that you're in the leadership, I'd like you to tell Carl Albert that I would appreciate it if he would keep the Boston-Austin axis going."[97]

The End of the Albert Speakership

The Albert-O'Neill team led Congress for six years. When Albert announced his retirement, his reasons were probably varied, including what he wrote in his memoirs, "already (10 years earlier) I had had one major heart attack. My doctors told me that my heart just could not take too much more. I was still young enough and still healthy enough to enjoy many years with my family and friends."[98]

But those friends were equally aware that the last few months of the Albert regime had seen a number of unflattering allegations about his behavior. Though none of them were confirmed, the numerous negative reports were becoming public, and caused the Speaker personal embarrassment and jeopardized his ability to lead. By 1976, some of the Republican efforts to take over Congress by capitalizing on its institutional unpopularity started a "Congressional Speaker Reform Committee" and a newsletter called "The Naked Truth" that focused not just on policy but also congressional scandals. They called O'Neill "corrupt" and accused Albert of "keeping a South Korean spy on his payroll," a charge stemming from the nationally publicized "Koreagate" scandal.[99] That scandal alleged that a South Korean rice dealer had given too generously to members of Congress and that they had returned the favor by acting favorably on his behalf. Though no one ever confirmed an Albert role in that scandal, the allegations alone were damaging.

The *National Journal* wrote stories about scandals ascribed to Albert, giving a high profile exposure to what had been circulating in the Capitol halls for months: "In the past year, the diminutive Albert has shown up in the gossip and social columns of the Washington press almost as often as he has in the political sections. He has been chided for his alleged fondness for young women and liquor, for his supposed erratic behavior and for what his critics consider a lack of forceful direction. . . . His admirers say they hope he will not hang on to the point where he obscures the reputation he gained in earlier years as a gifted and energetic legislator."

The most prominent rumors concerned Albert's drinking. At one point, his car was involved in a hit and run accident. He returned to the scene a few minutes later and negotiated a cash settlement for the damage he had done to a van and to a parked car. "The police drove Mr. Albert home. And that, too, was that — even though witnesses said the Speaker was 'obviously drunk.'" The next day, reporters questioned Albert about the incident. Albert denied that he had been drinking. The event must have been well attended because Albert began his comments by quipping, "I wonder what it is that brought so many attractive people in here today."[100]

Later, there was a fire at Albert's apartment that rumors suggested had begun when Mrs. Albert fell asleep while smoking. That fire took place after another fire three years earlier had damaged the Albert's previous residence. In the second fire, which occurred while the Speaker was in New York, Mrs. Albert was slightly injured.[101] Though nothing more came of that event, surely it too added to the stress.

Finally, a small media firestorm took place over a photo taken during the 1975 Gerald Ford State of the Union address. In the photo, Albert appeared to be asleep. Though Albert denied that, the event simply added to the list that led to a feeling by some that Albert had passed his most effective years.[102]

Another factor that may have played into Albert's decision was that Tip O'Neill had earned his chance to be promoted to the top spot. Albert had, O'Neill later told Jim Wright, intended to serve only six years or so from the outset. When the time came for O'Neill to contemplate organizing the House should Speaker Albert retire, O'Neill asked Albert if he should begin planning to be Speaker. O'Neill reported to Wright that Albert told O'Neill to begin planning.[103] Albert's years as Speaker included the long struggle that culminated in the end of the Vietnam War and the resignation of Pres. Richard Nixon following impeachment hearings. But now the Albert era was ending, and the O'Neill era was at its dawn. The spirited election of a new majority leader would keep the Austin-Boston connection together for one last time.

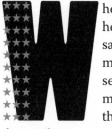**W**hen Tip O'Neill was elected Speaker in January 1977, he became the third Speaker of the House from Massachusetts in thirty years. In addition to John McCormack — O'Neill's principal mentor in the House — who served from Sam Rayburn's death in 1961 until retirement in 1971, Speaker Joe Martin, the Republican from the Attleboro suburbs south of Boston, had been Speaker during the two post–New Deal Congresses in which the Republicans had wrested majority control of the House from the Democrats.

To many, O'Neill exemplified the old-style Boston "pol." Even the most casual observer of U.S. politics is familiar with O'Neill's aphorism that "all politics is local." A large, gregarious, backslapping backroom operator, O'Neill cultivated a reputation as an astute — even ruthless — practitioner of pork barrel politics. For example, even as he sought to cut weapons systems and the Defense Department budget as Speaker during the 1980s, he pushed for additional funds for weapons systems that brought jobs to Massachusetts.[1]

Like many urban politicians, O'Neill continually came under the scrutiny of reporters and political enemies who assumed that O'Neill's glad-handing manner was a thin veil for a politician "on the take."[2] After several news organizations, most notably the *Boston Herald,* investigated O'Neill's financial dealings, and a particularly close call with the influence-peddling "Koreagate" scandal of the mid 1970s, O'Neill emerged largely unscathed but nevertheless determined to avoid such improper appearances in the future. Still, if O'Neill himself was not comfortable with the shadier side of machine politics, he was certainly forgiving and defending of friends and colleagues who had been caught practicing influence-peddling and questionable fundraising techniques. From the scandal in John McCormack's office to John McFall to Frank Thompson to Dan Rostenkowski, many O'Neill contemporaries and close friends would at one point or another succumb to ethical lapses that ended their political careers.

Of course, being an old-style pol was not inconsistent with O'Neill's position as a self-proclaimed keeper of the New Deal faith. And, to O'Neill, it was an article of faith that the national government could play a role in making the lives of U.S. citizens better. Although its critics would contend that the New Deal was little more than an electoral scheme that used the public coffers to protect Democratic incumbents, disparate elements of the Democratic Party, including O'Neill, believed in a beneficial role for government.[3] Indeed, what united (to varying degrees) O'Neill to Sam Rayburn, Phil Burton, Richard Bolling, and Jim Wright was the belief that government could be used to redress inequities in society. As a member of Congress, a partisan Democrat, and eventually the Speaker, O'Neill kept this faith throughout his three decades–long House career.

If the Austin-Boston alliance was the New Deal coalition's primary manifestation in the House, O'Neill is probably its most appropriate and obvious personal beneficiary. A sometime guest at Rayburn's Board of Education in the late 1950s, his role in leadership circles increased after McCormack became Speaker. O'Neill was appointed, often at McCormack's suggestion, to increasingly important positions of party responsibility from the 1950s through the 1970s. From his extraordinary appointment to the Rules Committee in only his second term in the House to his last-minute appointment as co-chairman of the Democratic Congressional Campaign Committee in 1970, McCormack's preferment of his protégé put O'Neill on a path toward higher positions of leadership that culminated in his decade-long Speakership.

Not only did O'Neill benefit from the Austin-Boston connection, but he also protected and perpetuated the alliance, promoting the careers of members of both the Texas and Massachusetts delegations throughout the 1970s and 1980s and protecting the means by which the alliance was perpetuated: the leadership's ability to appoint allies and associates to high-level positions, most notably the majority whip post. Along with Speaker Albert, in 1973 O'Neill had appointed Texan Jim Wright to the "leadership ladder" by making him one of three deputy whips. And, in 1976, O'Neill's friendship may have served to encourage Wright to run for majority leader and key colleagues to support Wright's candidacy.

In all, O'Neill was perfectly cast as a character in the Austin-Boston connection; he was utterly faithful to the New Deal as both a political philosophy and an electoral strategy. Still, to treat O'Neill as merely reflective of the "old order" in House Democratic politics is misleading. O'Neill had one foot in the old order, but the other constantly probed the possibilities of change in the House and tried to keep pace as a new generation of younger, more liberal members entered the House. Indeed, although intensely loyal personally to McCormack to the end, by the late 1960s, O'Neill was starting to demonstrate his independence from the aging Speaker on a range of issues and procedural questions in the House. This transitional status between the old order and the emerging "new politics" of the 1960s is probably best exemplified by O'Neill's break from the Speaker (and his friend Lyndon Johnson) on Vietnam and O'Neill's championing of many, if not all, of the internal House reforms of the 1970s. This increased independence endeared O'Neill to the growing number of young liberal members of Congress while maintaining his strong ties to the House establishment. These twin strengths, when added to O'Neill's personal popularity, made him a seemingly undeniable player in House leadership politics.

"McCormack's Man"

That O'Neill would become the face of the Democrats for the national media during the Reagan administration was something that few would have predicted for him early in his political career. The first Democratic Speaker of the Massachusetts House, when O'Neill went to the U.S. House in 1952, he harbored plans to return home to run for governor when the time was right. But, of course, he would stay in the U.S. Congress for three decades, retiring in 1986.

An influential Democrat in Massachusetts state politics, O'Neill had many friends and associates from Curley and McCormack to the Kennedy family. As O'Neill told it, when John F. Kennedy decided to give up his House seat to challenge Sen. Henry Cabot Lodge in 1952, Kennedy informed O'Neill that the seat would be open more than a year in advance of his announcement to give O'Neill a head start in mounting a campaign to succeed him. After winning a close race for the Democratic nomination, O'Neill won the Massachusetts 11th congressional district with nearly 70 percent of the vote. Kennedy, who had a continually antagonistic relationship with John McCormack, told O'Neill, "Tip, don't do what I did down there. Be nice to John McCormack."[4]

In part, Kennedy's feud with McCormack could be traced to personal and Massachusetts politics. As a well-funded outsider, Kennedy had little need for the resources the Massachusetts party could provide, and thus he felt no obligation to follow their orders. For example, Kennedy was the lone Democrat in the Massachusetts congressional delegation who refused to sign a petition McCormack circulated trying to get a presidential pardon for James Michael Curley. Moreover, Kennedy and McCormack had more than one battle over patronage in Massachusetts politics.

But Kennedy's advice to O'Neill to be nice to McCormack was not merely a reminder to avoid personal conflict and to leave internecine Massachusetts Democratic feuds out of his congressional dealings. Kennedy specifically advised O'Neill not to buck the "to get along, go along" norms of party loyalty that Rayburn and McCormack defended. Kennedy had been an outsider in the House. O'Neill said of Kennedy's career in the House, "He was a maverick, didn't follow the leadership of Rayburn and McCormack, and they resented him very much." Indeed, in his pursuit of the 1960 Democratic presidential nomination, Kennedy worried about Rayburn's chairing of the nominating convention and confided to O'Neill that "Rayburn had a personal dislike for me."[5] Moreover, Rayburn's negative attitude toward Kennedy was emblematic of Rayburn's antipathy toward what he regarded as the House's "showhorses" who claimed credit for the diligent legislative efforts of its "workhorses."[6] Richard Bolling, close to both Rayburn and Kennedy, said that even after Kennedy became president, "the Speaker viewed Kennedy as if he were still a backbencher."[7]

In contrast to Kennedy's style of being a dilettante more interested in the Washington social scene than the internal workings of the House, O'Neill threw himself into the House's work and quickly allied with McCormack. McCormack and O'Neill had themselves once been rivals in Massachusetts politics and had first taken one another's measure on opposite sides of a bitter contest over which candidates would represent the Massachusetts delegation to the 1948 Democratic convention.[8] Despite this early rivalry, O'Neill had so impressed the then–Majority Leader McCormack that McCormack encouraged O'Neill to try to build a Democratic majority in the Massachusetts House. When O'Neill successfully built that legislative majority to become Speaker of the Massachusetts House, he counted McCormack among the principal supporters, financiers, and inspirations of the effort.

Soon after he arrived in Washington, O'Neill became McCormack's regular companion, breakfasting daily with McCormack in the House dining room and joining McCormack's frequent, if brief, appearances at "cocktail parties, receptions, and fund-raisers" on Washington's early evening social scene. At breakfast, O'Neill would learn about the internal politics of the legislative process as McCormack would hold court on matters in the House. In the evenings, McCormack would introduce O'Neill to key lobbyists and members of the executive branch, from which O'Neill's connections "downtown" proliferated. At first mistaken for McCormack's bodyguard, O'Neill soon came to be well-connected in Washington circles and well-known as "McCormack's man."[9]

As "McCormack's man," O'Neill understood well that loyalty would put him on a glide path toward greater influence in the House. Describing his sense of party loyalty, O'Neill conveyed McCormack's command of the Massachusetts and even the New England delegations: "we followed along the line pretty well. The entire Massachusetts delegation pretty nearly voted as a unit at all times, the New England delegation, particularly the Democrats, followed the leadership of McCormack."[10] Throughout O'Neill's House career, McCormack's hand guided and elevated O'Neill. This mutually beneficial relationship was probably never made explicit, but with each of these men well-schooled in the patronage-based politics of Curley's Boston, it was a familiar and comfortable alliance. O'Neill would loyally serve his senior colleague, and, in return, McCormack would look for opportunities to advance the interests of his talented protégé.

When the Democrats took back control of the House after the 1954 Eisenhower midterm elections, their replenished numbers allowed for the awarding of more and better committee assignments than when O'Neill first came to the House in the 83d Congress. Still, few could have predicted that O'Neill would land the influential appointment that he did. When the Democrats organized the 84th Congress, O'Neill became only the second second-term representative to be appointed to the influential Rules Committee. O'Neill's 83d Congress classmate, fellow Massachusetts representative and Washington roommate, Eddie Boland, was appointed to the Appropriations Committee the same year. Both of these plum appointments, of course, were primarily McCormack's doing. Describing his appointment to Appropriations, Boland told political scientist Richard F. Fenno Jr. that he "got on the committee by going to see John McCormack . . . McCormack looks after the Mass. people, and takes care of vacancies."[11]

These committee appointments played to the strengths of each of McCormack's protégés, and each appointment encouraged different career paths in the House. Eddie Boland's placement on Appropriations would likely lead to a career as one of the House's "Cardinals," an appropriations subcommittee chairmanship, where a detail- and policy-oriented member might become influential in federal spending policy. O'Neill's placement on the Rules Committee and the consequent responsibility to the party and the House leadership, on the other hand, solidified O'Neill's distinctly political, rather than policy-oriented, career. To be sure, Boland would become himself a player in internal House politics, but his ultimate influence would be made within the Appropriations Committee.[12]

In terms of seniority, O'Neill was appointed just behind Rayburn protégé Dick Bolling, and, therefore, any hope of someday chairing the committee was unlikely to be fulfilled. Still, an appointment to Rules gave the young congressman a key post from which he could both influence all manner of legislation pertaining to his district and forward the interests of (and thus his career in) the House Democratic Party. On the day Rayburn told O'Neill of his appointment to Rules, the Speaker mentioned McCormack's role in the decision and emphasized the importance of the post to the party as well as the requirement that O'Neill demonstrate party loyalty when required. O'Neill recalled the brief exchange: "He [Rayburn] says, John McCormack tells me you're a former Speaker of the House. I says, that's right. And you know what loyalty is. I says, that's right. He says, you know what it means to get legislation to the floor — you could be opposed to the legislation but I would expect you to get votes for me to get it on the floor. I says, that's party loyalty. He says, you're going on the Rules Committee." But, of course, it was not only party loyalty that was required; O'Neill was to be loyal specifically to McCormack. Of the eight Democrats on the Rules Committee, O'Neill described Representatives Howard W. Smith and Bill Colmer as the conservatives largely independent of the leadership, with the remaining six members equally divided among Rayburn and McCormack loyalists: "Jim Delaney, Madden, myself: we were McCormack people on the committee. Bolling and Thornberry, and the old judge . . . from Arkansas — Trimble: they were considered to be Rayburn people. And so if Rayburn had a problem on the committee, he would contact his men; while McCormack . . . always talked to Madden, Delaney, and myself."[13] Whereas loyalty to McCormack usually meant loyalty to the party, on those occasions, like on funding for Catholic schools during the Kennedy administration, where loyalty to McCormack meant parting ways with other leaders of the party (even O'Neill's friend President Kennedy), O'Neill sided with the majority leader.[14] Speaking for the party and McCormack on the Rules Committee was particularly important in the 1960s as a conservative coalition of committee Republicans and conservative southern Democrats, headed by Rules Chairman Howard W. Smith (D-VA), often would vote together to keep legislation from the House floor. When a confrontation between Rayburn and Smith in February 1961 led to a House expansion of the Rules Committee (such that the conservative coalition would generally lose rather than win close votes), O'Neill not only provided a loyal vote for the top party leaders but also kept tabs on the internal politics of the committee and alerted McCormack to potential trouble.

And with Rayburn's death and perennial McCormack rival and liberal Dick Bolling also on Rules, McCormack's grip on the committee was not assured without other liberal allies to do the leadership's bidding. McCormack put it plainly, "O'Neill was my man on the committee. A Roman Catholic that represented my views. When he spoke, he spoke for me."[15]

McCormack's appointment of O'Neill to Rules was the beginning of a pattern of preferment that led to a long series of internal appointments that would elevate O'Neill through the ranks of the House leadership and, by McCormack's retirement, put O'Neill within striking distance of the top party leadership. Much of House leadership in the mid-twentieth century was informal and highly personal; leaders led primarily through the use of small circles of influence. Nothing symbolized this informal, personal style better than the Board of Education cultivated by Garner and then Rayburn. As O'Neill recalled, McCormack "invited" him to attend these exclusive late afternoon gatherings "on many occasions," and O'Neill boasted that "John McCormack would never bring anybody else in but me."[16]

Although not a regular at "Board" meetings during Rayburn's tenure, O'Neill attended regularly enough to get to know Rayburn and the other influential House leaders present. Indeed, O'Neill's relationship with McCormack gave the young House member the rare opportunity to become known by Speaker Rayburn. Describing his relationship with Rayburn as "extremely cordial" and "very friendly," O'Neill recalled frequent and "long conversations" with the normally taciturn Speaker. O'Neill's loyalty to McCormack gave him stature with Rayburn. Having proven himself as someone who would "go along," O'Neill remembered, "I got along extremely well with the old Speaker."[17]

O'Neill's stock in the House rose when McCormack became Speaker. As McCormack continued the Board of Education, largely unchanged in its meeting time, tone, and even membership, one reporter noted, "several of the regulars of the Rayburn era are usually present when the board convenes. . . . The only new member . . . is Representative Thomas P. O'Neill, Jr. . . . a long time close friend and political associate of Speaker McCormack."[18] O'Neill was now well-placed to influence legislation and politics in the House of the 1960s.

After fifteen years on Rules and nearly a decade as a regular at the Board of Education, McCormack conferred O'Neill's first official party leadership position when he appointed him co-chairman of the Democratic Congressional Campaign Committee in 1970. For years, younger Democrats had complained that longtime DCCC chairman Mike Kirwan (D-OH) was too complacent in the position he had held since 1947 and seemed ready to press this point in the 1969 House organizational caucus (the same organizational caucus at which Morris Udall would challenge McCormack). Many of the same younger, more liberal members who supported Udall's challenge also called for increased caucus (rather than top leadership) control of the Campaign Committee. Forestalled, just as was Udall's challenge to McCormack, the liberals had to be satisfied with McCormack's promise to take "unspecified steps . . . to strengthen the committee."[19]

Among these unspecified steps was McCormack's appointment of O'Neill to the committee and, when Kirwan died in the midst of the summer stretch of the 1970 midterm elections, O'Neill's appointment to chair the committee. Speaker McCormack and Majority Leader Albert quickly appointed a temporary replacement to guide the party's electoral activities until November. Taking the extraordinary step of appointing co-chairs, McCormack and Albert each appointed a protégé from his home state to take over. Close Albert associate Rep. Ed Edmonson (D-OK) joined O'Neill as co-chairman of the DCCC for the 1970 election cycle. Both stayed on after the 1970 elections, although O'Neill became the sole chairman for the 1972 election cycle when Edmondson resigned to run for the U.S. Senate.[20]

O'Neill was something of an innovator as DCCC chairman, especially compared to Kirwan. During O'Neill's chairmanship, the DCCC broke with Kirwan's long-standing practice of giving all Democratic incumbents equal support regardless of need and began targeting specific "opportunity" districts where the committee's scarce campaign funds could be strategically deployed. He also curried favor with his colleagues and made important contacts with Democratic officials throughout the country by traveling to congressional districts for campaign fundraisers. In addition, O'Neill's DCCC actively identified weak Republicans and aided Democratic challengers who had a chance of unseating them. As O'Neill recalled, "I loved this work, which was a natural extension of what I had accomplished in Massachusetts in 1948, when, at John McCormack's urging, a few of us worked feverishly to make the state house Democratic."[21]

In less than two decades in the House, O'Neill had emerged as a top party leader. His close association with McCormack catapulted him nearly to the top of the House Democratic Party. Appreciating the mentoring and support he had received from McCormack, O'Neill remained a loyal "McCormack Man" throughout his career. When the Sweig-Voloshen influence-pedaling scandal threatened McCormack, O'Neill was one of seven (three of them members of Congress) to be character witnesses for McCormack's aide Sweig. As one of McCormack's key defenders, when a constituent wrote O'Neill questioning the Speaker's integrity, O'Neill replied, "From my years of close contact with the Speaker in the House, I feel that I am qualified to state that he is most able, dedicated, and one of the greatest legislative leaders in the history of our government. This is the period of the year when Congress is appointing Committees and awaiting hearings. Because of the lack of action, it is customary for newsmen to choose one individual and blast away. This is just what they have done to the Speaker of the House." Especially notable is that when criticism of McCormack came from within the House, O'Neill remained loyal to the Speaker. By December 1967, when many Democratic members had come to the conclusion that McCormack had outlived his usefulness as Speaker, O'Neill said, "there are those who criticize McCormack today in his leadership, but they never criticize him in front of me because . . . they know I'm close to him." And when the criticisms of Richard Bolling and other House liberals reached a crescendo in 1967 and 1968, O'Neill's support of McCormack remained unwavering. In an undated letter from this time, O'Neill reaffirmed his gratitude and support to the Speaker, writing that "It has been my great honor and privilege to have served with you in the House" and that his accomplishments were "due to your great and inspiring leadership."[22]

The Next Boston Speaker

When McCormack announced his retirement in 1970, it seemed likely that neither of the two top leadership posts would be occupied by a northern Democrat. Most people conceded that Majority Leader Albert would be elevated to Speaker (and, indeed, the only serious contender who could challenge Albert was Wilbur Mills of Arkansas), but the two most likely contenders for majority leader were majority whip and Louisianan Hale

Boggs and Arizona's Morris Udall. In turn, the long-held belief that the top party leadership required geographical balance meant that Tip O'Neill and other liberal northerners would receive serious consideration for appointment as whip.

That O'Neill was a leader from the Northeast, popular, with substantial experience and a following would be the characteristics that catapulted him into the top House leadership. Still, O'Neill was not alone in his ambition. From the urban ethnic Midwest, Chicago's Dan Rostenkowski and Detroit's James O'Hara offered similar kinds of regional balance to the Democratic leadership dominated by Oklahoma's Albert and Louisiana's Boggs. A weaker, though still serious, case for regional balance might be made for Appalachian Ohio's Wayne Hays. And, from the northeast, New York's Hugh Carey was also widely considered a potential top House leader.

By the same token, there were many members of Congress from the West (particularly California) who believed that the geographical composition of the leadership should reflect the party's increasing reliance on the West for key votes. In addition to Udall, who had challenged John McCormack in late 1968 and who hoped to be the party's first "southwestern" leader, a whole range of Californians from insiders like John McFall to conservatives like Bernie Sisk and the ultimate outsider-liberal, Phil Burton, believed that they represented the future of the House Democrats.

Finally, among the rivals in O'Neill's path was another McCormack protégé from Massachusetts, Eddie Boland. Somewhat ironically, it was Boland, O'Neill's closest friend, Massachusetts colleague, and Washington roommate, who represented the greatest threat to his prospects for advancement. Inasmuch as the Democratic Party prized geographical balance in its House leadership, in all likelihood there was room for only one New England Democrat in the top leadership posts and certainly only room for one liberal McCormack protégé from Massachusetts. Both ambitious, O'Neill and Boland saw each other as rivals. Describing their rivalry, one-time majority whip Tony Coelho told John Farrell, "Both of them were perceived as the next Bostonian Speaker."[23]

Who, O'Neill or Boland, would enter the top House leadership? Or would Boston be shut out of the leadership in favor of another northern establishment Democrat like Rostenkowski, O'Hara, or Carey? Or, for that matter, would the party leadership finally reflect the gains Democrats had made in California and the West? These questions would be determined by the Democrats' 1971 race for majority leader, although each of these contenders would make his move in a different way. O'Hara would run for majority leader, and although he had a good reputation among liberals in the House, he would never step out of the shadow of fellow liberal Morris Udall in his bid to step over Majority Whip Hale Boggs. Carey and Rostenkowski would, like O'Neill, side with the establishment choice for majority leader, Hale Boggs, and each would receive Boggs's serious consideration for the whip post. Boland, on the other hand, would, in the end, throw his support to Udall in the hopes of being Udall's appointment as whip.

McCormack's retirement set off one of the most hotly contested leadership races in the second half of the twentieth century. With Majority Leader Albert advancing to the Speakership with only symbolic opposition from Michigan's John Conyers, the real race, it seemed, would be to succeed Albert as majority leader. Although in the end the pool of candidates would include Majority Whip (and eventual victor) Hale Boggs, his most formidable challenger Morris Udall, as well as O'Hara, Bernie Sisk, and Wayne Hays, both Tip O'Neill and Eddie Boland gave some thought and received some encouragement to make a run for the majority leadership.

One congressional staff member handwrote a letter to O'Neill advising him "in case you haven't seen it," although surely he had, that "the total number of House Democrats in the 92nd Congress will be 63 from New England, New York and Pennsylvania. Give it some thought you can make the Majority Leader's spot." Surely others saw this possibility and recognized O'Neill's strengths as a potential leader. Representative Edward J. Patten (D-NJ) encouragingly described O'Neill as "The Ideal Majority Leader."[24] Although these and other House insiders perceived that O'Neill had a better shot at the leader's post than Boland, once Boland announced, O'Neill refused to run against his friend and roommate. Still, this rivalry caused more than a little friction between the two, and O'Neill would eventually complain that Boland hadn't really worked for the position; some speculated that he had cut a deal with Udall to serve as a "stalking horse" in the campaign.

The deal that more likely took place between Udall and Boland was similar to that struck between Boggs and Rostenkowski in which Boland, in exchange for delivering northeastern votes and making a seconding speech for Udall, would be appointed whip. Udall regarded Boland's support as a key endorsement on his way to victory. Not only did Udall expect incorrectly that O'Neill would follow his roommate's lead, but Udall believed that Boland was a good ambassador for the campaign to recruit a host of last-minute uncommitted votes. He sent Boland a list of "Appropriations Committee Types," members from the northeast, and other "colleagues who might really be impressed . . . by a personal pitch from you." In all, Udall told Boland, "You can wrap this up all by yourself if you can swing a few of these undecideds."[25]

The Udall-Boland alliance was formidable and potentially very troublesome to O'Neill's future. If Udall won, O'Neill's support of Boggs would leave him at odds with the new majority leader. Moreover, if Udall's later contention that he would have appointed Boland whip actually was the case, then O'Neill's hopes for advancement would have been dashed. No amount of personal influence and popularity would have helped O'Neill convince his fellow Democrats that the party needed another Massachusetts member in the top leadership. Had this scenario played out, O'Neill would have little hope to advance in the leadership. The only possibility that would remain for O'Neill was to challenge his friend at some later point, but this was unlikely. The same personal loyalty to Boland that kept O'Neill from challenging his roommate for the 1971 majority leader's race would likely have kept O'Neill from challenging him in subsequent years.

O'Neill personally liked Mo Udall but did not forgive him for his 1968 challenge to Speaker McCormack. Indeed, according to O'Neill, McCormack made a personal appeal to his protégé when he telephoned him and said, "Tom, I hope you're not supporting Udall." O'Neill's loyalty to McCormack won out. Udall recounted, "At a critical juncture somebody brought word that Tip O'Neill had said he couldn't buy me under any circumstance" because of the challenge to McCormack. O'Neill later would acknowledge as much in his memoirs: "Mo Udall was a beautiful guy and a close friend, but he had made a big mistake a couple of years earlier when he had challenged McCormack for Speaker. . . . I liked Mo, but I was loyal to McCormack."[26] O'Neill backed Boggs for majority leader. And Boggs's good fortune in victory would turn things in O'Neill's, and not Boland's, favor.

For many of the same reasons that Udall prized Boland's support, O'Neill was quite a catch for the Boggs campaign. If not a candidate himself, O'Neill's close association to McCormack, his influential position on Rules, and otherwise strong personal following made him a potentially pivotal player in the majority leader's race. Keeping himself "available" until the very last weeks of the campaign, O'Neill attracted the attention of both Udall and Boggs as a key to garnering the support of northeastern members. Interestingly, by remaining uncommitted, O'Neill seems to have convinced both Udall and Boggs of his support. On January 14, 1971, Udall wrote to O'Neill that if he had O'Neill's support, "you can be sure that I'll do my utmost to be a practical, responsible, totally available floor leader who is sensitive and concerned about you and the special problems of your constituency." Although this is a typical campaign letter for leadership races, at the bottom of the letter Udall handwrote to O'Neill: "HAVE TALKED TO EDDIE — I WON'T FORGET YOUR HELP. MO." This came the same day that Boggs received O'Neill's promise of support by telephone and wrote to O'Neill both to thank him for his support and assistance in reaching out to other northeastern undecided members.[27]

Just as Udall had given Boland a list of members to contact on his behalf, Boggs gave O'Neill a list of eighteen members, "All of [whom] had been pledged to Eddie Boland." Somewhat surprisingly given Boland's support of Udall, O'Neill reports that "every one of them agreed to vote for Boggs."[28] The Boggs camp believed that O'Neill's assistance put the majority whip over the top; upon hearing from O'Neill, Boggs told aide Gary Hymel, "I've just been elected," knowing that along with his own support, O'Neill could deliver a substantial bloc of northeastern votes.[29]

With Boggs's second ballot victory, O'Neill had bested Boland and was now in the running for whip. With Albert of Oklahoma the new Speaker and Boggs of Louisiana the new majority leader, the new leadership team needed regional balance. One close observer contended that O'Neill's eventual appointment to the post "was an obvious move to provide more geographic balance to the new leadership team."[30] Still, O'Neill was merely a contender for whip, and he was neither Albert's nor Boggs's first choice.

Tradition had it that the majority leader selected the whip. In the midst of the majority leader's campaign, Boggs had made a deal with Dan Rostenkowski to elevate the Chicagoan to whip in exchange for the support that the Illinois Democrat and the Daley machine could provide Boggs's candidacy. In many ways, Rostenkowski was a good choice in that he was an urban ethnic Democrat who could help provide regional balance to the leadership team. But Albert vetoed the appointment of Rostenkowski.

Even prior to meeting with Boggs, Albert had tipped his hand regarding his preferences for the whip post as well. Perhaps in his haste to avoid conflict with Boggs, Albert, for a brief time, even voiced support for caucus election rather than leadership appointment of the whip. It was widely assumed that Udall was in a good position to win such an election. Moreover, it was generally assumed that Udall as whip was acceptable to the incoming Speaker. Even once Albert backed off his support of electing the whip, it was reported that he wanted either Udall or James O'Hara appointed whip. "But Mr. Boggs is said to have balked at naming either of these two men or any others who did not support him [and, indeed, ran against him] for majority leader."[31]

With Rostenkowski, Udall, and O'Hara off the list and with Texan Olin Teague's selection as caucus chairman exacerbating the need for regional balance, Boggs and Albert cast about for another urban, ethnic politician who could provide regional balance to the leadership team. They narrowed the list to two Irish members, Hugh Carey of New York and Tip O'Neill of Massachusetts.

It is unclear if O'Neill was the beneficiary of good fortune or John McCormack's hand. Hugh Carey, an ambitious politician and future governor of New York, was a serious competitor. Although O'Neill had provided key support, so had Carey, whom Boggs selected to give a seconding speech on his behalf in the caucus. But Carey's appointment was not to be. Carey was eliminated from consideration when senior members from New York expressed reservations about Carey to Albert. Failing to win the support of his own delegation did not bode well for Carey's candidacy, and O'Neill emerged as the remaining whip candidate acceptable to both Albert and Boggs. According to O'Neill, the two senior New Yorkers who weighed in with Albert against Carey were John Rooney and Jim Delaney.[32]

That it was, in part, Delaney's handiwork that cleared the way for O'Neill is notable in that Delaney had not only been O'Neill's Rules Committee colleague, but he had also been one of "McCormack's men" on the committee.[33] If the senior New Yorker knew that both Carey and O'Neill were in the running for the whip spot, this is yet another example of a close McCormack associate clearing the way for O'Neill to rise up the House Democratic leadership ladder.

According to Rostenkowski, O'Neill's appointment was a case of "being in the right place at the right time. They needed somebody North, and Tip was acceptable." This view minimizes O'Neill's own efforts. In one sense, O'Neill benefited from having "made himself available" to a serendipitous process of elimination. But O'Neill had done more than merely remain available for the post. O'Neill rounded up signatures of New England Democrats in support of Albert's Speakership election.[34] And, of course, O'Neill helped deliver crucial votes to Boggs in the last week of the majority leader's race. O'Neill's longtime association with and loyalty to McCormack put him in the running, but his active support of both Albert and Boggs solidified his position.

Moreover, O'Neill was a rare, if not unique, commodity among the pool of leadership candidates. From the Rules Committee and the Board of Education in the 1950s to the 1960s to providing key support for Boggs and Albert in their races to succeed up the leadership ladder, O'Neill had ingratiated himself with southerners and the top leadership while maintaining and expanding his liberal credentials. He was acceptable to north and south, young and old, and nearly universally liked. This is something that could not be said for Rostenkowski, for example. Despite being the establishment choice, as O'Neill told a *Congressional Quarterly* correspondent upon his selection as whip, "I haven't found any members of the Democratic Study Group who don't feel they now have a voice in the leadership. . . . I know that when the leadership meets, the views of the liberals will be expressed."[35]

Personality aside, the Austin-Boston axis played a large role in O'Neill's elevation to majority whip. As he had for so many years, McCormack worked the phones, calling both Albert and Boggs to put in a good word for his protégé. According to O'Neill, it was McCormack who asked him to round up commitments to support his loyal Majority Leader Albert.[36] And, although ostensibly neutral, McCormack had aided Boggs's campaign for the majority leadership and had advised O'Neill against supporting Udall. Finally, it is perhaps not a coincidence that New Yorker Jim Delaney, a close McCormack associate, advised Albert and Boggs against selecting Hugh Carey as whip.[37] In all, as John A. Farrell described it, "old John McCormack had intervened — yanking the strings which tied him to Boggs and Albert on O'Neill's behalf."[38]

John McCormack, selected into the leadership three decades earlier, settled a score against his western foe Udall, gave important support to Boggs in a close race, and secured for O'Neill this one last key appointment on his way up the leadership ladder. Even as he was leaving the House, McCormack was not only the good mentor "yanking the strings" and "working the phones" to assist O'Neill, but he was also perpetuating the alliance and the influence of Massachusetts in the House Democratic Party as he had since he became majority leader in 1940. Just as McCormack had brought regional balance to the House leadership in 1940, O'Neill's appointment as whip in 1971 also helped maintain the regional balance within the leadership. As *New York Times* congressional reporter Marjorie Hunter reported, "With the appointment of Mr. O'Neill, Massachusetts retains a position of Democratic Congressional leadership that it had been on the verge of losing for the first time in 30 years."[39]

Being Elected up the Leadership Ladder

Although McCormack's preferment could place O'Neill on the Rules Committee, as DCCC chairman, and help him be appointed whip, to advance to majority leader and eventually to Speaker, O'Neill would have to win election by the Democratic caucus. While being McCormack's protégé helped O'Neill build a resume that enhanced his credibility as a potential House leader, it would be Boggs's tragic death and O'Neill's skills, especially his likability and popularity, that would help him ascend to the Speakership only six years after McCormack's retirement.

The personal coalition O'Neill was building was broad indeed. He was acceptable to much of the House establishment, such as southerners and committee chairs, primarily because of his association with McCormack. In the mid- to late 1960s, O'Neill also started expanding his base of support among younger, more reform-oriented liberals. This broad acceptability and personal popularity were particularly important at a time when the House was democratizing. Increasingly, it was no longer enough merely to be the anointed establishment candidate. Aspiring leaders had to develop a following among the increasing number of young, liberal members coming to the House.

Appealing simultaneously to these younger members and the House establishment was particularly difficult in the late 1960s. Throughout the 1960s and early 1970s, younger members increasingly pushed for internal reforms that stripped establishment committee chairmen of their dominance of the legislative process, opened up the House to greater "sunshine" in the form of press and public scrutiny, and otherwise democratized the internal processes of the House. During this time, O'Neill developed genuine credentials and accomplishments as a House reformer. To be sure, he was not as much a leader of the reform movement as was Dick Bolling or Mo Udall, but he did help implement many House reforms, such as the Hansen Committee's reform package and the use of the recorded teller system that democratized the House and opened up the legislative process. Some members suspected that O'Neill preferred that House adopt the Hansen Committee reforms rather than Bolling's bolder reforms. In addition to the reforms contained in the Hansen proposal, Bolling would have also re-aligned committee jurisdictions, further threatening established committee chairmen and even establishment-oriented outside groups, most notably organized labor.[40] Perhaps it was this position, flanked on the left as he was by Bolling, Udall, and eventually Phil Burton, that allowed O'Neill to deliver genuine reform accomplishments to young liberals while maintaining his strong ties with older members.

In addition to internal reforms, O'Neill's early opposition to the Vietnam War uniquely helped his reputation, among the House's top establishment leaders, to younger more liberal members. Indeed, for all of McCormack's help it may have been O'Neill's key departure from McCormack and Albert on Vietnam that solidified his future in the leadership as young liberals came to trust his instincts and respect his courage on that defining issue. In the end, O'Neill was well-positioned as an "establishment" champion of the peace movement with a reputation for sympathy for the House reform movement.

This broad base of acceptability, along with his institutional position, keyed O'Neill's advancement. As whip, O'Neill was on the leadership ladder, and he also could leverage his accomplishments from his previous position as Democratic Congressional Campaign Committee head into a great deal of support in a future race for majority leader. Just as his early efforts in Massachusetts legislative elections helped to propel then-minority leader O'Neill to be Speaker of the Massachusetts House, O'Neill was successful at turning his dual roles as the House Democrats' top campaigner and top vote-counter into member support when he ran for majority leader in 1973.

If all had proceeded according to form, when Albert retired, Boggs would be elevated to Speaker (though likely not without opposition), and O'Neill would make the race for majority leader. But when, less than two years after his election as majority leader, Boggs disappeared in an Alaskan plane crash, O'Neill temporarily assumed majority leader responsibilities. But running to succeed Boggs permanently presented O'Neill with a difficult situation. As whip, the majority leader's race was his to lose, but campaigning for a leadership position that would only be open if Boggs was dead would be unseemly, particularly in the small-town atmosphere of the House. Ambitious members such as Sam Gibbons and Phil Burton moved ahead with campaigns for leadership posts anyway. Whereas Gibbons had been planning a possible run for caucus chair, he started making calls in his campaign to succeed Boggs. Burton was even more brazen as reports circulated that he had begun talking about making the whip post elective so he could mount a campaign for it only "48 hours after Hale disappeared."[41]

The delicate situation in which O'Neill had to begin running for majority leader while Boggs's family still held out hope that he would be found alive was the majority whip's first hurdle in the race. The day after the 1972 elections, Tip O'Neill, with Boggs's son Tommy by his side, called Lindy Boggs seeking her approval to run to succeed her husband as majority leader.

If Lindy Boggs's approval was key to O'Neill's beginning his run for majority leader, to seal the deal, O'Neill would need key southern support. Working closely with Gary Hymel, a native Louisianan and Boggs aide, O'Neill made inroads with southern establishment members. In Louisiana, Hymel helped O'Neill land the support of Armed Services chairman Edward Hébert. Just as Boggs had believed that he "had it won" when O'Neill pledged his support just two years earlier, O'Neill's victory for the majority leadership required key support from Boggs's own state delegation.

To have the support of Lindy Boggs and Hébert was not unusual for O'Neill, who uniquely maintained popularity with liberals and acceptability to key southern House members. Although early in his career McCormack may have had to rely on Sam Rayburn to nurture his relationships with southerners, this position of being a liberal acceptable to the South was one that McCormack had enjoyed increasingly throughout his years in the House. Indeed, by the end of his career, when liberals like Udall would challenge him, it was McCormack's appeal to strong southern committee chairs and delegations that helped stave off the end of his leadership career.

Despite O'Neill's broad appeal, Sam Gibbons was determined to give O'Neill his only contested race for leadership advancement. Gibbons, who represented a Tampa congressional district since 1962, attracted a great deal of attention in the 1960s as a southerner who could champion liberal causes, particularly when leaders "needed a white southerner who could get [legislation] through." A key backer of the 1970 Legislative Reorganization Act, Gibbons lent his support and efforts to all manner of House reforms ranging from instituting the recorded teller vote system to weakening the seniority rule. On substantive policy issues, Gibbons was enigmatic even when compared to other liberal southerners. Although Robert L. Peabody is correct that Gibbons had "solid labor credentials," Gibbons had voted against repealing the "right to work" provisions of Taft-Hartley in 1965, the same vote that kept organized labor from supporting Udall for majority leader in 1971. Although he was a southern member of Ways and Means, Gibbons voted in a 1969 committee meeting to cut the oil depletion allowance that was so central to Texas and Louisiana members of Congress. And even though he was an early LBJ supporter on Vietnam, Gibbons opposed the war by the 1970s.[42]

Having had a taste of member-to-member campaigning in 1969 when he had to line up commitments to become Florida's new member of the House Committee on Ways and Means, Gibbons believed that he could successfully challenge O'Neill for majority leader or, at least, leverage a somewhat successful challenge into being selected majority whip. However, Gibbons's policy positions seemed contradictory, and Gibbons went into the campaign with no strong base in any wing of the party. Although Gibbons dropped out of the race before a caucus vote, an analysis of the O'Neill-Gibbons race sheds important light on the strength of O'Neill's political support specifically and the Austin-Boston alliance generally in the early 1970s.[43] By the same token, closely examining the support that Gibbons received provides, for the first time, some insight into the cracks, such as they were, in O'Neill's support and the Austin-Boston alliance.

When Gibbons announced he would run against O'Neill on November 1, 1972, few observers held out much hope that he would be successful. As *New York Times* reporter R. W. Apple summed up Gibbons's strategy, "Mr. Gibbons apparently hopes to win support both among Congressional reformers, whom he has supported in the past, and among Southerners." In his letter to Democratic colleagues announcing his candidacy, Gibbons cited, among other strengths, his "desire to build bridges between my fellow Democrats from all regions of the country."[44]

If Gibbons were to win, it would be with a coalition of members from different backgrounds, regions, and ideologies who could be united only under an anti-O'Neill umbrella. It was a difficult bridge to build, though Gibbons was adroit at "narrowcasting" discrete and sometimes contradictory messages to the various groups he had identified. Gibbons divided House Democrats into seven key groups at which he would aim his campaign: "a. Southerners; b. DSG; c. Cities (urban); d. Chairmen; e. New Members; f. Blacks; g. Women" and carefully tailored his announcement letters appealing for support to each.[45] His letters to southerners would emphasize that "we must stop inroads of Republicanism [in southern states]" and "maintain our Committee chairmen," and, to committee chairmen themselves, his appeals would promise assistance in "seeing that the important legislation your committee reports gets through legislative impasses." To members of the Democratic Study Group (DSG), Gibbons promised to "rally various factions" of the party but cautioned that although he had supported George McGovern's candidacy, "we can't afford to get ourselves caught in another presidential election like the last one . . . but must work towards getting the best Democrat nominated." In truth, however, Gibbons's only hope for victory was to build a bridge that could encompass a broad coalition of disparate elements of the House Democratic Party disaffected with O'Neill.

Gibbons explored each opportunity. First, O'Neill was the establishment candidate. Not only was he the McCormack protégé and Rules Committee member who had been DCCC chairman, but O'Neill was on the "leadership ladder" as majority whip and acting majority leader since Boggs's disappearance. Moreover, despite the Speaker's customary pledge to remain neutral, a rumor was widely circulated that Albert preferred O'Neill's elevation to majority leader. When a somewhat sympathetic Wilbur Mills asked Gibbons if he had confirmed that Albert was for O'Neill, Gibbons could only respond, "The Speaker told me he could work with me."[46] Although O'Neill's establishment ties would be potent elements in any campaign for a leadership post, in the midst of a democratizing revolution in the House Democratic caucus, the automatic elevation of an appointed whip, even a popular one, seemed like an anachronism, and Gibbons hoped that it would invite a backlash from reformers.

To counter O'Neill's strength as the establishment choice, Gibbons tried to position himself as an outsider, despite his ten years in the House and his recent placement on the Ways and Means Committee. In his letter to colleagues announcing his candidacy, Gibbons emphasized that he had "been in Congress long enough to learn how it operates but not so long that he has a vested interest in preserving the status quo." Perhaps building upon some of the lingering resentment that led to Udall's strength (such as it was) in 1968 and 1971, Gibbons appealed to those members who wanted "Leadership for a Change." Railing against an established "escalator" system of advancement, Gibbons promised to open up the House, claiming that "reform of the House will not be a reality until the *appointed* whip does not automatically move up the leadership ladder."[47]

Gibbons also subtly tapped into Democrats' dissatisfaction with the national party's poor performance in the 1972 elections and declining public approval of Congress as further justification for wholesale change. In his letter announcing his candidacy, Gibbons wrote that his campaign slogan would be "Leadership for a Change" and that House Democrats needed not only to present "positive and imaginative legislative proposals" but to help manage the "Democratic National Committee and the Democratic National Convention." Only through innovation could the deplorable drop in confidence in Congress (from 42 percent in 1966 to 21 percent in 1972 according to the Harris Poll) be rectified. Gibbons concluded, "We must infuse new ideas into our system if we are to regain public confidence."[48]

Still, it is hard to translate such broad dissatisfaction with a system into a campaign against one man, particularly when O'Neill had also called for wholesale changes in the Democratic National Committee in the wake of the Nixon landslide. Even when it came to considering the "escalator system" in the House, many potential Gibbons supporters did not know where to place their anger. When the subject of democratizing, or "opening up," the House came up in conversation with Rep. Dante Fascell, the most liberal member of Florida's Democratic delegation, Fascell said to Gibbons that "opening" the House up "starts with the Speaker, Wayne Hays and O'Neill."[49] More generally, many of the members who might support Gibbons's candidacy did not so much oppose O'Neill as they did the top "establishment" leadership, once again controlling succession.

Opening up House leadership had a more general meaning for many of the more policy-oriented younger members to whom Gibbons was trying to appeal: they wanted to democratize the legislative process itself. Observing in his campaign planning documents that "O'Neill running on personality, it seems, not issues," Gibbons sought to run a leadership campaign that, as House leadership campaigns go, was unusually focused on issues and ideas. Other members too saw the majority leader's race as an opportunity to have a more substantive debate about issues and policies. Admitting that he was "NOT impressed with O'Neill," incoming freshman Texan Dale Milford told Gibbons that "we should run this on the ISSUES."[50]

Leadership races can have broad consequences for policy and the overall direction of the party, but they rarely involve substantive debates on policy direction, and this race was no exception. Gibbons's emphasis on issues never really transcended the internal world of House politics. In his campaign he emphasized "issues" of "Secrecy, scheduling, and seniority" as examples of "the often mentioned problems of the House which contribute to the criticism of Congress." By "secrecy," Gibbons meant legislative secrecy and called for increased "sunshine" in the legislative process to "build public confidence." In addition, Gibbons's call to end "secrecy" also included "the updating and codification of the precedents of the Chair so that members will have an up-to-date reference as we prepare for the parliamentary side of the legislative process." Another issue was scheduling. In addition to the common leadership campaign promises of making a more member-friendly legislative schedule (both in terms of scheduling district work periods and recesses and the daily schedule), Gibbons also offered the possibility of switching to a two-year clock (as opposed to the status quo one-year clock) for authorizations to speed up the appropriations process. Finally, when it came to the issues of seniority and recent efforts at "spreading the action," Gibbons lent his support to the growing call to have committee chairmen confirmed by the caucus at the beginning of each Congress.[51] These calls to action proposed democratizing the legislative process and breaking the leadership's near-monopoly control over arcane information regarding the process, but they would not turn the leadership election into a referendum on the direction of the national party.

Gibbons received ample encouragement from would-be supporters and even some O'Neill supporters to continue to press on the issues. Jerome Waldie of California, while reluctant to support Gibbons over O'Neill, added, "unless he [O'Neill] is willing to support the issues expressed in your letter, I will not consider my commitment binding to him." Jonathan Bingham of New York, similarly reluctant to commit to Gibbons, offered to call John B. Oakes, the *New York Times* editor, to get Gibbons "some attention," because "you are putting out ideas and Tip isn't and I think you should smoke him out."[52]

For many of these same reasons, the Gibbons forces also believed that they could reach out to members newly elected in the 1972 elections. Discussing potential supporters, Lionel Van Deerlin (D-CA) mentioned to Gibbons that he had met "the new congresswoman from Colorado [Pat Schroeder] who knows the woman who beat Celler [Elizabeth Holtzman, D-NY]—they are certainly going to be different—I think you would have appeal with that group." However strong Gibbons's appeal might be among these younger members, Tip O'Neill had more resources with which to woo them to his side. Just three days before announcing he would run to succeed Boggs as majority leader, O'Neill sent a letter to incoming House freshmen congratulating them on their victories, reminding them of his past support as whip and DCCC chairman, and offering his future assistance: "I am well aware of the problems which confront a newly-elected Member of Congress, including the hiring of staff, obtaining office space and attending to the other incidentals in establishing your Congressional office. I want to personally offer my own services in assisting you in whatever way possible. I cordially invite you to visit the Whip Office . . . or my Congressional office . . . during any of your trips to Washington. In addition, I am sure that anyone of my staff will be more than happy to assist you with the myriad chores involved in setting up a Washington office."[53] Whatever appeal a "change-oriented" candidacy might have among incoming freshmen, O'Neill's promises to use his many resources to help them "settle in" in Washington likely better met their more immediate and pressing needs.

In all, Gibbons's efforts to appeal to liberal and younger members never gained enough traction to even "smoke O'Neill out" on the issues, much less compete with him for the majority leader's post. Although O'Neill was by no means spared the disaffection that many younger and most liberal members had with the leadership generally, he did seem to many the most acceptable among the top leaders and thus a bad place to start the revolt. Explaining his decision not to re-run for majority leader, Udall said that "O'Neill had most of Boggs's strengths with few of his liabilities." Other outsiders like Waldie, who had introduced the caucus resolution seeking a vote of "no confidence" in John McCormack, were generally supportive of O'Neill; he told Gibbons of two "hang-ups" that would keep him from supporting Gibbons's challenge to O'Neill: "1) committed to Bernie [Sisk] if he decides to go; 2) of the 3 leadership posts, Tip has been the best." The second of Waldie's "hang-ups" was repeated almost verbatim by Missouri's Billy Hungate. This same sentiment was echoed, in a somewhat different form, by the consummate insider Dan Rostenkowski. Bitter to the end in his feud against Speaker Albert, Rostenkowski also told Gibbons, "I've been asked about your campaign by the press and others: I have to tell them you're running for the wrong office — you'd get more votes running against Albert." Indeed, when Rostenkowski received Gibbons's letter asking for support in the majority leader's race, Rostenkowski told him, "I pledge you my support now if you will run for Speaker."[54]

If there was scant support for Gibbons among liberals, there was little more to be found among fellow southerners, though occasionally he would gain expressions of southern support. As the House Democrats became more liberal, many southerners (conservative and liberal alike) believed that the image of the national party would hurt them at home. Particularly in light of Republican success with its "southern strategy" and Democratic weakness among non-black southern constituencies due to civil rights and Vietnam and exemplified by George McGovern's landslide loss, many southerners believed that they had to take control of the direction and image of the national party. Some southern House Democrats saw this leadership race (especially due to the loss of the southerner Boggs) as key to re-asserting a southern component to the party. As Walter Flowers (D-AL) said to Gibbons, "the National Party had better recognize the South or we will be the minority party or turn Republican. . . . I don't want it [majority leadership] to go to the NE again and I don't think appointed Whip should move up." Still, Flowers's discontent did not translate into automatic support for Gibbons; indeed Flowers told Gibbons that he did not like his choices: "It disturbs me that only you and Tip have surfaced — you would think there would be ten running."[55]

Generally speaking, Gibbons could not gain support among his fellow southerners. Peabody reports that O'Neill encountered only one southerner "outside the Florida delegation, a Texan, who announced outright he was for Gibbons." This was most likely Bob Eckhardt, who openly wrote to Gibbons of his support and who had rarely displayed shyness about being a maverick within the Texas delegation and the House Democratic Party. The archival record confirms that there were few other southern commitments for Gibbons. Admitting to Gibbons that he was "scared to death when I was labeled one of the four most liberal southerners," Williamson Stuckey of Georgia told Gibbons, "Won't vote for O'Neill; won't vote for that red-neck Waggoner — don't know that I'll vote for you! Committed only to Mo Udall: At th[e] point, you're my candidate — I would 'break my neck for you.'" Other southern and southwestern members expressed their support for Gibbons's candidacy: David Bowen (D-MS) offered that he was "favorably disposed," and Harold Runnels of New Mexico promised Gibbons that he "will help you in any way I can." And, of course, Gibbons received broad, if not universal, support from his own Florida delegation. Indeed, once Gibbons entered, O'Neill released Claude Pepper from his commitment; O'Neill told Pepper that he would "understand if a man of our Delegation ran."[56] Still, these few exceptions demonstrate that Gibbons's support from southerners was largely limited to his own Florida delegation.

Any in-roads that Gibbons could make with southern members would necessarily promise to moderate and southernize the image of the House Democratic Party while "maintaining" the committee chairmen. But such promises would probably weaken his support among liberals. This exemplifies the central problem with Gibbons's multifaceted campaign: his employment of contradictory tactics in his efforts to appeal to disparate elements of the House.

In addition to straddling the ideological split within the party, there were many other contradictions in Gibbons's campaign. For example, although Gibbons repeatedly complained that O'Neill used his position as DCCC chairman to curry favor with members, Gibbons offered to use his membership on Ways and Means for the same purpose. With that committee still serving as the House Democrats' "committee on committees," Gibbons dangled promises of favorable committee assignments to incoming members in exchange for leadership support. In his letter to incoming freshmen, Gibbons offered "to work towards getting you on the assignment of your choice."[57] Clearly what was at issue was not a candidate's use of institutional position to aid in his campaign, but rather that, as whip and former DCCC chairman, O'Neill had more resources to use.

Also, while running an anti-establishment campaign, Gibbons hoped to counter O'Neill's strength as the "establishment" choice by getting some establishment support of his own. O'Neill's association with Speaker Albert gave him a leg up in this regard, and Gibbons believed that his cause would similarly benefit if he could get a commitment from the powerful and respected Ways and Means chairman, Wilbur Mills. Gibbons's notes on the 1973 leadership race reveal that he was in frequent contact with Mills. This reveals another glaring contradiction for Gibbons: should he have succeeded in getting Mills's support and this had his desired effect of attracting more establishment southern support, Gibbons would likely have sacrificed many of his "Leadership for a Change" reformer credentials and a lot of his potential liberal support.

Moreover, for all of his general calls for bold reforms, Gibbons was more reticent when it came to proposals to strip his own Ways and Means committee of its power as the Democratic Committee on Committees. He wrote, "I believe that complaints about the Committee on Committees could be remedied by expanding this committee to include in its membership the Speaker and Majority Leader. Certainly the leadership needs this extra leverage to help meet its responsibilities."[58] This represented "reform" compared to the status quo, but it was weak reform compared to switching this power entirely to the leadership-dominated Steering and Policy Committee, which would happen shortly.

If Gibbons regarded Mills's support as key, he should have known from his many conversations that it would not be forthcoming. Although Mills generally seemed supportive, he repeatedly sent Gibbons subtle signals advising against challenging O'Neill. Seeking a new compromise with Gibbons each time they spoke, Mills was his subtlest on November 10:

"Mr. Mills asked 'What are you up to? We can't lose you from the Ways and Means Committee.'" A week and a half later, Mills asked Gibbons if he was "irretrievably involved" and suggested that Gibbons might make a good chairman of the Democratic Congressional Campaign Committee. When it became clear that Gibbons could not win, Mills offered to try to broker a deal to get Gibbons appointed whip in exchange for backing out. When discussing the various members who hoped to be appointed whip, Mills seemed to favor Gibbons when he said, "If you know by the 30th or 31st that you don't have the votes, then it would be well for you and I to sit down with the Speaker and Tip."[59]

If he could ignore Mills's gentle hints, Gibbons did not ignore the repeated advice and predictions he heard from other members that he had no chance to beat O'Neill. In addition to frequent assessments that he could not break through O'Neill's support by broad groups of members, Gibbons's Ways and Means colleague Rostenkowski told him that most of the Illinois delegation supported O'Neill. Chet Holifield of California conceded that "Tip's capabilities are not the same as yours, Sam, but he'll have the Catholic vote" and he "has the votes." Jonathan Bingham of New York concluded that O'Neill "is in good shape" Gibbons would counter that his polling was "indecisive" and that O'Neill must not have it locked up because "he is still working."[60]

It is difficult in House leadership races to induce members to support a campaign that is likely to lose if for no other reason than members do not want to draw the ire of the new majority leader. Even close supporters and friends expressed reticence about Gibbons's futile effort. The fact that Don Fraser of Minnesota, with whom Gibbons had worked closely on the legislative reform efforts, would support but "not work openly" for the challenger was instructive. O'Neill's support was so strong that some close associates failed to offer even secret support for Gibbons's candidacy. Carl Perkins (D-KY) told Gibbons, "You're a devil of a good fellow, Sam. I don't think I have a better friend than you. I want to talk to you about this. I don't want to make a commitment at this time." Even from within the Florida delegation, Gibbons was advised that he could not beat O'Neill. Bob Sikes told Gibbons, "You must realize that Tip has a lock on it — has DSG, leadership, etc." The Gibbons campaign, too, was coming to this realization, and by the end of November they identified the perception that Gibbons could not win as his primary problem. Notes for campaign planning observed that "SMG says the worse thing against him is the psychological issue that he can't win."[61]

Although the perception that Gibbons could not win was more likely a result of O'Neill's strength than its primary cause, such a perception never helps in a House leadership race. According to O'Neill, Gibbons's support primarily amounted to a thin coalition of "southern conservatives and 'way out liberals.'" Two weeks after his first conversation with Gibbons, Sikes wrote to him, "I do not recommend that you go through with your campaign until the caucus show-down unless you have firm commitments on about one-third of the votes, or unless you have positive evidence of many uncommitted members who can be swung to you. It is not going to help you or your delegation to take a one side beating."[62] Indeed, had Gibbons stayed in the race, he was in for such a one-sided beating, and little evidence existed (even with optimistic assumptions) that Gibbons had anywhere near the support that Sikes suggested he needed to stay in the race.

According to John A. Farrell, "By Thanksgiving O'Neill had between 150 and 180 commitments." More than three weeks before Gibbons would drop out, many believed that the race was over. On December 1, 1972, Robert Leggett (D-CA) wrote to O'Neill conveying his belief "that we have the Majority Leadership locked up on your behalf." In the end, although Gibbons estimated that he had about 60 firm commitments, Leo Diehl, O'Neill's chief aide in the campaign, said that Gibbons received "at most 25 votes and that's giving him everything."[63]

A look inside the Gibbons campaign sheds doubt on his assessment of 60 votes. Gibbons labeled his supporters by number with his top supporters recorded with a "1," those who had given a vague expression of support with a "2," and those uncommitted as a "3." Adding even the uncommitteds to Gibbons's total reveals that the Floridian's support seems never to have exceeded 30, and this count itself likely overestimated Gibbons's strength. When Kika de la Garza told Gibbons, "I am not happy with Tip ... and You [Gibbons] let us down on depletion — the hell with both of you," Gibbons registered de la Garza as an "uncommitted — 3" whose support he would still try to get.[64] Similarly, despite Wilbur Mills's efforts to get Gibbons to take another party leadership post and Dan Rostenkowski's close ties to O'Neill, both were listed as "uncommitted — 3."

With these caveats in mind, Table 7-1 breaks down Gibbons's supporters and hopefuls in these three categories. It seems that the O'Neill camp was probably closer to an accurate gauge of Gibbons's support. Giving Gibbons, as Leo Diehl put it, "everything," the 30 supporters identified in

TABLE 7-1. SAM GIBBONS'S SUPPORTERS, MAJORITY LEADER'S RACE, 1973

Strongest Supporters, "1"	Weak Supporters, "2"	Uncommitteds, "3"
Bennett (FL)	Bingham (NY)	Garza (TX)
Diggs (MI)	Bowen (MS)	Gaydos (PA)
Eckhardt (TX)	Flowers (AL)	Heckler (WV)
Fascell (FL)	Hamilton (IN)	Mazzoli (KY)
Fraser (MN)	Holifield (CA)	Milford (TX)
Fuqua (FL)	Stuckey (GA)	Mills (AR)
Lehman (FL)	Van Deerlin (CA)	Pickle (TX)
Perkins (KY)		Rostenkowski (IL)
Pepper (FL)		Stokes (OH)
Runnels (NM)		Waldie (CA)
Sikes (FL)		
Udall (AZ)		
Vanik (OH)		

the Gibbons papers is not far off from the 25 Diehl estimated. What then were Gibbons's strengths and, by contrast, O'Neill's weaknesses?[65]

Gibbons was a talented legislator and a relatively popular House Democrat of considerable accomplishments. Moreover, he had only a few years prior secured the support of over 140 colleagues in a member-to-member campaign to place him on the Ways and Means Committee. Why was his support for majority leader so lackluster? Or, alternatively, why was O'Neill's support so seemingly impenetrable?

When it comes down to it, leadership campaigns are about comparing the choices the caucus is given in light of the candidates who have decided to run. Many observers mistakenly touted Gibbons as the more liberal candidate in the race; this also seemed to be the attitude of liberal members who counseled Gibbons to run on the issues. However, Gibbons's supporters and even some outside observers claimed that "O'Neill had preempted the liberal reformer's issues just enough to make Gibbons's campaign hopeless," perhaps underestimating O'Neill's genuine liberal accomplishments and credentials.[66]

As southerners went in the early 1970s, Gibbons was, in fact, something of a liberal. His Americans for Democratic Action (ADA) rating generally placed him in the most liberal half of the Democratic Party, but he was not even the most liberal member of the Florida delegation, nor could he compete with O'Neill and other northerners on the support of liberal causes on a broad range of issues. On most issues O'Neill was to the left of Gibbons. And on race issues, Gibbons likely had some difficulty. Along with New Jersey's Frank Thompson, he was instrumental in stripping Adam Clayton Powell, who had called Gibbons a "racist," of his powers as chairman of the Education and Labor Committee in 1966.[67] In all, the characterization of Gibbons as a liberal was not so much a stretch as was the contention that Gibbons was a more liberal alternative to O'Neill.

As for the South, Gibbons was neither conservative enough nor "establishment" enough to rally key southern committee chairs or the deans of southern state delegations, a fact that the O'Neill camp recognized. Peabody speculates that when Gibbons sent out a poll late in the campaign asking members whether he should stay in the race, O'Neill supporters returned their ballots hoping to keep Gibbons in the race to forestall the emergence of a more formidable southern challenger.[68]

A December 1972 assessment of the majority leader's race in Gibbons's office read: "If defeated for Majority Leader major reason would be you favor too many changes that the 'Old Guard' could not go along with" and "You and Tip represent different points of view on policy issues."[69]

In the end, Gibbons's candidacy was hurt by O'Neill's experience and personality, as well as the lack of regional balance a Gibbons candidacy offered to the leadership of the 93d Congress. Moreover, Gibbons's overall lack of leadership experience worked against his joining the leadership ranks at the majority leader level. Indeed, the fact that there was speculation that the majority whip post might become an elective position gave many members an "out" from having to tell Gibbons that they preferred O'Neill. In a personal conversation, Carl Perkins suggested that Gibbons could win an elective whip post ("McFall and Brademas no good, he says") and that, given O'Neill's commanding lead, "this is the realistic position to take." Perhaps Martha W. Griffiths of Michigan summarized most of the points that members seemed to acknowledge when she wrote to Gibbons that she thought O'Neill had the leader's job secure in part because "you and Albert are both from the south." She continued, "Why don't you try for Whip?"[70]

It was, in part, Gibbons's ambition to be a member of the leadership that led him to drop out of the race for the majority leadership. He worried that if he continued his campaign, he might "become like O'Hara — no longer a viable candidate." Far preferable, it seems, was a second withdrawal scenario. Having been advised that it was "more statesmanlike to get up in the Caucus, announce that because of the support for Mr. Albert, which you go along with, and in order to maintain close working relationship at leadership level, you are withdrawing since Mr. Albert's first choice is O'Neill," Gibbons backed out of the leadership race in late December 1972.[71]

As much as O'Neill's appointment to whip was due to a serendipitous process of elimination and, of course, his opportunity to run for majority leader due to the unexpected tragedy of Hale Boggs's death, O'Neill's 1973 election as majority leader seemed so matter of course. His success as DCCC chairman and his innovations during his brief tenure as whip confirmed the expectations of many that O'Neill was a talented political leader. And he was popular among broad categories of members. Just prior to the unanimous caucus vote elevating O'Neill to majority leader, Gibbons told his former rival, "Tip, I can tell you something that nobody else in this room can. You haven't got an enemy in the place." Or, as Spark Matsunaga said in his seconding speech, "Tip O'Neill is the man which the job itself seeks."[72]

The Speakership would soon seek Tip O'Neill as well. Both the fact that he had no enemies "in the place" and this typical pattern of succession dating back for decades, put O'Neill in good stead for elevation to the Speakership. Still, when Speaker Carl Albert announced his retirement in 1976, despite his obvious lock on succession, O'Neill worked quickly and vigorously to guarantee succession to the Speaker's chair.

Even in the face of almost assured victory, O'Neill was a stalwart campaigner. For years, O'Neill had told the story of his first election when his neighbor, Mrs. O'Brien, stopped him on election day to chastise him for not asking for her vote. Despite their closeness, Mrs. O'Brien told the young politician, "people like to be asked." O'Neill frequently told this story when it otherwise seemed embarrassing to ask a longtime friend for support that might have been assumed; he reportedly told Boggs this story when he asked to be appointed majority whip. Following this logic and although he was not challenged in his ascent to the Speakership, he left no stone unturned and no member, no matter how close, unasked. O'Neill even formally asked roommate Eddie Boland for his support.[73]

Leaving nothing to chance, O'Neill sewed up his elevation to the Speaker's chair quickly and without incident. By late 1975, O'Neill already claimed to have lined up the commitments needed to succeed Albert as Speaker.

What started with a career as "McCormack's Man" ended with O'Neill stepping out of the old Speaker's shadow to establish his own independent and broader following in the House. If McCormack was too out of touch with younger members, O'Neill had become one of their key allies in the reform movement. If McCormack was too conservative on Vietnam, O'Neill was an early opponent of the war who had real influence in the House and the party. And if liberals' complaints about McCormack had included that he was not combative enough with Richard Nixon, the same could not be said of Tip O'Neill, who led much of the political fight in the impeachment against Nixon.

Nevertheless, it did all start with John McCormack. Upon hearing that O'Neill had officially become the caucus nominee for Speaker, McCormack wrote to the man he once described as his "best friend in Washington," "I am very happy exceedingly so. Some years ago I . . . had the definite thought that some day you would be Speaker." Whether that "some years ago" was five years earlier when McCormack helped secure for O'Neill a whip appointment, seven years earlier when he appointed him to chair the Democratic Congressional Campaign Committee, or more than twenty years prior when he first helped O'Neill secure his spot on the Rules Committee, McCormack and the Austin-Boston alliance more generally played a determinative role in O'Neill's rise in the House. And on the day that O'Neill was sworn in as Speaker, symbolizing their role in his elevation, McCormack and Albert escorted their protégé to the Speaker's chair.[74]

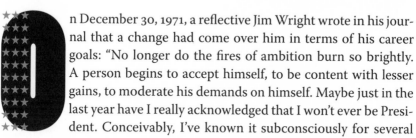

CHAPTER 8
JIM WRIGHT
THE LAST TEXAN

n December 30, 1971, a reflective Jim Wright wrote in his journal that a change had come over him in terms of his career goals: "No longer do the fires of ambition burn so brightly. A person begins to accept himself, to be content with lesser gains, to moderate his demands on himself. Maybe just in the last year have I really acknowledged that I won't ever be President. Conceivably, I've known it subconsciously for several years, but only in this year have I said it to myself, and you know, it's kind of a relief." He continued, "Probably I could win the Senate race against John Tower this year. . . . [But] I'm no longer willing to pay the price I once would gladly pay for escalation up the political ladder. I'm not willing to humble myself, to go hat in hand to the fat cats and beg for money. It's false pride, I know — a weakness, not a strength. But there it is, and that's me. I'm unwilling to go through the sheer physical torment of a state-wide campaign. Then, too, a sort of personal conservatism creeps in with middle age. There's the comfort of familiarity in my Congressional Office, the gradual accumulation of seniority (that crutch I once vowed never to embrace) and an unwillingness to venture boldly and risk the relative security (financial and otherwise) of my present job."[1]

These entries were revealing in ways that Wright perhaps did not understand himself as he wrote them. No longer would he pursue political ambitions outside of the House as he had when he ran in a special election for the Senate in 1961. And though his ambition had been tempered, the seniority that he was building in the House would allow him a different sort of pursuit, leadership in the House of Representatives. In short order, he would become deputy majority whip and would move up in seniority on the Public Works Committee where by 1976, he would be in line to be chair. Then, in December of 1976, he would find an outlet for his political ambition in the chamber where he had, by that time, spent twenty-two years. And though his ambition had turned inward, his biographer John

Barry concluded that "ambition burned in him as fiercely as in anyone in Washington."[2]

In the most hotly contested majority leader race in history, he would win that post. In so doing, he would continue in the political tradition of his Texas predecessors John Nance Garner and Sam Rayburn and would eke out a narrow victory, continuing the Austin-Boston connection for one last time. The contest would maintain the old Democratic coalition against the reform agenda of Wright's principal challenger, Phillip Burton of California.

The Field of Four

The year 1976 was a year of the improbable election. Jimmy Carter had emerged miraculously onto the national stage to become president. The election of Carter, the obscure former governor of a southern state, would set the stage for a majority leader election with another improbable victor. With the retirement of Speaker Carl Albert in 1977, Majority Leader Thomas P. "Tip" O'Neill had no challenger for the top position in the House. In an ordinary year, Democratic Whip John McFall of California would be next in line for the majority leadership, but this was no ordinary year. As the contest unfolded, four principal contestants emerged.

McFall, a native of Buffalo, New York, was a moderate Democrat from the Central Valley of California who had been elected to Congress in 1956. He had served on the Appropriations Committee where he had been a close ally of Wright's Texas colleague, Appropriations Chairman George Mahon. He had been appointed whip, the third-highest position in his party, by Speaker Albert four years earlier, showing himself to be an "inside player" in House politics. As whip, he had been "a very charming and able fellow, but no boat rocker." His leadership status came by remaining loyal to the leadership and waiting his turn to move higher in the leadership. As whip, though he had been well-organized and hardworking, he had been labeled an old-style Democrat and had been unable to build a constituency among the new breed of Democrats who came to the House following Watergate.[3]

Not only had McFall worked his way into the upper echelons of the House, but he enjoyed the support of establishment-oriented members of the California delegation as well, including Chet Holifield, the dean of the delegation. Holifield reported that "one of my interests is McFall — I'm committed to him for whip (though I think Brademas would be acceptable). McFall was whip for Calif. delegation; delegation is split, what with Burton in the fight. McFall did well in research position."[4]

Because of a strong push for reform in the House, even his appointment as whip had been difficult, as there had been a movement in the House, led by Phil Burton, to make the position elective — the thought was that McFall could not have won the position in an election. Burton, who came from a district less than fifty miles from McFall's, always indicated "without exactly saying it that he doesn't even regard McFall in his league." Upon the presumed death of Hale Boggs, Burton had begun an "intense campaign" to make the whip position elective, thinking he could win election with the change in rules. As late as January 3, 1973, he believed he had the votes to pull off such a reform. But on that day, Burton lost the vote in caucus 123–114, thus assuring that the whip would be appointed and that his ambition to move up in the leadership would be postponed.[5] This episode was an interesting precursor of things to come. Burton campaigned hard to become caucus chair less than two years later. And in the majority leader race, he would confidently predict a victory up to the day he narrowly lost.

Burton, from San Francisco, had emerged as one of the strongest personalities in the Democratic delegation in the House. A large man with a penchant for food and drink, Burton was a physical presence with a roguish charm. Burton had fueled his political ambition in the House by becoming Democratic caucus chair late in 1974. Rather than waiting to climb the seniority ladder, Burton had become the first member of Congress to actively campaign for the caucus chair. Before that time, the caucus chair, in the words of Jim Wright, "was not a position to be sought but one to be bestowed." Elected to Congress first in 1964, Burton was the youngest and least experienced of the candidates for majority leader but had emerged as a true leader among the "ultraliberals" in the House. Burton was aware that his personality would be an issue in the race, remarking that the voting would be "personal and chemical in a way," with members having "a great variety of reasons for voting the way they do."[6]

Richard Bolling had long had the ambition to lead in the House. Standing over six feet tall and weighing more than two hundred pounds, Bolling was a handsome and imposing man. Elected to Congress initially in 1948, he had represented Pres. Harry Truman's home district in Congress. While Truman did not initially support Bolling, by early in his career, Bolling later remembered, "it was generally understood that I was a Truman protégé and considered a 'comer' by Speaker Sam Rayburn." He had run against Carl Albert for majority leader in 1961 when John McCormack became speaker upon the death of Sam Rayburn. Early in his career, Bolling had been tapped by Rayburn as a young man with a great deal of potential and soon became a regular at Rayburn's Board of Education, where influential members met with the Speaker at the end of the day. As a member of the Rules Committee, Bolling had earned the reputation as one of the most influential members of the House. At age sixty, he was the oldest and most senior candidate in the field. His reputation as a Rayburn protégé had by now worn thin, with a close associate of Wright assessing that role: "you can't be that forever." His abrasive personality also worked to his disadvantage.[7]

Finally, Jim Wright became a candidate. Wright had served in Congress since 1954 and had emerged as a leader in the powerful Texas delegation. Prior to coming to Washington, Wright had been mayor of Weatherford, Texas, and a member of the Texas House of Representatives, where he had earned a reputation as "the most liberal member of the House." Wright had worked for the repeal of the poll tax, anti-lynching legislation, and the admission of African Americans to the University of Texas Law School.[8] As a result, he expressed surprise at continually being called a "conservative" as he entered the majority leader race. His Public Works Committee membership, suggested by Speaker Rayburn, had allowed him to do favors for many colleagues over time.

Pres. John Kennedy, in the last speech he ever delivered, had said that with Wright's leadership, no city "is better represented in the Congress of the United States than Fort Worth." As early as 1966, journalist Sarah McClendon speculated that Wright might be the next Speaker. While McClendon's report was ill-timed and had no real merit, it demonstrated that even a decade before the 1976 majority leader's race, Wright had been seen by some, including Pres. Lyndon B. Johnson, as being worthy of promotion to the highest levels in the House. By 1976, *Texas Monthly* deemed Wright "a low-key, skillful technician, capable, when the need arises, of studied virtuoso showmanship." Further, it speculated, before Carl Albert's resignation, that Wright might attain House leadership, including majority leadership and eventually the Speakership.[9]

Wright had also nurtured a record for innovative thinking in national politics, advocating strategies for peace with the Soviet Union, paying down the national debt, reforming campaign finance, promoting Latin American political development, and providing adequate water supplies for the western United States. Finally, Wright had written a well-received book, published originally in 1965 and in its third edition by 1976, about the relationship between citizens and their government.[10]

Wright had become one of the House's strongest orators and floor managers and represented the center of the party ideologically. He had served as deputy whip, appointed to the post by Tip O'Neill at the request of John McCormack, who valued the "Boston-Austin" connection that had characterized McCormack's own relationship with Rayburn. Wright's job as deputy whip, as part of a team that included both Speaker-elect O'Neill and McFall, had been "persuading Southern Democrats to support the leadership" and "providing ideological balance to the leadership team."[11]

In Congress, Wright had a more conservative voting record than the other three contestants for majority leader, as table 8-1 illustrates. Of course, the attempt to rate a congressional member's ideology from an interest group, such as the Americans for Democratic Action scores used here, is potentially misleading. It can misrepresent the voting record of the member in juxtaposition to his constituency. Both Bolling and Burton represented districts with constituencies more supportive of liberal voting records than McFall and Wright. And though Wright's scores indicated a more conservative bearing, a Texas reporter remarked, "It's hard to pin him down."[12]

Wright's conservatism and Texas district allowed him to emphasize geographical diversity and the leadership's need to reach out to all types of members: "The leadership team ought to be balanced. We need someone who can communicate with moderate members and who can bring guys along who might not have voted with our programs."[13]

The Burton Campaign

Burton was the most openly ambitious of the candidates for the leadership post. He had begun to earn a reputation as an astute deal maker in Congress. Supporters argued that this "political genius" would serve the Democratic Party well in the leadership. But fellow liberal Morris Udall of Arizona saw a distinction. Burton, he said, was a deal maker, but not a coalition builder. "He'd rather do something in a devious way if given a choice, and pit one member against another." Burton openly began his campaign as soon as it was known that Speaker Albert would retire. He campaigned extensively at the Democratic National Convention in 1976, setting up a hospitality suite at the convention under the auspices of the Democratic caucus to entertain and woo House members.[14]

TABLE 8-1. ADA RATINGS OF THE FOUR CANDIDATES
FOR MAJORITY LEADER IN 1976

Year	Richard Bolling	Phillip Burton	John McFall	Jim Wright
1970	56	89	44	22
1971	65	92	46	24
1972	75	100	44	19
1973	52	100	48	40
1974	70	91	48	30
1975	79	89	68	32
1976	75	90	65	30

Source: J. Michael Sharp, *Directory of Congressional Voting Scores*, 3d ed. (CQ Press, 2000).

Burton was an energetic, brilliant, and hard-charging campaigner who could be overbearing and imposing in his tactics. The Bolling campaign had one case in point. Martha Keys of Kansas told Burton that she supported Bolling, but afterwards she began to receive $100 checks from California with notes to the effect that "Phil Burton said you might need this."[15]

Burton campaigned, first, from his position as a member of the Democratic Study Group (DSG), the organization through which Burton had worked to push reform in the House. To underscore his relationship with that group, Burton named Abner Mikva, head of the DSG, as the leader of his campaign. In truth, Burton was a committee of one. He often acted on his own counsel without input from his supporters, with even his brother John, also a member of the California congressional delegation, feeling left out.[16]

Mikva assessed the field of competitors in this way. McFall, he believed, was an "amiable nonentity," a characterization that became prescient as the campaign developed. Bolling was an "extremely bright, good looking fellow who had a snippy air about him." Again, this was a commonly shared assessment. Wright was "an unctuous evangelical with a pocketful of chits from the Chicago and New York City guys." Mikva continued, "None of us took him seriously."[17]

In a ploy to attract the votes of reform minded members of Congress, Burton released his income tax records, going back to 1971, showing that he really had no appreciable income beyond his congressional salary and almost no assets.[18] It also implicitly laid down the challenge to his opponents to follow suit. None did.

Secondly, Burton differentiated himself from his opponents by pointing to his early opposition to the Vietnam War, another indication of his break from the Democratic establishment. Such opposition proved two points:

he had the courage of his convictions, and he was willing to break with the established leadership when convictions came into play. Of course, this was a potential double-edged sword for Burton. As majority leader, he would have to work within the leadership rather than to challenge it openly. To that end, Burton emphatically promised to work with Speaker Tip O'Neill. Asked whether he could work with O'Neill, Burton answered easily: "Sure."[19]

Burton's personality often caused him problems, especially when he had been drinking. For example, in a Washington restaurant, a Texas supporter of Wright introduced himself to Burton. Burton bristled and asked the visitor what he was doing in Washington. The man replied, "I'm here to see if Jim Wright can help us with the farm bill." Burton exploded, "F— Jim Wright. F— the farm bill. I will single-handedly sink all this redneck Texas special interest s—." The visitor silently left. Burton later explained that his crude behavior was intentional. "I don't even want Jim Wright to have a meeting with a favored constituent without feeling me breathing down his f— neck."[20]

Burton wanted to build on his reputation for reform in the House. A letter sent by fourteen supporters in the House pointed to his reform agenda, including specifically his leadership by example in releasing his financial records and his coalition building for reform. He was proud of his leadership of the Watergate Class of 1974, a reform-minded group that had wanted to shake things up in the tradition-laden organization. Burton had helped Democratic Congressional Campaign Committee Chair Wayne Hays allocate funds for that class and had reminded them of his role in the allocation of those funds.[21]

Beyond that, Burton had led the revolt against the seniority system when he had persuaded the party to oust three chairmen — Bob Poage of Agriculture, Wright Patman of Banking and Currency, and Edward Hébert of Armed Services — from their positions. Such leadership differentiated Burton from Wright, a Texan like Poage and Patman, who had openly supported Patman during the caucus.[22]

But Burton had, during the same meeting, successfully worked to assure the reelection of Wayne Hays as chairman of the House Committee on Administration. Unpopular among many of his colleagues, Hays was a close friend with Burton. Burton interceded on Hays's behalf to help him keep his committee chairmanship when the young members of the party had wanted to remove him. Then, in May of 1976, a scandal broke out around Hays. He had employed as a secretary a young woman named Elizabeth Ray with whom he reportedly had sexual relations. She came to work, by her own report, only a couple of days a week for just a few hours. Moreover, "I can't type. I can't file. I can't even answer the phone." The scandal that ensued forced Hays to resign, with Burton helping draft his letter of resignation. While Burton himself was not implicated in the scandal, this was no way to begin a campaign.[23]

It was widely thought that Burton had made a deal where Hays would be reelected as chair of the House Administration Committee in exchange for Hays supporting Burton for caucus chair. When Hays was forced out, it embarrassed the Burton campaign and meant that Hays, "one of the few people remaining in Congress who could be counted on to deliver votes," would not be a factor in favor of Burton. And here is where the feelings of Tip O'Neill emerged in the campaign, despite his official neutrality in the race. It was no secret that O'Neill thought Burton too strident, too unappreciative of the traditions of the House, and a dangerous choice as majority leader. But his only public statement that tipped his hand was when he told reporters that Burton "had tried to persuade the leadership to go easy" on Hays, a charge Burton disputed.[24]

Burton felt betrayed by a Herblock cartoon published in *The Washington Post* four days before the election that portrayed Burton as a wheeler-dealer used car salesman with specific reference to his relationship with Wayne Hays. Coming when it did, Burton deemed it "below the belt," leaving a terrible impression on the incoming freshmen. After the cartoon appeared, the Burton forces sent out a "Dear Colleague" letter arguing that the cartoon had been unfair. One of the signers of the letter was Norman Mineta, a congressional newcomer pledged to support Burton. But Burton remained suspicious because if Mineta wanted to move up in congressional influence, the advancement of a more senior Californian might keep him from moving up the leadership chain. There may have been reason for concern, for Mineta had, according to Wright's records, agreed to support Wright after the first ballot.[25] Such an event might help explain why Burton was so unsure of his numbers of supporters. He had obtained pledges through arm-twisting techniques, and in a secret ballot such tactics might not pay off.

The Bolling Campaign

Bolling had long wanted a leadership position in the House. As early as 1961, he had challenged Carl Albert for majority leader when Sam Rayburn died and John McCormack succeeded to the Speaker's chair. Bolling later regretted that move because he developed an admiration for Albert, whom he saw as an "under-appreciated leader and Speaker." When the position came open in 1976, Bolling warmed to the task of organizing a campaign. On June 5, he announced that since Albert was retiring, he was supporting O'Neill for Speaker and declaring his candidacy for the majority leadership.[26]

His campaign would be difficult, for while Bolling was widely respected in the House as a master legislator and intellectual leader, he was also seen as abrasive and arrogant. To those whom he did not like, the foremost perhaps being Phillip Burton, Bolling could be very rude. If such people called on the phone, Bolling would have short and trivial conversations. When the phone call was over, Bolling would remark, "I wouldn't give that prick the time of day if I had the only watch in town." *Dun's Review* offered this description: "Bolling has always been a respected — if not particularly popular — legislator. Brilliant, brooding and often acerbic, Bolling has the reputation of not suffering fools gladly." Bolling himself concluded, "As everyone knows, I'm not shy about mentioning my capabilities" and he remarked to his colleague Morris Udall that "I think I'm too arrogant to win." He also had alienated some more traditional members of Congress when he wrote a book critical of what Bolling believed to be the outmoded congressional process.[27]

Bolling also had a long list of friends, including Gillis Long of Louisiana. Bolling tapped him to chair his majority leader campaign. Long, in comments at a Bolling breakfast early in the campaign, revealed both Bolling's strategy and his concerns. One of the central campaign coordinators would be Bolling's wife, Jim Bolling, a longtime Democratic political activist. Jim Bolling would coordinate Bolling's personal contacts, through visits, phone calls, and mailings with current members of the House and the Democratic nominees standing for election. She also was to develop a list of outside contacts in members' districts that might influence the majority leader vote. Finally, she would try to organize a brunch for new members' wives and organize speaking engagements in their districts during the campaign. Participants at the breakfast were given a list of uncommitted members who could be contacted and encouraged to vote for Bolling, an activity that would be coordinated by Christopher Dodd of Connecticut. Finally, James Symington, like Bolling a member of the Missouri delegation, was to meet with the retiring members of Congress to have them encourage their successors to back Bolling.[28] Symington was appropriate for this role because he was himself retiring from the House to seek election to the Senate.

In his statement, Long also indicated that Bolling was primarily concerned with stopping the election of Phillip Burton. "Until you analyze this race in terms of who can win in a head to head contest against Burton," Long said, "you can not fully appreciate the importance of Dick Bolling's campaign. In reality, on the last ballot some of the members will not be voting for their first choice; they will in fact be voting against the candidate they oppose the most. . . . I think that you will have to agree that Jim Wright simply cannot beat Burton because many of Bolling's people will go with Burton. The same thing is even more true when you analyze it in terms of a McFall versus Burton runoff."[29] The central message: not only did Bolling want to be majority leader, but his greatest fear was that if he were not in the race, Phillip Burton would be elected.

Bolling's strategy to block Wright and McFall was announced by Jim Bolling, speaking to a group working for Bolling's election. Wright "has one of the worse [sic] civil rights records in the Congress, and McFall, who is presently Whip, I would characterize as quite colorless and a conservative member." In a letter meant for a friend of a current congressman, hoping that friend would influence her friend (who was not identified) to vote for Bolling, Jim Bolling wrote, "Wright and McFall bases are too narrow, they can expect little or no labor, black, liberal, or freshman 94th Congress votes."[30]

Behind the scenes, Jim Bolling was pursuing a negative strategy against Wright as well. She wrote, in a memo to her husband, that a committee had been formed to try to help Jim Wright pay off his personal debt. In a memo of June 6, 1976, she made notes to her husband about the employment of two members of the Wright family:

> think about the mmes Wrights
> #1 Mab Wright
> — believed to be employed by the Guide Office, US Capitol. When contacted, office reported "Mrs Wright not in office today; expected tomorrow"
> #2 Betty (Hay) Wright
> 1972 — Ass't to chair, public works Chairman Jim Wright
> 73, 74, 75 Betty Wright listed as ass't to the chair
> 1976 — Betty Wright is Administrative Assistant.

These thoughts were clearly aimed at making a nepotism issue against Wright. Although no record exists that this information was ever spread directly to other members of Congress, after the election was over,

Mrs. Bolling complained that *The Washington Post* was privy to this information and had not made use of it.[31]

Jim Bolling was in charge of beginning a relationship with incoming members' wives. She sent each one a letter congratulating them and enclosing a "newcomer's guide" and a cookbook.[32]

Bolling hoped to be able to use Carl Albert, the retiring speaker, to help his campaign. In an August 2 memo, Jim Bolling wrote her husband that the Speaker was supposed to be "working the Oklahoma delegation and others" but that if he was not doing so, others needed to be assigned the task. Bolling had a note in his files dated June 7 that said that Albert "said he would do everything short of endorsing me out loud." The next day, his notes say: "Carl A. said he might try to dissuade Wright." Wright, however, has said that Albert actually encouraged him to run.[33]

Bolling also thought that he might have Tip O'Neill's support. O'Neill's close friend and alter-ego Edward Boland supported Bolling, and O'Neill had served on the Rules Committee with Bolling. On Rules, remarked one colleague, Bolling "had carried the mail for a lot of people over the years." Bolling did use Boland as a conduit to O'Neill, once sending Boland an editorial from the *Kansas City Times* that was titled, "Bolling is the best, most likely choice" and adding a note, "Dear Eddie, I would say that the major press now seems to feel that we have a winner — thought you and Tip might like to see the attached clips."[34]

There was a bit of an air of superiority from the Bolling camp about Wright's record in Congress. As a member of the Public Works Committee, Wright could help members get congressionally funded projects in their districts. However, Jim Bolling wrote that members should be reminded that all of those bills had to pass through the Rules Committee on which Bolling was the ranking member.[35] Such a reminder suggested that Bolling wanted to use his position just as Wright did but also reflected the insider's perspective that Rules is a more important committee than Public Works.

Bolling found the prospect of being an administrative leader uncomfortable. He had a greater interest in working on legislation than he did in interacting on a regular basis with other members of the House and having to craft compromises with combating egos. His ambition to accomplish overall goals and to keep Burton from the leadership, however, drove him to campaign for the post. He could not quite bring himself to go schmooze prospective members of the House at the Democratic National Convention and did not campaign extensively for colleagues across the country as did Burton and Wright, but he did go personally to each Democratic member's office to touch base and ask for their support. Such politicking was uncomfortable for Bolling but essential to success.[36]

Bolling received the endorsement of *The New York Times* for the position. The *Times* saw Bolling as "qualified by intellect, experience, philosophical outlook and political skill to manage the new administration's legislative program" while being able to "articulate and defend the interests of the House as a great democratic institution."[37] While a *Times* endorsement might have solidified Bolling's core intellectual and liberal support, it hardly could help in reaching out to moderate, southern, and western voters.

The Wright Campaign

In March, Wright first verbalized his thoughts of running for majority leader after a meeting with Congressman Harley Staggers of West Virginia. On the car trip back to Washington, Wright discussed possible strategies for election with his senior advisor and close friend Craig Raupe. As they talked, they became encouraged. Raupe, who to Wright "was as near as I've had to a brother," turned his attention to managing the campaign. Once the decision was made to run, Wright warmed to the task. "I was not a reluctant candidate. I found the thought of being majority leader very appealing."[38] Wright was the last of the four candidates to enter the campaign; the others began with a significant head start. However, Wright felt that he had a good chance to woo moderate and conservative members as McFall's campaign languished.

Despite the rumors that since Speaker-designate Tip O'Neill's friend Edward Boland was supporting Bolling, O'Neill too was supporting him, there were crosscutting rumors that O'Neill was not happy with the choice between Burton and Bolling. "He feared and distrusted Burton. He served on Rules for years with Bolling and could not tolerate his arrogance." He also did not think that either would share influence with him easily. However, as incoming Speaker, O'Neill could not afford to take a position in the race because he would have to work with whichever candidate won. Bolling, nevertheless, thought that O'Neill was with him. A memo to Jim Wright from his associate Marshall Lynam on November 23 reported that Bolling associate Gillis Long of Louisiana had told a reporter that O'Neill's friend Edward Boland was supporting Bolling and that O'Neill was trying to make his influence known through Boland.[39]

Wright remembered that he had only one conversation with O'Neill regarding the majority leader race. O'Neill approached Wright and said, "I hear you're thinking about running for majority leader." Wright replied: "Yes, I'm thinking about it, but I'm in position to take over as Chair of Public Works and am worried about the time commitment majority leader would entail." "Jim," O'Neill replied, "Majority leader wouldn't take any more time than Public Works." Wright interpreted the statement as an indication that O'Neill was not opposed to his running. No one knows who O'Neill ultimately supported, though Wright believes it might very well have been McFall on the first ballot and thereafter him. But, Wright notes, "If Tip was as good a politician as I think he was, probably all four of us felt that way."[40]

Wright's campaign strategy relied primarily upon his two strongest constituencies within the House — the Texas delegation and the membership of his Public Works Committee.[41] Unity in the Texas delegation was a long-standing tradition. As Wright began to seek endorsements, he knew that his home delegation would be crucial. Moreover, as a longstanding member of Public Works, a large committee with twenty-nine Democratic members, support from his fellow committee members would be essential.

He also took advantage of the fact that like President-elect Carter, he was a moderate and also a southerner. Said Wright, tongue-in-cheek, "I'd be able to communicate with President-to-be Jimmy Carter, since both of us obviously were free from accent." During the last days of the campaign, he underscored his advantage in working with Carter by wearing a golden peanut lapel pin, a gift from the president-elect.[42]

The support of Illinois congressman Dan Rostenkowski would become a boon to Wright. Rostenkowski disliked both Bolling and Burton. Bolling remembered, "Rostenkowski hated me. He had to find someone else. He came up with Wright."[43] Though certainly Rostenkowski was not the only member of Congress to encourage Wright, he had a special place in the campaign. As a product of the Chicago political machine of the inimitable Mayor Richard Daley, Rostenkowski was able to set up an appointment between Wright and Daley. Daley left the meeting impressed with Wright and made known his support to the members of the Chicago congressional delegation and to Mayors Frank Rizzo of Philadelphia and Abraham Beame of New York. Suddenly, the Wright coalition had spread beyond his two primary constituencies of the Public Works Committee and the Texas delegation.

Robert Remini reports that Rostenkowski worked for the election of

Wright with O'Neill's blessing. Burton, Bolling, and McFall all had flaws that would be long-term liabilities for the leadership, and O'Neill and Rostenkowski thought Wright a far superior option. Wright did not know about any involvement of O'Neill in the process but appreciated the support Rostenkowski gave him in taking him to Chicago to meet with Mayor Daley. He knew that Daley lobbied for him with two other big-city mayors. Wright was unaware that up until that point in the race, Daley had backed Bolling. Rostenkowski's support might have indicated that O'Neill supported Wright as well. O'Neill and Rostenkowski were close personal friends and shared golf outings from coast to coast. (Wright recalled going to the Bing Crosby golf tournament in California when he was majority leader, an irony since Wright was not a golfer. But Wright said that O'Neill and Rostenkowski would make so many deals during those outings that he went "out of self-defense.")[44]

A *New York Times* editorial suggested that Wright's strategy would be to "renew the alliance between the Southwest and the Northeast that has dominated the House since 1940." In the judgment of the *Times,* as in Bolling's thoughts, Wright would have a difficult time succeeding. "It is doubtful that Mr. Wright, a middle-of-the-roader, can gain leadership of what has become a predominantly liberal party in the House." Indeed, Wright did focus on the connection in a widely distributed letter: "the Democratic party cannot make it without the South and the Southwest. . . . If ours is the party we claim it to be, its leadership must represent more than just one ideological faction."[45]

Wright, reflecting on his views of the legislative process, suggested that in dealing with fellow members of Congress, it was always important to remember three things:

> (1) "Men of goodwill and sincere purpose often disagree. And this can happen without either antagonist being a sycophant, a demagogue, or a rascal. Or even stupid, for that matter."
> (2) "Congressmen are, after all, just people, [with] finite knowledge and fallible judgments."
> (3) "Most Congressmen earnestly want to do the right thing."[46]

Part of Wright's appeal would be to proceed from these three tenets and, implicitly, contrast his candidacy from those of his competitors.

Toward the end of the campaign, a friend of Wright's, Nick Masters, learned of the strategy Bolling's camp was using against Wright. He reported that Wright would be charged with not having the support of the

Texas delegation, that he had a terrible civil rights record, and that he was too beholden to Texas oil interests. Wright and his advisors responded strongly to each of the three.

First, he drafted an endorsement letter that was signed by all but two of his Texas colleagues. The only two that did not sign were Jack Brooks and Bob Eckhardt, both of whom had pledged to support Burton before Wright entered the race. Brooks, of course, wanted on the leadership ladder, and if Wright was majority leader, Brooks, a Rayburn protégé, would have his leadership plans derailed. He had also been most unhappy with Boggs as majority whip, claiming that Boggs had never told "us how they are going to vote — never call back to get answers." Eckhardt had long been friendly with Wright but felt that Wright had become more conservative over time and that Wright had embellished a story about his role in a 1947 oil tax bill in Texas to establish his liberal credentials. Even so, it was thought that Brooks and Eckhardt would have supported Wright had he announced his candidacy earlier.[47] In the Texas caucus, however, Wright refused to pressure his colleagues to change their commitments. In the first place, they probably would not have, but in the second, such tactics would be harmful in the long run. But Wright did not give up entirely on getting the support of Brooks and Eckhardt. In a letter to financial supporter and friend Bernard Rapoport, Wright wrote to apologize for having seen Rapoport only briefly at the Democratic National Convention: "I was massaging Democratic nominees." He said too that he respected Brooks's and Eckhardt's commitments but that he would not mind "a gentle hint that it might be nice for the Texans to stand together behind a Texan. They might resent any more overt intrusion."[48]

The fact that he was a southern candidate also meant that his opponents wished to focus on the liabilities that they perceived in his record, particularly with regard to civil rights and defense spending. Wright responded to the civil rights charges in a letter to his colleagues. While regretting that he had opposed the 1964 Civil Rights Act on grounds "which I thought at the time to be valid but which I no longer believe to be correct," he pointed out his long record of backing other civil rights legislation, a list that he enclosed with his letter. He noted that his votes were risky in his district: "I have probably as good and long-standing a record of support for basic civil and human rights as anyone from my part of the country could be expected to have and still survive in the politically turbulent years that are behind us. My record in this regard is quite different from that of most of my colleagues from the geographic area I represent."[49]

To combat the charge that he was too tight with Texas oil, Wright asked that his oil supporters take a low profile. He also used word of mouth to debunk this charge.[50] While Wright had always been friendly to independent oil producers, he was no friend of "big oil," though many members from non-oil states and in the media seemed not to be able to differentiate between the two.

John McFall was the candidate most similar to Wright in ideological support within the Democratic caucus. He knew that McFall's campaign was languishing, so Wright appealed to McFall's supporters by asking them to support him on a second ballot should McFall be eliminated in the first.

Wright campaigned heavily at the Democratic convention of 1976, though his operation was so low key that the *Congressional Quarterly* did not even notice. While Burton relied on members to come to the parties he hosted, Wright made prior appointments with as many of the candidates for election to the House as he could. He set up individual breakfasts, lunches, or cocktail hours with each. Since he had not yet formally declared himself a candidate, he did not solicit support but rather told the potential freshmen that he was considering running and that he wanted to help them in their elections. Later, he followed through on the offer of campaign assistance by appearing for twenty-one successful freshman candidates during the campaign. Such cultivation yielded relationships that turned into at least a dozen votes in the election, and Wright thought that all twenty-one supported him.[51]

On July 27, Wright formally announced his campaign in letters to his colleagues. He had eight different versions of his letter, one that he sent to his opponents telling them, "I felt I owed you the courtesy of letting you know directly from me," and one to each of the following: Texas supporters, verbal supporters, uncommitted members, those committed to another, those with whom he had no contact, the California delegation, and retiring members.[52]

An undated tally sheet in Wright's records shows that he had either specific commitments or good intelligence on most members of the House. It reveals at least sixty-seven firm commitments to Wright, including all of the members of the Texas delegation except Brooks and Eckhardt. More interestingly, at least twenty-five members had told Wright that he was their second choice, with most of those committed to McFall on the first ballot. Additionally, there was a little intrigue revealed as well. Californian Norman Mineta, under immense pressure from Burton and McFall, was committed to Wright after the first ballot. And a member of the New York delegation, James Hanley, was committed to Burton but privately told Wright he would vote for him.[53]

On the morning of the caucus, former Wright aide turned journalist and playwright Larry L. King wrote an article favorable to Wright. President Carter had suggested in an interview that he had a "favorite" for the majority leader post, but he knew that the president could not involve himself in internal House matters. However, King, a writer-in-residence for the *Washington Star*, used Carter's announcement as fodder for speculation. King suggested that Carter's candidate must be Jim Wright and outlined the reasons for his speculation. The Wright campaign made sure that all members with votes had a copy on their doorsteps the next morning. On each one, they had stuck a label: "See inside. Larry L. King on the Critical House Majority Leader Race."[54]

He also knew that a major battle would be over gaining the support of new incoming members of the House. While much of the attention in the contest was by necessity focused on incumbents, the new members of Congress, elected in 1976 for the first time, would be real targets of opportunity. Not having been around in Congress, they would not know any of the candidates well. Not having engaged in political bargaining on issues with the candidates, their loyalties would be weak and uncertain. To appeal to these incoming members, Wright decided to pursue their support in two ways. First, he orchestrated political support for their campaigns in the form of campaign contributions from Texas supporters. In order to accomplish this task, he enlisted the help of his staff. They solicited donations from Wright supporters that were to be sent to prospective members of Congress running to become freshmen members. Marshall Lynam, one of Wright's close associates, remembers soliciting a donation from Arthur Temple, a wealthy lumber executive from Diboll in deep East Texas. Lynam, along with Craig Raupe and others, convinced Temple to write a check to a number of candidates for election, one of them being Barbara Mikulski, then running for her first term from Maryland. Another Wright supporter, Bernard Rapoport, an insurance executive from Waco, recalls writing ten blank $1000 checks to be sent as campaign contributions to potential Democratic members of the House. Wright's archives contain many more records of the same activity, with forty-seven letters indicating contributions sent by third parties to candidates in support of the Wright campaign. Many of the checks were in the amount of $50.00, showing that they were mostly symbolic, even during the relatively inexpensive campaigns of that era. Still, in all, the Wright campaign was estimated to have raised $50,000 for candidates in this manner.[55]

In addition to offering financial support, Wright offered to come to the districts and campaign for these candidates. The offer of money was one thing, but giving of himself was even more effective. His campaigning for candidate Allen Ertel of Pennsylvania was perhaps the best example. Wright made twenty-five appearances with Ertel before different groups on one day during the campaign, even though Ertel was given little chance of winning by pundits. When Ertel was elected, it underscored Wright's ability as an effective campaigner.[56]

Wright also wooed incoming House members by hosting the freshmen congressmen when they came to Washington. He invited them to come to a luncheon after the general election. Then, finding out that his scheduled luncheon would preclude the other three candidates having a chance to speak with the incoming class, Wright invited them to come as well: "I introduced each of the other candidates with complimentary and glowing things to say about him. I tried to say the most complimentary thing I could say and to point up some of the really constructive things that each of them had done and gave each of them the opportunity to talk with the incoming members at the luncheon. That seemed to be the decent thing to do and I suppose that the incoming members appreciated the fact that I could be that decent about it and not try to monopolize them."[57]

At the luncheon, each candidate had the opportunity to address the freshmen. Burton, having been very popular with the class of 1974, hoped that he could use his record of helping incoming members as a way to seek their support, mentioned that he had helped push reforms through Congress working with the class of 1974. After he had spoken, Wright added: "We're fortunate to have with us today the president of the class of '74, Carroll Hubbard of Kentucky. Would you care to say anything, Carroll?" "I sure would," Hubbard replied, "I'm for Jim Wright." Burton's appeal had backfired.[58]

The McFall Campaign

McFall's strategy was low key. He argued that his record as whip had been good, and based on that, he deserved to be promoted. He was in the traditional position to move up, especially given the fact that by general assessment, he had been a good whip. Journalist John Barry suggested that McFall "played the inside game well and, generally popular, had the advantage of being in the leadership ladder."[59]

His campaign was largely a two-man operation, McFall and his top aide, Irving Sprague. McFall mostly went about his job as whip and hoped that his record, combined with tradition, would make him a serious candidate. He also relied on "the growing network of deputy and regional whips" to get the word out. "I'm not aggressive in buttonholing people. That's not my style. My style is to say 'I hope I can have your support.'"[60]

Retiring Speaker Carl Albert, McFall reported with pride, "said I was the best whip of the last 25 years." Indeed, McFall had put together a track record. He had helped develop a whip advisory system that informed members about key votes, an improvement in the floor information system. He also developed speech cards to help Democratic congressional candidates. And the Democrats had overridden more vetoes under Gerald Ford than in any presidency since Andrew Johnson's in the 1860s.[61]

But among those who vied for the position, it was generally felt that McFall was not up to the task of winning the election. He was not comfortable asking people for their support and not terribly sage in being able to interpret the coy responses of his colleagues when he did ask. One member recalled that if a member of the House would tell McFall "John, you'd be a helluva leader," he counted that as a commitment, though such an interpretation might be far from the reality. Moreover, there was concern even among those who might be predisposed to help McFall that his amiable personality might not resonate well with the majority leader's position. They doubted that "such a pleasant and easy going guy would be forceful enough to knock heads, as a Majority Leader occasionally was required to do."[62]

McFall's biggest liability, however, came when he became embroiled in a scandal that crippled his already flagging chances. McFall had admitted that he received $4000 dollars from Korean lobbyist Tongsun Park, putting it into his office account. Many members of Congress had such accounts, and McFall's was not the largest, but allegations that he had used the money to finance interest-free loans through which he was able to pay his California taxes, buy his daughter a car, and help finance her college tuition crippled his campaign.[63]

The scandal had begun when it was revealed that in the spring of 1973, representatives of the Korean embassy launched a plan to "buy off" congressmen to obtain legislation favorable to Korea. Congressman Donald Fraser called the scheme "outright subversion" revealing "a calculated intent by the K[orean] CIA to use clandestine means to sway American public opinion and official policy." On October 24, 1976, in the middle of the majority leader campaign, the *Washington Post* broke the story. The story claimed Tongsun Park was the mastermind of the plot. McFall had written two letters on behalf of Park to Korean president Park Chung Hee, one in 1971 and another in 1973.[64] The scandal would be the focus of great attention over the next year, but for now, it simply acted as the final blow to McFall's chances for election.

McFall had become a weak fourth candidate by the end of the campaign. In the question and answer session with new members the day before the election, McFall generated only twenty minutes of questions in the allotted thirty-minute time.[65] His candidacy had never really taken off, and by now it had almost completely fizzled.

Meet the Press

The day before the balloting, all four candidates made a joint appearance on the NBC Sunday morning broadcast of "Meet the Press," allowing an open exchange of ideas.

Burton seemed in campaign mode from the beginning of the broadcast, arguing that he alone was best qualified "in bringing my colleagues of diverse points of view together for common action." When asked about his relationship with Wayne Hays, Burton suggested that because of his working with Hays, the reform agenda passed by the House was better than it otherwise would have been. But he also distanced himself from his friend, saying that he had no idea about the events in which Hays had become embroiled. He suggested that office accounts such as the one that Tongsun Park had contributed to in McFall's office should be outlawed, reestablishing his credentials as a reform candidate. He expressed confidence that he would win the election.[66]

Bolling's presentation included references to his twenty years of experience on the Rules Committee and his success as floor leader in the major budget reform bill that had passed the House only two years earlier. In response to the charge that he was "stuck-up" and "lacked tact," Bolling responded by listing his legislative successes in civil rights and budget reform as well as his relationship with Sam Rayburn. Bolling also made it clear that he did not want Burton to win, at almost any cost. Asked if he had entered the race "with the avowed purpose of blocking Mr. Burton," Bolling replied, "Well, that is no secret. That is certainly true."[67]

Wright was asked about his ideology from the very start, with a question about why he voted with the Democratic majority only 62 percent of the time in the previous year. Wright argued that he was in the "mainstream" of the party and that the job of majority leader was not, after all, ideological. He was asked why, in this bitter race, he continued to speak highly of each of his opponents. Was that a ploy? "No," Wright replied, "I don't seek election on the basis of their being poor candidates. They aren't poor candidates. They are able men. I honor them all." Wright scored points with some members of Congress by refusing to answer a question about how he would vote on an internal House disciplinary procedure. Bob Sikes of Florida had been charged with violating House rules with some financial indiscretions. Wright's "none of your business" response was popular among House insiders who thought such information to be private.[68]

McFall spent almost all of his time answering questions about the "Koreagate" scandal and his relationship with Park and trying to defend his overall record and his office account. He wished to focus on his "imaginative and innovative" leadership, but that did not become the agenda of the program. His candidacy had lost its vibrancy.

The Whip Position

As the major battle was being fought for majority leader, a lesser conflict was being waged for whip. Wright's Texas colleague Jack Brooks was interested, but Indiana's John Brademas mounted a successful multifaceted campaign for the position, in part on the advice of Tip O'Neill, who discouraged Brademas from running for majority leader. Said O'Neill, "If you run and lose, you're finished. . . . If you don't run you'll be the whip." One of the issues in 1976 was whether the whip position should continue to be appointed by the leadership or whether it should be elected by the caucus. If the whip position was made elective, Brademas had collected commitments from half the caucus. And Brademas was also trying for support if the whip position remained appointive, seeking a commitment that if Bolling were elected majority leader, Brademas would be appointed whip.[69]

The Balloting

Even as the day of the caucus approached, the media continued to see the race as a two-candidate operation, with Wright and McFall out of the calculation. Speaker-elect O'Neill apparently saw it the same way. He invited both Bolling and Burton over for a drink after the voting, whichever one won. He did not invite Wright.[70]

The morning of the vote, the candidates anxiously awaited the results. Wright recalled that he did not do any campaigning that morning, reasoning that "the hay was either in the barn or it wasn't by then." Wright received a couple of phone calls from members committing to him. The evening before Wright had received a call from Gillis Long of the Bolling camp assuring Wright that if Bolling was eliminated in the second ballot, "he and everyone he could influence would be trying to help me."[71] This was an interesting phone call, for it might have reflected an understanding in the Bolling camp that Wright was pulling ahead of Bolling.

On the morning of the vote, each candidate was nominated and seconded. Peter Rodino of New Jersey, a member who had arrived in Washington at the same time as Bolling and was well known from his leadership of the House Judiciary Committee during the Watergate investigation, nominated Bolling. He emphasized Bolling's "profound understanding of the work of this house" and characterized Bolling as "a man of the House." Gillis Long of Louisiana, Andrew Young of Georgia, and Tim Wirth of Colorado made seconding speeches. Long, of the Louisiana Long family, was Bolling's close friend and campaign coordinator. He also emphasized Bolling's expertise: "I was impressed with his openness, his knowledge on a broad range of issues, his understanding of the workings of the Congress, and his evenhandedness in dealing with the members." Young, a former associate of Martin Luther King Jr. and an ally of President Carter, represented African American leadership in the House. Wirth, who had emerged as one of the leaders of the "Watergate" class in the House, took a slightly different approach, commenting that Bolling's name "has become synonymous with reform," an apparent attempt to cut into Burton's support.[72]

Next came the nomination of John McFall by B. F. Sisk, his friend and colleague. Sisk's speech was that of a good friend but contained a good deal of irony, considering McFall's difficulties from the Koreagate scandal. McFall, he said, was "a man of truly outstanding ability, unquestioned integrity, and rare dedication to the House." Seconding speeches came from Tom Steed of Oklahoma, a co-member of Appropriations, John Murtha of Pennsylvania, and Harold "Bizz" Johnson. Johnson was, like Sisk and McFall, a member of the California delegation. Murtha emphasized the fact that McFall was an asset in the leadership who had been "the most helpful person I have met in this House," and Johnson focused on his upgrading of the whip office.[73]

Burton was nominated by Yvonne Brathwaite Burke of California and seconded by Jim Florio of New Jersey, Charles Rose of North Carolina, and Abner Mikva of Illinois, his campaign manager. The speeches addressed Burton's commitment to reform and his strong personality. Burke pointed to his early opposition to the war in Vietnam and his leadership in reform. Further, Burton "can earn us a respect among the people of the nation, a respect I say we have earned, but have been denied." Florio addressed Burton's personality: "Some would characterize him as being too direct, too blunt, too open, but . . . the American people demand these characteristics." Rose promised through a story that Burton would lead the charge for further reform. He said that there was a group of dairy farmers who had advertised their milk as coming from contented cows. But in that area, there was one independent-minded farmer who claimed that his cows were never contented. Rather, they "were constantly striving to do better." Burton was like those farmer's cows: "he wants you and me to make this place better." And as for Burton's strong personality, Mikva said, there is no question that "Phil is an enthusiast."[74]

Wright chose Texas colleague Charles Wilson to make his nominating speech, and Wilson sounded some of Wright's themes. He pointed to Wright's voting for the Civil Rights Acts of 1965, a vote that was "about as popular in Fort Worth as terminal cancer," to his well-known "persuasive powers," to the geographic diversity that would come with Wright's selection (a Speaker from the Northeast, a whip from the Midwest, and a caucus chair from the West), and to Wright's connection with incoming president Carter.[75] Incoming freshman congressman Allen Ertel stressed Wright's courtesy to others in the House and complimented Wright for helping him win his election when his election seemed hopeless. Finally, Dan Rostenkowski sounded the themes Wright thought would help him win. Wright, Rostenkowski said, "has never demagogued against this institution" and "hasn't engaged in backbiting or petty intrigue." These references were to Bolling, who had written books critical of House traditions, and Burton, who was known for his hardball politics. And Rostenkowski said that Wright, like Rayburn before him, always respected the word of other members.[76]

As the ballots were being cast, Burton had his campaign manager Mikva stand behind Norman Mineta in line to make sure that he was voting correctly. Mikva was incredulous: "That's crazy," he told Burton. Mineta knew why Mikva had been put in line behind him and showed Mikva his ballot clearly marked "Burton."[77] His pledge to Burton had been fulfilled, but there were more ballots yet to go.

On the first ballot, Burton emerged as the leader with 106 votes followed by Bolling with 81, Wright with 77, and McFall with 31. After the first ballot, each candidate expressed surprise at the number of ballots he had received, for each thought they had more hard commitments than the results indicated. Wright recalls: "I thought I was being very hard-nosed about it. I was trying very diligently to be conservative in my appraisal of my own strength. I was deliberately not counting people who I thought I'd get. But it turns out that I actually thought on the day of the vote that I would get about eight more on the first ballot than I received."[78]

Bolling too was surprised. It had been reported by Gillis Long through a reporter to Wright associate Marshall Lynam that Bolling had felt he had 93 commitments as of November 23, a far cry from the 81 votes he ultimately received. Burton thought that he had 117 votes, 10 more than he actually received.[79]

There was very little time between the ballots. Wright had several associates go around and talk to folks who had suggested to him that they might support him on the second ballot, especially McFall supporters. The results of the second ballot were as follows: Burton received 107 votes, Wright 95, and Bolling 93. Indeed, Wright thought that of the 18 votes he picked up on the second ballot, perhaps 16 had come from McFall supporters, more than went to Bolling and Burton combined.

Wright was, of course, ecstatic about the outcome of the vote. No matter how razor-thin the margin, it accomplished his goal of making the final run-off. He was a bit surprised that he did not beat Bolling by more votes but was happy with the outcome. After the vote, Wright recalled, "we took the list of those we knew to be committed to Bolling and my friends fanned out like a bunch of June bugs and tried to nail down each one of them." The Bolling camp speculated that Burton had diverted some of his support to Wright so that he could eliminate Bolling. Burton's thought was, according to the Bolling camp, that he could defeat Wright on the third ballot. Burton always specifically denied that he had engaged in such tactics. Apparently, one of Burton's supporters actually asked Burton about that tactic as a way of eliminating Bolling. "Are you crazy?" Burton replied, "No. We play straight football."[80]

The vote was indicative of the persistent cleavages that had appeared when the Watergate class came on the scene. Whoever won the race would be confronted with difficult challenges. Regardless, the third ballot was the deciding one, and it came out with a one-vote margin. On the third ballot, Wright prevailed, 148–147.

Reflections

Wright learned of his election when two of his colleagues came in the door of the Speaker's lobby, one of them smiling and holding one finger in the air. Said Wright, "I didn't know whether he meant there was one more vote to be counted or that one finger meant w-o-n, or what. Then I saw Ray Roberts come in, and when he jumped in the air, I knew that there was good news. I was kind of stunned. It dawned on others a bit before it did me, I think, because I was suddenly surrounded by people reaching over, shaking hands and congratulating me. I was overwhelmed by a tide of emotion, and when the announcement was made, I was still in a kind of state of euphoria."[81]

Wright's first congratulatory reward was a kiss from his wife, who had been in the gallery. Then he received a bottle of Dom Perignon courtesy of Texas Senator Lloyd Bentsen. And soon after came a congratulatory phone call from President-elect Carter. To the press, in reference to Lyndon Johnson's 1948 Senate election margin of 87 votes, Wright joked: "We Texans are not new to landslides." He went on, on a serious note, to pledge to work for progressive legislation.[82]

After the initial celebration, Tip O'Neill invited Wright to come to his office for a drink. A few minutes later, Wright headed back to his office in the Rayburn building through a gauntlet of well-wishers. Wright turned to his assistant Marshall Lynam and said, "Marshall, tomorrow I want to talk to Gary Hymel and find out what the hell a Majority Leader is supposed to do."[83]

Trying to interpret the reasons for Wright's victory and the other candidates' losses is complex. The ballots themselves were secret, and one can never be certain how key members of Congress might have voted. However, Burton attempted to reconstruct the vote on the final ballot for the purpose of assessing his chances to challenge Wright in the future or perhaps to assess who his friends and enemies in the House were. Myron Struck of *Roll Call* compiled his list by checking with his sources in congressional offices and with newspapers in congressional districts. He provided a list to Burton, indicating how he thought 280 of the 295 voters cast their ballots. Additionally, Jim Wright's tally before the election indicates that ten of the remaining voters had committed to him. Combining those two tallies gives Wright 150 votes to Burton's 141 and leaves five as unknown. Since Wright received only 148 votes, obviously there are at least two errors in the data. However, for the purposes of explaining patterns

TABLE 8-2. BURTON-WRIGHT MAJORITY LEADER VOTE ANALYSIS

	Burton	Wright
Region		
Northeast	42 (57%)	32 (43%)
Midwest	41 (63)	24 (37)
South	20 (21)	75 (79)
West	34 (64)	19 (36)
Mean ADA Score	77.90	45.78
Mean Years Service	5.39	10.67
Members Elected 1974 (Watergate)	52 (71%)	21 (29%)
New Members (elected 1976)	24 (55%)	20 (45%)
Leadership (committee chairs and party leaders)	7 (30%)	16 (70%)
N	137	150[a]

[a]Votes are counted primarily according to data collected by Myron Struck for Phil Burton, Majority Leader 1976 Notebook, PBP. Of the fifteen members that Struck listed as "uncertain," ten were listed in Wright's tally as for Wright (Tally sheet, n.d.). Accordingly, the Wright support in this chart is two higher than his actual total. Excluded from this analysis are the five members who were not listed in either the Burton or Wright calculations and the votes of caucus members from Washington, D.C., Guam, Puerto Rico, and the Virgin Islands, all of whom probably supported Burton. In looking over the Struck tally that had been prepared for Burton, Wright said that he thought the listing pretty accurate, though he thought there to be a few errors. Wright interview, October 17, 2006.

in the vote, those few errors do not affect analysis of overall voting trends, as indicated in table 8-2.

Wright's major source of support was the South, where he outpolled Burton by a nearly four to one margin. In the other three regions, Burton won handily, though Wright did receive notable support in all three of the other regions. Particularly, Wright seemed to receive support from Chicago (where Mayor Daley and Dan Rostenkowski worked the delegation), New York City, New Jersey, and Boston.

In terms of ideology, there was a wide disparity between Burton voters and Wright voters, with Burton supporters averaging a score of nearly 78 on the Americans for Democratic Action (ADA) ratings for 1976 compared to an average of 46 for Wright. These differences did not reflect universal patterns. For example, Dawson Mathis of Georgia (ADA score: 16) supported Burton while Frederick Richmond of New York (ADA score: 95) supported Wright. But the overall trend was very strong.

Similarly, the length of experience in the House seemed to play a large role, with those having long service being much more likely to support

Wright. Perhaps it was a positive feeling about Wright's respect for the traditions of the House (Wright had spoken out against removing his Texas colleagues Wright Patman and Bob Poage from their committee chairs when the seniority system came under challenge and had told a journalist in the Meet the Press appearance that internal House affairs regarding the discipline of Robert Sikes of Florida was "none of your business"). Perhaps it was Burton's advocacy of sweeping reforms that led more senior members to oppose him while encouraging young members to support him. Burton fared especially well among members of the Watergate class of 1974 and won more narrowly among the freshman class of 1976, a class where Wright had campaigned diligently in the districts of the prospective members. Finally, another indicator came from the support of senior leaders in the party, including the committee chairs, Speaker, whip, and caucus chair. There, Wright won handily, receiving 16 votes to Burton's 7.

With only a single vote having been necessary to change the outcome, speculations as to the cause of Wright's victory are as numerous as the individual reasons for each member's vote. Wright thought that had Bolling survived the second ballot, he might have enjoyed the same type of victory that Wright had. Clearly, the election was about ideology, personality, and respect for the traditions of the House. Bolling's arrogance toward other members of Congress hurt him, and Burton's crude exercise of influence hurt him. The fact that neither of them could tolerate the other but that Wright got along with both is instructive. Burton was once characterized as "an absolute political genius" and Bolling as an "intellectual beacon of the House," but neither seemed able to grasp the fact that Wright was viable as a candidate because he had the ability to work with others. Perhaps that was why both underestimated his candidacy. Wright himself reflected, "Everything a member does in the total years of his service has some bearing on their decision in selecting their leaders."[84]

After the caucus vote eliminating him from the race, Bolling went back to his office and talked with his staff. He wanted to avoid a "pity party" and asked his staff to discuss the loss now and then move on. No one said anything, and after a pause, he went into his private office. The only sign of his frustration was that he slammed the door "so hard that the walls shook." Reflecting on the vote, Jim Bolling, still obviously flustered from losing, was interviewed by a student at Hamilton College named Steve Talevi. In her comments, she said that part of Wright's success was because of two factors: (1) that Burton had thrown some of his support to Wright in the second ballot to eliminate Bolling; and (2) that members of the Public Works Committee had supported Wright so that they could move up the seniority ladder on the committee. She said that many members were angered that Burton had eliminated Bolling with such backhanded tactics and thus supported Wright in the runoff. As to the Public Works Committee, the cigar-smoking Mrs. Bolling simply said that they had played "s—house politics."[85]

Commenting on a paper written by Bruce Oppenheimer and Robert Peabody for the American Political Science Association, Mrs. Bolling wrote on the paper's margins: "Perhaps [the] single most obvious key influence on the outcome of the election was [the] *Washington Post*'s withholding of information of Wright's nepotism and murky personal-political finances." She also thought the paper presented Wright "as pioustistic [*sic*] and [as a] 'hale fellow well met' that you could look rather naïve in a couple of years."[86]

In the evening following the vote, however, the Bollings went to dinner and drank two toasts that night. The first was in sorrow at their loss and the second was that Phillip Burton had been defeated. Thus, though Bolling had not himself won the position as he had hoped, he was happy that he had achieved his secondary goal — keeping the position from his archenemy Burton.[87]

For his part, Burton handled the defeat with good grace in public, telling the caucus, "Jim, first of all, you have proven one thing to me, you count a lot better than I do." To a friend, he said, "My good friend. Just relax. It's all over. Sala and I are going on vacation. It's okay. I'm not disheartened." However, as he departed from the meeting and rode down the elevator, he appeared bitter and implied that his defeat was the result of his reputation for backroom dealing. Perhaps the irony in Burton's loss was best summarized in the reflections of his younger brother John. When John had come into politics, Phil offered him advice on how to be successful, and this was "kind of funny coming from him, he always had a theory that you try to get along with people that don't have the same political persuasion, which he used to do. But then he didn't get along with people who had the same political persuasion, which is what cost him the majority leader position."[88]

Despite Burton's protests, though, his biographer John Jacobs revealed that he *was* devastated, and he never fully recovered from the loss and often "viewed his colleagues through a prism." Burton would have loved to challenge Wright again. Early in 1978, asked by a reporter if he planned to challenge Wright, Burton replied, "I certainly don't plan to wait until the next century," and later in 1978 he reported that "we're counting the votes, and if they are there, we'll go." It was even speculated that there was spreading disaffection with Wright "among labor leaders, consumer groups, and reportedly, even Speaker Tip O'Neill." For his part, O'Neill never commented on these reports but was later flattering in his public assessment of Wright's leadership.[89]

Wright was confident that Burton could not successfully challenge him. In a confidential memo from Myron Struck to Burton, Struck reported on a conversation he had had over breakfast with Craig Raupe, a close aide to Wright. Raupe reported that "We know that Burton could challenge us. We're not naïve. But that would be a mistake, I think. That race wouldn't be close." By the fall of 1978, even some of Burton's supporters apparently told him that this "might not be a propitious time to challenge Wright." And when votes at the Democratic caucus meeting were not encouraging, Burton announced: "I chose not to run. . . . I don't think things fit for me." Burton knew that Wright had consolidated his position as leader, and though he still would have liked to have the majority leader job, by that time "he knew he could never beat Wright and decided not to challenge him again."[90]

Burton's inability to make a strong challenge came in part because of Wright's performance, though Burton thought it "lackluster." However, Bolling, among others, thought Wright had done a good job: "I'm a very strong supporter of Mr. Wright's." Wright had visited eighty-three congressional districts in his first term in the majority leader's chair and had solidified his support. Wright's tally showed the firm support of 133 members "absolutely for JW," 62 "probably for JW," 60 "don't know," and 24 "probably against JW." While political skill and making use of his new position as majority leader might explain some of his strength within the caucus, a more telling measure came in early 1980. The *U.S. News and World Report* conducted a survey of House members in which Wright was identified as both the most respected member of the House and as the most persuasive in debate.[91]

Some of Burton's supporters, citing his ideological commitment, his love of a good fight, and his acumen in getting things done, argued that things would have been very different had Burton been elected majority leader. Burton's biographer John Jacobs reports that these partisans thought Burton "might have given President Jimmy Carter a legislative record to run on for 1980." Conceding that claim improbable, Jacobs argues that with Burton in office, there might not have been such easy approval of Ronald Reagan's program of tax cuts, massive defense spending increases, adventurism in Central America, or "the nearly wholesale purchase of so many Democratic members of Congress via corporate honoraria and campaign contributions." Ralph Nader made a similar argument. "The defeat of California dynamo Phil Burton [by] conservative Texas Democrat Jim Wright occurred because liberals like Max Baucus of Montana and Barbara Mikulski supported Wright against this effective, brilliant, and compassionate leader."[92] His suggestion was that the election of Wright was a sellout to the ideals of Democrats.

Such claims are at best problematic and probably completely unfounded. Carter came to office with an inexperienced group of legislative advisors who hampered his legislative success. After a year, Craig Raupe reported colorfully that "I gave Carter credit for being new, and for the people being new, for months . . . and months . . . and months. Now I think they're just fuck-ups. Pure and simple."[93] Carter also had attitudes about legislating that precluded the kind of deal making that had been Burton's *modus operandi*. Carter's view of the presidency has been described by Charles O. Jones as that of a "trusteeship presidency." That view of the office is that the president should act "to represent the public or national interest, downplaying short-term electoral considerations." In terms of his relationships with Congress, Carter wished to present completed packages of legislation to Congress and was reluctant to consider the individual interests of members of Congress through patronage and public works programs. Wright once reported that Carter was difficult to help because the president did not want to make deals about public works issues to obtain votes necessary to pass his legislative priorities. Wright recalls that he had great respect for Carter but that the two of them had distinct differences on water development projects. Wright, a westerner, had long advocated expanding water resources. Carter saw them as boondoggles. Said Wright, "Every time I see Carter he makes me feel like a political whore."[94]

The claim that Burton could have headed off the Reagan revolution is perhaps even more improbable. In the first place, such claims probably give too much credit to the majority leader. After all, the Speaker is the most important leader of the House party. In the second place, Burton's successes in putting together coalitions had been on an *ad hoc* basis. He had not been charged with trying to push an entire legislative agenda through the House, a far different task. Burton's abrasive personality might have proved, over time, a challenge to maintaining a congenial relationship with the whole party. Moreover, as the voting indicated, the Democratic Party in the House had become fractured over time. Younger members had little appreciation for the traditions of the House that the older members held dear, and the more conservative members of the party, primarily from the South, felt an increasing isolation within the caucus.

Finally, the assessment that Burton might have been able to hold off the use of money to influence his colleagues both through honoraria and campaign contributions is inapposite. Indeed, Burton himself could oversee the uses of such inducements to persuade colleagues to his position. There is no evidence that he would have been able to stem the tide of money that continues to plague Congress in the twenty-first century.

McFall fell quickly after the majority leader's election. He not only lost that election but was not reappointed whip. Then, in the election of 1978, because of the "Koreagate" scandal in which he had been implicated, he was not reelected to Congress. Clearly, by the time of the majority leader election, his "old-style politics" had fallen into disrepute in a House where a huge percentage of the members had been elected post-Watergate. Mc-Fall commented on his fall, a comment that showed that he did not ever grasp the seriousness of the Koreagate scandal: "The problem was I didn't even know I'd done anything wrong."[95]

Interpreting Wright's victory, *The New York Times* suggested that Wright was elected in the last ballot as much because of the fear of Phil Burton as because of his own characteristics. One midwestern liberal in the House said, "I was afraid of Phil Burton; he is too hungry for power." Wright, in contrast, had gradually built seniority while showing respect for the traditions of the House. He had worked within the party and had not made many enemies in the chamber. He promised to be a conciliator who would follow the lead of Speaker O'Neill, to work as a "politician who can find a consensus, not one who will try to shape it," and to be "a good listener."[96]

At the end of his first year as majority leader and Carter's as president, Wright had an opportunity to reflect on the year. Despite his criticisms of Carter's congressional operation, he wrote in his journal, "His first year, on balance, has gone well. Yet hardly anyone appreciates how well. If we measure it by the number of important initiatives recommended by the President and enacted by the U.S. Congress, the productivity will exceed that of any similar period, save two, in modern history. Those two would be the first year of FDR's Presidency (1933) and the first year of LBJ's (1965). Excepting those, Carter's year has outpaced that of any other president in the last sixty years or more. But the public is unaware of this. When I explain it to people, they are astonished. The news media have daily high-lighted the confrontations, those few bills on which Congress has refused a Presidential request, or given him something different or less than he wanted. And so people have begun to ask. 'Why doesn't the president have any influence with Congress?'"[97] Wright perhaps was seeing what the future would hold for Carter and even to some extent for himself.

Indeed, by any measure, Carter's first year had its successes in terms of congressional action, though those successes were not universal. Working with a Democratic Congress, Carter achieved a success rate of 75.4 per-cent. The score was lower than either President Kennedy's or Johnson's, comparable with Richard Nixon's (working with a Congress controlled by the other party), and better substantially than Gerald Ford's. Wright had reason to feel successful; bleaker days for the Carter administration were to come.

Generally, Wright thought that Tip O'Neill had done well as Speaker. In a confidential memo, Burton's friend Myron Struck said that Wright's assessment was positive, saying that O'Neill had made only one mistake. He had not handled the abortion issue well. "He just couldn't handle it, and religious groups were harassing him. Wright had to engineer the compromise," said Wright confidant Craig Raupe. A Catholic, O'Neill thought he was in a no-win situation on abortion and asked Wright to handle the issue. Further, Wright's assessment was that the O'Neill Speakership might last only three or five years longer. "That's when the dog-fight will occur. I don't think his health will hold out much longer."[98] Of course, that prediction was wrong on both counts. O'Neill's tenure would last a full decade, and Wright would be elected Speaker without opposition. By the time of Wright's election as Speaker, the struggle of the 1976 election would be a distant memory. McFall lost in his reelection bid in 1978, Bolling retired from Congress following the 1982 elections, and Burton died in April of 1983.

Regardless of how scholars might interpret 1977, one could hardly quibble with Wright's own words: "Within three days — December 6 — I'll celebrate the anniversary of my election as Majority Leader. What a tumultuous day that was! And what a tumultuous year it has been."[99]

he Austin-Boston alliance was established during the later years of Franklin Roosevelt's New Deal and in the aftermath of FDR's thwarted efforts to pack the Supreme Court in 1937 and the failure of his 1938 "purge" of conservative congressional Democrats. The loss of FDR's enormous congressional majorities and the rise of the inter-regional Conservative Coalition of Republicans and conservative southern Democrats jeopardized the gains of Roosevelt's New Deal.

FDR and the liberal Democrats needed their own unique inter-regional alliance, and it was the Austin-Boston connection of Sam Rayburn, John McCormack, and their successors and protégés who would preserve the New Deal's major policy gains in public welfare (Social Security and workman's compensation); labor-management issues (the National Labor Relations Board); public scrutiny of the stock market in the Securities and Exchanges Act; and the regulation of energy for public use in the Public Utilities Holding Act. It was this remarkable coalition that lasted for a full fifty years in the most contentious century in world and American history. The Austin-Boston connection would keep the fractious Democratic Party united throughout the 1940s and 1950s in the era of World War II; the dawn of the atomic age; the postwar international conflicts with the Soviet Union; the corrosive years of McCarthyism; and the ultimate triumph over legalized segregation. The alliance remained in place in the 1960s and 1970s through the national traumas of the assassinations of Pres. John F. Kennedy and the Reverend Martin Luther King Jr.; the escalation and eventual end of the bloody Vietnam War; the investigation and resignation of Pres. Richard Nixon; and the internecine Democratic squabbles between Pres. Jimmy Carter and Speaker Tip O'Neill. In the 1980s, its last decade, the Austin-Boston connection of Tip O'Neill and Jim Wright successfully thwarted Pres. Ronald Reagan's multiple efforts to dismantle the public welfare programs that had been so instrumental in providing Americans with the safety nets that would enable the nation to never again face the despair of the Great Depression.

First and foremost, the Austin-Boston alliance stabilized the inherently fragile New Deal coalition, divided as it was among disparate interests and regional rivalries. The Austin-Boston alliance helped cope with the deepening rifts in the New Deal coalition, when the party's deep ideological and regional divisions suggested the value of selecting ideologically moderate legislative leaders who could reach out to the northern and southern factions. Indeed, in developing his classic hypothesis that legislative parties select ideological "middleman" as leaders, political scientist David B. Truman argued that this was primarily due to "the depth and persistence of the [regional and ideological] cleavages in both parties." Austin-Boston leaders would chart a moderate policy course that avoided legislative proposals that would threaten intraparty unity, especially those involving civil rights. From the perspective of northern members and their allies, this strategic reality established a de facto "southern veto" over liberal legislation.[1]

To be sure, the "middleman's" course and the southern veto came at a price. Far more moderate than would satisfy the most ardent New Dealers or, later, the most progressive "new politics" liberals, the Austin-Boston leadership seemed to some to be unnecessarily deferential to southern interests, though the southerners also often balked at intraparty compromise and sided instead with Republicans in the famed "conservative coalition." While it is true that Austin-Boston leaders like Rayburn and McCormack were uniquely situated to protect the core policies of the New Deal and to bridge intraparty divides, it is also true that they did so, in part, by delaying, deflecting, and studiously ignoring policies that would undermine intraparty unity.

In some respects this moderation protected key elements of the New Deal from outright southern revolt; in others it merely perpetuated a racist status quo as Austin-Boston House leaders tolerated, worked closely with, and advanced the careers of some of the House's most ardent segregationists and forgave their dissent from national party stances. Eventually, the Austin-Boston leaders' strategy of delay and avoidance of race questions turned to a cross-regional *balancing* role when the 1948 Dixiecrat Revolt and the 1954 *Brown v. Board of Education* Supreme Court decision made it impossible to ignore race and civil rights politics any longer. Several efforts at such balancing from the late 1940s to the 1950s are illustrative. It was John McCormack who, rather than push the Rules

Committee in a more progressive direction, arranged for segregationist William Colmer of Mississippi to be returned to the committee's membership even over Rayburn's objections. And, even as Harry Truman argued for a "strong civil rights plank" in the Democrats' 1952 platform, John McCormack was one of the well-placed "Northern organization leaders" who "joined with Southern moderates" to forge a compromise position that watered down the Democratic position.[2] When Senators Strom Thurmond and Richard B. Russell penned their "Southern Manifesto" in 1956, most nationally oriented southern Democrats avoided signing. With Texans Sam Rayburn and Lyndon Johnson refusing to sign, the Speaker and the Senate majority leader opted for national leadership rather than regionalism. Following Rayburn and Johnson's lead, Texas was only one of two southern states (the other was Tennessee) to have a majority of its House delegation refuse to sign the manifesto. When the 1960 Civil Rights Act passed the House, only five southerners and four Texans voted in favor of the bill — notable among them were Rayburn protégés Jim Wright and Homer Thornberry of Texas along with Carl Albert of Oklahoma. Well-placed in the House and in the Democratic Party more generally, these middlemen were key participants in the compromises that steered a moderate course on potentially explosive legislative matters.

Although some have sought to vilify congressional leaders for their tolerance of the southern veto, in fairness to the Austin-Boston House leaders, such compromises were part and parcel of managing the New Deal coalition. These were, after all, the same strategic realities that led Franklin Roosevelt to provide lukewarm support, at best, for anti-lynching legislation in the late 1930s. And it was these strategic concerns to avoid antagonizing the South, more generally, that gave shape to the New Deal policy program as it would proceed and, just as notably, where it would not proceed. As Katznelson, Geiger, and Kryder put it, "The South's veto did more than divide the Democratic party from time to time. It also specified the basis on which a party alliance could be forged. If the South was prepared to block the national party on some issues, principally those that concerned race and labor, solidarity between the regions nonetheless could be achieved on terms more acceptable to the South. By discovering just such common ground, the Democratic party in the 1940s defined the landscape and moral geography of postwar American liberalism." If a united (or at least an arrested) Democratic Party was necessary for the perpetuation of New Deal policies, then civil rights and pro-labor legislation would languish in Congress.[3]

Eventually, of course, the southern veto on civil rights gave way, and the Lyndon Johnson-led 88th and 89th Congresses produced historic, progressive victories in the 1964 Civil Rights Act and the 1965 Voting Rights Act. Johnson's famous declaration that Democrats had lost the South for a generation was met by a Republican "southern strategy" to capitalize on that disaffection among southern white voters, a strategy that went a long way to ridding the Democratic congressional parties of their most conservative members. A subsequent decline in moderate Republicans in the Northeast and the Midwest meant that Democrats and Republicans were at once both more internally unified parties and more polarized from one another. Although this went a long way to increasing congressional partisanship more generally, it also changed the strategic aims of Democratic leadership selection. Writing in 1977, Garrison Nelson predicted, "As the Democratic Party becomes more philosophically united, and as the ancient regional conflicts recede, it is likely that the Democratic leadership will no longer need their controlled succession system and that the membership will no longer tolerate it."[4] Indeed, the Austin-Boston alliance's ability to stabilize intraparty leadership selection was no longer the necessity it had been from the 1930s to the 1950s, and leadership conflict within the Democratic Party increased significantly.

A second overall impact of the Austin-Boston alliance was a decline of congressional partisanship in the mid–twentieth century. The selection of Austin-Boston leaders (and other ideological "middlemen") served to mute interparty disagreement during Congress's "textbook" era. Compared to the late nineteenth and early twentieth centuries as well as the post-reform era from the 1970s to the end of the twentieth century, the mid-twentieth century Congress is noted for its diminished partisanship.[5] Indeed, coupled with the selection on the Republican side of Massachusetts representative Joe Martin as the Republican leader, the inauguration of the Democrats' Austin-Boston alliance in 1940 served to decrease the ideological gulf between the two parties' floor leaders in the House.

Figure 9-1 presents the ideological distance between House Democratic and Republican floor leaders.[6] High levels of interparty difference between the Democratic and Republican floor leaders (over 1.0) reveal themselves from 1899 to 1938 but drop precipitously in 1939–40 and remain low for the next fifty years. The fact that the Democratic majority routinely selected "middlemen" leaders facilitated the kinds of bipartisan and cross-partisan coalitions that typified the era. In addition to muting the overall differences between Democratic and Republican floor leaders,

FIGURE 9-1. IDEOLOGICAL DIFFERENCES BETWEEN DEMOCRATIC AND REPUBLICAN
FLOOR LEADERS, 1899–2007

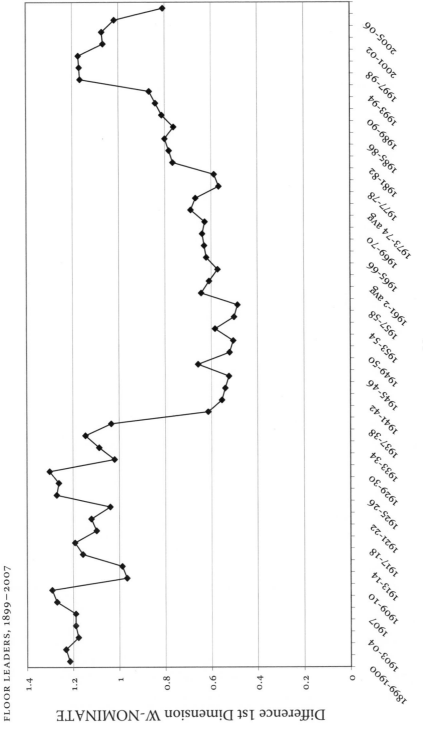

this moderation also provided for cooperative relationships with Republicans, particularly Republican leader Martin, on those occasions that Democratic leaders needed Republican votes to compensate for Democratic defections. With high levels of interparty disagreement prior to the New Deal's "third stage" and a resurgence from the Reagan to the Clinton administrations, the fifty-year trough where the interparty differences are relatively low represented in figure 9-1 roughly approximates the era where the Austin-Boston alliance dominated the House Democratic Party.

If the drop in interparty polarization was a long-lasting consequence of Austin-Boston-era leadership selection, the eventual demise of the alliance also coincided with the resurgence of interparty differences: by the late 1990s and the first Congresses of the twenty-first century, the ideological distance between Democratic and Republican floor leaders increased, exemplifying the hyper-partisanship of the contemporary congressional era. Indeed, the pairings of Democrat Dick Gephardt of Missouri against Republican Dick Armey of Texas and Democrat Nancy Pelosi of California against Republican Tom DeLay of Texas portray ideological distances not seen since 1939.

In retrospect and in light of contemporary partisan norms, some critics of the Austin-Boston leaders might argue that they were so moderate and cautious as well as permissive and deferential to southerners that the Democratic Party leadership lost de facto control of the House to a conservative coalition of southerners and Republicans. It is true that the conservative coalition was unusually prominent during the "textbook" era and predominantly effective when it did appear. Still, when one considers the broad range of issues that Congress confronts and the entirety of the legislative process, the conservative coalition was no match for the top, elected party leadership. For one, the conservative coalition was not likely to appear on a full range of issues. The Democratic leadership, by contrast, played on a wide-open field, facilitating bargains on (and coordinating them across) numerous issue areas. The conservative coalition was rarely more than an "issue specific" alliance focusing on labor issues and, of course, civil rights, ultimately confirming James Patterson's conclusion that "except on race legislation, southern congressmen were never 'solid.'"[7] Indeed, as strong as the conservative coalition got in the 1960s and 1970s and as party voting (votes on which at least 50 percent of Democrats vote against at least 50 percent of Republicans) decreased to its lowest levels in the early 1970s, in no Congress did the percent of conservative coalition appearances exceed the percentage of party votes. By the late 1960s and early 1970s, the conservative coalition was a potent rival for party dominance of floor voting, but by no means did it wholly supplant or displace party.

Moreover, the conservative coalition never *organized* the House as the Austin-Boston leaders did: the majority leader defeats of John O'Connor in 1937 and Clifton Woodrum in 1940 saw to that. Although conservative coalition leaders had a prominent beachhead in the House Committee on Rules where some positive gains were made for conservative policies, the scholarly consensus is that the conservative coalition's primary effectiveness was as a "blocking alliance" capable of "stalemating liberal bills." The conservative coalition was, on some issues, able to get conservative bills to the floor over majority party opposition. However, given its lack of organizational strength and the limited policy scope of the conservative coalition's influence, recent research has led to a more qualified assessment of the nature of the coalition's strength in the House. In doing so, it has corrected the overblown impression "that this [conservative] coalition, rather than the Democratic party, really ruled the roost" from 1937 to the 1970s.[8] None of this is to say that the Austin-Boston alliance was able to negate the influence of the conservative coalition throughout the "textbook" era, only that the effectiveness of the conservative coalition was frequently checked and limited in policy scope.

Viewed at a more personal level, it seems obvious that the conservative coalition's impact was less impressive than legend suggests and certainly less than if conservative coalition leaders — John O'Connor and Clifton Woodrum, for example — were at the helm of the formal Democratic leadership and, by extension, the House's legislative process. And any claim that Eugene Cox or Howard Smith (as influential as they were) were more influential in the House than Sam Rayburn (or for that matter perhaps even John McCormack) is simply untenable.

The third and most notable overall impact of the Austin-Boston alliance was that it persisted and did, in fact, run the House for a half-century. This persistence and historical longevity should not be taken lightly. There are two ways that the alliance could have lost control of the House: being displaced by intraparty rivals or losing majority control of the House to the Republicans. On both scores, the Austin-Boston alliance was remarkably successful at precluding its rivals.

In intraparty politics, the alliance perpetuated itself by establishing a "leadership ladder" of succession and a system of preferment of like-minded protégés, all while precluding and beating back intraparty challenges both from the right and from the left. If the caution and moderation of the party leadership elicited challenges and complaints from both conservative southerners and, especially as time went on, liberals, Austin-Boston provided a solid cross-regional alliance and starting block of votes that advantaged allied candidates for leadership posts.

At several points, the Austin-Boston alliance withstood intraparty turbulence and some potentially fatal challenges. When Democrats lost majority control of the House in 1946 and 1952 (having lost seats mostly in non-southern districts), southern Democrats remained and constituted about half of the caucus (a little more than half in the 80th Congress and just slightly less than half in the 83d Congress). The conservative element of the party well could have re-asserted its influence, toppling the leadership as Republicans frequently do after disappointing elections.[9] Indeed, southerners did prevail on a reluctant Rayburn to assume the minority leader post in 1946 in part to keep Boston's John McCormack from becoming the party's top leader.

Victories of liberal Democrats, particularly in the 1958 election and thereafter, reduced southern power to less than 40 percent of the caucus, a figure that waned to less than a third by the mid-1960s and thereafter. Thus, in the 1960s and the reform era of the 1970s, the threat to the Austin-Boston alliance was no longer from the right but, instead, from an increasingly vocal and vehement left frustrated with internal congressional structures, including leadership structures, that they deemed overly protective of conservative interests at the expense of liberal progress. When Rayburn died in 1961, liberals — including some in the Kennedy administration — explored the possibility of displacing John McCormack or supporting Richard Bolling's challenge to Carl Albert for majority leader in 1962. Liberal enough for many House Democrats, increasingly acceptable to southern Democrats who noted their own waning influence, and already on the "leadership ladder," both McCormack and Albert easily maintained their posts and appointed Hale Boggs as whip. Still frustrated, liberals complained that the leadership lacked liberal zeal, was too solicitous of southern Democrats, and provided weak leadership overall. Even after the historically productive 89th Congress, liberals wondered what more could have been accomplished with more aggressive leadership.

The loss of the White House in 1968 further increased liberal anxiety about congressional leadership. Without the legislative wizardry of Lyndon Johnson, the task of building legislative coalitions and, indeed, combating the Nixon administration would fall to a cautious and aging John McCormack. Again, the Austin-Boston alliance persisted as McCormack handily beat back a high profile (if ultimately ill-fated and little-supported) challenge from Morris Udall of Arizona. Despite Udall's loss, the unique challenge to a sitting Speaker showed that the younger generation of Democratic members was looking for new leadership. Upon McCormack's retirement two years later, Udall tried again for leadership, challenging (along with B. F. Sisk of California, Wayne Hays of Ohio, and James G. O'Hara of Michigan) Majority Whip Hale Boggs for the majority leader's post. Despite the complexities of the multicandidate race and with Boggs's personal performance in question, McCormack and Albert's hand-picked whip nevertheless won a second-ballot victory with some, Tip O'Neill among them, opting for the establishment choice of Boggs and showing their continued loyalty to John McCormack by refusing to support Mo Udall.[10]

The liberal challenges to the alliance persisted in the 1970s, but Tip O'Neill's easy victory over Sam Gibbons in the 1973 majority leader's race, due in part to his successful stint as chairman of the Democratic Congressional Campaign Committee (to which McCormack appointed him) and as majority whip (to which Albert and Boggs had appointed him) demonstrated the continued potency of the Austin-Boston alliance, particularly when the alliance's candidate was unusually talented and capable as well as personally popular. Of course, it also did not hurt that O'Neill was from the liberal Massachusetts end of the Austin-Boston alliance. Upon Albert's retirement three years later, O'Neill succeeded to the Speakership unopposed. Still, during this time it would seem that the emergence of younger, liberal members (particularly the large "Watergate baby" class of 1974) put liberals clearly in control of the caucus. In the race to succeed O'Neill as majority leader, San Francisco's Phil Burton, then the forceful and dynamic chairman of the Democratic caucus, was the presumptive favorite, but an alliance of the more moderate-conservative wing of the party and more "establishment" liberals associated with O'Neill and the Austin-Boston forces balked at choosing the very liberal and personally abrasive Burton. Although one Burton opponent, Jim Wright of Texas, was reputed to be too conservative for the increasingly liberal House Democratic Party of the 1970s, Wright's victory over Burton — by a mere one-vote margin — and the Texan's succession to the Speakership upon Tip O'Neill's retirement in 1986 perpetuated the Austin-Boston alliance (and forestalled California's emerging claim to more liberal Democratic leadership) into the Reagan era and the beginning of George H. W. Bush's presidency.

All the while, Democrats had to concern themselves with interparty competition and the potential for Republican gains. Indeed, it was the success of Reagan-era conservatism, continued Republican in-roads in the South, and eventually the Newt Gingrich–led "Republican Revolution" that posed the most significant challenges to Democratic control of the House. As frustrating as it was to the most liberal elements of the Democratic Party, the Austin-Boston alliance's accommodation of southerners was an important ingredient in Democrats' maintaining control of the House, with the exception of only two Congresses, from the New Deal until Gingrich became Speaker in the 104th Congress.

None other than Minority Leader Gerald Ford argued in the late 1960s in support of a Republican "southern strategy" that aimed to force southern Democrats to choose between supporting the national Democratic Party and the Johnson administration on the one hand or their more conservative congressional districts on the other hand.[11] That Republicans would successfully pursue this "southern strategy" for much of the next twenty years further highlights the electoral value of the moderating influence of the Austin-Boston alliance for blunting and delaying potential Republican gains. By the same token, the success of the Reagan landslide in 1980 allowed Republicans to win the presidency only six years after Watergate and to capture the Senate. Republican gains in the House of Representatives were significant enough that then-backbench House member Newt Gingrich organized a rump effort in November and December 1980 to try to persuade southern Democrats either to switch to the Republican Party prior to organizing the 97th Congress in order to vote for a Republican Speaker or to get a compromise conservative Democratic Speaker that both the southern Democrats and Republican members would support. During this time, O'Neill and Wright worked hard to better include and to secure the support of the caucus's most conservative members. Although critics might deny the functional nature of the Austin-Boston alliance, Republican leaders like Ford and Gingrich (as well as Democratic leaders O'Neill and Wright) understood that it was both the stability and moderation in the top leadership and the continued accommodation of southerners that accounted for the longevity of Democratic control of the

House as well as the maintenance (if not the expansion) of New Deal policies into the Reagan era.

Joe Bailey certainly had no idea what he had initiated with his mentoring of John Nance Garner and Sam Rayburn. But Bailey's selection as minority leader did foreshadow the increasing political influence of Texas in House Democratic politics. And Garner, though he represented the southern wing of the Democratic Party in the House and tried to maintain southern power in the House with his support for John McDuffie of Alabama as his successor, became the real architect of the Austin-Boston alliance by advancing the careers of both Sam Rayburn and John McCormack. Those men, in turn, advanced the careers of their protégés, perpetuating the alliance for decades until it finally came to an end with Jim Wright.

With the retirement of Tip O'Neill and Wright's elevation to the Speakership, the majority leadership moved to the West in keeping with the earlier efforts by Mo Udall of Arizona and Phil Burton of California. Tom Foley of Washington was chosen majority leader — the first western Democratic leader. And, with Wright's resignation as Speaker, Foley was elevated to that position. His majority leader was Richard Gephardt of Missouri. After the 1994 elections, Gephardt became the first Democratic minority leader since Sam Rayburn occupied the post in the first two years of the Eisenhower administration. When Gephardt left the post, Nancy Pelosi — clearly liberal and representing the same district that Phil Burton had — beat her more conservative rival, Steny Hoyer of Maryland, to become the first woman floor leader in congressional history and, after the Democratic takeover in 2006, the first woman Speaker of the House. Speaker Pelosi, the daughter of Rep. Thomas D'Alesandro of Maryland, was born in 1940 when her father's House service began in the 76th Congress at the time of the creation of the Austin-Boston Connection. D'Alesandro left the House to become the first Roman Catholic mayor of Baltimore. His daughter moved west to California. She was first elected to the House in 1987, and two years later, the Austin-Boston Connection ended with the resignation of Jim Wright. As the nation's first woman Speaker, Nancy Pelosi unites the legacy of the ethnic diversity of the eastern cities with the dynamism of the emergent West as the Democrats seek to create a new interregional alliance that will succeed in the twenty-first century much as the Austin-Boston connection did in the twentieth century.

NOTES

Abbreviations

AS   Adolph Sabath Papers, Manuscript Dept., Special Collections Division, Howard-Tilton Memorial Library, Tulane University Library, New Orleans, Louisiana.

CA   Carl Albert Papers, Carl Albert Center Congressional Archives, University of Oklahoma, Norman.

CAU   Records of the House Democratic Caucus, Library of Congress, Washington, D.C.

CK   Claude Kitchin Papers, Manuscripts Department, Library of the University of North Carolina at Chapel Hill, Southern Historical Collection, Chapel Hill.

DNC   Democratic National Committee, Library and Research Bureau, Franklin D. Roosevelt Library, Hyde Park, New York.

EPB   Edward P. Boland Papers, John J. Burns Library, Boston College, Chestnut Hill, Massachusetts.

FDR   President's Personal File, Franklin D. Roosevelt Library, Hyde Park, New York.

FDRO   President's Official File, Franklin D. Roosevelt Library, Hyde Park, New York.

FDRP   Franklin D. Roosevelt Press Conferences, Franklin D. Roosevelt Library, Hyde Park, New York.

FEH   F. Edward Hébert Papers, Manuscript Dept., Special Collections Division, Howard-Tilton Memorial Library, Tulane University Library, New Orleans, Louisiana.

FJT   Frank J. Thompson Papers, Seeley G. Mudd Manuscript Library, Princeton University, Princeton, New Jersey.

FMV   Fred M. Vinson Papers, Wendell H. Ford Research Center and Public Policy Archives, University of Kentucky, Lexington.

HB   Hale Boggs Papers, Manuscript Dept., Special Collections Division, Howard-Tilton Memorial Library, Tulane University Library, New Orleans Louisiana.

HH   Herbert Hoover Papers, Herbert Hoover Presidential Library and Museum, West Branch, Iowa.

HR   Henry Rainey Papers, Library of Congress, Washington, D.C.

HST   President's Secretary's Files, Harry S. Truman Library and Museum, Independence, Missouri.

HSTO   President's Official File, Harry S. Truman Library and Museum, Independence, Missouri.

JB   Joseph W. Bailey Papers, Dallas Historical Society, Dallas, Texas.

JBW   James B. Wells Papers, Center for American History, University of Texas, Austin.

JF   James Farley Papers, Library of Congress, Washington, D.C.

JFB   James F. Byrnes Papers, Robert Muldrow Cooper Library, Clemson University, Clemson, South Carolina.

JFK   John F. Kennedy Papers, John F. Kennedy Presidential Library and Museum, Boston, Massachusetts.

JJM   John J. McFall Papers, Holt-Atherton Dept. of Special Collections, University of the Pacific, Stockton, California.

JM   John McDuffie Papers, W. S. Hoole Special Collections, University of Alabama, Tuscaloosa.

JN   John C. (Jack) Nichols Papers, Carl Albert Center Congressional Archives, University of Oklahoma, Norman.

JNG   John Nance Garner Papers, Center for American History, University of Texas, Austin.

JO   John J. O'Connor Papers, Lilly Library, Indiana University, Bloomington.

JOH   James O'Hara Papers, Bentley Historical Library, University of Michigan, Ann Arbor.

JPT   Joseph P. Tumulty Papers, Library of Congress, Washington, D.C.

JR   Joseph Robinson Papers, Special Collections Division, University of Arkansas, Fayetteville.

JWB   Joseph W. Byrns Papers, Gorham-MacBane Public Library, Springfield, Tennessee.

JWM   John McCormack Papers, Howard Gotlieb Archival Research Center, Boston University, Boston, Massachusetts.

JWP   Jim Wright Papers, Special Collections, Mary Couts Burnett Library, Texas Christian University, Ft. Worth.

LBJ   Lyndon B. Johnson Papers, Lyndon Baines Johnson Library and Museum, Austin, Texas.

LBS   Lewis B. Schwellenback Papers, Library of Congress, Washington, D.C.

MKU   Morris K. Udall Papers, Special Collections, University of Arizona Library, Tucson.

MS   Morris Sheppard Papers, Center for American History, University of Texas, Austin.

PBP   Phillip Burton Papers, Bancroft Library, University of California, Berkeley.

RB Richard Bolling Papers, Miller Nichols Library, University of Missouri — Kansas City.

SG Sam Gibbons Papers, Special Collections, University of South Florida Libraries, Tampa.

SR Sam Rayburn Papers, Center for American History, University of Texas, Austin.

TPO Tip O'Neill Papers, John J. Burns Library, Boston College, Chestnut Hill, Massachusetts.

WB William Bankhead Papers, State of Alabama, Dept. of Archives and History, Montgomery.

WH Walter Gardner Hall Papers, Woodson Research Center, Fondren Library, Rice University, Houston, Texas.

Chapter 1. Introduction

1. See Frederick Jackson Turner, *The Significance of Sections in American History* (New York: Henry Holt, 1932); V. O. Key Jr., *Politics, Parties and Pressure Groups*, 4th ed. (New York: Thomas Crowell, 1964); Walter Dean Burnham, *Current Crisis in American Politics* (New York: W. W. Norton, 1982), pp. 92–117.

2. Richard Franklin Bensel, *Sectionalism and American Political Development: 1880–1980* (Madison: University of Wisconsin Press, 1984), p. 23.

3. It is very hard to defeat a congressman in his own party primary absent a scandal, because the congressman has all the advantages of incumbency and the party is that congressman's political base. Julius Turner, "Primary Elections as the Alternative to Party Competition in 'Safe' Districts," *Journal of Politics* (1953): 197–210; Harvey L. Schantz, "Julius Turner Revisited: Primary Elections as the Alternative to Party Competition in 'Safe' Districts," *American Political Science Review* (1976): 541–45.

4. On Cannon's power and the revolt, see Joseph Cooper and David W. Brady, "Institutional Context and Leadership Style: The House from Cannon to Rayburn," *American Political Science Review* (1981): 411–25; and Peter Swenson, "The Influence of Recruitment on the Structure of Power in the U.S. House, 1870–1940," *Legislative Studies Quarterly* (1982): 7–36.

5. Where nearly half of the House Democratic caucus was southern in the 72d Congress, less than one-third of the membership was from the South in the 73d, 74th, and 75th Congresses. After the New Deal, in only one Congress, the 80th, did southern Democrats outnumber non-southern Democrats.

6. James T. Patterson, *Congressional Conservatism and the New Deal: The Growth of the Conservative Coalition in Congress, 1933–1939* (Lexington: University of Kentucky Press, 1967).

7. Ibid., p. 167; Bensel, p. 160.

8. Paul T. David, Ralph M. Goldman, and Richard C. Bain, *The Politics of National Party Conventions*, rev. ed. (New York: Vintage Books, 1964), p. 187.

9. Sidney M. Milkis, *The President and the Parties: The Transformation of the American Party System since the New Deal* (New York: Oxford University Press, 1993), p. 82.

10. The term "uneasy truce" is from Milkis, *President and the Parties*, p. 79; the description of the "third stage" is from David L. Porter, *Congress and the Waning of the New Deal* (Port Washington, N.Y.: Kennikat Press, 1980), p. xi.

11. See Milkis, *President and the Parties*, especially chapters 4–6, and Sidney M. Milkis, *Political Parties and Constitutional Government: Remaking American Democracy* (Baltimore: Johns Hopkins University Press, 1999), pp. 84–102.

12. Indeed, though they differ in critical respects, both Richard Bensel and David Brady focus on the importance of committee organization for overcoming New Deal divisions; Bensel, pp. 149–55; Brady, *Critical Elections and Congressional Policy Making* (Palo Alto: Stanford University Press, 1988), especially chapter 4.

13. V. O. Key Jr., *Southern Politics in State and Nation*, new ed. (Knoxville: University of Tennessee Press, 1984), pp. 5–12.

14. Although many political scientists are apt to ignore or discount personal factors in explanations of congressional politics, close examination reveals its continuing importance. Lewis G. Irwin, for example, argues that personal relationships — friendly and unfriendly — constitute an important and overlooked goal in legislative battles; see *A Chill in the House: Actor Perspectives on Change and Continuity in the Pursuit of Legislative Success* (Albany: SUNY Press, 2002).

15. "Family affairs" is from John Bibby and Roger H. Davidson, *On Capitol Hill: Studies in the Legislative Process* (New York: Holt, Rinehart, and Winston, 1967), p. 143; Robert L. Peabody, *Leadership in Congress: Stability, Succession, and Change* (Boston: Little, Brown, 1976), p. 498.

16. Nelson W. Polsby, "Two Strategies of Influence: Choosing a Majority Leader," in *New Perspectives on the House of Representatives*, 2d ed., ed. Robert L. Peabody and Nelson W. Polsby (Chicago: Rand McNally, 1969), p. 331.

17. Ross K. Baker, *Friend and Foe in the U.S. Senate* (New York: Free Press, 1980), esp. chap. 1.

18. Not all of these relationships were between members of the same party who represented nearby districts, but many of these great personal and political alliances were. One who represented a nearby district might often represent the same types of constituents and share similar political values.

19. Some of these mentor-protégé relationships seemed to fill important emotional needs. The relationship between Sam Rayburn and Lyndon Johnson, for example, is frequently described as a father-son relationship, where Rayburn

seemed to look on Johnson as the son he never had and Johnson looked upon Rayburn as a kind a substitute for his far-less-successful father.

20. Baker, p. 248.

21. Ibid., pp. 6–7.

Chapter 2. Joe Bailey

1. Champ Clark, *My Quarter Century in American Politics,* vol. 1 (New York and London: Harper & Brothers, 1920), pp. 9–10; D. B. Hardeman and Donald C. Bacon, *Rayburn: A Biography* (Austin: Texas Monthly Press, 1987), p. 27; Alfred Steinberg, *Sam Rayburn: A Biography* (New York: Hawthorn Books, 1975), p. 38; Chauncey M. Depew, *My Memories of Eighty Years* (New York: Charles Scribner's Sons, 1924), p. 183.

2. Samuel G. Blythe, "The Great Bailey Myth," *The Saturday Evening Post,* May 27, 1911, n.p., JB.

3. Claude G. Bowers, *Beveridge and the Progressive Era* (New York: The Literary Guild, 1932), pp. 184–85; Claude Bowers, *My Life* (New York: Simon and Schuster, 1962), p. 69.

4. Sam Hanna Acheson, *Joe Bailey: The Last Democrat* (New York: Macmillan, 1932), pp. 12, 15; Clark, vol. 1, pp. 245–46; Joseph W. Bailey to O. B. Colquitt, Apr. 26, 1911, Texas State Archives, Austin.

5. Ronnie Dugger, *The Politician* (New York: W. W. Norton, 1982), p. 58.

6. Escal F. Duke, "The Political Career of Morris Sheppard, 1875–1941," Ph.D. dissertation, University of Texas, 1958, pp. 184–86.

7. Bowers, *My Life,* pp. 69–70.

8. Acheson, pp. 13–18.

9. Ibid., p. 28; Alwyn Barr, *Reconstruction to Reform* (Austin: University of Texas Press, 1971), p. 210.

10. Acheson, pp. 30–31, 37; Barr, p. 210.

11. Acheson, pp. 45–47.

12. In an effort to allow the Committee on Coinage, Weights, and Measures the right to circumvent the House Rules Committee to gain access to the floor, Bailey claimed that "there are not two committees of the House more important than the Committee on Banking and Currency and the Committee on Coinage, Weights, and Measures." This amendment to the House rules, known as the Bailey amendment, failed by a vote of 114 to 181; *Congressional Record,* Jan. 10, 1896, pp. 568–73.

13. Acheson, pp. 47–48, 55

14. Richard B. Cheney and Lynne V. Cheney, *Kings of the Hill: Power and Personality in the House of Representatives* (New York: Continuum, 1983), pp. 99–108.

15. Depew, pp. 125–27.

16. Acheson, p. 58; Clark, vol. 1, pp. 245–46.

17. *Congressional Record*, Feb. 23, 1897, p. 2161. Bailey's bitter patronage dispute with the Cleveland administration was shared by many Democrats. Congressman Zebulon Vance of North Carolina, for example, declared that, though he should rejoice at the election of a president, many of his constituents desired jobs, and he could get none of them appointed. He was reminded of a client of his who had inherited a farm from his father. There were so many difficulties about the title and getting possession of it and delay that the son said, "I almost wished father had not died." Depew, pp. 125–27.

18. Clark, vol. 2, pp. 9–10.

19. Rupert N. Richardson, *Colonel Edward M. House: The Texas Years, 1858–1912* (Abilene, Texas: Hardin-Simmons University, 1964), p. 124.

20. Clark, vol. 2, pp. 9–10, 343.

21. Acheson, p. 129.

22. Robert C. Cotner, *James Stephen Hogg: A Biography* (Austin: University of Texas Press, 1959, 1974), p. 482. However, in that era, it was not unusual for people in leadership positions in the House to leave for the Senate. Henry Clay, of course, left the House and the Speakership for the Senate. Later, so did James G. Blaine, John G. Carlisle, Charles F. Crisp, and Frederick H. Gillett. Among minority leaders like Bailey who left the House for the Senate are John Sharp Williams and Oscar W. Underwood. Bailey was at the end of a period in House history when "only a handful of men had pursued substantial lifetime careers within the House, and they were often the occasion for puzzled comment. Committee chairmen, minority leaders, and even speakers of the House would leap at the chance to leave that body and become freshmen senators (or sometimes governors)." See H. Douglas Price, "The Congressional Career Then and Now," in *Congressional Behavior*, ed. Nelson Polsby (New York: Random House, 1971), pp. 14–27.

23. Cotner, p. 483.

24. Quoted in Bob Charles Holcomb, "Senator Joe Bailey, Two Decades of Controversy," Ph.D. dissertation, Texas Technological College, 1968, p. 175.

25. Cotner, p. 563.

26. Richardson, pp. 166, 168–69.

27. Seth S. McKay and Odie B. Faulk, *Texas after Spindletop* (Austin: Steck-Vaughn Company, 1965), p. 18; "The Laborer and His Hire — Another Standard Oil Lesson," *Hearst's Magazine*, Feb. 1913, pp. 174–88.

28. Alfred Henry Lewis, "The Hon. (?) J. W. Bailey," *Cosmopolitan Magazine*, Apr., 1913, pp. 601–605. Lewis also suggests that while he was in the House, Bailey came in contact with wealthy individuals and that he was "bedazzled by their millions." One of those persons was former Governor Francis of Missouri who

came to Washington as Cleveland's secretary of interior and who later put Bailey in touch with Henry Pierce of the Waters-Pierce Oil Company, an acquaintance that led to the great Bailey political scandal.

29. David Graham Phillips, "The Treason of the Senate," *Cosmopolitan Magazine,* July, 1906, pp. 627–36 esp. 627; William A. Cocke, *The Bailey Controversy in Texas, with Lessons from the Political Life-Story of a Fallen Idol,* vol. 1 (San Antonio: Cocke Co., 1908), pp. 306, 310–11.

30. Acheson, p. 148.

31. Ibid., p. 149.

32. Tom Connally as told to Alfred Steinberg, *My Name is Tom Connally* (New York: Thomas Y. Crowell, 1954), p. 48.

33. Holcomb, p. 253.

34. Acheson, p. 175; Phillips, pp. 627–36.

35. Acheson, pp. 226, 228.

36. Ibid., p. 232.

37. Ibid., p. 233.

38. Cocke, p. 207; Dugger, p. 57.

39. Dugger, p. 58.

40. James Presley, *Saga of Wealth* (Austin: Texas Monthly Press, 1983), pp. 81–82.

41. M. M. Crane to Morris Sheppard, Apr. 30, 1912, MS.

42. Blythe, n.p.

43. Holcomb, p. 497; Duke, p. 131.

44. Joseph W. Bailey telegram to O. B. Colquitt, Mar. 4, 1911, JB.

45. Holcomb, p. 497; Acheson, p. 297; George P. Huckaby, "Oscar Branch Colquitt: A Political Biography," Ph.D. dissertation, University of Texas, 1946, pp. 331–32.

46. Acheson, pp. ix–xi.

47. McKay and Faulk, p. 23.

48. Evan Anders, *Boss Rule in South Texas* (Austin: University of Texas Press, 1982), p. 106; John Nance Garner to J. B. Wells, Sept. 21, 1921, JBW.

49. Anders, p. 95. Still, there were limits to Bailey's support. In 1901, for example, Wells seriously considered running for governor. Bailey was very slow to express support, perhaps because, like E. M. House, he feared Wells's Catholicism would defeat him but, most likely, because a man like Wells could challenge Bailey on the political stage and one day threaten him politically. Joe Robert Baulch, "James B. Wells: South Texas Economic and Political Leader," Ph.D. dissertation, Texas Tech University, 1974, pp. 218–24.

50. Anders, p. 95, 97.

51. Ibid., pp. 70–72.

52. Baulch, p. 261; J. B. Wells to Willacy, Nov. 3, 1906, JBW; Baulch, pp. 268, 271.

53. Anders, p. 97.

54. Alwyn Barr, "John Nance Garner's First Campaign for Congress," *West Texas Historical Association Yearbook* (1972): 105–10.

55. Rayburn traced his desire to become Speaker to Bailey's speech. That, of course, suggests that Bailey spoke about the Speakership, and, since he was the Democratic nominee for Speaker in 1897, it seems likely that he would have talked about the Speakership at that time.

56. Sam Rayburn interview with V. J. Young, 1956, SR; Steinberg, p. 8.

57. Steinberg, p. 51.

58. When in the House, Bailey's congressional district had been the 5th Congressional District, which, when Bailey entered the House, consisted of eleven counties: Archer, Baylor, Clay, Collin, Cooke, Denton, Montague, Rockwall, Wichita, Wilbarger, and Wise counties. That district had a population of slightly over 140,000, and 6.2 percent of the population was black. When Bailey left the House, the district consisted only of Collin, Cooke, Denton, Fannin, Grayson, and Montague counties due to redistricting. This district had a population of over 193,000 people with an 8.6 percent black population. Rayburn was elected to represent a newly drawn 4th Congressional District that consisted of Collin, Fannin, Grayson, Hunt, and Rains counties and overlapped much of Bailey's old district.

59. Cocke, p. 294; Ed Steger to Joe Bailey, Sept. 11, 1899, JB; Ed Steger to Joe Bailey, June 22, 1907. JB; Cocke, pp. 290–93.

60. "Political Ball Is to Start Rolling again on Monday," *Dallas Morning News*, Aug. 1, 1920, n.p., JB; Hardeman and Bacon, p. 488, footnote 53.

61. C. Dwight Dorough, *Mr. Sam* (New York: Random House, 1962), p. 79; Jim Wright interview with James Riddlesperger, May 12, 2005, Fort Worth, Texas.

62. Acheson, pp. 237–38.

63. Jim Wright interview; Hardeman and Bacon, p. 483, footnote 14.

64. A. M. Kennedy was a strong Bailey man, having been the floor leader of the pro-Bailey forces during the 1907 Bailey investigation; Cocke, p. 207.

65. Hardeman and Bacon, p. 49; Dorough, p. 81; Steinberg, p. 19.

66. Huckaby, p. 237.

67. Cocke, p. 207; J. H. Collard to J. W. Bailey, Apr. 25, 1913, JB; Virgie Turner to J. W. Bailey, Nov. 5, 1912, JB; and A. Parr to J. W. Bailey, Nov. 7, 1912, JB.

68. Hardeman and Bacon, p. 48.

69. Anthony Champagne, *Congressman Sam Rayburn* (New Brunswick: Rutgers University Press, 1984), p. 32; "Let's Give Sam a Fair Deal," *Bonham Dailey Favorite*, June 16, 1948, n.p., in "Scrapbook 1935–1954," SR.

70. Champagne, p. 32.

71. Randell had been involved in the Texas militia and had been city attorney in Denison and county attorney in Grayson County. He was a joiner, involved in the Masons, the Knights of Pythias, the Red Men, and the Woodmen of the World. Frank W. Johnson, ed. and updated by Eugene Barker with the assistance of Ernest William Winkler, *A History of Texas and Texans*, vol. 5 (Chicago and New York: The American Historical Society, 1914), pp. 2640–41. Randell was a significant enough figure in Grayson County politics that as early as 1897, he was delivering major addresses. In that year, he spoke in behalf of the Sons of the Confederate Veterans at the dedication of the Confederate monument on the courthouse square in Sherman. *An Illustrated History of Grayson County, Texas*, Sherman Public Library, p. 92.

72. Bailey left the Ways and Means Committee in 1899, and Randell was named to the committee in 1907. "The Movement Comes of Age," Texas State Library and Archives Commission, www.tsl.state.tx.us/exhibits/suffrage/comesofage/randell-folsom.html; Joe Bailey to C. B. Randell, Jan. 23, 1900, JB.

73. Obviously, this was a remarkably bad political choice for Randell. After all, his Texas successor on Ways and Means, John Garner, became minority leader, Speaker, and vice president. And, if nothing else, Randell could have been a power in Congress because of his position on Ways and Means. Randell, however, was in the House at a time (or at least the tail-end of the time) when even those in more important positions would leave the House to become a freshman senator. See Price, pp. 6, 18.

74. Acheson, p. 279.

75. Duke, p. 131–32; Hardeman and Bacon, p. 484, footnote 29; Blythe, n.p.; M. M. Crane to Morris Sheppard, Apr. 30, 1912, MS.

76 Holcomb, p. 474; Brian Hart, "Choice Boswell Randell," *The New Handbook of Texas* (Austin: Texas State Historical Association, 1996), p. 439.

77. Bailey never debated Randell on the issue of receiving gifts and fees, although Bailey did debate Texas Atty. Gen. Robert Davidson on the question. Joe B. Frantz, *Texas: A History* (New York: W. W. Norton, 1984), p. 153.

78. Holcomb, p. 49; C. B. Randell to Ermina Folsom, Nov. 25, 1910, Ermina Thompson Folsom Papers, Texas State Library, www.tsl.state.tx.us/exhibits .suffrage/comesofage/randell-folsom.html.

79. "Events at Saturday's Caucus Come to Light," *Dallas News*, Apr. 18, 1911, n.p., "Scrapbook 11, 1908–1911," MS; "Sheppard Supported Randell for Chairman," *Brownwood Daily Bulletin*, n.d., n.p., "Scrapbook 14, 1912–1920," MS.

80. C. Richard King, "Woodrow Wilson's Visit to Texas in 1911," *Southwestern Historical Quarterly* (1961): 184–95. When the papers quoted Texas Democratic Chairman Shelby Williams as saying that the Texas convention at Galveston had instructed Texas Democrats to support Joe Bailey for president the

year before, Wilson supporter Congressman Robert Henry declared that there would be a "practically unanimous vote for the nomination of Woodrow Wilson" (pp. 190–91).

81. Ibid., 188, 190, 195.

82. "Randell Speaks to Small Crowd," *Ballenger Banner Leader,* May 17, 1912, n.p., "Scrapbook 14, 1912–1920," MS. In the same scrapbook is a political cartoon portraying Randell as speaking to a nearly empty audience in a large auditorium. The cartoon is entitled "The Plaint of Randell," who is saying, "Wolters and Sheppard have framed up on me."

83. "Hot Fight in Texas over Bailey's Seat," *Chicago Evening Post,* July 11, 1912, n.p., "Scrapbook 14, 1912–1920," MS; Thomas Campbell to Morris Sheppard, Apr. 30, 1912, MS; Thomas Ball to Morris Sheppard, Apr. 23, 1912, MS; Duke, p. 153.

84. Joe Bailey to Sam Rayburn, Nov. 9, 1912, JB; Sam Rayburn to Joe Bailey, Nov. 15, 1912, JB.

85. D. B. Hardeman, compiled by Larry Hufford, *D. B.: Reminiscences of D. B. Hardeman* (Austin: AAR/Tantalus, 1984), p. 141; Acheson, p. 354.

86. Connally as told to Steinberg, p. 91; Dorough, p. 138.

87. Choice was born in 1857, his son Andrew in 1880 (Johnson and Barker, pp. 2640–41). Rayburn quoted in Champagne, p. 98; Steinberg, p. 53.

88. Champagne, pp. 100–101.

89. Ibid., p. 101.

90. Ibid., p. 103.

91. Ibid., p. 103.

92. Quoted in Steinberg, pp. 45–46.

93. Hardeman and Bacon, pp. 76–85.

94. Quoted in Steinberg, p. 54.

95. Ibid., p. 36; James A. Clark with Weldon Hart, *The Tactful Texan: A Biography of Governor Will Hobby* (New York: Random House, 1958), pp. 123–24.

96. "Andrew L. Randell Funeral Thursday," *Sherman Daily Democrat,* Mar. 16, 1931, p. 1; Norman D. Brown, *Hood, Bonnet, and Little Brown Jug* (College Station: Texas A&M University Press, 1984), p. 61; Mike Cox, "KKK," TexasEscapes.com, www.texasescapes.com/MikeCoxTexasTales/227-KKK-in-Texas.htm.

97. His wife had died in 1913, and his other son had died in infancy (Records of West Hill Cemetery, Sherman Public Library, Sherman, Texas).

98. Choice Randell's real threat was that his vote, combined with the vote of other candidates, would force Rayburn into a run-off. In 1917, the Texas legislature had passed a law providing that if the winner of a primary did not get more than 50 percent of the vote, there would have to be a run-off primary with the candidate who finished second (Steinberg, p. 102). Randell lived in Sherman until his death in 1945.

99. There may have been a special honor associated with Bailey's sponsorship since President Taft had offered Bailey an associate justiceship on the court to replace Justice Peckham. But Bailey realized that he did not have a judicial temperament and declined the nomination (Acheson, pp. 259–60). For Bailey's sponsorship of Rayburn to the Supreme Court bar, see Rayburn's certificate of admission to the bar, SR.

100. J. W. Bailey to Mr. and Mrs. W. M. Rayburn, Aug. 4, 1916, SR.

101. Duke, p. 273; Huckaby, p. 425.

102. Baulch, pp. 358–59; McKay and Faulk, pp. 78, 81; Joseph M. Ray, ed., *Thomason: The Autobiography of a Federal Judge* (El Paso: Texas Western Press, 1971), p. 25.

103. Pat Neff quoted in Brown, pp. 16–17; Acheson, p. 389.

104. Ray, 22–25.

105. Brown, pp. 88–92.

106. MacPhelan Reese, et al., *Speak, Mr. Speaker* (Bonham: Sam Rayburn Foundation, 1978), p. 35.

107. Connally as told to Steinberg, pp. 118.

108. Acheson, 372–94; Connally as told to Steinberg, p. 126; McKay and Faulk, p. 34; Steinberg, p. 76.

109. Acheson, p. 402; Frantz, p. 153; Connally as told to Steinberg, pp. 173–77.

110. Hardeman, compiled by Huffman, p. 141; Dorough, p. 453.

111. John Nance Garner to Fred M. Vinson, Nov. 13, 1931, FMV.

112. Dorough, pp. 84, 126; Jordan A. Schwarz, *The New Dealers* (New York: Knopf, 1993), p. 251.

113. Dorough, p. 12; Connally as told to Steinberg, p. 91.

Chapter 3. John Nance Garner

1. Joe B. Frantz, *Texas: A History* (New York: W.W. Norton, 1984), p. 178; Neil MacNeil, *Forge of Democracy* (New York: David McKay, 1963), p. 80.

2. O. C. Fisher, *Cactus Jack* (Waco: Texian Press, 1978), pp. 8–9.

3. Arthur M. Schlesinger Jr., *The Crisis of the Old Order, 1919–1933* (Boston: Houghton Mifflin Company, 1956), p. 227; "John Garner Hides His Grief under Jolly Talk on Way to Dying Mother," *Knoxville News Sentinel,* Sept. 18, 1932, n.p., Box 868, folder "Garner-Goldsborough," DNC; Owen P. White, "Cactus Jack," *Collier's Weekly,* Jan. 23, 1932, n.p., Scrapbook, 12-08-1931/2-20-1932, JNG.

4. Bascom Timmons, *Garner of Texas* (New York: Harper and Bros., 1948), p. 90; Frank Kent, "The Great Game of Politics," *Baltimore Sun,* Mar. 29, 1932, n.p., Scrapbook #3, Mar. 1, 1932–Apr. 18, 1932, JNG.

5. Allan A. Michie and Rank Ryhlick, *Dixie Demagogues* (New York: Vanguard Press, 1939), p. 28; John McDuffie to John Nance Garner, May 18, 1949, JM.

6. Michie and Ryhlick, pp. 27–28; Connally as told to Steinberg, p. 91.

7. Rayburn claimed that Garner was so thrifty that he would not buy ice, and that was why Garner drank his whisky with tap water. D. B. Hardeman and Donald C. Bacon, *Rayburn: A Biography* (Texas Monthly Press, 1987), p. 114.

8. James Reston Sr., *The Lone Star: The Life of John Connally* (New York: Harper and Row, 1989), p. 41; Hardeman and Bacon, pp. 485–86, footnote 8; Miller quoted in Robert Remini, *The House: The History of the House of Representatives* (New York: HarperCollins, 2006), p. 302; John McDuffie to John Nance Garner, Nov. 6, 1944, JM.

9. William "Fishbait" Miller claimed that Garner and Longworth engaged in drinking bouts. See Remini, p. 302.

10. Carl Albert interview with Ron Peters, May 9, 1979, CA. The drinking did not end once Garner retired from politics. As Garner described the routine of life to Sam Rayburn in a 1950 letter, "I am really enjoying life — in good health. Nothing to worry about. Strike a blow for liberty about 5 o'clock every afternoon and keep busy reading and 'piddling' around all the four ranches." John Nance Garner to Sam Rayburn, May 31, 1950, SR.

11. Hardeman and Bacon, p. 136. The few really intimate friends included John McDuffie of Alabama and Sam Rayburn. In one letter to Sam Rayburn, Garner even wrote, "Give John McDuffie my love, taking a good portion for yourself." John Nance Garner to Sam Rayburn, Sept. 6, 1932, SR. Many of Garner's letters were actually written and typed by his wife, Ettie.

12. Hardeman and Bacon, p. 137; Larry Hufford, ed., *D. B.: Reminiscences of D. B. Hardeman* (Austin: AAR/Tantalus, 1984), p. 41; John E. Lyle interview by Anthony Champagne, May, 1980, SR; Hardeman and Bacon, pp. 70, 115, 136; Carl Albert interview, CA.

13. *Congressional Record*, Apr. 6, 1922, pp. 5119–20.

14. Hardeman and Bacon, p. 136. Emmanuel Celler of New York once rose to the floor and began to speak with the traditional language, "Mr. Speaker, reserving the right to object. . . ." At that point, the temperamental Garner cut Celler off saying, "There is not reason to object" and then banged his gavel. When another Democrat made a motion Garner opposed, even though "yeas" outnumbered "nays," Garner held the motion defeated and moved on. In the early Hoover administration, when Garner was more Hoover ally than opponent, Garner told Majority Leader Rainey and Ways and Means Chairman Collier that they should keep quiet about their personal views on tax policy. They did. If you were a stranger calling on Garner, it would not be unusual for him to greet you by saying, "What the hell do you want?" See Raymond Clapper, "Garner Rule in House Is Iron-Fisted," *Dallas Journal*, Jan. 26, 1932, n.p., Scrapbook, 12-08-1931/2-20-1932, JNG.

15. According to Timmons, Garner believed that reading the *Congressional*

Record and committee reports would teach one the congressional trade. See Timmons, p. 112. McDuffie to Garner, Nov. 6, 1944.

16. Rexford G. Tugwell, *The Democratic Roosevelt* (New York: Doubleday, 1957), p. 226; John McDuffie to John Nance Garner, July 23, 1940, JM; Timmons, p. 286; John Nance Garner to Claude Kitchin, Oct. 5, 1922, CK.

17. Robert J. Smith, interview by Michael Gillette, May 15, 1979, LBJ.

18. Patrick Cox, "John Nance Garner," in *Profiles in Power*, ed. Kenneth E. Hendrickson Jr., Michael L. Collins, and Patrick Cox (Austin: University of Texas Press, 2004), p. 44; Joe Robert Baulch, "James B. Wells: South Texas Economic and Political Leader," Ph.D. dissertation, Texas Tech University, 1974, p. 149.

19. See generally, Evan Anders, *Boss Rule in South Texas* (Austin: University of Texas Press, 1982); see Baulch, pp. 365–66; and Fisher, pp. 20–21; Alwyn Barr, "John Nance Garner's First Campaign for Congress," *West Texas Historical Association Yearbook* (1972): 105–10.

20. Garner quoted in Barr, p. 106; Baulch, p. 204.

21. Baulch, pp. 214–17; Baulch, pp. 217–18 citing J. B. Wells to Garner, June 20, 1901.

22. Fisher, pp. 8–20; Timmons, pp. 15–26.

23. For biographical treatments of Garner's life, see Fisher, Timmons, and Marquis James, *Mr. Garner of Texas* (Indianapolis: Bobbs-Merrill Co., 1939). A discussion of the district is found in the special supplement of the *Uvalde Leader-News*, Nov. 23, 1958, n.p., JNG.

24. Data on the district is from Stanley B. Parsons, Michael J. Dubin, and Karen Toombs Parsons, *United States Congressional Districts, 1883–1913* (Westport, Conn.: Greenwood Press, 1990).

25. Barr, p. 110; J. A. Kemp to James B. Wells, Nov. 1, 1902; Monta J. Moore to James B. Wells, Oct. 22, 1902; J. W. McKnight to James B. Wells, Oct. 30, 1902; B. H. Carleton to James B. Wells, Nov. 2, 1902; W. H. Clendenin to James B. Wells, Oct. 22, 1902; James E. Luch to James B. Wells, Oct. 23, 1902; Edward M. House to James B. Wells, Oct. 8, 1902. All these letters are in JBW.

26. Garner's views toward Hispanics were unenlightened: "They are not troublesome people unless they become Americanized. The sheriff can make them do anything." He paid Hispanic workers in his pecan business one penny a pound for shelled nuts, about a dollar a day; Reston, p. 39.

27. Fisher, p. 20; Anders, pp. 12–19.

28. O. Douglas Weeks, "The Texas-Mexican and the Politics of South Texas," *American Political Science Review* (1930): 625–26.

29. Anders, p. 193. Anders writes that "solid majorities failed to satisfy the Duval chieftain. Often he strived for unanimity in the vote count."

30. Untitled, Scrapbook, Nov. 18, 1913 to Mar. 4, 1925, JNG; E. R. Garner to

John McDuffie, July 30, 1926, JM; John Nance Garner to Archer Parr, Nov. 20, 1901, JNG.

31. Timmons, p. 286, James, p. 83; "Maney Announces He Is a Candidate against Garner," Scrapbook, JNG; "John Garner Plans Visit to Corpus Christi Shortly," Scrapbook, JNG; Fisher, p. 22.

32. See especially James, pp. 133–36. Garner incorrectly claimed that he never wrote letters more than one page in length when he did write (Fisher, p. x). John McDuffie, for one, recognized the extent to which Garner depended on his wife, Ettie. McDuffie wrote, "After all, Mr. Garner owed much of his success to Mrs. Garner, whom I often-times designated as 'Congressman.'" John McDuffie to Bascom N. Timmons, Dec. 20, 1948, John McDuffie Papers, W. S. Hoole Special Collections, University of Alabama, Tuscaloosa.

33. Fisher, p. 22.

34. Marquis James's book, *Mr. Garner of Texas,* is a Garner campaign biography. Bascom Timmons was one of Garner's closest friends, so close that Garner chose Timmons to be his spokesman at the 1940 Democratic convention (see Fisher, p. 149). Cecil Dickson was often used by Garner as a witness when Garner felt he needed someone he trusted to listen in on a conference. See Fisher, p. vii.

35. William S. White interview by Dorothy Pierce McSweeney, Mar. 5, 1969, LBJ.

36. John Nance Garner to Sam Rayburn, Aug. 3, 1932, SR; Ettie Garner postscript to John Nance Garner letter to Sam Rayburn, Aug. 27, 1932, SR; John Nance Garner to Sam Rayburn, Sept. 6, 1932, SR.

37. Anders, pp. 121–23.

38. See the discussions of military appointments in an exchange of letters between Wells and Garner. James B. Wells to John Nance Garner, Mar. 2, 1916; James B. Wells to John Nance Garner, June 14, 1916. See also B. L. Cain to John Nance Garner, June 23, 1916. This letter is brimming with gratitude for the appointment of his son to West Point. Garner received the letter but then sent it to Wells. The letter to Garner in part says, "I am for Judge Wells. First, Last and Always and with me are all my friends in Cameron County." The letters are in JBW.

39. An example of a military appointment for a friend is Wells to Garner, June 24, 1916, JBW. In this letter, Wells sought an appointment as second lieutenant for an old friend. Wells also wrote Garner parenthetically, "Everybody down here thinks that you are all-powerful, and I hope you are!" For an example of help for pensioners, see James B. Wells to John Nance Garner, Jan. 8, 1916, JBW.

40. James B. Wells to John Nance Garner, May 6, 1916, JBW; Baulch, p. 305; James B. Wells to John Nance Garner, May 28, 1914, JBW.

41. John Nance Garner to James B. Wells, June 19, 1916, JBW; James B. Wells to Mrs. John Garner, June 7, 1916, JBW. Wells wrote, "Pardon my writing this letter

to *you* [his emphasis], but, frankly, I rely upon your brain and your heart to keep old John constantly advised, and aid him."

42. John Nance Garner to James B. Wells, June 12, 1914; Garner to Wells, June 19, 1916; John Nance Garner to Joe K. Wells, undated, all in JBW.

43. "Hornby Praises Garner's Work," Scrapbook #1, Nov. 18, 1913/Apr. 4, 1925, JNG; Timmons, pp. 36–38; Baulch, p. 253.

44. Fisher, p. 25; Timmons, pp. 61–62; Fisher, p. 26.

45. Ronnie Dugger, *The Politician: The Life and Times of Lyndon Johnson* (New York: W. W. Norton, 1982), pp. 322–23. An interesting treatment of Garner's actions in Parr's behalf is William Robert Smith interview by Michael Gillette, LBJ.

46. Baulch, pp. 228, 309.

47. George Rothwell Brown, "Heraldings," Jan. 11, 1932, Scrapbooks 12-08-1931/02-20-1932, JNG.

48. Timmons, pp. 39–40; Hardeman and Bacon, pp. 107–108; Timmons, pp. 61–62; Fisher, p. 30; MacNeil, pp. 79–84.

49. Ronald M. Peters Jr., *The American Speakership* (Baltimore: Johns Hopkins University Press, 1990), p. 97.

50. Anders, p. 122; John Nance Garner to James B. Wells, Jan. 17, 1915. JBW.

51. "Notes on Remarks of John N. Garner — Sixty-Second Congress," President's Individuals File — Garner, John Nance, HH.

52. "Notes on Remarks of John N. Garner — Sixty-Second Congress," President's Individuals File — Garner, John Nance, HH.

53. "Garner's Pork Barrel Philosophy" attached to memorandum from J. Bennett Gordon to Mr. Joslin, July 20, 1932, President's Individuals File — Garner, John Nance, HH. Garner claimed he was misquoted by a reporter when he spoke at Pleasanton, Texas, in Atascosa County and that what he had actually said was: "Too often the disposition of the people is this: If a man from Massachusetts gets a hog in an appropriations bill, they expect a man from Texas will at least try to get a ham." See Fisher, p. 33.

54. Michie and Ryhlick, p. 23.

55. Timmons, p. 88; James F. Byrnes, *All in One Lifetime* (New York: Harper & Brothers, 1958), pp. 32–33; Timmons, p. 88; Garner to Kitchin, Oct. 5, 1922; "Stand on Tariff Beats Hayden for Democratic Post," Scrapbook, 11-18-1913/03-04-1925, JNG.

56. Timmons, p. 42.

57. Baulch, p. 361. Nor was only Garner mentioning the Speakership at that time. Bascom Timmons, Garner's reporter ally, was writing about the possibility. Timmons, however, also wrote that Finis Garrett, Henry Rainey, and Cordell Hull were possibilities as well. See Bascom Timmons, "Garner Is Boomed to Next Speaker," *Ft. Worth Record,* Nov. 8, 1922, n.p., Scrapbook, 11-18-1913/03-04-1925, JNG. At the same time, he was thinking about being Speaker, he was consider-

ing retirement (Timmons, p. 95). Congressman John Box of Texas took Garner's retirement seriously enough that he made it known that he would like to replace Garner as whip. See John C. Box to Claude Kitchin, Henry D. Flood, Finis J. Garrett, and John N. Garner, Mar. 5, 1921, CK.

58. David Burner, *The Politics of Provincialism: The Democratic Party in Transition 1918–1932* (New York: Alfred A. Knopf, 1967), p. 104.

59. Timmons, p. 95; Garner to Kitchin, Oct. 5, 1922.

60. John Garner to Claude Kitchin, Jan. 6, 1923, CK; Hardeman and Bacon, p. 136; Byrnes, pp. 34–35.

61. Robert Dean Pope, "Senatorial Baron: The Long Political Career of Kenneth D. McKellar," Ph.D. dissertation, Yale University, 1976, pp. 88–89.

62. Joseph P. Tumulty to John Nance Garner, Aug. 8, 1928, JPT; John Nance Garner to Joseph P. Tumulty, Aug. 14, 1928, JPT; Pope, p. 186.

63. John Garner to John McDuffie, Apr. 16, 1931, JM.

64. Richard B. Cheney and Lynne V. Cheney, *Kings of the Hill* (New York: Continuum, 1983), pp. 156–57, and Peters, pp. 104–106.

65. Timmons, p. 123.

66. One news report noted that Garner had persuaded southern Democrats to provide greater recognition to other regions, though it stated that Garner had done so not to aid his own quest for the Speakership but in the interest of party harmony and to help ensure future Democratic victories. See J. R. McDonell, "Party War Looms over Speakership," *Washington Post,* July 6, 1932, n.p., JWB.

67. John D. Erwin, "Byrns Leading in Speaker Race," *Evening Tennessean,* Nov. 16, 1932, n.p., JWB.

68. A Nashville paper claimed that Garner's enemies wanted to turn to Byrns as an alternative for Speaker but that Byrns had refused to be a party to that effort. However, a Washington paper claimed that Byrns had been a candidate against Garner for Speaker but withdrew in the latter stage of the race. Compare Charles S. Hayden, "Byrns Returns to Washington," *Nashville Banner,* Nov. 23, 1931, n.p. with McDonnell, JWB.

69. Will P. Kennedy, "Rainey's Election as Leader Seen," *Washington Star,* Nov. 24, 1931, n.p., JWB.

70. Peters, pp. 114–18.

71. Crisp and John Rankin of Mississippi were the southern possibilities for majority leader after John McDuffie and Joe Byrns withdrew from the majority leader's race. See "Byrns Not in Leader Race," *The Knoxville News-Sentinel,* Scrapbooks, JWB. Ayres was considered a northern rival of Henry Rainey's for the majority leadership. See Charles S. Hayden, "Byrns Returns to Washington," *Nashville Banner,* Nov. 23, 1931, n.p., Scrapbooks, JWB.

72. George Rothwell Brown, "Heraldings," Jan. 11, 1932, Scrapbook, 12-08-31 to 02-20-32, JNG. See also Fisher, p. 69; Childs, p. 111; and Hardeman and Bacon, p. 114. William B. Bankhead to John N. Garner, telegram, Nov. 13, 1931, WB.

73. Fisher, p. 78.

74. John Nance Garner to John McDuffie, Sept. 24, 1931, JM; Jordan A. Schwarz, "John Nance Garner and the Sales Tax Rebellion of 1932," *Journal of Southern History* 30 (1964): 162; Jordan A. Schwarz, *The Interregnum of Despair* (Chicago: University of Illinois Press, 1970), p. 236.

75. Tugwell, p. 226.

76. Joseph Tumulty to John Nance Garner, Feb. 2, 1932, JPT.

77. Henry Rainey to James Farley, Aug. 27, 1932, JF; John Garner to James Farley, Aug., 1932, JF.

78. Lionel V. Patenaude, *Texans, Politics and the New Deal* (New York and London: Garland Publishing, 1983), p. 26; John Nance Garner to James Farley, July 23, 1932, JF; Patenaude, p. 27.

79. Edward Angly, "Garner on Way East, Averse to Taking Stump," *New York Herald Tribune,* Sept. 16, 1932, n.p., DNC.

80. "Garner Assures Business Heads Here He's Safe," *New York Herald Tribune,* Oct. 13, 1932, n.p., DNC.

81. "John Garner Hides His Grief under Jolly Talk on Way to Dying Mother," *Knoxville News Sentinel,* Sept. 18, 1932, n.p., DNC; "Nation Misled by President Says Garner," *New York Herald Tribune,* Oct. 15, 1932, n.p., and "Garner to Let Campaign Rest on the One Speech He Made," *New York Times,* Oct. 25, 1932, n.p., DNC; "Denies that Garner Is a Member of the Klan; His Secretary Charges Senator with 'Falsehood,'" *New York Times,* Oct. 29, 1932, n.p., DNC.

82. John Garner to Joseph Tumulty, Oct. 16, 1936, JPT.

83. Unable to get Garner, Colmer convinced Speaker Joe Byrns and Majority Leader William Bankhead to attend the event. William M. Colmer interview, Former Members of Congress Oral History Project, Box 3, Oct. 27, 1978, Library of Congress, Washington, D.C.

84. John N. Garner to Franklin D. Roosevelt, Nov. 17, 1934, FDR; Patenaude, pp. 35–36.

85. Patenaude, p. 36.

86. Raymond Moley to Franklin D. Roosevelt, Sept. 19, 1934, FDR; Roosevelt quoted in Michael J. Romano, "The Emergence of John Nance Garner as a Figure in American National Politics, 1924–1941," Ph.D. dissertation, St. John's University, 1974, p. 237–38.

87. Romano, pp. 239–40.

88. John Garner to Jim Farley, July 1, 1937, JF.

89. Romano, pp. 247, 251–52; James Farley, Columbia University Oral History Transcript, JF.

90. Romano, pp. 257, 267, 281, and 288.

91. Ibid., p. 307; James Farley to Claude Bowers, Feb. 8, 1940, JF; see also Romano, pp. 293–94; James Farley to Claude Bowers, Dec. 21, 1939, JF; Claude Bowers to Jim Farley, Jan. 19, 1940, JF.

92. John Garner to Lewis B. Schwellenbach, Apr. 21, 1941, LBS; John Garner to Sam Rayburn, Jan. 3, 1942, SR; John Garner to Harry Truman, Nov. 26, 1951, HST; Harry Truman to John Garner, Dec. 11, 1948, HST; Ettie R. Garner to Harry Truman, Jan. 5, 1946; Harry Truman to Mrs. Garner, Jan. 9, 1946; Lt. Colonel R. B. Marlin to General Vaughan, Jan. 16, 1946; Harry Truman to Mrs. Garner, Jan. 18, 1946, all in HSTO; John Garner to Harry Truman, Nov. 23, 1950, HST; Walter Hall to Sam Rayburn, Oct. 27, 1952, WH.

Chapter 4. Sam Rayburn

1. John McDuffie as told to Mary Margaret Flock, *To Inquiring Friends If Any* (Mobile: Azalea City Printers, n.d.), pp. 255–58.

2. J. Bernard McDonnell, "McDuffie, of Alabama, Close to Garner and Plain Spoken," *Washington Post*, Jan. 23, 1933.

3. Ibid; Memorandum titled "The Speakership," JO.

4. McDonnell, p. 2.

5. Ralph Neal Brannen, "John McDuffie: State Legislator, Congressman, Federal Judge, 1883–1950," Ph.D. dissertation, Auburn University, 1975, pp. iv, 20, 145, 163, 167, 173.

6. McDuffie, pp. 260–61.

7. James Hamilton Lewis to Henry Rainey, Dec. 16, 1930, HR; Henry Rainey to James Hamilton Lewis, Dec. 19, 1930, HR.

8. Henry Rainey to V. Y. Dallman, Mar. 4, 1931, HR.

9. For example, James T. Igoe wrote O'Connor that Cullen was conferring with Garner and had stated that he agreed with Garner on the organization of the House. See James T. Igoe to John J. O'Connor, Nov. 14, 1931, JO.

10. Document titled "Internal Feud in Tammany May Destroy Its Chance to Obtain Speakership," JO; John J. Cochran to John O'Connor, Nov. 16, 1931, JO; Igoe to O'Connor, Nov. 14, 1931.

11. Will P. Kennedy, "Rainey's Election as Leader Seen," *Washington Star*, Nov. 24, 1931, n.p., Scrapbooks, JWB; "Post Gallery of Notables," *Washington Post*, Feb. 2, 1932, n.p. Scrapbooks, JWB.

12. McDuffie, p. 261. Even Rainey supporter Adolph Sabath, however, realized that McDuffie's withdrawal had prevented a House Democratic schism along regional lines. He wrote McDuffie, "above all, you are a true Democrat with

the interest of the Party at heart." Adolph J. Sabath to John McDuffie, Nov. 27, 1931, JM.

13. Brannen, p. 169.

14. McDuffie, p. 273; "Warm Fight Looms over Speakership," *New York Times*, Nov. 10, 1932, p. 2.

15. J. E. Rankin to John J. O'Connor, Feb. 28, 1933, JO.

16. Adolph Sabath, "Memoirs of Adolph Sabath, c. 1881–1930's, dictated to J. L. Tupy," pp. 542–43, AS.

17. J. Bernard McDonnell, "Rainey Backed by Roosevelt; Seen Speaker," *Washington Post*, Dec. 30, 1932, p. 1; Henry Rainey to James Farley, Dec. 6, 1932, and Dec. 14, 1932, JF; "House Speakership Contest Grows Hectic with Roosevelt Withholding Influence," *New York Daily Mirror*, Dec. 31, 1932, p. 1, Scrapbooks, JWB.

18. John O'Connor to Basil O'Connor, n.d. (stamped received Dec. 13, 1932), JO; Joseph W. Byrns to Franklin D. Roosevelt, Dec. 8, 1932, FDRO; "Roosevelt Advisors Backing McDuffie for the Speakership," otherwise unidentified newspaper clipping attached to Joseph W. Byrns to Franklin D. Roosevelt, Dec. 8, 1932, FDRO; "Byrns Seeks Tammany's Help in Aspiring to Speaker's Chair," *Cincinnati Enquirer*, Nov. 16, 1932, n.p., attached to Joseph W. Byrns to Franklin D. Roosevelt, Dec. 8, 1932, FDRO. Byrns had met with Curry and asked for his support for the Speakership on November 15, 1932. It was claimed that Curry, along with other political bosses such as Hague, were keeping an open mind in the Speaker's race. Garner had, of course, done the same thing in 1931 when he sought the Speakership. See "Byrns Seeking Curry's Aid in Speaker's Race," *New York Herald Tribune*, Nov. 16, 1932, n.p., Scrapbooks, JWB.

19. Franklin D. Roosevelt to Joseph W. Byrns, Dec. 27, 1932, FDRO; Franklin D. Roosevelt to John N. Garner, Dec. 27, 1932, FDRO.

20. John McDuffie to Jouett Shouse, Feb. 3, 1933 (two letters), JM; untitled and undated three-page memorandum, JO; Frank Freidel, *Franklin D. Roosevelt: Launching the New Deal* (Boston: Little Brown, 1973), p. 305. John O'Connor noted to his brother Basil that "our friend" Jouett Shouse was advocating McDuffie for Speaker. See O'Connor to O'Connor, n.d. (stamped received on Dec. 13, 1932). Unfriendly to McDuffie, the *Mobile Post* ran an editorial calling McDuffie "a power company baby." "Watch Alabama's Power Boys Meet the Issue," *Mobile Post*, Jan. 6, 1933, n.p., JWB.

21. Freidel, p. 306.

22. Untitled and undated three-page memorandum, JO.

23. "Joseph W. Byrns Looms as Rainey's Successor for House Leadership," *Nashville Banner*, Aug. 20, 1934, Scrapbooks, JWB; "Democratic Candidates Off Varying Claims Fitting Them for Office," *Springfield Republican*, Feb. 12, 1933, p. 1, JO.

24. Freidel, p. 306; memorandum titled "The Speakership," JO.

25. Will P. Kennedy, "Three Men Claim Enough Votes to Win Speakership," *Washington Evening Star,* Dec. 26, 1932, n.p., JWB.

26. Sam Rayburn to Jacob Le Roy Milligan, July 25, 1932, SR; Brannen, p. 175; D. B. Hardeman and Donald C. Bacon, *Rayburn: A Biography* (Austin: Texas Monthly Press, 1987), p. 146. Garner, of course, was being a political realist, but he long thought Rayburn could and should be Speaker and told Cecil Dickson, a Rayburn friend since 1922, of that belief. His only concern about Rayburn, a concern that was expressed by Garner in a variety of contexts, was that Rayburn was "very modest and self-effacing." Cecil Dickson interview with Anthony Champagne, June 29, 1980, SR.

27. Brannen, p. 176.

28. Phil D. Swing to Clarence Lea, Nov. 14, 1932, JM; Brannen, p. 179. The promise of a steering committee was made by McDuffie in his public announcement of his candidacy for the Speakership. See "McDuffie Comes out for the Speakership," *New York Times,* Nov. 28, 1932, p. 2.

29. McDuffie, pp. 276–77.

30. Undated memorandum titled "re Speakership," Box 23, JO.

31. Frank Hague to John J. O'Connor, Jan. 9, 1933, JO; James M. Curley to John J. O'Connor, Jan. 5, 1933, and Jan. 20, 1933, JO; telephone memorandum, n.d., JO.

32. Sabath., pp. 544–45.

33. Ibid., pp. 545–46.

34. Brannen, pp. 179–80. The *New York Times* reported that Garner had promised to remain aloof from the Speakership race. See "Three Lead in Race to Be Next Speaker," *New York Times,* Dec. 24, 1932, p. 4. John Rankin to Franklin Roosevelt, Dec. 31, 1932, FDR; Franklin D. Roosevelt to John Rankin, Jan. 27, 1933, FDR; Brannen, p. 180; "Roosevelt Key to Naming of Next Speaker," *New York Herald Tribune,* Dec. 31, 1932, p. 6, JO.

35. John McDuffie to A. M. Tunstall, Dec. 2, 1932, JM; "Asserts M'Duffie Will Be Speaker," *New York Times,* Dec. 30, 1932, p. 3.

36. Charles Hand to John McDuffie, Dec. 16, 1932, JM.

37. J. Bernard McDonnell, "Rainey Backed by Roosevelt; Seen Speaker," *Washington Post,* p. 1, and "Statement Issued by John McDuffie, Dec. 30, 1932," JM. McDuffie's statement announced, "If Governor Roosevelt has written or said he has not endorsed any candidate in the Speakership contest I am in no wise surprised. No candidate for that high office could expect Mr. Roosevelt to undertake to dictate the election of the next Speaker. As one candidate for the Speakership I would not be the source of such embarrassment to him."

38. John McDuffie to E. W. Pettus, Jan. 10, 1933, JM; John McDuffie to Grover C. Hall, Feb. 14, 1933, JM.

39. John McDuffie telegram to Robert Jackson, Feb. 28, 1933, JM.

40. John McDuffie to Robert M. Harris, Mar. 1, 1933, JM; Journal of the First Democratic Caucus of the 73d Congress, Mar. 2, 1933, CAU; Sabath, pp. 545–46. The *New York Times* concurs with Sabath that even some Texas votes went to the Rainey-Byrns coalition so that Congressman Buchanan of Texas could become chairman of the Appropriations Committee. Tammany Rep. Tom Cullen was made assistant leader in exchange for the Tammany votes. See "Garner Forces Beaten," *New York Times*, Mar. 3, 1933, p. 3.

41. McDuffie, pp. 278–79.

42. McDuffie, p. 278; Brannen, p. 182.

43. "Rainey to Take Garner's Place at House Helm," *Chattanooga Times*, Mar. 3, 1933, n.p., Scrapbooks, JWB.

44. John McDuffie to Roy L. Nolen, Mar. 9, 1933, JM; "Garner Forces Beaten," *New York Times*, Mar. 3, 1933, p. 1.

45. Arthur Krock, "In Washington — McDuffie Will Leave House after Courageous Career," *New York Times*, Feb. 1, 1935, n.p., JPT; Brannen, p. 181.

46. Ted Morgan, *FDR: A Biography* (New York: Simon and Schuster, 1985), p. 377.

47. Journal of the First Democratic Caucus of the 73d Congress.

48. Byrns disagreed with Garner's economic views. He had opposed the sales tax and questioned the desirability of a balanced budget. See "The Speakership Contest," *New York Times*, Nov. 19, 1932, p. 14. "Rainey to Take Garner's Place at House Helm," *Chattanooga Times*, Mar. 3, 1933, n.p., Scrapbooks, JWB.

49. "Rainey to Take Garner's Place at House Helm"; "Garner Forces Beaten," p. 1.

50. Sabath, p. 547; "Garner Forces Beaten," p. 1.

51. "Garner Forces Beaten," p. 3; Bruce J. Dierenfield, *Keeper of the Rules: Congressman Howard W. Smith of Virginia* (Charlottesville: University Press of Virginia, 1987), p. 47. Interestingly, Dierenfield identifies the Garner forces as "the Democratic congressional faction led by John W. McCormack of Massachusetts and Sam Rayburn of Texas" (p. 47).

52. McDuffie, p. 285.

53. Franklin D. Roosevelt telegram to John N. Garner, Aug. 20, 1934, FDR; John N. Garner to Franklin D. Roosevelt, Aug. 21, 1934, FDR; John O'Connor to Thomas J. O'Brien, Aug. 20, 1934, JO; John O'Connor to Loring M. Black Jr., n.d., JO; John O'Connor to George W. Lindsay, Dec. 17, 1934, JO; John O'Connor to Huey P. Long, Dec. 13, 1934, JO; John O'Connor to Thomas G. Ryan, Dec. 17, 1934, JO.

54. William Bankhead to John O'Connor, Nov. 19, 1934, JO.

55. John O'Connor to Joseph Monaghan, Dec. 26, 1934, JO; John O'Connor to Francis Condon, Dec. 26, 1934, JO; James F. Dulligan to William P. Connery,

Dec. 10, 1934, JO; James F. Dulligan to David Walsh, Dec. 11, 1934, JO; Dulligan to Connery, Dec. 10, 1934.

56. O'Connor to James J. Dooling, Dec. 17, 1934; John McDuffie to John O'Connor, Dec. 17, 1934, JO.

57. Jones had offices in the National Press Building in Washington, D.C. See Sam M. Jones to James F. Dulligan, Jan. 7, 1935, JO, and James F. Dulligan to Sam M. Jones, Jan. 8, 1935, JO.

58. O'Connor, for example, tried to get a friend to complain to a reporter for the *Washington Herald,* John T. Lambert, that an article had featured John Mc-Cormack for floor leader even though, O'Connor claimed, McCormack "doesn't have a chance." The race, wrote O'Connor, was between him and Bankhead, and he sought help in convincing Lambert to give him "a better break especially as to the attitude of my own New York delegation toward me." John O'Connor to John J. Crehan, Dec. 27, 1934, JO.

59. Memorandum titled "Pennsylvania's 'Unit Rule,'" JO.

60. James F. Dulligan, one of O'Connor's leading supporters, wrote the press agent, Sam Jones, who had been hired to assist O'Connor, "We were very much satisfied with the outcome and I look forward to bigger and better things for him." James F. Dulligan to Sam M. Jones, Jan. 8, 1934, JO.

61. McDuffie, p. 285; Brannen, p. 182.

62. "M'Duffie Gives Up Speakership Race," *New York Times,* Aug. 22, 1934, n.p., JM.

63. Dennis S. Nordin, *The New Deal's Black Congressman: A Life of Arthur Wergs Mitchell* (Columbia: University of Missouri Press, 1997), pp. 23, 30, 41, 44–45, 62–63, 89, 280.

64. McDuffie, pp. 286–88; Franklin D. Roosevelt to John McDuffie, Feb. 11, 1935, FDR; Brannen, p. 204; John McDuffie to John Rankin, Feb. 21, 1944, JM.

65. Hardeman and Bacon, p. 163; J. Bernard McDonnell, "Byrns Is Strong Contender in Race for Speakership," *Washington Post,* Jan. 29, 1933, p. 2.

66. McDonnell, p. 2; "Unexpected Passing of House Ruler in Midst of Adjournment Push Blow to Democrats," unidentified newsclipping, June 4, 1936, p. 1, Scrapbooks, JWB.

67. Genevieve Forbes Herrick, "In Capital Letters," *The Sunday Star,* 1934, Scrapbooks, JWB.

68. Marshall McNeil, "Joe Byrns Advanced by Friends for the House Speakership," *Washington Daily News,* July 15, 1932, n.p., Scrapbooks, JWB; Jewell Morrell Galloway, "The Public Life of Joseph W. Byrns," master's thesis, University of Tennessee, 1962, p. 53; editorial, "Garner Loses Caste," *Nashville Tennesseean,* Mar. 26, 1932, n.p., Scrapbooks, JWB.

69. Galloway, p. 2; Rodney Dutcher, "'Folksy' Nashville Congressman Is Ad-

vanced to No. 2 Job in Our Government: Has Friends Galore," *Knoxville News-Sentinel*, Dec. 30, 1934, n.p., Scrapbooks, JWB.

70. "Byrns in the Lead," *Nashville Banner*, Aug. 26, 1934, n.p., Scrapbooks, JWB.

71. Alfred Steinberg, *Sam Rayburn: A Biography* (New York: Hawthorn Books, 1975), pp. 106, 123–24; C. Dwight Dorough, *Mr. Sam* (New York: Random House, 1962), p. 253; "Rayburn Quits Campaign for Speakership," *Houston Chronicle*, Dec. 13, 1934, Scrapbooks, SR; Irvin M. May Jr. to Anthony Champagne, Oct. 11, 1982. May was a close friend of Marvin Jones and is Jones's biographer. Attorney General to Franklin D. Roosevelt, Dec. 30, 1935; Attorney General to Franklin D. Roosevelt, Aug. 15, 1938; Franklin D. Roosevelt to Attorney General, Sept. 12, 1938; H. P. Fulmer to Franklin D. Roosevelt, May 3, 1940, all in FDR; "Marvin Jones press release," Sept. 15, 1934, FDRO.

72. Cecil B. Dickson to Sam Rayburn, Oct. 6, 1934, SR.

73. Secretary of Commerce Daniel Roper to Marvin McIntyre, n.d., FDRO; Louis Howe to Jim Farley, Feb. 8, 1935, FDRO.

74. Adolph Sabath to Franklin D. Roosevelt, Nov. 17, 1934, FDR; Franklin D. Roosevelt to Adolph Sabath, Nov. 20, 1934, FDRO; Josh Lee to Louis Howe, Sept. 21, 1934, and Josh Lee to Louis Howe, Oct. 6, 1934, FDRO; Louis Howe to Josh Lee, Oct. 6, 1934, FDRO; Dutcher, n.p.

75. William Bankhead to Jim Farley, Aug. 27, 1934, WB; Victor Hanson to Harry Ayers, Nov. 17, 1932, and Victor Hanson to William Bankhead, Nov. 19, 1932, JM. Victor Hanson was publisher of the *Birmingham News* and *Birmingham Age-Herald* and strongly advocated McDuffie's candidacy for Speaker and Bankhead's deference to McDuffie's ambitions.

Judge Leon McCord wrote McDuffie, "Now if Mr. Will Bankhead insists on cluttering up your chances; if Senator John Bankhead is to run his [Will's] race for Speakership then they had just as well get ready for some stiff opposition down this way. You can beat John Bankhead for the Senate. I have very high regard for the Bankheads but I am not willing to see them claim every honor within our party." Leon McCord to John McDuffie, Nov. 15, 1932, JM.

76. In the telegram, McDuffie told Bankhead that he thought he could be elected Speaker and that he would make a formal announcement of his candidacy. He asked for Bankhead's support and sought a meeting with Bankhead. John McDuffie telegram to William Bankhead, Nov. 22, 1932, WB. William Bankhead to Eugene E. Cox, Nov. 17, 1932, WB; John McDuffie to A. M. Tunstall, Dec. 2, 1932, JM.

77. William Bankhead to A. R. Brindley, Aug. 21, 1934, WB; J. L. Milligan telegram to William B. Bankhead, Aug. 21, 1934, WB; William Bankhead to Henry M. Bankhead, Aug. 28, 1934, WB; "Byrns Favored for Speaker of National House,"

Miami Herald, Oct. 9, 1934, n.p., WB; INS news service, *Byrns Spikes Rumors of Federal Post,* Aug. 30 [1934], Scrapbooks, JWB.

78. One report suggested that both Rayburn and Bankhead needed northern running mates to satisfy concerns about sectional balance. Possible northerners were listed as John O'Connor of New York, John McCormack of Massachusetts, Robert Crosser of Ohio, Adolph Sabath of Illinois, and William Arnold of Illinois. The same article suggested an alliance between Byrns and James M. Mead of New York. "Byrns-Mead Combination Is Favorite," *Nashville Banner,* Nov. 25, 1934, n.p. Scrapbooks, JWB. Another article dealing with sectional balance suggested that balance was achieved with a Byrns-Bankhead leadership, because Bankhead's move to floor leadership made John O'Connor of New York chair of the Rules Committee. Lyle C. Wilson, "Plan to Cinch Speaker's Job for Byrns Seen," *Evening Tennessean,* Oct. 8, 1934, n.p., Scrapbooks, JWB.

79. Walter Chamblin Jr. to John McDuffie, Nov. 21, 1934, JM.

80. Ibid.

81. Ibid.

82. John McDuffie to Walter Chamblin Jr., Nov. 24, 1934, JM.

83. Walter Chamblin Jr. to Sam Rayburn, Oct. 10, 1934, SR; Mariette R. Garner to Sam Rayburn, Oct. 12, 1934, SR; Hardeman and Bacon, p. 165.

84. "President Watching Speakership Race," unidentified newspaper clipping, Scrapbook, SR; Dorough, p. 253 (quotation); "Rayburn Quits Campaign for Speakership," *Houston Chronicle,* Dec. 13, 1934, n.p., Scrapbook, SR; Robert T. Bartley interview by Anthony Champagne, Jan. 7, 1982, SR; Steinberg, p. 125; Hardeman and Bacon, p. 165; Cecil Dickson interview.

85. Hardeman and Bacon, p. 165; William Bankhead to Ed Crump, Dec. 17, 1934, WB; Walter Chandler telegram to William Bankhead, Dec. 22, 1934, WB; William Bankhead to John E. Miller, Dec. 17, 1934, WB; Elliott Thurston, "Byrns Leading Many Seekers of Speakership," *Washington Post,* Aug. 21, 1934, n.p., Scrapbooks, JWB; "Byrns Favored for Speaker of National House," *Miami Herald,* Oct. 9, 1934, WB; William Bankhead to Robert Doughton, Dec. 13, 1934, WB; William Bankhead to John McDuffie, Dec. 12, 1934, WB.

86. William Bankhead to Sam Rayburn, Sept. 11, 1934, WB.

87. Sam Rayburn to William Bankhead, Sept. 13, 1934, WB.

88. Sam Rayburn to William Bankhead, Nov. 3, 1934, WB; William Bankhead to Sam Rayburn, Nov. 13, 1934, WB.

89. William Bankhead to John McDuffie, Aug. 27, 1934, WB; George Huddleston to William Bankhead, Aug. 29, 1934, WB; John McDuffie to William Bankhead, Aug. 29, 1934, WB; John McDuffie to William Bankhead, Dec. 3, 1934, Box 13:11, WB.

90. "State Funeral for Speaker Byrns to be Held Friday in House Chamber,"

Cincinnati Times Star, June 4, 1936, p. 42, Scrapbooks, JWB. That Byrns had two previous heart attacks is noted by J. M. Galloway, "Speaker Joseph W. Byrns: Party Leader in the New Deal," *Tennessee Historical Quarterly* (1966): 69. Interestingly, Byrns had long-standing senatorial ambitions. He had seriously pursued a Senate seat in 1923 even though, as he wrote, "I am giving up a certainty of a powerful place in the House for an uncertainty." See Joe Byrns to John Byrns, June 16, 1923, JWB. At that time, he gave up his quest for a Senate seat because, he wrote, "Feel sure I could have won but was unwilling to pay price in money, work, worry and possibly health." See Joe Byrns to John [Byrns], Sept. 5, 1923, JWB. Cecil Dickson interview.

91. "Byrns Slated for Speaker When New Congress Meets," *Cincinnati Enquirer,* Aug. 21, 1934, n.p., Scrapbooks, JWB; John D. Erwin, "Joe Byrns Jr., Says His Father Wanted Only One More Term," *Nashville Tennesseean,* June 5, 1936, p. 1, Scrapbooks, JWB. See also file titled "Material on Death of Sen. [*sic*] Byrns Clippings Memorial Addresses Picture of funeral in Washington," JWB.

92. Ruth Finney, "The National Round-Up," *Washington Daily News,* Oct. 30, 1934, n.p., Scrapbooks, JWB; Sam Rayburn to William Bankhead, Nov. 20, 1935, WB; William Bankhead to Sam Rayburn, Nov. 23, 1935, WB; Bascom N. Timmons telegram to the *Dallas Times Herald, Houston Chronicle,* and *San Antonio Express,* June 6, 1936, Scrapbook, SR; Dorough, p. 248.

93. Hardeman and Bacon, pp. 207–208. Rayburn was one of sixty members appointed to represent the House at the funeral in Nashville. See "House Committee for Byrns Rites," *Nashville Tennesseean,* June 5, 1936, p. 1, Scrapbooks, JWB. Cecil Dickson interview.

94. William B. Bankhead to John J. O'Connor, June 10, 1935, JO; "Bankhead Speaker; Byrns Rites Planned," *Washington Daily News,* June 4, 1936, p. 1, 42, Scrapbooks, JWB.

95. William Bankhead to James H. Farley, Nov. 12, 1936, JF.

96. Dorough, p. 252; Robert A. Waller, "The Selection of Henry T. Rainey as Speaker of the House," *Capitol Studies* (1973), p. 162; Walter Judson Heacock, "William Brockman Bankhead: A Biography," Ph.D. dissertation, University of Wisconsin, 1952, p. 201; James MacGregor Burns, *Roosevelt: The Lion and the Fox* (Fort Washington, Pa.: Harvest Books, 1956), pp. 340–41; James T. Patterson, *Congressional Conservatism and the New Deal: The Growth of the Conservative Coalition in Congress, 1933–1939* (Lexington: University of Kentucky Press, 1967), p. 53; Hardeman and Bacon, p. 210.

97. May to Champagne. See also Joseph M. Ray, ed., *Marvin Jones Memoirs* (El Paso: Texas Western Press, 1973), pp. 117–18. In Jones's published version, Rayburn did not ask to be released from his promise to support Jones. Instead, Jones decided not to run for the leadership, and so, to Rayburn's pleasure, he released

Rayburn from his promise. Ruth Finney, "Rayburn Appears Likely Choice for House Leader," *Washington Daily News,* Nov. 13, 1936, n.p.; "Rayburn Leading in Race for Next House Leadership," *Dallas Morning News,* Nov. 22, 1936, n.p.; Robert C. Albright, "Gallery Glimpses," *Washington Post,* Dec. 27, 1936, n.p. Albright wrote, "Representative John Rankin . . . runs in every leadership contest, because it's good fun and he likes a scrap." These newsclippings are located in scrapbooks at SR.

98. George W. Stimpson, "Texas Is Again Chief Issue in Congress Fight," *Houston Post,* Dec. 3, 1936, n.p.; Ruth Finney, "Both O'Connor and Rayburn 'Sure' of Post," *New York Herald Tribune,* Dec. 1, 1936, n.p. Both are in scrapbooks at SR; Albright, "Gallery Glimpses," *Washington Post,* Dec. 27, 1936, n.p.; Robert C. Albright, "Rayburn-O'Connor Battle Will Enliven Opening of New Congress," *Washington Post,* Dec. 6, 1936, n.p.; Robert C. Albright, "Floor Leader Victory Seen for Rayburn," *Washington Post,* Jan. 3, 1937, n.p.; "Rayburn Leading in Race for Next House Leadership," *Dallas News,* Nov. 22, 1936. All the above clippings are in scrapbooks at SR. See also U.S. Congress, *Official Congressional Directory,* 74th Cong., 2d sess. (Washington, D.C., 1935), p. 161.

99. "An Old Custom," *New York Times,* Dec. 30, 1936, n.p.; Will P. Kennedy, "Taylor Supports Rayburn in Fight," unidentified newspaper clipping; Robert Albright, "Floor Leader Victory," *Washington Post,* Jan. 3, 1937, n.p., all in Scrapbooks, SR.

100. John O'Connor to W. W. Howes, July 1, 1936, JO; Lionel V. Patenaude, *Texans, Politics and the New Deal* (Garland, 1983), pp. 52–63; Patterson, p. 53; Rodney Dutcher, "New Deal," *St. Louis Star Times,* Dec. 3, 1936, n.p.; and "The Congress," *Time,* Dec. 14, 1936, n.p., both in Scrapbooks, SR; Burns, p. 341; Hardeman and Bacon, p. 211; "Statement of Representative Thomas F. Ford," FDR; J. O. Fernandez to John O'Connor, Aug. 7, 1936, JO.

101. Raymond Z. Henle, "Signs Indicate Roosevelt Wants Rayburn for Leader of House," *Toledo Blade,* Dec. 18, 1936, n.p.; Joseph Alsop Jr., "Two States Back Rayburn for Floor Leader," *New York Herald Tribune,* Dec. 4, 1936, n.p. Both clippings are in FDR. Michael Stack to Franklin D. Roosevelt, Dec. 18, 1936, FDR.

102. Michael J. Stack to Franklin D. Roosevelt, Dec. 18, 1936, FDR.

103. See O'Connor's listing of Catholics in a folder labeled, "Catholic Senate and House 1936," JO.

104. John O'Connor to Charles West, Dec. 28, 1936, JF; John O'Connor telegram to James Farley, JF.

105. John O'Connor to Patrick H. Drewry, July 9, 1936, JO; Patrick H. Drewry to Martin F. Smith, Oct. 26, 1936, JO; Don Gingery to John O'Connor, June 22, 1936, JO.

106. Hardeman and Bacon, p. 212. Interestingly, Arthur Wergs Mitchell, the

black Democratic machine congressman from Chicago who was personally allied with John McDuffie, was opposed to Rayburn. He supported O'Connor, arguing, "We feel that our interest will be better taken care of under the leadership of Mr. O'Connor. . . . I can assure you that a vote for him will be greatly appreciated by the fourteen millions of Negroes in the United States." See Nordin, p. 152. The unusual relationship between McDuffie and Mitchell was, of course, a personal one, and Mitchell's loyalty did not transfer to Rayburn, who, Nordin claims, Mitchell considered a populist, and Mitchell disdained populists (p. 152).

107. Hardeman and Bacon, p. 212; see the folder labeled "Itineraries, March 4, 1933–August 31, 1940," JF; "Columbia University Oral History Project Transcript, August 3, 1957," JF; David McKean, *Tommy the Cork: Washington's Ultimate Insider from Roosevelt to Reagan* (Hanover, N.H.: Steerforth Press, 2004), pp.73–74.

108. John O'Connor to Jim Farley, Dec. 28, 1936, JF; Adolph Sabath to James H. Farley, Dec. 22, 1936, JF; John O'Connor telegram to James H. Farley, Jan. 4, 1937, JF.

109. Alsop, "Two States Back Rayburn for Floor Leader"; Patterson, p. 53. The death sentence in the Holding Company Act would, absent compelling reasons, break up the companies after a certain date.

110. Robert S. Allen interview with Anthony Champagne, June 13, 1980, SR; John McCormack interview with Anthony Champagne, Mar. 11, 1980, SR; and Cecil Dickson interview. McCormack noted that "O'Connor was quite arrogant." Dickson said that O'Connor was hot-tempered and was "domineering." Patterson, p. 53.

111. Richard Bolling, *Power in the House: A History of the Leadership of the House of Representatives* (New York: E. P. Dutton and Company, 1968), 177; Bolling, 135.

112. In 1937, Rayburn returned the favor to Crosser, endorsing him for a judgeship on the U.S. Court of Appeals for the District of Columbia. James Roosevelt to Sam Rayburn, Sept. 24, 1937, FDR.

113. J. J. Kurlander to Marvin McIntyre, Jan. 2, 1937, FDRO. O'Connor, however, had said of Father Coughlin, "I will kick him from the Capitol to the White House," so he had not endeared himself to the radio priest. Typescript of an untitled article by Paul Mallon, *Philadelphia Ledger*, Oct. 1, 1936, n.p., JO.

114. Ira P. DeLoache to Sam Rayburn, Nov. 25, 1936, SR; Sam Rayburn to Ira P. DeLoache, Nov. 27, 1936, SR; Sam Rayburn to J. J. Kurlander, Jan. 12, 1937, SR; J. J. Kurlander to Sam Rayburn, Dec. 30, 1936, SR; J. J. Kurlander to Robert Crosser, Dec. 31, 1936, SR; Walter L. Hensley to Sam Rayburn, Jan. 7, 1937, SR; J. J. Kurlander, "One Vote for Rayburn as Floor Leader," *Cleveland Press*, Dec. 18, 1936, n.p., Scrapbook, SR; J. J. Kurlander, "Congressman Rayburn," *Cleveland Plain Dealer*, Dec. 23, 1936, n.p., Scrapbook, SR.

115. Anthony Champagne, *Congressman Sam Rayburn* (New Brunswick: Rutgers University Press, 1984), pp. 86–87; W. A. Thomas to Sam Rayburn, Nov. 11, 1936, SR.

116. Sam Rayburn to Clarence F. Lea, Sept. 22, 1936, SR.

117. "Rayburn as Speaker," *Abilene Morning News*, Dec. 19, 1936, n.p., Scrapbook, SR; "Excerpts from Jerry Voorhis, *Confessions of a Congressman*," pp. 26–27, CA.

118. Kirke Simpson, "A Washington Bystander," *Fort Worth Star-Telegram*, July 24, 1936, n.p., Scrapbook, SR; Lyle Boren interview with Anthony Champagne, May 28, 1985, SR; U.S. Congress, *Official Congressional Directory*, 75th Cong., 2d sess. (Washington, D.C., 1937), 161–72.

119. Albright, "Rayburn-O'Connor Battle Will Enliven Opening"; Jack Nichols to Wesley E. Disney, Dec. 8, 1936, JN; Lyle Boren interview; U.S. Congress, *Official Congressional Directory*, 75th Cong., 2d sess., 161–72. O'Connor and Nichols may have been personal friends as well as political allies. O'Connor bought Nichols thirty-six cocktail glasses, a shaker, ice tub and tongs, and a stirrer and spoon on Dec. 8, 1936, from R. H. Macy Co. He paid $20.14. See John O'Connor to R. H. Macy Co., Dec. 8, 1936, JO.

120. John O'Connor to Kenneth Romney, Oct. 13, 1936, JO.

121. John O'Connor to Kenneth M. Romney, Aug. 19, 1936, JO.

122. Hardeman and Bacon, p. 499, footnote 21; Charles Faddis Press Release, Dec. 23, 1936, JF.

123. James Roosevelt interview with Anthony Champagne, May 17, 1984, SR.

124. Basil O'Connor to Franklin D. Roosevelt, Dec. 14, 1936, JO.

125. Albright, "Rayburn-O'Connor Battle Will Enliven Opening"; "Roosevelt Keeps Hands Off in Fight," *Baltimore Sun*, Dec. 18, 1936, n.p., Scrapbook, SR; FDR Press Conference, Dec. 18, 1936, #330, vol. 8, pp. 179–80, FDRP; "House Fight Grows Hot," *Daily Tribune*, Sioux City, Iowa, Dec. 12, 1936, n.p. The editorial was sent from John O'Connor to Margaret LeHand by franked mail and was postmarked December 16, 1936. FDR. Roosevelt arrived in Charleston from his trip to South America on Dec. 14, 1936.

126. John O'Connor to James H. Farley, Dec. 28, 1936, JF.

127. Leroy D. Brandon, compiler under the direction of South Trimble, "Unofficial List of Members of the United States House of Representatives and Their Places of Residence," 75th Cong., corrected to Nov. 14, 1936 (Washington: GPO, 1936), JO; Lyle Boren interview.

128. Nor was his belief that he had the majority leadership by a landslide the only O'Connor miscalculation. In 1935, he thought the president in political trouble because of "huge spending, Utility Bill and taxes." John O'Connor to William B. Bankhead, Sept. 7, 1935, JO.

129. "Roosevelt Keeps Hands Off in Fight," *Baltimore Sun,* Dec. 18, 1936, n.p., Scrapbook, SR.

130. News Teletype, Dec., 18, (1936), JR; Joe T. Robinson to John J. O'Connor Telegram, Dec. 19, 1936, JR; HGM (a Robinson secretary) to Sam Rayburn, Dec. 19, 1936, JR; HGM (a Robinson secretary) to John N. Garner, Dec. 19, 1936, JR.

131. "Broken Pledge Laid to Guffey in House Fight," *New York Herald-Tribune,* Dec. 13, 1936, n.p., Scrapbook, SR; Carl B. Albert interview with Anthony Champagne, Dec. 6, 1979, SR; Robert L. Peabody, *Leadership in Congress: Stability, Succession, and Change* (Boston: Little Brown, 1976), pp. 493–95. In the 1932 Speakership race, John Rankin wrote President Roosevelt and asked him to be neutral. Roosevelt responded, "You may be quite sure that I have been and shall be wholly neutral in regard to the Speakership. That question certainly is not related to any executive function." John Rankin to Franklin D. Roosevelt, Dec. 31, 1932, FDR; Franklin D. Roosevelt to John Rankin, Jan. 27, 1933, FDR. Sam Rayburn to William Bankhead, Nov. 5, 1936, WB; C. P. Trussell, "Bankhead Neutral over Speakership," *Baltimore Sun,* Dec. 16, 1936, n.p., WB; Sam Rayburn to William Bankhead, Nov. 13, 1936, WB. According to Rayburn's letter, Bankhead's expression of neutrality was privately conveyed in a letter of November 10, 1936. Albright, "Rayburn-O'Connor Battle Will Enliven Opening." Any sense of indebtedness that Bankhead might have felt toward O'Connor must have been weakened by O'Connor's efforts to replace Bankhead as majority leader in 1935 when Bankhead was incapacitated by a heart attack. Heacock, "William Brockman Bankhead," p. 205.

132. "O'Connor Bloc Hits Meddling in House Fight," *Washington Post,* Dec. 5, 1936, n.p., Scrapbook, SR; "O'Connor Letter Turns Boomerang," *Baltimore Sun,* Dec. 5, 1936, n.p., Scrapbook, SR.

133. Typed statement by John W. McCormack, Scrapbook, SR; Hardeman and Bacon, p. 212; Will P. Kennedy, "Capitol Sidelights," *Washington Star,* Sept. 30, 1934, n.p., Scrapbook, JWB; Lester Ira Gordon, "John McCormack and the Roosevelt Era," Ph. D. dissertation, Boston University, 1976, pp. 149–50; Bascom N. Timmons telegram to *San Antonio Express, Houston Chronicle,* and *Dallas Times Herald,* Jan. 4, 1937, Scrapbook, SR; Timmons telegram, Jan. 4, 1937.

134. Robert S. Allen to John O'Connor, Jan. 8, 1937, JO; Hardeman and Bacon, p. 213; Arthur Krock, "In Washington: How Both Sides Won in a 'Battle,'" *New York Times,* Jan. 6, 1937, CA; John O'Connor to Royal S. Copeland, Jan. 13, 1937, JO; John O'Connor to Basil O'Connor, Jan. 5, 1937, JO; John O'Connor to Edward H. Crump, Jan. 8, 1937, JO. O'Connor's reference to the new governor of Tennessee is a comment about former congressman Gordon Browning. Browning had been a leader in Joseph Byrns's efforts to become Speaker. O'Connor seemed to assume Browning would continue to be opposed to Rayburn's ambitions even after Byrns's death. O'Connor's anger with the Tennessee delegation was also in-

spired by Congressman Sam McReynolds, a close friend of Speaker Byrns, who supported Rayburn as "a former Tennessean." Dorough, p. 255. John O'Connor to Sidney Hillman, Mar. 22, 1937, JO.

135. O'Connor's finances were not the best. His net income, according to federal income tax returns, in 1931 was an impressive $49,311.38, but in 1937 his net income was only $3,946.34 (JO). Krock, "In Washington: How Both Sides Won in a 'Battle'"; Hardeman and Bacon, p. 213; Edward J. Flynn, *You're the Boss* (Viking Press, 1947), 150–51; Steinberg, p. 164; and Bankhead to Rayburn, Aug. 10 and Sept. 29, 1938, WB. Roosevelt's frustration with O'Connor comes through in this letter that he wrote to O'Connor: "I know that you will not mind if I tell you with what very deep regret I have noted your statement made after my recovery message was sent to the House on Thursday. Frankly, it was the only discordant note among the members of the Democratic Party in the House of Representatives and coming from the Chairman of the Rules Committee can only make my regret the greater." Franklin D. Roosevelt to John O'Connor, Apr. 16, 1938, FDR. "Rayburn—Excerpts from *Secret Diary of Harold Ickes*," II, p. 174, CA.

136. Joseph W. Byrns Jr. to John O'Connor, Apr. 6, 1938, JO.

137. One of Rayburn's talents was an ability to form strong friendships with people of all ideologies. Gene "Goober" Cox of Georgia was "uncouth, foulmouthed, [and] belligerent. . . . He was forever losing his temper, and once he got into a fistfight on the House floor with doddering Adolph Sabath." Rayburn's friends could not understand why Rayburn even tolerated him, but Rayburn seemed to enjoy his company, and Cox was totally loyal to Rayburn. See Hardeman and Bacon, p. 305. Cox, an ultra-reactionary and racist, served on the Rules Committee, and Cox could and did move legislation out of the committee when requested by Rayburn. Interestingly, when Roosevelt sought to purge Cox along with O'Connor, Rayburn intervened and protected Cox from the purge. See Steinberg, pp. 168–69. Secretary of the Treasury Henry Morganthau noted that there was thought of turning patronage over to Fay, O'Connor's opponent, as a way of strengthening Fay with Tammany leaders. Defeating O'Connor, noted Morganthau, "is one of the most important fights that the President has taken on because if O'Connor is re-elected and goes back on the Rules Committee, matters would become very difficult." See Henry Morganthau Diaries, Sept. 7, 1938, vol. 138, p. 249, Franklin D. Roosevelt Library, Hyde Park, N.Y.

138. Sam Rayburn to William Bankhead, Aug. 15, 1938, WB; John O'Connor to Howard Chandler Christy, July 15, 1938, JO; William Bankhead to Sam Rayburn, Sept. 12, 1938, WB; Sam Rayburn to William Bankhead, Oct. 3, 1938, WB. Of course, Rayburn was writing about O'Connor's loss in the Democratic primary; O'Connor did receive the Republican nomination and ran in the general election, but Rayburn wrote, "Of course, our trouble from the Party standpoint is over as

far as O'Connor is concerned it matters not what the result of the November election may be in that district. He will be compelled to seek his assignments from the Republicans."

139. James F. Byrnes to John Nance Garner, Sept. 29, 1938, JFB; "Columbia University Oral History Project Transcript May 10, 1957," JF.

140. Lyle W. Dorsett, *Franklin D. Roosevelt and the City Bosses* (Port Washington, N.Y.: Kennikat Press, 1977), p. 65.

141. John O'Connor to Abraham S. Nettles, Jan. 18, 1940, FDR; John J. O'Connor to Philip B. Perelman, Aug. 21, 1940, JO.

142. Sam Rayburn to John O'Connor, Sept. 20, 1940, JO. Rayburn did seem to have the talent to avoid lasting grudges with political enemies. Steinberg, p. 28.

Chapter 5. John W. McCormack

1. Robert Remini, *The House: The History of the House of Representatives* (New York: HarperCollins, 2006), pp. 394, 419.

2. Nelson W. Polsby, *How Congress Evolves* (Oxford University Press, 2004), pp. 36–40.

3. Garrison Nelson, "Irish Identity Politics: The Reinvention of Speaker John W. McCormack," *New England Journal of Public Policy* (1999–2000): 13–14. It should be mentioned that McCormack did have a penchant for high stakes poker — an anomaly in an otherwise vice-free life. That fondness for poker no doubt benefited McCormack's relationship with John Nance Garner, also a frequent poker player. When Tip O'Neill, another well-known gambler, played poker with McCormack on one occasion, he lost so much money that McCormack let him win back much of his losses and urged O'Neill not to play again, since he considered O'Neill an amateurish player. Jim Wright interview with James Riddlesperger, May 12, 2005, Fort Worth, Texas.

4. Garrison Nelson, "The Matched Lives of U.S. House Leaders: An Exploration," paper presented at the 1978 Annual Meeting of the American Political Science Association, New York, N.N., pp. 44–45.

5. Nelson, "Irish Identity Politics," pp. 15–29.

6. Jim Wright tells of occasions when he saw Rayburn invite McCormack to dinner with him. An invitation to dinner with Rayburn was prized by the members and also considered practically to be a summons — if invited, members went with Rayburn. McCormack, however, would always decline, telling Rayburn that he "had a date tonight with Mrs. McCormack." Jim Wright interview, May 12, 2005.

7. Garrison Nelson, "House Leaders and Race Politics," paper presented at the 1990 Annual Meeting of the New England Political Science Association, Portland, Maine, Apr. 20–21, 1990, pp. 18–20.

8. Ibid., pp. 21–27.

9. Rayburn actually was not baptized until late in life, where he then joined his father's Primitive Baptist faith. For political reasons, he kept his religion uncertain — either Methodist or Baptist — for many years, until he finally became a Primitive Baptist. Elder Ball, the minister of the Primitive Baptist Church in Tioga, Texas, baptized him and also was the minister at Rayburn's funeral.

10. See the treatment of McCormack's rise to congressional power in Lester Gordon, *John McCormack and the Roosevelt Era,* Ph.D. dissertation, Boston University, 1976.

11. James E. Sargent, "Clifton A. Woodrum of Virginia: A Southern Progressive in Congress, 1923–1945," *Virginia Magazine* (1981), pp. 341–46, 349, 352; James E. Sargent, "Woodrum's Economy Bloc: The Attack on Roosevelt's WPA, 1937–1939," *Virginia Magazine* (1985), pp. 205–206; Richard Bolling, *Power in the House* (New York: E. P. Dutton, 1968), p. 151; James T. Patterson, *Congressional Conservatism and the New Deal: The Growth of the Conservative Coalition in Congress, 1933–1939* (Lexington: University of Kentucky Press, 1967), pp. 172, 237, 303, 327, 340.

12. Henry N. Dorris, "Push Plan to Defer House Leader Test," *New York Times,* Sept. 19, 1940, p. 15; undated, untitled planning document in a folder titled "House Majority Leader Contest," JOH; Bolling, pp. 151–52.

13. Robert A. Caro, *The Years of Lyndon Johnson: The Path to Power* (New York: Alfred A. Knopf, 1982), pp. 606–64. Indeed, Caro wrote that "polls early in 1939 showed that about sixty additional Democrats could expect to lose their seats in 1940" (p. 611). In 1938, eighty-two Democrats had lost seats in the House (p. 610).

14. *New York Times,* Sept. 26, 1940, p. 1. When it was requested that the vote be taken by teller (a process whereby members more publicly display their preferences), the motion failed 108 to 85.

15. Minutes of the caucus meeting, "76th 1939–1940," CAU.

16. Alfred Steinberg, *Sam Rayburn: A Biography* (New York: Hawthorn Books, 1975), p. 235.

17. "Rayburn Draft Growing," unidentified newspaper, dated Nov. 12, 1946, quoted in D. B. Hardeman and Donald C. Bacon, *Rayburn: A Biography* (Austin: Texas Monthly Press, 1987), p. 324; Sam Rayburn to J. Percy Priest, Nov. 29, 1946, in H. G. Dulaney and Edward Hake Phillips, eds., *Speak, Mister Speaker* (Bonham, Tex.: Sam Rayburn Foundation), p. 137; Sam Rayburn to John H. Kerr, Dec. 16, 1946, in Dulaney and Philips, p. 137.

18. Hardeman and Bacon, p. 324. Still, C. Dwight Dorough claims that Truman "had nothing to do with the draft because there were rumors that he might have a Cabinet post for the Speaker" though he "naturally thought it a good idea to keep

him in a position of legislative leadership." C. Dwight Dorough, *Mr. Sam* (New York: Random House, 1962), p. 388.

19. Sam Rayburn speech in Congress, Jan. 7, 1947, in Dulaney and Phillips, p. 139.

20. Dorough, pp. 388–89.

21. Nelson, "House Leaders and Race Politics," pp. 27–35.

22. Bolling, p. 177; Richard Bolling interview by Nelson Polsby, July 28, 1961, quoted in Polsby, p. 194, footnote 5.

23. Dorough, p. 431; Sam Rayburn to John McCormack, Nov. 11, 1952, SR.

24. Rep. Thomas Lane's nomination speech of John McCormack for majority leader, "87th, 1961," CAU.

25. Garrison Nelson, "Irish Identity Politics," p. 8; Polsby, pp. 36–37.

26. Polsby, pp. 36–39.

27. Morris Udall interview by Nelson Polsby, Jan. 19, 1962, quoted in Polsby, p. 38; Tip O'Neill with William Novak, *Man of the House* (New York: Random House, 1987), pp. 120–22; Jim Wright interview, May 12, 2005.

28. Polsby, pp. 39–40; Harry S. Truman to John W. McCormack, Jan. 8, 1962, JWM; Bolling, p. 209; John W. McCormack to H. G. Dulaney, Dec. 14, 1967, JWM.

29. "Gamble for the Gavel," *Newsweek*, Jan. 6, 1969, pp. 24–25; "Old Jawn," *Newsweek*, Mar. 6, 1967, p. 28.

30. *Congressional Record*, Jan. 17, 1967, p. 675.

31. Ibid., pp. 675, 681.

32. The following exchange took place:

THE SPEAKER: The Chair will state that the matter is not one of personal privilege. Does the gentleman seek further recognition?

RIVERS: Yes. I positively do. Have you overruled me?

THE SPEAKER: There is a difference between overruling and ruling.

RIVERS: Mr. Speaker, I most respectfully ask to be recognized for a long minute.

THE SPEAKER: Without objection, the gentleman is recognized for 1 minute (Ibid., p. 681).

33. Ibid., p. 681; "Old Jawn," p. 28.

34. Bolling, pp. 149–50; "Congressional Reform Bill Dies in Rules Committee," *CQ Almanac* 1968, p. 658; "Session Summary, Party Leaders, Turnover in 1967," *CQ Almanac*, 1967, p. 25.

35. Press release, Oct. 28, 1967, JWM.

36. Bob Sikes (D-FL), *Congressional Record*, Oct. 30, 1967, p. 30432; "House Democrats Plan Revolt against Speaker" *Business Week*, Apr. 6, 1968, p. 41. Early in 1967, revelations of ethical violations concerning Adam Clayton Powell Jr., who

chaired the House Education and Labor Committee, led to a Democratic caucus effort to exclude him from the House membership. McCormack opposed this effort, but when the caucus succeeded in expelling Powell, McCormack was named as the defendant in the subsequent court case. The Supreme Court ruled eight to one against the House in *Powell v. McCormack,* and Powell was seated in 1969 but not returned to his chairmanship. For many House liberals, still smarting from the loss of forty-eight seats in the 1966 House elections, McCormack's inability to handle this issue effectively was further evidence of the need for his being replaced as Speaker.

37. Kika de la Garza to John McCormack, Nov. 21, 1968, JWM.

38. Mike Kirwan to John McCormack, Nov. 21, 1968; John Flynt to John McCormack, Dec. 12, 1968; Clem Zablocki to John McCormack, Nov. 26, 1968; Mario Biaggi to John McCormack, Dec. 6, 1968; John McCormack to Mario Biaggi, Dec. 17, 1968, all in JWM.

39. Richard T. Hanna to John McCormack, Nov. 18, 1968; John McCormack to Richard T. Hanna, Dec. 2, 1968; Wayne Aspinall to John McCormack, Nov. 27, 1968; Jerome Waldie to John McCormack, Dec. 1, 1968, all in JWM.

40. Carl Albert to John McCormack, Nov. 30, 1968, JWM; John McCormack to Carl Albert, Dec. 6, 1968, JWM.

41. Jim Wright to John McCormack, Nov. 27, 1968, JWM.

42. William Randall to John W. McCormack, Dec. 12, 1968, JWM; Patrick J. Maney, "Hale Boggs: The Southerner as National Democrat," in *Masters of the House,* ed. Roger H. Davidson, Susan Webb Hammond, and Raymond W. Smock (Boulder: Westview Press, 1998), p. 243.

43. Brock Adams to Carl Perkins, Dec. 19, 1968, JWM. Perkins forwarded his copy of Adams's material to McCormack.

44. Ray Roberts to John McCormack, Dec. 19, 1968, JWM; Carl Perkins to John McCormack, Dec. 19, 1968, JWM.

45. Edith Green to John McCormack, Dec. 1, 1968, JWM.

46. Bob Poage to John McCormack, Nov. 18, 1968, JWM; Jack Brooks to John W. McCormack, Dec. 21, 1968, JWM.

47. Hale Boggs and F. Edward Hébert to John McCormack, Dec. 11, 1968, JWM.

48. Richard Ichord to John McCormack, n.d., JWM; John McCormack to Richard Ichord, Dec. 16, 1968, JWM.

49. "Memo of Telephone Call between Mr. T in Washington and Mr. M in Arkansas," MKU.

50. "Memorandum of Telephone Conversation December 19, 1968 between Phil and Frank, December 20, 1968," MKU.

51. The southern challenger to McCormack was, of course, Clifton Woodrum of Virginia. Memo, n.d., MKU.

52. Morris K. Udall to John W. McCormack, Nov. 27, 1968, JWM; John W. McCormack to Morris K. Udall, Dec. 10, 1968, JWM; "Some Notes on Caucus Held by Democrats on Wednesday, January 29," MKU; handwritten notes, n.d., MKU.

53. Larry L. King, "The Road to Power in Congress," in *Education of a Congressman: The Newsletters of Morris K. Udall,* ed. Robert L. Peabody (Indianapolis: Bobbs-Merrill, 1972), pp. 296–97.

54. Ibid.

55. Morris K. Udall to John McCormack, Dec. 26, 1968, JWM; Morris K. Udall to "Dear Democratic Colleague," Dec. 26, 1968, JOH.

56. Frank Thompson to John McCormack telegram, Dec. 26, 1968, JWM; Robert G. Sherrill, "Insurgents in Caucus: Club Business on the Hill," *Nation,* Jan. 27, 1969, pp 102–104.

57. Charles Bennett to John McCormack, n.d., JWM; Sherrill, pp 102–104.

58. Memorandum, n.d. [from second week of 1971], JOH; John McCormack memorandum, n.d., JWM; memorandum, n.d. [from second week of 1971].

59. "January 1969 Head Count," MKU; Jim Wright interview, May 12, 2005.

60. "Some Postmortem Thoughts on the Speaker Contest, Jan. 3, 1969," MKU; "Memorandum for Speakership Race File," Jan. 7, 1969, MKU; "Some Postmortem Thoughts on the Speaker Contest, Jan. 3, 1969."

61. "Some Thoughts on How to Win While Losing," MKU.

62. Les Gapay, "The Leaderless Majority," *Nation,* Feb. 9, 1970, n.p., CA; Jerome Waldie to John McCormack, Feb. 2, 1970, CA; Look News Release, "Leading Democratic Congressman Calls for Resignation of House Speaker McCormack," Apr. 20, 1970, RB.

63. Handwritten on the back of a clipping titled "Switch? Brooke not that unhappy," RB; Joe Lastelic, "Speaker John McCormack Loses His Patience with Reporters," *Kansas City Times,* Mar. 17, 1970, p. 6A, RB.

64. Jerome Waldie to John McCormack, Feb. 2, 1970, TPO. When McCormack's close associate John Rooney of New York traveled to California, he clipped some of Waldie's statements from local California papers and sent them to the Speaker. With these clippings is a handwritten note to John McCormack reading, "Mr. Rooney, NY, was in California & clipped these from local papers for your files," JWM.

65. John McCormack press statement, n.d., JWM; "Such Ingratitude" *Nation,* Feb. 23, 1970, pp. 195–96; Jerome Waldie to John McCormack, Dec. 1, 1968, JWM.

66. Jack Beidler to Walter P. Reuther, Mar. 11, 1970, JOH.

67. United Press International teletype, n.d., CA.

68. Gapay, p. 135.

69. "Carl Albert in Line for Speaker's Chair," n.p., n.d., CA.

Chapter 6. Sam Rayburn's Boys

1. Bolling said, "Well, I've been described in various ways; as a Rayburn lieutenant or a Rayburn leg man or a Rayburn flunky. It depends on who's talking. But, you see, I enjoyed working for Mr. Rayburn and found it a creative role to play. Mr. Rayburn and I although rather different in ages and different in some respects in background, saw things very much alike. I'm a good deal more liberal than he was although he was always liberal enough. There was a congenial, effective working relationship." See Richard Bolling interview by Ronald J. Grele, Nov. 1, 1965, JFK.

2. Richard Bolling interview with Anthony Champagne, June 26, 1980, SR; Carl Albert interview with Ron Peters, May 11, 1979, CA.

3. Bolling interview, June 26, 1980, SR.

4. Sam Rayburn to F. Edward Hébert, Nov. 29, 1946, FEH; C. Dwight Dorough, *Mr. Sam* (New York: Random House, 1962), p. 431; Bolling interview, June 26, 1980, SR.

5. Leslie Carpenter, "Albert 'Deal' Is Hinted," *Tulsa Tribune*, Oct. 6, 1961, n.p., CA. Bolling claimed that he would have run against McCormack if the president had not been Catholic. He said, "Well you see, I'm a Protestant and there was too much religious issue around, and I don't like it. This may be mawkish on my part, but the last thing I will ever do is exacerbate that kind of fuss. I figured that if a Protestant ran against McCormack that it would be taken as — that would be used — that would be part of the news. I think, frankly, that McCormack would have been easier to beat than Albert because there were an awful lot of people who wanted to defeat him. But there were also an awful lot of people who didn't want me in leadership." Bolling interview, Nov. 1, 1965, JFK.

6. Carl Albert with Danny Goble, *Little Giant: The Life and Times of Speaker Carl Albert* (Norman: University of Oklahoma Press, 1990), p. 199.

7. Both sides in the Albert-Bolling battle for majority leader seemed to think that the other side acted improperly in campaigning for the job before Rayburn's death. Robert Peabody, *Leadership in Congress* (Little, Brown, 1976), pp. 73 (Nelson Polsby is the author of this chapter, which deals with the Albert-Bolling race for majority leader).

8. Hale Boggs to Carl Albert, Nov. 13, 1961, CA; Doris Fleeson, "Kennedy Ponders the Speakership," no publisher listed, n.p., attached to Hale Boggs to Carl Albert, Nov. 13, 1961, CA.

9. Bolling interview, Nov. 1, 1965, JFK. Bolling made a similar comment right after the election of Albert. He said that the White House was wise to stay out of the race "so long as I wasn't very close." Untitled, *Time*, Jan. 12, 1962, n.p., Scrapbook, RB. Milton Viorst, "Ask Wagner's Help in House Leader Fight," *New York Post*, Dec. 19, 1961, n.p., Scrapbook, RB; *Time*, Jan. 12, 1962.

10. "Kennedy Bad Boys at It Again," *Chicago Sunday Tribune*, Dec. 3, 1961, CA;

handwritten note appended to an undated letter from Carl Albert to John Mc-Cormack, CA; "Rep. Albert to J.F.K.," *Washington Star,* Dec. 14, 1961, n.p., Scrapbook, RB.

11. Albert interview, SR; Albert, pp. 167–69.

12. Paul Duke, "Rayburn Exit to Make House an Even Tougher Administration Barrier," *Wall Street Journal,* Oct. 6, 1961, pp. 1, 20, CA; Frank Boykin to John McCormack, Dec. 2, 1961, CA.

13. Doris Fleeson, "Rayburn Ponders His Course," *Washington Evening Star,* Oct. 3, 1961, Scrapbook, n.p., HB; "Decline and Fall," *Time,* Sept. 7, 1959, p. 11, RB; Associated Press, "Speakership Succession," Oct. 6, 1961, n.p., Scrapbook, HB.

14. Cabell Phillips, "Compromise Gains on Speaker Issue," *New York Times,* Oct. 16, 1961, p. 17; Robert E. Baskin, "Representative Bolling Faces Big Odds in Bid to Become Speaker," *Dallas Morning News,* Nov. 23, 1961, p. 12, Scrapbook, HB; William S. White, "Kennedy's Congressional Crisis," *Washington Evening Star,* Nov. 15, 1961, p. A-23, Scrapbook, HB; Phillips, "Compromise Gains on Speaker Issue."

15. Carl Albert, of course, was not the only person to receive such encouragement. Hale Boggs also received supporting mail and press coverage. See Clarence Cockrell to Hale Boggs, Oct. 14, 1961, and *Congressional Quarterly,* "Speaker Rayburn's Illness Raises Questions of Successor," Oct. 5, 1961, n.p., HB; "Washington Whispers," *U.S. News and World Report,* Sept. 25, 1961, p. 33, CA; Judge Stephen Chandler to Carl Albert, Oct. 10, 1961, CA; W. A. "Gus" Delaney Jr. to Carl Albert, Oct. 12, 1961, CA. This, of course, was a remarkably unrealistic plan. Douglas Kiker, "Liberal, Dixie Demos Form Anti-McCormack Coalition," *Atlanta Journal,* Oct. 26, 1961, n.p., CA.

16. Kiker, "Liberal, Dixie Demos"; Hale Boggs interview by T. H. Baker, March 13, 1969, "Early Draft of an Oral History for the LBJ Library," HB.

17. Charles V. Gilmore to Carl Albert, Oct. 31, 1961, CA; Carl Albert to Charles V. Gilmore, Nov. 1, 1961, CA.

18. Don Gosney and Kay Blackburn to Burr Harrison, Dec. 6, 1961, HB.

19. Peabody, p. 74; Allan Cromley, "High-Ups Are High on Albert," *D.C. Times,* Sept. 15, 1961, n.p., CA; "Albert in Line to Step Ahead," *Daily Oklahoman,* Oct. 6, 1961, n.p., CA.

20. Cromley, "High-Ups Are High on Albert"; Carl Albert to Sam Rayburn, Sept. 16, 1961, CA.

21. Albert interview, SR; Albert, p. 255. Kerr had the money to provide considerable funding for Albert, and Kerr's oil interests also gave him access to the money of other oil men. When Kerr died on January 1, 1963, he left an estate of $20.8 million to his widow and children. Lawrence Sullivan to Carl Albert including an *Associated Press* news ticker, Mar. 1, 1963, CA.

22. Anne Hodges Morgan, *Robert S. Kerr: The Senate Years* (Norman: University of Oklahoma Press, 1977), p. 224.

23. Bolling interview, Nov. 1, 1965, JFK.

24. Leslie Carpenter, "House Speaker Fight Expected," no publisher, n.d., n.p., CA.

25. Morgan, pp. 221, 224, 302 footnote 135; Office of the White House Press Secretary, "Remarks of the President at Big Cedar, Oklahoma," Oct. 29, 1961, CA.

26. When Bolling announced, he was at Rutgers University for a three-day stint as politician-in-residence. The *Times* reported his announcement was on November 20. "Bolling in House Race," *New York Times*, Nov. 21, 1961, p. 30; Peabody, pp. 73, 77; Richard Bolling to Carl Albert, Nov. 28, 1961, CA.

27. "Bolling Reported Quitting Fight for House Majority Leadership," *New York Times*, Jan. 3, 1962, p. 12; Roy Wilkins telegrams, Dec. 15, 1961, RB; Carl Albert to Herbert Brannan, Dec. 5, 1961, CA.

28. Jack Williams, "Sam Rayburn's Departure to Recuperate Puts Bolling and others in Spotlight," *Kansas City Star*, Sept. 1, 1961, p. 1, Scrapbook, RB; Duke, "Rayburn Exit to Make House"; Arthur Krock, "Rayburn's Successor," *New York Times*, Oct. 8, 1961, n.p., Scrapbook, RB; Jack Williams, "Cannon's Support Goes to McCormack," *Kansas City Times*, Oct. 17, 1961, n.p., Scrapbook, RB; "McCormack Favored in Poll," *Roll Call*, Oct. 11, 1961, n.p., RB; "Kennedy 'Hands-Off' in House," no publisher, Oct. 29, 1961, n.p., Scrapbook, RB.

29. Dan Irwin, "Bolling Bids for Majority Leader Job," *New York Herald Tribune*, Nov. 21, 1961, n.p., Scrapbook, RB; "A Strong Majority Leader," *New York Times*, Dec. 11, 1961, p. 30; "The Battle for House Leader," *New York Times*, Dec. 24, 1961, p. 4–6. Bolling was supported by civil rights organizations in the leadership battle. John D. Morris, "Bolling Reported Quitting Fight for House Majority Leadership," *New York Times*, Jan. 3, 1962, p. 1; "Needed — A Leader Who Leads," *New York Post*, Nov. 22, 1961, n.p., and "Bolling for Floor Leader," *St. Louis Post-Dispatch*, Nov. 21, 1961, n.p. in Scrapbook, RB; "One Bid for House Job Is Discounted," *Kansas City Times*, Nov. 23, 1961, n.p., Scrapbook, RB.

30. Carl Albert to Max Morgan, Nov. 30, 1961, CA; Carl Albert to Homer Thornberry, Nov. 27, 1961, CA; Jim Wright interview with James Riddlesperger, July 21, 2005, Fort Worth, Texas; Mrs. Nona Bolling and Larry Bodinson, interview with James Riddlesperger and Anthony Champagne, Feb. 26, 2000, Kansas City, Missouri; Homer Thornberry to Richard Bolling, RB.

31. Albert to Thornberry; Joe O'Connell to Carl Albert, Dec. 29, 1961, CA. Although not on the list, Albert also got the support of New York Congressman Adam Clayton Powell, probably the most controversial African American politician of the time. See Don Irwin, "Powell on Albert's Bandwagon in Contest for House Leadership," *New York Herald Tribune*, Dec. 1, 1961, n.p., CA. Thus, Albert

was in the odd situation of having the support of Powell as well as reactionary seg-regationists like Howard Smith of Virginia and William Colmer of Mississippi.

32. Peabody, pp. 86, 96, footnote 45; Carl Albert to Howard W. Smith, Nov. 11, 1961, CA; Carl Albert to Howard Smith, Nov. 19, 1961, CA.

33. Peabody, p. 88; untitled, *Time,* Jan. 12, 1962, n.p., Scrapbook, RB.

34. Bolling interview, Nov. 1, 1965, JFK. Morris, "Bolling Reported Quit-ting Fight," p. 1. There is an undated document in Bolling's files that provides a state-by-state count of votes for Bolling. The count is divided among "Possible" votes, "Probable" votes, "Sure" votes, and "No" votes. Bolling lists 138 "Possible" votes, 30 "Probable," 8 "Sure," and 88 "No." He would, of course, have needed most of his "Possible" votes to win. The folder containing this untitled and undated document is "Misc./personal/etc," RB; *Time,* Jan. 12, 1962, RB.

35. Bolling interview, Nov. 1, 1965, JFK. Bolling did say that McCormack tried to continue the close working relationship that had existed between Bolling and Speaker Rayburn, but Bolling simply did not have the bond with McCormack or the respect for McCormack that he had for Rayburn, and that effort by McCor-mack "just didn't work. I don't think it's anybody's fault."

36. Untitled, *Wall Street Journal,* Nov. 24, 1961, n.p., Scrapbook, RB. However, in one interview Bolling did say that while he was not interested in the whip posi-tion, supporters might pressure him to take the job. See "Bolling Has High Hopes for Majority Leader Job," *Time,* Dec. 27, 1961, p. 3, Scrapbook, RB.

37. Nola Bolling and Bodinson interview.

38. Milton Viorst, "Why Bolling Quit Race for Party Leader," *New York Post,* Jan. 3, 1962, n.p. Scrapbook, RB; *Time,* Jan. 12, 1962; Nola Bolling and Bodinson interview; Kevin Phillips, "Boggs Boomerang," *Washington Post,* May 1, 1971, p. A-15, MKU; Ronald Sarro, "Troubled Leadership," *Washington Star,* June 17, 1971, pp. A-1, A-6, MKU.

39. "Rep. Carl Albert Has Come a Long Way from Bugtussle," *Daily Oklaho-man,* Aug. 6, 1970, p. 26, CA; John W. Seder, "Mystery Contender," *New York Times Magazine,* n.d., p. 12, CA; Wilbur Mills to Carl Albert, May 21, 1970, CA; Murray Seeger, "Reports and Comment," *Atlantic Monthly,* n.d., p. 6, CA.

40. Sam Gibbons notes on conversation with Wilbur Mills, Nov. 16, 1972, SG; Sam Gibbons notes on conversation with Wilbur Mills, Nov. 10, 1972, SG; Sam Gibbons notes on conversation with Bob Sikes, Nov. 8, 1972, SG; Bolling, p. 95.

41. Albert interview, CA.

42. Thomas H. Ferrell and Judith Haydel, "Hale and Lindy Boggs: Louisiana's National Democrats," *Louisiana History* (1994): 394; Boggs interview, HB.

43. F. Edward Hébert with John McMillan, *Last of the Titans: The Life and Times of Congressman F. Edward Hébert of Louisiana* (Center for Louisiana Stud-ies, University of Southwestern Louisiana, 1976), p. 161.

44. Ferrell and Haydel, pp. 390–94.

45. Larry L. King, "The Road to Power in Congress," *Harper's Magazine*, June, 1971, pp. 42, 44, 48; "Leadership Wrap-Up," Jan. 22, 1971, MKU; Bob Woodward, "Ford's Friendship with Nixon Ran Deep," *Dallas Morning News*, Dec. 29, 2006, p. 10A; Albert interview, CA.

46. Jack Anderson, "McCormack Left a Power Vacuum," *Washington Post*, Mar. 10, 1972, p. D19.

47. King, "The Road to Power in Congress," *Harper's Magazine*, June, 1971, p. 45; Shirley Elder, "Boggs Couldn't Refuse a Fellow Democrat," *Evening Star and Daily News*, Oct. 17, 1972, p. A-6, Scrapbook, HB; John Fischer, "The Easy Chair," *Harper's Magazine*, Oct., 1970, p. 21, CA; Cile Sinex, "Bella and Hébert: Improbable Friends," *States Item*, Aug. 3, 1972, pp. 22–23, Scrapbook, HB; Les Gapay, "The Leaderless Majority," *Nation*, Feb. 9, 1970, n.p., CA; Albert interview, CA; "Rep. Carl Albert Has Come a Long Way From Bugtussle," p. 26; Peabody, pp. 158–59, 187–88.

48. Peabody, p. 159.

49. Albert interview, CA.

50. And, it should be added, he was willing to brag about it. These acts of considerable political courage were written up by Argyll Campbell for Hale Boggs to give to columnist Jack Anderson who was writing an article on congressional courage and integrity. See Argyll Campbell for Hale Boggs to Jack Anderson, Aug. 20, 1965, HB.

51. King, "The Road to Power in Congress," *Harper's Magazine*, June, 1971, p. 42.

52. Patrick J. Maney, "Hale Boggs: The Southerner as National Democrat," in *Masters of the House*, ed. Roger H. Davidson, Susan Webb Hammond, and Raymond W. Smock (Boulder: Westview Press, 1998), p. 249.

53. Jack Beidler to Walter P. Reuther, Mar. 11, 1970, JOH.

54. Undated handwritten notes to James O'Hara, JOH.

55. Charles C. Diggs to James G. O'Hara, Dec. 14, 1970, JOH.

56. See Peabody, p. 181; undated memorandum titled "Brooks Record," JOH.

57. Hubert Humphrey to Bill Welsh, Oct. 30, 1970, JOH; "Majority Leader Lobby Group," JOH.

58. Memorandum to O'Hara Floor Group, "Subject: Where We Stand," JOH. This memorandum is mistakenly dated 1/13/70. But because of its content and its similarity to a revised memo dated 1/15/71, it is obviously from 1971. "Memorandum re CQ Poll," n.d., JOH. The CQ Straw Poll was released January 11, 1971; memorandum to O'Hara Floor Group.

59. Memorandum to O'Hara Floor Group, "Subject: Where We Stand," Jan. 15, 1971, JOH; untitled memorandum, second week of 1971, JOH.

60. Untitled memorandum, second week of 1971; "Results of CQ Straw Poll

for House, Senate Leadership" *Congressional Quarterly Weekly Report,* Jan. 11, 1971, p. 1.

61. Larry L. King, "The Road to Power in Congress: The Education of Mo Udall and What It Cost," in *Education of a Congressman: The Newsletters of Morris K. Udall,* ed. Robert L. Peabody (Indianapolis: Bobbs-Merrill, 1972), p. 305; Peabody, p. 183; Maney, p. 245; King, "The Road to Power in Congress," *Harper's Magazine,* June, 1971, pp. 45–48, HB. Richard Bolling thought that Udall initially "had no support from anyone in the House for the position of Majority Leader." "Research for *Power in the House* revision July 1973," RB; Morris K. Udall to Files, "Leadership, Jan. 21, 1971," MKU.

62. King, "The Road to Power in Congress," *Harper's Magazine,* June, 1971, p. 55, HB. Wilbur Mills was especially important to Boggs in keeping the southern delegations in line. Maney, p. 245.

63. Daniel Rapoport, *Inside the House* (Chicago: Follett Publishing, 1975), p. 79. Though Boggs thought he did have Chisholm's support, and she did get the seat on the Education and Labor Committee, Jim O'Hara thought Chisholm supported him. See King in Peabody, ed., p. 315.

64. King in Peabody, ed., p. 313. And Udall thought Boggs "made hay" with the freshmen members. See Morris Udall to Files, "Leadership," Jan. 21, 1971, MKU.

65. Maney, p. 249; Albert, p. 325; Andrew J. Glass, "Congressional Report: Uncommitted Democrats hold key to choice of new House majority leader," *CPR National Journal,* Jan. 9, 1971, p. 69.

66. Morris K. Udall, "Memorandum of Telephone Conversation," MKU.

67. Ibid.; "The Periscope," *Newsweek,* Jan. 18, 1971, p. 13, MKU.

68. Peabody, p. 160; Maney, p. 245; King in Peabody, ed., p. 302.

69. "The Periscope," p. 13; memo to files, Jan. 14, 1971, MKU; "Udall Press Release," Jan. 18, 1971, MKU; King in Peabody, ed., pp. 306–307.

70. Morris K. Udall to files, Jan. 16, 1971, MKU papers; King, "The Road to Power in Congress," *Harper's Magazine,* June, 1971, p. 58.

71. Albert, p. 326; Peabody, p. 173; "MKU Leadership 71, 12-03-70," MKU.

72. Wright interview, July 12, 2005.

73. Peabody, pp. 207–208, 281; James L. Merriner, *Mr. Chairman: Power in Dan Rostenkowski's America* (Carbondale: Southern Illinois University Press, 1999), pp. 120–21; Albert, p. 327; King in Peabody, ed., p. 322.

74. King in Peabody, ed., p. 323; Albert, p. 329.

75. TB to Morris K. Udall, "Office Memo, 1-27-71 Leadership Postmortem (highly confidential)," MKU. The memorandum notes that Peabody thought Bolling voted for Boggs in the belief that he could defeat Boggs in a future Speakership race.

76. "Comments on Peabody Draft Re Leadership Race, 1971," MKU; Patrick J.

Maney, "Hale Boggs, Organized Labor, and the Politics of Race in South Louisiana," in *Southern Labor in Transition, 1940–1995*, ed. Robert H. Zieger (Knoxville: University of Tennessee Press, 1997), p. 246; "Boggs Seen as Next Speaker," *New Orleans States-Item*, Mar. 27, 1972, n.p., Scrapbook, HB; Jim Wright, *Balance of Power* (Atlanta: Turner Publishing, 1996), pp. 190–91. Interestingly, Jim Wright notes that Begich arranged for a back-up speaker in case Boggs's Washington commitments made it impossible for him to make the trip. That back-up was Jim Wright.

77. Carl Albert to John McCormack, Oct. 23, 1972, CA.

78. On these two pivotal classes (1964 and 1974), see Jeff Fishel, "Representation and Responsiveness in Congress: the 'Class of Eighty-Nine,' 1965–1970" in *American Politics Series, A Sage Professional Paper*, ed. Randall B. Ripley (Beverly Hills: Sage, 1973) and Burdett Loomis, *The New American Politician: Ambition, Entrepreneurship, and the Changing Face of Political Life* (New York: Basic Books, 1988).

79. Transcript of the House Democratic Caucus, Jan. 21, 1971, CAU.

80. Ibid.

81. O'Neill quoted in Paul R. Clancy and Shirley Elder, *Tip: A Biography of Thomas P. O'Neill, Speaker of the House* (New York: MacMillan, 1980), p. 122; see Peabody, p. 216. Indeed, it was assumed that a likely winner of a whip election in 1971 would be Morris K. Udall of Arizona. Transcript of the House Democratic Caucus.

82. Sam Gibbons notes on conversation with Mo Udall, Nov. 8, 1972, SG; Memorandum "Suggestions and Observations," n.d., SG; Sam Gibbons notes on conversation with Wilbur Mills, Nov. 10, 1972, SG.

83. Sam Gibbons notes on discussion with Wilbur Mills, Dec. 11, 1972, SG; Sam Gibbons notes on conversation with Dan Rostenkowski, Nov. 10, 1972, SG.

84. Transcript of the House Democratic Caucus, Jan. 2, 1973, CAU; John A. Farrell, *Tip O'Neill and the Democratic Century* (Boston: Little, Brown, 2001), p. 391.

85. Indeed, the first elected Democratic whip would be Californian, and former Bernie Sisk aide, Tony Coelho in 1987.

86. Transcript of the House Democratic Caucus; Tip O'Neill quoted in *Congressional Quarterly Almanac* 1973, p. 27; Peabody, p. 259.

87. Transcript of the House Democratic Caucus.

88. Peabody, p. 259; Farrell, p. 391; *Congressional Quarterly Almanac* 1973, p. 27.

89. Peabody, p. 259.

90. Peabody, pp. 247–51; Rostenkowski repeated this rumor to Gibbons; see Sam Gibbons notes on conversation with Dan Rostenkowski; "Those Who Have Suggested Gibbons for Whip" undated [mid- to late Dec. 1972], SG; Sam Gibbons notes on conversation with Chet Holifield, Dec. 7, 1972, SG.

91. Sam Gibbons notes on discussion with Wilbur Mills, Dec. 11, 1972.

92. Sam Gibbons notes on discussion with John Beckler, "SMG & John Beckler," Nov. 29, 1972, SG.

93. Clancy and Elder, p. 124.

94. It is important to note that many southerners consider Oklahoma a "border state" rather than a southern state.

95. Sam Gibbons notes on discussion with Jake Pickle, Nov. 13, 1972, SG. Pickle added, "Wright in general would be an activist as you would, Sam." "Those Who Have Suggested Gibbons for Whip" undated [mid- to late Dec. 1972], SG; Sam Gibbons notes on discussion with Kika de la Garza, Nov. 13, 1972, SG.

96. The other two were Spark Matsunaga of Hawaii and Richard Fulton of Tennessee.

97. Tip O'Neill with William Novak, Man of the House (New York: Random House, 1987), p. 226.

98. Albert, p. 372.

99. Matt Pinkus, "Running Away from Ford, against Congress," CQ Weekly Report, Aug. 21, 1976, p. 2259.

100. Daniel Rapoport, "Congress Report/It's Not a Happy Time for House, Senate Leadership," National Journal, Feb. 7, 1976, p. 169; "Congressmen, Cars, Laws, and Favoritism," Washington Post, Sept. 18, 1972, p. A22; see generally, Steven Waldman, "Governing under the Influence; Washington Alcoholics: Their Aides Protect Them, the Media Shields Them," Washington Monthly, Jan. 1988; Speaker's Daily Press Conference, Sept. 11, 1972, CA.

101. Martin Weil and E. J. Bachinski, "Rep. Albert Apartment Hit by Fire," Washington Post, May 15, 1974, p. B1.

102. "Sleeper of the House," no publication listed, n.d., n.p. CA.

103. Jim Wright interview, July 21, 2005.

Chapter 7. Back to Boston

1. See, for example, John A. Farrell, Tip O'Neill and the Democratic Century (Boston: Little, Brown, 2001), p. 687.

2. Paul R. Clancy and Shirley Elder, Tip: A Biography of Thomas P. O'Neill, Speaker of the House (New York: MacMillan, 1980), pp. 186–88; see also pp. 493–94.

3. See Samuel Beer, "In Search of a New Public Philosophy," in The New American Political System, ed. Anthony King (Washington, D.C.: American Enterprise Institute, 1978), pp. 5–44.

4. Tip O'Neill with William Novak, Man of the House (New York: Random House, 1987), pp. 104–105; Clancy and Elder, p. 85.

5. Thomas P. O'Neill Jr. interview with Charles T. Morrisey, May 18, 1966, JFK.

6. O'Neill said that Rayburn disliked Kennedy because "number one, he didn't

feel as though he did his homework; number two, he wasn't dependable; number three, he was a maverick along the line; number four, when he did show up on the floor, he would make a speech and he would get tremendous coverage of the speech, and the Speaker would know that there had been members of the Committee who had worked long and tirelessly and they wouldn't even get their name in the paper. Here was Kennedy coming along without having done the work and taking the credit, or taking the headlines. He resented it and it was a resentment that he built up against him through the years. Let's just say that he never liked the fellow." Thomas P. O'Neill Jr. interview by John F. Stewart, Dec. 6, 1967, JFK.

7. Richard Bolling, *Power in the House* (New York: E. P. Dutton), p. 201.

8. The differences were purely due to local politics; as minority leader, O'Neill represented younger members who hoped to occupy Democratic seats at the convention, whereas McCormack, allied with James Michael Curley, led the old-guard-machine slate of delegates. Both sides, however, were vying to cast their ballots for Harry Truman for the presidential nomination.

9. Clancy and Elder, pp. 85–86; O'Neill, pp. 120–21.

10. O'Neill interview with John F. Stewart.

11. The other member to have been placed on Rules that early in his career was Rep. Howard W. Smith of Virginia. Edward P. Boland interview by Richard F. Fenno Jr., June 9, 1959, Center for Legislative Archives, National Archives and Records Administration.

12. Boland is best known as the author of the "Boland amendment" that prohibited the use of federal dollars in aid to the Nicaraguan Contras in the 1980s and sparked the Iran-Contra arms-for-hostages scandal of the Reagan administration.

13. Clancy and Elder, p. 89; O'Neill interview with John F. Stewart.

14. See the discussion of this in Farrell, pp. 186–88. Pres. Lyndon Johnson would call the Speaker to complain that O'Neill was using his position on Rules to hold up key administration legislation. Farrell, pp. 195–98.

15. Quoted in Farrell, p. 167.

16. Joseph Cooper and David W. Brady, "Institutional Context and Leadership Style: The House from Cannon to Rayburn" *American Political Science Review* (1981): 411–25; O'Neill interview with John F. Stewart. On second thought, O'Neill acknowledged that McCormack likely also brought his fellow Rules Committee members Delaney and Madden to the Board of Education.

17. O'Neill interview with John F. Stewart.

18. "Rayburn's 'Board of Education' Keeps Role under McCormack," *New York Times*, Jan. 29, 1962, p. 27.

19. "House Democrats Crush Udall's Challenge to McCormack's Leadership of Chamber," *Wall Street Journal*, Jan. 3, 1969, p. 3.

20. See Robin Kolodny, *Pursuing Majorities: Congressional Campaign Com-*

mittees in American Politics (Norman: University of Oklahoma Press, 1998), pp. 120–21.

21. O'Neill, p. 207.

22. "Sweig's Defense Makes Its Case in a Day," *Wall Street Journal,* July 7, 1970, p. 3; Thomas P. O'Neill Jr. to constituent, Jan. 31, 1967, TPO; O'Neill interview with John F. Stewart; Thomas P. O'Neill Jr. to John W. McCormack, JWM.

23. Farrell, p. 283. Boland represented Springfield in central Massachusetts rather than any Boston district.

24. Jim Bradley to Tip O'Neill, n.d., TPO; Edward Patten to Tip O'Neill, Dec. 21, 1970, TPO.

25. Boland's expectation that he would be appointed whip seems to have been confirmed by Udall; see Larry L. King, "The Road to Power in Congress: The Education of Mo Udall and What It Cost," in *Education of a Congressman: The Newsletters of Morris K. Udall,* Robert L. Peabody (Indianapolis: Bobbs-Merrill, 1972), pp. 313–14. Bernie Sisk, too, sought out Boland as a potential supporter and appointee as whip; see Robert Peabody, *Leadership in Congress* (Boston: Little, Brown, 1976), p. 185; Morris K. Udall to Edward P. Boland, n.d., EPB.

26. Tip O'Neill, p. 217; Udall quoted in King, p. 325.

27. Morris K. Udall to Tip O'Neill, Jan. 14, 1971, TPO. This is also cited in Farrell, p. 285. Hale Boggs to Tip O'Neill, Jan. 14, 1971, TPO.

28. O'Neill, p. 217. If this assessment is accurate, then it is more than a little interesting that O'Neill could better deliver Boland's supporters to Boggs than Boland could deliver them to Udall. This is but one more of a series of mysteries surrounding Boland's support of Udall. Most notably, why did Boland's loyalty to McCormack not keep him from supporting Udall as it did O'Neill?

29. O'Neill, p. 217.

30. Marjorie Hunter, "O'Neill New Democratic Whip; Albert Set Back on Rules Plan," *New York Times,* Jan. 23, 1971, p. 17.

31. Ibid.

32. O'Neill, p. 220. Another account suggests that only one New Yorker pulled the rug out from under Carey. A Carey associate said that it was "a case of the pig-shit Irish being jealous of the lace-curtain Irish"; quoted in King, p. 323.

33. Rooney, too, was friendly with McCormack. Indeed, McCormack likely first learned of Jerome Waldie's 1970 motion to vote "no confidence" in the Speaker from Rooney. As he was preparing to respond to Waldie's criticisms (which were first made public in California newspapers), McCormack was armed with clippings. A McCormack aide wrote an untitled and undated memorandum to McCormack stating, "Mr. Rooney, New York, was in California & clipped these from local papers for your files"; JWM.

34. Quoted in Farrell, p. 291; O'Neill, p. 211.

35. *Congressional Quarterly Almanac* 1971, p. 10.

36. O'Neill, p. 211.

37. Tip O'Neill identified that Representatives John Rooney and Jim Delaney of New York had met with Albert in this regard (*Man of the House*, p. 220). In interviews at the JFK Library with both Morrisey and Stewart, O'Neill identifies Delaney as a close McCormack associate on Rules and one of a few members other than O'Neill that McCormack would bring to the Board of Education meetings.

38. Farrell, p. 290.

39. Hunter, p. 17.

40. One more important "sunshine" reform would be added to O'Neill's list of accomplishments: O'Neill was instrumental in the adoption of the ultimate "sunshine" reform when the House instituted live gavel-to-gavel televised coverage of its proceedings on C-SPAN on March 19, 1979. On O'Neill's role and motivations in promoting the Hansen reforms at the expense of the Bolling reforms, see Roger H. Davidson and Walter J. Oleszek, *Congress against Itself* (Bloomington: Indiana University Press, 1977), p. 200.

41. Peabody, p. 244; Sam Gibbons notes on conversation with Chet Holifield, n.d., SG.

42. Sam M. Gibbons quoted in Arthur Levin and Alice Parson, "Sam M. Gibbons," *Ralph Nader Congress Project, Citizens Look at Congress* (Washington, D.C.: Grossman Publishers, 1972), p. 7; Peabody, p. 243; Levin and Parson, pp. 8–10.

43. Only one extended treatment of this race exists in the literature, and it was conducted prior to the availability of either Gibbons's or O'Neill's papers; see Peabody. The O'Neill papers have very little information on his leadership races, but the Gibbons papers reveal important details of this race.

44. R. W. Apple Jr., "Democratic Chief to Fight for Post," *New York Times*, Nov. 1, 1972, pp. 1, 21; Sam Gibbons to James O'Hara, Nov. 8, 1972, JOH.

45. "Plans," n.d. [early Nov. 1972], SG.

46. Sam Gibbons notes on conversation with Wilbur Mills, Nov. 21, 1972, SG.

47. "Basic Elements in the Gibbons Campaign," SG.

48. Sam Gibbons to James O'Hara, Nov. 16, 1972, JOH.

49. Sam Gibbons notes on conversation with Dante Fascell, Nov. 8, 1972, SG.

50. "SMG & John Beckler," Nov. 29, 1972, SG; Sam Gibbons notes on conversation with Dale Milford, Nov. 20, 1972, SG.

51. Gibbons to O'Hara, Nov. 16, 1972.

52. Sam Gibbons notes on conversation with Jerome Waldie, Nov. 20, 1972, SG; Sam Gibbons notes on conversation with Jonathan Bingham, Dec. 6, 1972, SG.

53. Sam Gibbons notes on conversation with Lionel Van Deerlin, Nov. 13, 1972, SG; Tip O'Neill to Dear Democratic Colleague, Nov. 9, 1972, TPO.

54. Peabody, p. 241; Sam Gibbons notes on conversation with Jerome Waldie;

"Those Who Have Suggested Gibbons for Whip," SG; Sam Gibbons notes on conversation with Dan Rostenkowski, Nov. 10, 1972, SG.

55. Sam Gibbons notes on conversation with Walter Flowers, Nov. 13, 1972.

56. Peabody, p. 244. The fact that Eckhardt wrote a letter to Gibbons expressing his support is significant in light of the fact that Gibbons was not asking his supporters to make their choice public. Eckhardt, it seems, was quite willing to let Gibbons and others, possibly O'Neill, know where he stood. Bob Eckhardt to Sam Gibbons, Dec. 12, 1972, SG. Sam Gibbons notes on conversation with Williamson Stuckey, Nov. 11, 1972, SG; Sam Gibbons notes on conversation with David Bowen, Nov. 9, 1972, SG; Sam Gibbons notes on conversation with Harold Runnels, Nov. 15, 1972, SG; Sam Gibbons notes on conversation with Claude Pepper, Nov. 9, 1972, SG.

57. "Letters," n.d. [early Nov. 1972], SG.

58. Sam Gibbons to James O'Hara, Nov. 16, 1972.

59. Sam Gibbons notes on conversation with Wilbur Mills, Nov. 10, 1972, SG; Sam Gibbons notes on conversation with Wilbur Mills, Nov. 21, 1972; Sam Gibbons notes on conversation with Wilbur Mills, Dec. 11, 1972, SG.

60. Sam Gibbons notes on conversation with Dan Rostenkowski, Dec. 4, 1972, SG; Sam Gibbons notes on conversation with Chet Holifield, Dec. 7, 1972, SG; Sam Gibbons notes on conversation with Jonathan Bingham.

61. Sam Gibbons notes on conversation with Don Fraser , Nov. 15, 1972, SG; Sam Gibbons notes on discussion with Carl Perkins, Nov. 11, 1972, SG; Sam Gibbons notes on conversation with Bob Sikes, Nov. 13, 1972, SG; "SMG & John Beckler."

62. Peabody, p. 263; Bob Sikes to Sam Gibbons, Dec. 6, 1972, SG.

63. Farrell, p. 321; Robert Leggett to Tip O'Neill, Dec. 1, 1972, TPO; Leo Diehl quoted in Peabody, p. 264.

64. Sam Gibbons notes on conversation with Kika de la Garza, Nov. 13, 1972, SG.

65. Although it is important to note that we cannot be sure that the archives have a record of all of Gibbons's supporters, to the extent that these committed members are representative of his overall support we can learn something about both Gibbons's strengths and O'Neill's weaknesses in 1973 such as they were.

66. Clancy and Elder, p. 130.

67. John Jacobs, *A Rage for Justice* (Berkeley: California University Press, 1995), p. 148.

68. Peabody, p. 264, footnote 25.

69. Undated Memorandum, "Suggestions and Observations," n.d., SG.

70. Sam Gibbons notes on discussion with Carl Perkins, Nov. 21, 1972, SG; Martha W. Griffiths to Sam Gibbons, Dec. 14, 1972, SG.

71. "Suggestions and Observations"; "Reasons for Not Having a Poll," n.d., SG.

72. Peabody, p. 258; Folder, "Democratic Caucus 1973," TPO.

73. See, O'Neill, pp.219–20; Tip O'Neill to Edward P. Boland, July 7, 1976, EPB.

74. "Best friend in Washington" quote from Mollie Boast, "Thomas P. O'Neill Jr.," *Ralph Nader Congress Project*, p. 1; John W. McCormack to Tip O'Neill, Dec. 7, 1976, TPO; Farrell, p. 19.

Chapter 8. Jim Wright

1. Jim Wright's journal, Dec. 30, 1971, JWP

2. Ibid., Jan. 8, 1973; John M. Barry, *The Ambition and the Power — The Fall of Jim Wright: A True Story of Washington* (New York: Viking Press, 1989), p. 12.

3. Michael Barone, Grant Ujifusa, and Douglas Matthews, *The Almanac of American Politics, 1972* (Boston: Gambit, 1972), p. 70; Richard Lyons, "McFall, Victim of Korean Scandal, Will Also Lose Job as House Whip," *New York Times*, Dec. 7, 1976, p. 33; Shirley Elder, "Burton Wears Thin," *The Sentinel Montgomery County*, Oct. 2, 1975, n.p., JJM; Michael Barone, Grant Ujifusa, and Douglas Mathews, *The Almanac of American Politics, 1978* (New York: E. P. Dutton, 1977), p. 75.

4. Sam Gibbons notes on conversation with Chet Holifield, Dec. 7, 1972, SG. The reference to McFall's "research position" is that, along with Brademas, the Californian led a special DCCC organization designed to provide House Democrats with politically oriented issue information for their re-election efforts.

5. Untitled newsclipping, *Lodi News*, n.p., Dec. 28, 1972, JJM; Joseph Albright, "Phil Burton — Almost King of the Hill," *San Francisco Chronicle*, May 15, 1975, p. 11, JJM; untitled newsclipping, *Fresno Bee*, n.p., Jan. 3, 1973, PBP; untitled newsclipping, *San Francisco Chronicle*, n.p., Jan. 3, 1973, PBP.

6. Joyce Purnick, untitled newsclipping, *New York Post*, Dec. 7, 1974, n.p., PBP; Jim Wright interview with Robert Peabody, Mar. 18, 1977, JWP; Barone, Ugifusa, and Matthews, *Almanac of American Politics, 1972*, p. 51; Thomas P. Southwick, "House Leadership Race: Wide Open Contest," *CQ Weekly Report*, Oct. 9, 1976, p. 2895.

7. Richard Bolling, "How Dick Bolling Got to Congress and Stayed There," *Kansas City Star*, Feb. 13, 1983, p. 14, RB; Bruce Oppenheimer and Robert L. Peabody, "How the Race for House Majority Leader Was Won — By One Vote," *Washington Monthly*, Nov. 1977, p. 48; Southwick, p. 2898.

8. Oppenheimer and Peabody, p. 50.

9. "Remarks at the Breakfast of the Fort Worth Chamber of Commerce, November 22, 1963," *Public Papers of the President* (1963), p. 888; Sarah McClendon, "Jim Wright to Be Next House Speaker," *El Paso Times*, Mar. 10, 1966, p. 1; Griffin Smith Jr. and Paul Burka, "The Best, the Worst, and the Fair-to-Middlin'," *Texas Monthly*, May 1976, p. 109.

10. See "The Jim Wright Slant on Washington," Dec. 22, 1958, JWP; "The Jim Wright Slant on Washington," Feb. 16, 1959, JWP; Jim Wright, "Clean Money for Congress," *Harper's Magazine,* Apr. 1967, n.p., JWP; "The Wright Slant on Washington," Feb. 18, 1965, JWP; Jim Wright, *The Coming Water Famine* (New York: Coward-McCann, 1966); Jim Wright, *You and Your Congressman* (New York: Coward-McCann, 1965).

11. Tip O'Neill with William Novak, *Man of the House* (New York: Random House, 1987), p. 226; Barbara Sinclair, *Majority Leadership in the U.S. House* (Baltimore: Johns Hopkins, 1983), p. 33.

12. Richard L. Lyons, "Soothing Bridge-Builder," *Washington Post,* Dec. 7, 1976, p. A6.

13. *Congressional Quarterly Almanac* 1977, p. 6.

14. Barry, p. 18; John Jacobs, *A Rage for Justice* (Berkeley: California University Press, 1995), p. 303; Oppenheimer and Peabody, p. 51; Southwick, p. 2896.

15. B to JB memo, RB.

16. Jacobs, p. 309.

17. Ibid., p. 304.

18. Ibid., p. 310. He even went so far as to send a letter to his colleagues listing his income tax return for 1976 — his congressional salary of $44,600, interest of less than $100, and honoraria from speeches of $2500. House Majority Leader 1976 notebook, PBP.

19. Southwick, p. 2896.

20. Jacobs, p. 308.

21. Letter to colleagues from Michael Blouin, William Broadhead, Bob Eckhardt, Don Edwards, Joseph J. Fisher, James J. Florio, Robert W. Kastenmeier, Abner J. Mikva, George Miller, Norman Y. Mineta, Anthony Toby Moffitt, Richard L. Ottinger, Charles Rose, and John F. Sieberling, Dec. 2, 1976, PBP; Jacobs, p. 255.

22. Jacobs, p. 268.

23. Ibid., p. 297.

24. Southwick, p. 2897; Leo Remmert, "McFall Gets Leadership Nod in Struggle for House Post," *Sacramento Bee,* June 12, 1976, p. A5, JJM.

25. Jacobs, pp. 312, 318; tally sheet, n.d., JWP.

26. Nona Bolling and Larry Bodinson interview with James Riddlesperger and Anthony Champagne, Feb. 26, 2000; "Letter to Cong-Elect with copy of announcement," Nov. 16, 1976, RB.

27. Bolling and Bodinson interview; Gerald R. Rosen, "New House Leader?" *Dun's Review,* Nov., 1976, p. 55, RB; Barry, p. 20; Richard Bolling, *House Out of Order* (New York: E. P. Dutton, 1965); Bolling and Bodinson interview.

28. "Gillis Long's Comments at Bolling Breakfast," Sept. 9, 1976, Box 369, RB.

29. Ibid.

30. "Majority Leader" file, RB; "J.B. Notes" file, RB.

31. "Jim Wright" file, RB; Jim Bolling to Richard Bolling, June 6, 1976, RB. It should be noted that these charges were never made publicly and never substantiated. Jim Bolling to Bruce Oppenheimer, Oct. 4, 1977, RB.

32. "Majority Leader" file, RB.

33. Jim G. Bolling to Richard Bolling and Gillis Long, Aug. 2, 1976, RB; "Majority Leader Race Notes June 7, 1976," RB; Jim Wright interview with Ben Procter, Oral History, JWP, April 26, 1992, p. 16.

34. Southwick, p. 2898; Richard Bolling to Edward Boland, Nov. 30, 1976, EPB.

35. Mrs. Richard Bolling to Mrs. Estes Peterson, n.d., RB.

36. Bolling and Bodinson interview; Jacobs, p. 300.

37. "The Leadership of Congress," *New York Times,* Nov. 22, 1976, p. A24.

38. Barry, pp. 11–14; Jacobs, p. 303. Years later, he still had that competitive edge, even when it came to catching bigger fish than his friends on a fishing trip with friends. Jeff Guinn, "A Lion in Winter," *Fort Worth Star Telegram,* Aug. 26, 2001, p. 12G.

39. Jacobs, p. 300; Marshall Lynam to Jim Wright, Nov. 23, 1976, JWP.

40. Wright believes that out of personal loyalty and institutional tradition, O'Neill probably supported McFall on the first ballot and Wright thereafter. Jim Wright interview with James Riddlesperger, July 7, 2006; Jim Wright interview with James Riddlesperger, Mar. 19, 2002.

41. Marshall L. Lynam, *Stories I Never Told the Speaker* (Dallas: Three Forks Press, 1998), p. 153.

42. Jim Wright, *Balance of Power: President and Congress from the Era of McCarthy to the Age of Gingrich* (Atlanta: Turner Publishing, 1996), p. 266; Marjorie Hunter, "James Claude Wright," *New York Times,* Dec. 7, 1976, p. 32.

43. Jacobs, p. 300.

44. Robert V. Remini, *The House: The History of the House of Representatives* (New York: HarperCollins, 2006); Wright interview, July 7, 2006.

45. "The Leadership of Congress," p. A24; "Jim Wright" folder, RB.

46. Jim Wright, "Legislation and the Will of God," in *Congress and Conscience,* ed. John B. Anderson (Lippincott, 1970), pp. 25–27.

47. "General Notes on Whip Office," TPO; Gary A. Keith, *Eckhardt: There Once Was a Congressman from Texas* (Austin: University of Texas Press, 2007), p. 248; Lynam, p. 167. Interestingly, two accounts of the race differ on Wright's relationship with Jack Brooks. Jacobs, p. 315, writes that Brooks was "Wright's closest friend in the House — some said his only friend." But Barry, p. 30, wrote that they had "tension" and "had long been rivals." As with most conflicting accounts, there is perhaps some truth to each, but clearly Wright and Brooks had worked harmoniously for a number of years, since both had been in the Texas legislature

together. Eckhardt's support for Burton was a bit more high profile, and he co-signed a letter, sent to all Democrats, in support of Burton. Letter to Democrats, Dec. 2, 1976, PBP. Keith, p. 248.

48. Jim Wright to Bernard Rapoport, July 20, 1976, JWP.

49. "Jim Wright Folder," RB.

50. Barry, pp. 25–26; Lynam, p. 168.

51. Southwick, p. 2895; Oppenheimer and Peabody, p. 51; Barry, pp. 23–24; Lynam, pp. 160–61.

52. "Colleague Correspondence" file, JWP.

53. Tally sheet, n.p., JWP.

54. Lynam, p. 169; Barry, p. 27.

55. Lynam, pp. 155–58; Bernard Rapoport interview with James Riddlesperger, Dec. 13, 2001; "Meet the Press" file, JWP; Jacobs, p. 309.

56. Lynam, p. 163; Oppenheimer and Peabody, p. 53.

57. Wright interview, Mar. 18, 1977.

58. Lynam, pp. 169–70.

59. Barry, p. 14.

60. Daniel Rapoport, "Congress Report/It's Not a Happy Time for House, Senate Leadership," *National Journal,* Feb. 7, 1976, p. 170, Box 193, JJM; Southwick, p. 2898.

61. James M. Naughton, "4 Seeking House Leadership Post Press Claims in the Election Today," *New York Times,* Dec. 6, 1976, p. 1. McFall reported that Wright Patman had reported the same thing three weeks before Patman's death: "Mac, you're the best whip we've had for the last 42 years." *Sacramento Bee,* Nov. 9, 1978, p. A5, JJM. Southwick, p. 2899.

62. Jacobs, p. 305; Lynam, p. 163.

63. Warren Weaver Jr., "Rep. McFall's Tie to Seoul Lobby Draws Attention to 'Slush Funds,'" *New York Times,* Dec. 3, 1976, p. 28.

64. *1977 CQ Almanac* (Washington, D.C.: Congressional Quarterly, 1978), p. 820.

65. Ibid., p. 5.

66. Transcript, "Meet the Press," Dec. 5, 1976, RB.

67. Ibid.

68. Ibid.; Barry, p. 26.

69. Leadership staff member during this time period confidential interview with Doug Harris, Aug. 1, 2003; Barry, p. 29; "Memo to the File — Conversation with Thompy," June 16, 1976, FJT.

70. Barry, p. 27.

71. Wright interview, Mar. 18, 1977.

72. Transcript, Hearings before the Committee on Organizing Democratic Caucus for the 95th Congress, Dec. 6, 1976, pp. 41, 44, 46, PBP; Jacobs, p. 317.

73. Transcript, Hearings before the Committee on Organizing Democratic Caucus for the 95th Congress, pp. 48, 52; Jacobs, p. 317.

74. Transcript, Hearings before the Committee on Organizing Democratic Caucus for the 95th Congress, pp. 57–59, 62.

75. Ibid., p. 64. Though the appointment of Brademas as whip had not been announced, it was widely known that he was the likely appointee. Jim Wright interview with James Riddlesperger, Oct. 17, 2006.

76. Transcript, Hearings before the Committee on Organizing Democratic Caucus for the 95th Congress, pp. 70, 72.

77. Jacobs, p. 318.

78. Wright interview, Mar. 18, 1977.

79. Marshall Lynam to Jim Wright, Nov. 23, 1976, JWP; Jacobs, p. 316.

80. Wright interview, Mar. 18, 1977; Jacobs, p. 319; Oppenheimer and Peabody, p. 56.

81. Oppenheimer and Peabody, p. 47.

82. Wright, *Balance of Power,* p. 266; Mary Russell, "Rep Wright Is Elected House Majority Leader," *Washington Post,* Dec. 7, 1976, p. 1.

83. Lynam, p. 171.

84. Wright interview, Mar. 18, 1977; Sen. Gaylord Nelson quoted in Jacobs, p. vii; Barry, p. 14; Wright interview, Mar. 18, 1977.

85. Bolling and Bodinson interview; "Majority Leader" file, RB.

86. "Majority Leader" file, RB.

87. Bruce Oppenheimer and Robert Peabody, "The House Majority Leadership, 1976," paper presented at the Annual Meeting of the American Political Science Association, 1977, p. 66.

88. Transcript, Hearings before the Committee on Organizing Democratic Caucus for the 95th Congress, p. 82; David E. Rosenbaum, "O'Neill Is Speaker; Rep. Wright of Texas Wins Majority Post," *New York Times,* Dec. 7, 1976, pp. 1, 33; John Burton Oral History, California State Archives, University of California at Berkeley, Dec. 17, 1987.

89. Jacobs, p. 323; Abe Mellincoff, "The Old Pork Barrel," *San Francisco Chronicle,* Mar. 6, 1978, n.p., JWP; Gil Bailey, "Phil Burton: The 'Benevolent Steamroller' of Washington," *San Jose Mercury News,* July 7, 1978, n.p., PBP; "Washington Whispers," *U.S. World and News Report,* Mar. 29, 1978, n.p., JWP. O'Neill explained his retirement as Speaker in part as a consideration of the fact that Wright deserved a chance to be Speaker, having "been the loyal majority leader since 1977." O'Neill, p. 371. Such a statement shows O'Neill's respect for Wright both as a person and as a legislator; one would hardly pass over the gavel of an institution one loved to someone who you did not think up to the task.

90. Myron Struck to Phil Burton, n.d., PBP; Leo Remmert, "Burton May Delay

Bid for Leadership," *Sacramento Bee*, Nov. 11, 1978, n.p., PBP; John Fogarty, "Burton Won't Run for House Post," *San Francisco Chronicle*, Nov. 14, 1978, n.p., PBP; Barry, p. 30.

91. Transcript, Joe McCaffrey show, 1978, JWP; tally sheet, n.d., JWP; Richard E. Cohen, "They Won't Take Jim Wright for Granted This Time," *National Journal*, May 6, 1978, pp. 712–15, JWP; "Movers and Shakers in the Capitol," *U.S. News and World Report*, Jan. 14, 1980, p. 41, JWP.

92. Jacobs, p. 323; Ralph Nader, *Crashing the Party* (New York: St. Martin's, 2002), pp. 22–23.

93. Struck to Burton, n.d. Jim Wright believed that the Congressional liaison staff were nice people but that they were micromanaged from the White House. Wright interview, Oct. 17, 2006.

94. Charles O. Jones, *The Trusteeship Presidency: Jimmy Carter and the United States Congress* (Baton Rouge: Louisiana State University Press, 1988), pp. 2, 106–11; Bob Woodward, *Shadow: Five Presidents and the Shadow of Watergate* (New York: Simon and Shuster, 1999), p. 55.

95. Untitled newsclipping, *Sacramento Bee*, Nov. 9, 1978, p A5, JJM.

96. David Rosenbaum, "Surprise Vote by Democrats," *New York Times*, Dec. 8, 1976, p. 15.

97. Jim Wright's journal, Dec. 13, 1977.

98. Struck to Burton, n.d; Wright interview, Oct. 17, 2006.

99. Jim Wright's journal, Dec. 3, 1977.

Chapter 9. Conclusion

1. David B. Truman, *The Congressional Party: A Case Study* (New York: John Wiley and Sons, 1959), p. 106; Ira Katznelson, Kim Geiger, and Daniel Kryder, "Limiting Liberalism: The Southern Veto in Congress, 1933–1950," *Political Science Quarterly* (1993): 283–306.

2. Alonzo L. Hamby, *Beyond the New Deal: Harry S. Truman and American Liberalism* (New York: Columbia University Press, 1973), p. 487.

3. Katznelson, Geiger, and Kryder, p. 302. As Sean Farhang and Ira Katznelson write, "In the mind of the southern legislator . . . labor had become race"; "The Southern Imposition: Congress and Labor in the New Deal and Fair Deal," *Studies in American Political Development* (2005): 30.

4. David W. Rohde, *Parties and Leaders in the Postreform House* (Chicago: University of Chicago Press, 1991), pp. 58–59; Garrison Nelson, "Partisan Patterns of House Leadership Change, 1789–1977," *American Political Science Review* (1977): 939.

5. See Joseph Cooper and David W. Brady, "Institutional Context and Leadership Style: The House from Cannon to Rayburn," *American Political Science Review* (1981): 411–25.

6. Developed by Keith Poole and Howard Rosenthal, W-NOMINATE scores use all congressional roll call to develop an ideological (left-right) score for House leaders ranging from the most liberal (−1.0) to the most conservative (+1.0); these scores correlate highly with more traditionally used Americans for Democratic Action and American Conservative Union scores. For a complete discussion of these scores, see Keith Poole and Howard Rosenthal, *Congress: A Political-Economic History of Roll Call Voting* (New York: Oxford University Press, 1997).

7. David W. Brady and Charles Bullock, "Is There a Conservative Coalition in the House?" *Journal of Politics* (1980): 549–59; Katznelson, Geiger, and Kryder, p. 296; James T. Patterson, "A Conservative Coalition Forms in Congress, 1933–1939," *Journal of American History* (1966): 762.

8. See Eric Schickler and Kathryn Pearson, "Agenda Control, Majority Party Power, and the House Committee on Rules," paper presented at the 2006 Annual Meeting of the Midwest Political Science Association; See, Brady and Bullock, pp. 549–59; John F. Manley, "The Conservative Coalition in Congress," *American Behavioral Scientist* (1973), p. 224; Gary W. Cox and Mathew D. McCubbins, "Agenda Power in the U.S. House of Representatives, 1877–1986," in *Party, Process and Political Change in Congress: New Perspectives on the History of Congress,* ed. David W. Brady and Mathew D. McCubbins (Palo Alto: Stanford University Press, 2002), p. 129. Note that Schickler and Pearson Midwest Political Science Association paper has offered persuasive evidence that any effort to thoroughly dispel the conservative coalition's influence is itself overblown.

9. Robert L. Peabody argued that Republican "revolts" were due, in part, to disappointing election results and frustration at "their long period of minority status." *Leadership in Congress: Stability, Succession, and Change* (Boston: Little, Brown, 1976), p. 477. If Republicans retained their tendency toward conflict in leadership selection even after winning the majority, Democrats' consensus in leadership succession gave way when they lost the majority after 1994; see Douglas B. Harris, "Legislative Parties and Leadership Choice: Confrontation or Accommodation in the 1989 Gingrich-Madigan Whip Race," *American Politics Research* (2006): 200–201.

10. See Matthew N. Green, "McCormack versus Udall: Explaining Intraparty Challenges to the Speaker of the House," *American Politics Research* (2006): 3–21. On Boggs's personal troubles in 1968 and 1969 that caused unease among some members; see Peabody, pp. 156–61.

11. John F. Manley quoted an extended statement by Ford from the *Congressional Record* (1967), pp. 45407–45409; see Manley, "The Conservative Coalition in Congress," *American Behavioral Scientist* (1973): 233.

INDEX

abortion issues, 250

Adams, Brock, 135–36, 141–43

AFL-CIO, 160, 166–67

African Americans, 6, 9–11, 18, 91, 165, 222, 240

agrarian uprising, 19–20

Agriculture Committee, 81, 94, 102, 225

agriculture subsidies, 129

Albert, Carl, 1, 119–20; Civil Rights Act, voting for, 253; comments of, 149–50; involvement in "Koreagate," 186–87; as majority leader, 195–97, 222, 226; as McCormack protégé and supporter, 14, 130, 134, 216–18, 258–59; Oklahoma district of, 10; race for Speaker, 141–47, 148–61; relationship with Boggs, 141–47, 202; relationship with Wright, 189; retirement from Speaker, 220, 223, 227, 229, 237; stance on Vietnam War, 204; tenure as Speaker, 179–80, 183–85, 198, 200, 207, 210, 212

Albright, Robert C., 115

Allen, Robert, 116

American Federation of Labor, 40; *see also* AFL-CIO

Americans for Democratic Action, 156, 166, 215, 223, 244

Anderson, Charles Arthur, 109

Anderson, Jack, 163

Apple, R. W., 206

Appropriations Committee: Boland member of, 192–93, 199; Buchanan member of, 60, 99; Byrns chair of, 63, 77, 81, 86, 91–92; Cannon member of, 130; Mahon chair of, 220;

Texans chairs of, 102; Woodrum member of, 122

Armed Services Committee, 225

Armey, Dick, 256

Aspinall, Wayne, 134

Bailey, Joseph Weldon, 14–46, 51, 69, 125, 261

Bailey, Joseph Weldon Jr. "Little Joe," 45

Baker, Ross, 12, 13

Bankhead, William, 64–65, 74, 77, 81–90, 95–97, 99–103, 114–17, 122, 126, 159

Banking and Currency Committee, 149, 225

Barkley, Alben, 7, 70

Barry, John, 219–20, 236

Baucus, Max, 248

Beame, Abraham, 231

Begich, Nick, 175

Beidler, Jack, 146–47

Beiter, Alfred F., 104

Bennett, Charles, 142

Bensel, Richard, 7

Bentsen, Lloyd, 243

Beveridge, Albert, 18

Biaggi, Mario, 133

Bingham, Jonathan (Jack), 138, 209, 213

Bissell, Wilson, 20–21

Blanton, Thomas L., 50, 99

Boggs, Hale: Albert, relationship with, 153, 158; disappearance of, 211, 217, 221; race for majority leader, 179–80, 183; as Rayburn protégé, 14, 148, 150, 152; tenure as majority leader,

Boggs, Hale (*continued*)
179–80, 209–10; Udall, relationship with, 142; Waldie, relationship with, 146; as Whip, 1, 130, 134–37, 160, 233, 258
Boggs, Lindy, 161–62, 205
Boland, Edward, 169, 171, 192–93, 197–200, 217, 229–30
Boland, Patrick J., 104, 124
Bolling, Richard S.: Albert, rivalry with, 159–60, 258; ideas on government, 189; ideas on House reform, 203–204; McCormack, critic of, 122–23, 126, 128, 131, 134–38, 140, 145,159–61, 164, 166, 194, 196; Mills, rivalry with, 161; race for majority leader, 148–50, 152–58, 223–24, 226–30; race for Speaker, 245–47; as Rayburn protégé, 108, 164, 191, 193, 221–22; retirement, 250; Udall, rivalry with, 142, 174–75; ideas on appointed or elected Whip, 181–83
Bolling, Jim, 227–29, 245–46
Bolling, Nona, 158, 160
Boren, Lyle H., 110, 113
Bowen, David, 211
Bowers, Claude, 17–18, 71
Boykin, Frank, 152
Brademas, John, 182–86, 216, 220–21, 239
Brooks, Jack, 136, 166–67, 180, 185, 233–34, 239
Bryan, William Jennings, 17, 20–21, 81
Buchanan, James, 60, 64, 81, 86, 99
Burke, Yvonne Brathwaite, 240
Burleson, Albert Sydney, 36, 60
Burleson, Omar, 169, 173
Burns, James MacGregor, 105
Burton, John, 224, 246
Burton, Phillip: ideas on government, 189; race for majority leader, 197, 204, 220–21, 223–26, 227–28, 230–32, 234–36, 238–39, 259, 261; race for Whip, 180, 183–85
Bush, George H. W., 260
Byrd, Harry F., 98
Byrnes, James F., 60, 61–62, 83, 117
Byrns, Joseph W., 63–64, 76–103, 91–103, 114–17, 126
Byrns, Joseph W. Jr., 117

campaign finance reform, 222
Cannon, Clarence, 64, 130
Cannon, Joseph, 4, 6, 16, 48, 57–58
Carew, John, 76
Carey, Hugh, 174, 180, 197–98, 201–202
Carpenter, Leslie, 155
Carter, Jimmy, 220, 231, 235, 240–41, 243, 247–50, 251
Celler, Emmanuel, 150, 209
Chamblin, Walter, 97–98, 101, 108
Chandler, Stephen, 153
Chavez, Cesar, 167
Chicago Democratic Convention of 1963, 173–74
Chilton, Horace, 22, 35
Chisholm Shirley, 169
Civil Rights Act, 233, 241, 253–54
civil rights, 2, 10, 11, 119, 126, 137, 157, 160, 165–66, 210, 233, 238, 252–54
civil service, 20–21, 121
Civil War, 2, 52
Clark, Champ, 4, 16–19, 21, 57–59, 75, 102, 115
Clark, Joel Bennett, 75, 115
Clay, William, 144, 167
Cleveland, Grover, 20
Clinton administration, 256
Cochran, John J., 76, 124

Coelho, Tony, 184, 197

Collier, James, 77

Collier, John, 64

Colmer, William, 11, 126, 130, 141, 158, 169, 193, 253

Colquitt, Oscar B., 17, 29, 34, 37

Confederacy, 4, 10, 47, 110, 113

Congressional Speaker Reform Committee, 186

Connally, Tom, 25, 39, 44–45

Connery, William, 86, 121

conservative coalition, 7–8, 142, 193–94, 214, 252, 256–57

Constitution, U.S., 21–22, 69

Conyers, John, 198

Coolidge, Calvin, 62, 82

Corcoran, Tom, 118

cotton, 40, 46, 97

court packing, 7, 70, 251

Cox, Eugene "Goober," 90, 113, 124, 126, 128, 257

Crain, W. H., 52

Crane, M. M., 28

Crisp, Charles, 19, 21, 64, 77

Crosser, Robert, 86, 104, 109

Crump, Ed, 87, 99, 116

Culberson, Charles, 37, 42–44, 60

Cullen, Tom, 76, 83, 86, 89, 107, 113, 116

Curley, James Michael, 58, 83,120, 190–92

Curry, John, 63–64, 79, 83, 85–87, 89, 118

D'Alesandro, Thomas, 261

Daley, Richard 172–74, 200, 231–32, 244

de la Garza, Kika, 132, 185, 214

defense issues, 166, 188, 233, 248

Delaney, Jim, 193, 201–202

Delaney, W. A. "Gus," 153

DeLay, Tom, 256

Democratic Congressional Campaign Committee, 83, 91, 93–94, 96, 106, 189, 195, 203–204, 213, 217–18, 259

Democrats' Committee on Committees, 4, 45, 58, 121, 212

Depew, Chauncey, 16

DePriest, Oscar, 91

Deschler, Lew, 49–50

Dickson, Cecil B., 54, 94–95, 98–99, 101, 103

Diehl, Leo, 214–15

Dies, Martin Jr., 123

Dies, Martin, 110–11

Diggs, Charles C. Jr., 166–67

Dingell, John D., 110, 124, 143

Dodd, Christopher, 227

Dooling, James J., 89

Duke, Paul, 156

Dulligan, James, 89–90

Dunn, Pat, 52, 59

Eckhardt, Bob, 181–82, 211, 233–34

Edmondson, J. Howard, 156

Edmonson, Ed, 195

Education and Labor Committee, 167, 169–70

Edwards, Don, 141–42

Eisenhower, Dwight D., 192, 261

Ertel, Allen, 236, 241

Faddis, Charles, 111

Farley, James A., 86, 97, 153; relationship with Bankhead, 95, 101, 103; relationship with Byrns, 94, relationship with Garner, 66–67, 70–71, 78–79; relationship with McDuffie, 84, 91, relationship with O'Connor, 80, 83, 112, 116–18; relationship with Roosevelt, 106–107

Farmer's Alliance, 19
Farrell, John A., 182–83, 197, 202, 214
Fascell, Dante, 208
Faubus, Orval, 152
Fay, James H., 118
Federal Bureau of Investigation (FBI), 163
Fenno, Richard F. Jr., 192
Fernandez, Joe "Bathtub," 105–106
Finance Committee, 155
Fisher, O. C., 54
Fitzgerald, John F. "Honey Fitz," 120
Fleeson, Doris, 150–51
Florio, Jim, 240–41
Flowers, Walter, 211
Flynt, John, 133
Ford, Gerald, 163, 187, 237, 250, 260
Ford, Thomas, 105
Foreign Affairs Committee, 58
Francis, David, 25
Frantz, Joe, 44–45, 47
Fraser, Donald, 167, 213, 237

Garner, Ettie, 48–49, 54–55, 71, 98
Garner, John Nance, 13, 44, 47–72, 99, 102, 117, 149, 194, 220; as Bailey protégé, 14, 16, 24–25, 30–31, 36–37, 45, 261; as mentor to McCormack, 47, 116, 121–22, 126; as mentor to Rayburn, 9, 46, 97, 105, 108, 110, 113–15
Garner, Tully, 71
Garrett, Finis, 50, 60–61
Gephardt, Dick, 256, 261
Gibbons, Sam, 161, 180–81, 183–85, 204–13, 214–17, 259
Gilmore, Charles V., 153
Gingrich, Newt, 260
gold standard, 67
Great Depression, 6, 42, 65, 67, 73, 74, 252

Great Society, 119, 147, 169
Green, Edith, 135
Griffiths, Martha W., 216
Guffey, Joe, 86, 89–90, 98, 101, 106, 108, 114
Gunter, Nat, 20

Hague, Frank, 79, 83, 107
Hall, Walter, 72
Halleck, Charles, 136, 152–53
Hanley, James, 235
Hanna, Richard T., 133
Hardeman, D. B., 34, 38
Hardin, Sid, 53–54
Harding, Warren G., 61, 77
Hare, Silas, 19
Hare, Silas, Jr., 39
Harrison, Pat, 7, 70
Hayden, Carl, 60, 129–30
Hays, Wayne, 153–54, 163, 167–70, 172, 178–80, 182–84, 197–98, 208, 225–26, 238
Hearst, William Randolph, 66
Hébert, F. Edward, 136, 158, 162, 205, 225
Hensley, Walter L., 109
Hepburn Rate Bill, 29–30
Hicks, Louise Day, 171
Holifield, Chet, 155, 158, 169, 184, 213, 220–221
Holtzman, Elizabeth, 209
Hoover, Herbert, 59, 65–67, 74
Hoover, J. Edgar, 163
House Judiciary Committee, 21–22
House reform, 12, 137, 171, 175, 190, 203–204, 207–209, 212, 218, 221, 224–25, 238
House Un-American Activities Committee, 149, 152
House, E. M., 51–52

House, Edward, 23
Houton, Daniel, 145
Howe, Louis, 84, 95
Hoyer, Steny, 261
Hubbard, Carroll, 236
Hull, Cordell, 16, 59, 70, 83
Humphrey, Hubert, 166–67
Hunter, Marjorie, 202
Hurja, Emil, 97, 106
Hymel, Gary, 164, 200, 205, 243

Ichord, Richard, 136
Ickes, Harold, 117, 122
immigrants, 6, 61
imperialism, 22–23
income tax, 30, 57, 65
inheritance tax, 65
Internal Revenue Service, 32, 109
Interstate and Foreign Commerce
    Committee, 69, 81, 101–102, 104,
    109–10, 150
Interstate Commerce Commission,
    29–30, 40–41

Jackson, Robert, 78, 86
Jacobs, John, 246–48
James, Marquis, 54
Jeffersonian ideals, 22, 30, 81
Johnson, Harold "Bizz," 240
Johnson, Lady Bird, 162
Johnson, Lyndon B., 123, 162, 164, 166,
    186, 243, 250, 253, 259–60; relation-
    ship with Albert, 154, 158; relation-
    ship with Bailey, 27; relationship
    with McCormack, 127, 143–44, 147,
    153; and Vietnam, 190, 206; relation-
    ship with Wright, 222, 249
Johnson, Sam, 27–28
Johnston, Rienzi M., 29
Jones, Charles O., 248

Jones, Jesse, 67
Jones, Marvin, 64, 86, 94, 104, 113
Judiciary Committee, 81, 102

Keller, Kent, 113
Kelly, Edward J., 107
Kennedy, A. M., 34, 39
Kennedy, John F. 127–28, 147–48,
    150–56, 164, 186, 190–91, 193, 222,
    250–51, 258
Kennedy, Patrick "P.J.," 120
Kennedy, Robert, 150
Kennedy, Will, 115
Kerr, John H., 108, 125
Kerr, Robert, 154–56
Key, V. O. Jr., 10
Keys, Martha, 224
King, Larry L., 139, 235
King, Martin Luther Jr., 240, 251
Kirby, John H., 23–24, 69
Kirwan, Mike, 133, 195
Kitchin, Claude, 59–60, 61, 75
Kleberg, Robert J., 42, 52
Kleberg, Rudolph, 52
Korea, 237–38
"Koreagate" scandal, 186, 188, 239–4,
    249
Krock, Arthur, 86–87, 116, 156
Ku Klux Klan, 41, 44, 61, 68

labor issues, 40, 42, 47, 142, 167, 205,
    253
LaGuardia, Fiorello, 65
Landon, Alf, 68
Landrum, Phil, 137
Lane, Thomas J., 127
Latin American issues, 222
Lea, Clarence F., 109, 124
leadership ladder, 12, 14, 125, 176, 189,
    201–18, 226, 233, 236, 258

League of Nations, 43
Leggett, Robert, 214
Legislative Reorganization Act, 205
LeHand, Margaret (Missy), 112
Lesinski, John, 110
Lewis, Alfred Henry, 23
Lewis, John L., 47
liberal coalition, 142, 147, 214
limited government, 30
Lodge, Henry Cabot, 190
Long, Gillis, 227–28, 230, 240, 242
Long, Huey P., 85, 89, 105, 162
Longworth, Nicholas, 13, 49–50, 58, 62
Lyle, John, 50
Lynam, Marshall, 230, 235, 242–43

Mahon, George, 220
Maloney, Paul, 162
Maney, Patrick J., 134, 136
Mansfield, Joseph, 64
Mansfield, Mike, 150, 156
Marshall, John, 34, 39
Martin, Joe, 120, 124, 126, 136, 188,
    254–56
Masters, Nick, 232–33
Mathis, Dawson, 244
Matsunaga, Spark, 217
McCarthyism, 251
McClendon, Sarah, 222
McCooey, John, 83, 85–86
McCormack, John, 1, 9, 104, 119–47,
    151, 154, 165, 168, 251–53, 257–59;
    relationship with Albert, 158, 175–
    76, 186, relationship with Bankhead,
    101; constituency, 11; relationship
    with Curley, 58, 83; as candidate for
    Speaker, 150–57, 159–61, 170, 172; as
    Garner protégé, 47, 77, 116, 122, 261;
    as candidate for majority leader, 91,
    97–98, 100; as mentor to O'Neill,

174, 183, 190–218, 22; relationship
    with Rayburn, 113, 115, 149, 166;
    retirement, 164, 171; as Speaker, 222,
    226
McCormack, Harriet Joyce, 128
McCovey, John, 76
McDuffie, Cornelia, 91
McDuffie, John, 48–49, 51, 54, 62–65,
    73–88, 90, 91, 96, 97, 101, 107, 115,
    126
McFall, David, 24
McFall Resolution, 24–25
McFall, John, 176, 197, 224, 216, 228,
    230–32, 249–50; efforts to keep
    Speaker post appointive, 182–85;
    ethical lapses, 188, 249; relationship
    with Holifield, 220–21; candidate
    for Speaker, 234, 236–38, 240, 242;
    relationship with Wright, 234
McGovern, George, 207, 210
McIntyre, Marvin, 95, 109
McIntyre, Ross, 97
McKean, David, 107
McKinley presidency, 21
McLemore, Jeff, 52
McSweeney, John, 109
Mead, James M., 89, 91, 100, 104, 117
Medicare, 155
Mellon, Andrew, 65, 67
Mexican Americans, 53
Mexico, 18, 52, 53, 56, 58
Mikulski, Barbara, 235, 248
Mikva, Abner, 224, 241
Milford, Dale, 208
Milkis, Sidney M., 7, 8
Miller, Benjamin, 82
Miller, John, 99
Milligan, Jacob Le Roy "Tuck," 64, 77,
    82, 94, 96
Mills, Roger Q., 19, 22

Mills, Wilbur, 143, 145–46, 157, 160–
61, 163, 180–81, 184, 196, 207, 214; as
Chair of Ways and Means, 136–37,
163, 169, 171, 212–13; support for
McCormack, 136–37, 155, 170; as
Rayburn protégé, 148, 152
Mineta, Norman, 226, 234–35, 241
Mitchell, Arthur Wergs, 91
Moley, Raymond, 69, 95
Morris, Willie, 164
Mosier, Harold G., 109
Moss, John, 169, 176, 182
Murtha, John, 240

NAACP, 156
Nader, Ralph, 248
national debt, 222
National Labor Relations Board, 251
Neff, Pat, 43
Nelson, Garrison, 254
nepotism, 228, 246
New Frontier, 147, 155
Nichols, John C., 110, 113
Nixon, Richard, 134, 163, 187, 208, 218,
251, 259

O'Brien, Larry, 151
O'Brien, Tom, 89, 172, 113, 158
O'Connor, Basil, 76, 79, 111, 116
O'Connor, John J., 1–2, 7–9, 64,
74–83, 88–90, 99, 101–18, 97–118,
126, 257
O'Hara, James G., 133, 142, 145, 147,
165–68, 172, 175, 197–98, 201, 216
oil issues, 9, 174, 206, 234
O'Neill, Thomas P. (Tip), 1, 120, 158,
164, 174, 185, 239; relationship with
Bolling, 229; relationship with Burton, 225–26, 230; constituency, 11;
as McCormack protégé, 14, 128–29,

143, 171, 259; retirement, 260–61; as
Speaker, 175–76, 186–87, 188–218,
220, 223, 227, 230; ideas on Whip
position, 178, 180, 182–84; relationship with Wright, 231–32, 243, 247,
249–50, 251
Oakes, John B., 209
Oppenheimer, Bruce, 246

Park, Tongsun (see also "Koreagate"),
237–39
Parr, Archer, 34, 52–54, 57
Patenaude, Lionel, 69
Patman, Wright, 50, 113, 149, 158, 225,
245
Patten, Edward J., 198
Patterson, James T., 7, 108, 122–23
Peabody, Robert, 164, 174–75, 183, 211,
216, 246
Pelosi, Nancy, 256, 261
Penfield, W. L., 17–18
Pepper, Claude, 211
Perkins, Carl, 135, 213, 216
Phillips, David Graham, 23
Phillips, Kevin, 160, 174–75
Pickle, Jake, 182–83, 185
Pierce, Henry Clay, 24–28
Poage, Bob, 136, 158, 225, 245
poll tax, 9, 53, 222
Polsby, Nelson, W., 12, 159
post office department, 20–21
Pou, Edward, 64–65, 74, 77, 87
Powell, Adam Clayton, 132, 216
Priest, J. Percy, 124–25, 150
progressive Democrats, 36, 40, 42, 77,
92, 95,128
progressive Republicans, 65, 75
prohibition, 19, 29, 34, 37–39, 43, 54
Public Buildings and Grounds Com-
mittee, 81, 102

Public Utility Holding Company Act, 99, 104–105, 108, 111, 251
public welfare, 251
Public Works Commission, 219, 222, 229, 231, 246
public works programs, 9, 74
purge efforts, 7–8, 70, 108, 117–18, 251

race issues, 6, 9–11, 14–15, 18, 22, 36, 157, 161, 216, 252–53
railroad regulation, 20, 29–30, 40–41
Rainey, Henry, 59, 63–64, 66, 73, 75–88, 93–94, 96, 107, 115, 126
Rains, Albert, 152
Randall, William, 134
Randell, Andrew, 37, 39–42
Randell, Choice B., 35–37, 39, 41–42, 45
Rankin, John, 77–78, 81, 84, 91, 96, 100–101, 104, 113, 126
Rapoport, Bernard, 233, 235
Raupe, Craig, 230, 235, 247–48, 250
Ray, Elizabeth, 225–26
Rayburn, Sam, 1, 9, 120, 191, 220, 226, 251, 257, 261; as Bailey protégé, 14, 16, 30, 33–34, 37–38, 43–45; relationship with Bolling, 221–22, 238; relationship with Brooks, 233; constituency, 10–11, 45; as Garner protégé, 46, 47, 49–51, 61, 63–64, 66, 69, 71–72; ideas about government, 189; relationship with McCormack, 119, 122, 124–31, 147, 194, 205, 223, 252–53, 258; relationship with Roosevelt, 7–8; as Speaker, 73–118; successors, 148–87
Reagan, Ronald, 1, 14, 248, 251, 256, 260–61
Reed, Thomas Brackett, 4, 19–21
Rees, Thomas, 141, 176, 184
Remini, Robert, 231–32

Richmond, Frederick, 244
right to work, 142, 169, 205
Rivers and Harbors Committee, 81, 102
Rivers, Mendel, 131
Rizzo, Frank, 231
Roberts, Ray, 135, 144, 243
Robinson, Joseph, 113–14
Rodino, Peter, 240
Rooney, John, 201
Roosevelt, Franklin D., 1–2, 6–7, 76, 83, 96, 103, 115, 129, 251, 253; relationship with Farley, 106–107, 153; relationship with Garner, 55, 66–68, 70, 80, 87–88, 98; relationship with Jackson, 78–79, 86; relationship with McCormack, 122; relationship with McDuffie, 84, 90–91; relationship with O'Connor, 108, 111–12, 116–18; relationship with Rayburn, 95, 105, 109, 114; and Works Progress Administration, 122–23
Roosevelt, James, 111, 158
Roosevelt, Theodore, 22, 29, 57
Rose, Charles, 240–41
Rostenkowski, Dan, 137, 188, 197–98, 202, 213; relationship with Alert, 158, 173–74, 179, 210; relationship with Boggs, 164, 71–72, 200; relationship with O'Neill, 214, 231–32; candidate for Speaker, 143, 145–47, 169; ideas on Whip position, 181; relationship with Wright, 241, 244
Rules Committee, 12, 58, 81, 108, 164, 257; Bailey as member, 21; Bankhead as member, 95, 97, 102; Bolling as member, 148, 158, 175, 222, 229–30, 238; Colmer as member, 11, 130, 252–53; Cox as member, 113, 126; O'Connor as member, 7, 76, 89, 99, 101–103, 111, 117; O'Neill as mem-

ber, 174, 189, 192–95, 199, 201–203, 207, 218; Pou as member, 65, 74; Sisk as member, 169; Thornberry as member, 158

Russell, Richard B., 253

Russia, 71–72, 81

Sabath, Adolph, 78, 83–89, 95, 104, 107

Santa Fe railroad, 32, 35

Sayers, Joseph, 24

Scheuer, Jim, 167

Schlesinger, Arthur Jr., 48

Schroeder, Pat, 209

Schwarz, Jordan, 65

Seabury, Francis, 30–31

Securities and Exchanges Act, 251

segregation, 9–11, 161, 251–53

seniority system: advantages to Bolling, 175, 222; Burton's disregard of, 221, 225; advantages to Byrns, 93; as means of obtaining committee chairs, 4, 6, 178; criticism of, 143, 208–209, 245–46; as means of managing power, 58; and mentoring system, 13–14; advantages to McCormack, 129, 153; advantages to Rainey, 75–77; advantages to Rayburn, 97, 104; advantages to Southern representatives, 63–64; as point in Udall argument, 138; advantages to Wright, 219, 249

Sheppard, Morris, 29, 36–37, 42

Sikes, Robert (Bob), 132, 161, 169, 213–14, 239, 245

Simpson, Kirke, 110

Sisk, B. F. (Bernie), 158, 166–69, 172, 176, 197–98, 210, 240, 259

Smith, Al, 87, 122

Smith, Howard W., 88, 123, 158–59, 193, 257

Smith, T. S., 24

Social Security, 251

Southern Manifesto, 161, 253

Soviet Union, 81, 222, 251

Sparkman, John, 124

Sprague, Irving, 237

Staggers, Harley, 230

State Department, 17–18

statehood, 22

states rights, 30, 39–40

Steed, Tom, 151, 157, 240

Steering and Policy Committee, 212

Steger, Ed, 32, 35, 46

Stevenson, Adlai, 72, 149, 164

Struck, Myron, 243, 247, 250

Stuckey, Williamson, 211

Sumners, Hatton, 51, 64

Supreme Court, 24, 42, 76, 251–52; see also court packing

Symington, James, 144, 227

Taft-Hartley Act, 142, 169, 205

Talevi, Steve, 245

Tammany, 7, 63–64, 89, 99, 101, 103–108, 110, 116, 118; support in Speaker race, 76, 79, 80, 82–87

tariffs, 23, 60, 63, 81

tax issues, 77–78, 81, 93, 155, 248

Teague, Olin "Tiger," 163, 173–74, 185, 201

Temple, Arthur, 235

Territories Committee, 81,121

Thomas, W. A., 32–33, 44, 109

Thomason, Ewing, 43, 125

Thompson, Frank, 136–38, 141, 144, 159, 165, 188, 216

Thornberry, Homer, 157–59, 193, 253

Thurmond, Strom, 253

Tillman, Ben "Pitchfork," 26, 29

Timmons, Bascom, 51, 54, 60–61, 63

Tower, John, 219

Travis, Edmond, 33–34

Treen, David, 162

Truman, David B., 252

Truman, Harry, 71, 117, 124–25, 127, 129, 149, 151, 221–22, 253

Tumulty, Joe, 62, 66, 68

two-thirds rule, 7, 110

Udall, Morris K., 163, 166–67, 169, 173, 180, 183, 203, 207; relationship with Albert, 160; relationship with Boggs, 164–65, 170–71, 175; candidate for majority leader, 197–201; relationship with McCormack, 119, 128–30, 134, 168, 172, 195, 202, 205; relationship with O'Neill, 204

Udall, Stewart, 151

Underwood, Oscar, 58, 73, 75

United Farm Workers Organizing Committee, 167

utility companies, 103–104

Van Deerlin, Lionel, 209

veterans' issues, 50, 69, 77, 92, 169

Vietnam War, 119, 187, 251; Brooks's attitude toward, 166; Burton's attitude toward, 224, 241; Gibbons's attitude toward, 206, 210; O'Neill's attitude toward, 174, 190, 204, 218; Udall's attitude toward, 143–44

Vinson, Carl, 123–24

Vinson, Fred, 45, 71, 104, 113

Voorhis, Jerry, 109

Voting Rights Act, 164, 254

wages and hours bill, 7, 70

Waldie, Jerome, 134, 144–47, 176, 209–10

Walter, Francis "Tad," 110, 149, 152, 155

Warren, Lindsay R., 64, 77, 100, 108, 123

Washington, Booker T., 22

"Watergate" class, 220, 225, 240, 242, 245, 259

Watergate scandal, 220, 240, 249, 260

Waters-Pierce Oil Company scandal, 24–28, 30–31

Ways and Means Committee, 4, 12, 21, 64, 77, 88, 92; Bailey as member, 21; Boggs as member, 163, 169–71; Garner as member, 46, 47, 58–61; Gibbons as member, 205–207, 212–13, 215; Maloney as member, 162; McCormack as member, 83, 116, 121; Mills as member, 136–37, 152, 160–61; Rainey as member, 78–79, 81; Randell as member, 35, 37, 45; Rostenkowski as member, 172

Weeks, O. Douglas, 53

Wells, James B., 23, 30, 41–43, 51–57, 59–61

Wells, Joe K., 56

Wells, Tinie, 42

Wheeler, Joe, 21

Whelchel, Benjamin, 110

Whip position, change in process (to elect or to appoint), 174, 178–186, 200–201, 216, 221, 239

white supremacy, 20, 22

White, William S., 54

Wilkins, Roy, 156

Williams, Jack, 157

Williams, John Sharp, 18

Wilson, Charles, 241

Wilson, Woodrow, 29, 36–37, 39–41, 60, 75

Wirth, Tim, 240

Wolters, Jacob, 36, 37

women's right to vote, 30, 36, 38–39, 42–43

Woodrum, Clifton, 1, 9, 77, 87, 104, 108–109, 122–24, 126, 257
workman's compensation, 251
Works Progress Administration, 122
Wright, Jim, 33, 120, 185, 253, 259–61; relationship with Albert, 158, 173–74; constituency, 10; ideas about government, 189; relationship with McCormack, 14, 129, 134; relationship with O'Neill, 182, 187, 251; as Speaker, 219–50

Young, Andrew, 240

Zablocki, Clem, 133

ISBN-13: 978-1-60344-116-2
ISBN-10: 1-60344-116-6